THE SENSES
OF MAN

by Joan Steen Wilentz

With more than 100 illustrations by the author

THOMAS Y. CROWELL COMPANY

NEW YORK

Established 1834

To Ted

All illustrations are by the author
with the exception of those acknowledged
on page 323.

Copyright © 1968 by Joan Steen Wilentz

DESIGNED BY SUSAN GIBSON

Manufactured in the United States of America

L.C. Card 68-11073
ISBN 0-8152-0298-9

Apollo Edition, 1971

INTRODUCTION

Man is an irritable creature. Scratch him and he hurts. Pepper his soup and he sneezes. Flash a car's bright headlights in his eyes, and he says, "Damn!" These are irritants, of course, and they are disturbing ones. There are other kinds of "irritants." A boy strokes a girl's arm, barely touching the hair as his fingers move down to her wrist. A mother hums softly, lulling her baby to sleep. An acolyte wafts a censer, and a congregation bows its head. These don't seem to be irritants in the familiar sense of the word. Yet this is precisely what they are.

Man is like a sea animal living in a shell. As long as the animal's shell rests in the sand, nurtured in a quiet bath of sea water, its inhabitant appears impervious to the world outside. But let the water be stirred a bit, let a shaft of light, or perhaps a shadow of darkness appear, and the animal is alerted to action. So it is with man. The machinery of his nervous system hums so quietly that, like the sea creature, man may appear indifferent to the world. But if that world changes in the slightest, he may snap to attention.

What does he do then? He may take action—put iodine on his

scratch or slow his car down. Or he may do nothing, for if man has the ability to perceive, he also has the ability to ignore the perception. Without this we could only imagine a world of Red Queens and Mad Hatters. (It is just this inability to ignore the many stimuli impinging on man every second that characterizes certain acute mental disorders.)

This is how the outside world affects him. Man also is aware of an inner world. Right now as you read this page (when you are made conscious of it) you know where your left foot is. You know exactly how you're sitting without having to look. You know if your stomach is empty or if you've eaten a heavy meal. How do you know these things? No sights, sounds, smells, tastes, or touches told you. Fortunately you have a whole set of internal senses. You have only to see a failure in any of these systems to realize their importance. A person whose muscle-sensing system is disordered may not be able to stand without swaying or move without looking drunk. He may speak in a monotone and his face be devoid of expression. He may not recognize everyday objects—a key, a flashlight, a watch—when they are placed in his hands. Indeed the person may not even recognize his right hand as "his." Or he may feel the existence of a third hand.

As is true of disorders of any of man's senses, the afflictions are of different degrees of severity. They may involve the isolated and tragic loss of a sense itself—as in blindness and deafness—or they may involve distortions of the senses, leading to such bizarre phenomena as phantom limbs, visual hallucinations, strange echoes in the head, smells where there are no smells, tastes where there are no tastes, sensations that the skin is crawling with insects when there is nothing on it.

As in all fields of medical research, the anomalies and malfunctions have served as an important source for obtaining knowledge about the normal state. Indeed, up until a generation ago, the gross correlation of symptoms with diseased tissues was the only direct line to knowledge scientists had.

About forty years ago, however, a German investigator named Hans Berger revived the notion that the brain of an animal generates minute electric currents. He made the first brain wave recordings from normal human subjects. They were so crude that many scientists dismissed them as laboratory artifacts. But within a decade the tide had turned. Today the technique of electrophysiology is the prime tool in mapping man's brain.

In a normal human subject the surface currents of the brain can be read by attaching electrodes to the scalp. To get at the deeper structures of the brain, investigators must open the skull; they depend on the occasional cases of human neurosurgery or, more commonly, experiments with animals. Such work and the older techniques of destroying a part of an animal's brain, or using drugs to induce changes remain the three principal ways by which scientists can study the nervous system. Such methods have been used to correlate parts of the brain with certain changes in behavior and with certain emotional and sensory qualities, or with the ability of an animal to be conditioned in learning experiments. Still, when it comes to dealing with the senses of animals, a cat cannot tell what it sees; a monkey cannot report what it may hear. The problem of acquiring knowledge of sensations might have remained teasingly remote, except for an exciting turn in the history of science. The improvements brought about by technology based on solid state physics—the transistor, the tunnel diode—made it possible to produce miniaturized equipment that was both reliable and highly sensitive. These tools of the electronics engineers in the hands of the neurophysiologists provided the means for the study of things that were of new concern to the engineers themselves: how the ear hears or how the eye sees.

With tools available for recording the current generated from sites in or near a single nerve cell, scientists gained a new insight. This insight, instead of leading to a simplified theory, has led to the realization that the brain performs a vast integrating and coordinating function in which billions of cells may participate; in which excitation and inhibition, cooperative and non-cooperative interactions take place; and in which incoming signals may be modified or controlled by important feedback mechanisms generated within the nervous system itself.

The electrical dissection now possible has inspired some surprising new looks at man's sensory system. One theory of vision compares the structure of the photoreceptors with semi-conducting materials. Investigators of hearing postulate that a certain inner ear fluid may be a source of electrical energy, a living liquid battery. Our perceptions of smell and taste may depend on a complex code in which data on the molecular size, shape, and electric charge may all play a role.

But perhaps the fundamental revelation to emerge from current research is one that gives the lie to popular statements that compare man's brain to a giant computer. It is microscopic nerve cells that perform a computer-like function; each cell is a world unto itself yet, at the same time, each maintains a subtle relation with its neighbors, the whole system coordinating and signaling a pattern that gives meaning to the structure Sir Charles Sherrington so beautifully described as "the enchanted loom."

ACKNOWLEDGMENTS

The subject of this book, summed up in a single word, is communication. The book is concerned with how man communicates with himself and the world around him, and how the world informs man of itself. The research entailed has engaged the author in extensive communication with professionals in the field. Many read one or more chapters relevant to their research; many gave freely of their time in interviews; many supplied papers, photos, and suggestions for further research. In subtle and incalculable ways these contacts inspired the work with a sense of excitement and importance. The field of neurophysiology today seems to be undergoing a wave of discovery and synthesis comparable to what happened to physics in the twenties and thirties, and to molecular biology in the fifties. While in part this foment is due to advances in technology, in the main it stems from the particularly keen minds who have chosen this field as their life's work. Of these I should like to single out the following to thank for their generous help and encouragement: Dr. Tryphena Humphrey of the University of Alabama Medical Center, Dr. Nikolajs Cauna of the University of Pittsburgh School of Medicine,

Drs. Charles R. Noback and Werner Loewenstein of the College of Physicians and Surgeons of Columbia University, Dr. Ainsley Iggo of the University of Edinburgh, Drs. David H. Hubel and Torsten Wiesel of Harvard Medical School, Dr. George Wald and Mr. Paul Brown of Harvard University, Dr. Georg von Békésy of the University of Hawaii, Drs. M. L. Wolbarsht and T. H. Benzinger of the Naval Medical Research Institute, Bethesda, Maryland, Drs. Grant Rasmussen and Edward F. Evans of the National Institute of Neurological Diseases and Blindness, Dr. Ernst Ray Pariser of the Technological Laboratory of the Department of Interior's Bureau of Commercial Fisheries, Dr. J. Y. Lettvin of the Massachusetts Institute of Technology, Dr. Robert Gesteland of Northwestern University, Dr. John E. Amoore of the Western Regional Research Laboratory of the Department of Agriculture at Albany, California, Dr. James W. Johnston, Jr., of Georgetown University, Washington, D.C., Dr. Alan Rothballer of Albert Einstein Medical College of Yeshiva University, Dr. Harry Harlow of the University of Wisconsin, Dr. Harlow W. Ades of the University of Illinois, Dr. Edward S. Hodgson of Columbia University, Dr. Bela Julesz of Bell Telephone Laboratories, Dr. Hans Engström of the University of Göteborg, Sweden, and Dr. Ronald Melzack of McGill University, Montreal, Canada.

I am grateful to Dr. Humphrey for supplying me with photographs taken by the late Dr. Davenport Hooker which appear in his *A Preliminary Atlas of Early Fetal Activity*, to Dr. Cauna for his generous supply of photomicrographs of cutaneous receptors, to Dr. Engström for photos of the vestibular organs, to Dr. von Békésy for his photo of the arm-cochlea model, to Dr. Benzinger for photos of calorimetry equipment, and to Dr. Harlow for his photos of maternally deprived monkeys.

I should like to express my thanks to Dr. Noback, whose friendly words of advice and help accompanied my earliest formal introduction to neuroanatomy when I attended lectures given by him and Dr. Malcolm Carpenter at the College of Physicians and Surgeons of Columbia University in 1963–64.

I am also appreciative of the anecdotes and news stories supplied to me by fellow science writers Martin Mann of Time-Life, Inc., and Joan Hollobon of the Toronto *Globe and Mail*.

Lastly my thanks are due to the lay person of intelligence and curiosity for whom this book is intended. This role has been most nobly and sympathetically undertaken by my husband.

CONTENTS

I

What the Baby Saw

It may surprise mothers to learn that a baby is born some many months too soon—that compared to it, the soft wet bundle of fur that is a kitten, blind at birth, can far better fend for itself. Nevertheless, as medical school professors are fond of saying, "It is very hard to kill a baby."

What goes on in the first few months of life is a fascinating combination of care and contact. The elements of care are obvious. They include the warm bottle, the dry diaper, and the clean sheet. But what happens when the baby comes into contact with the hot, cold, hard, soft, sweet, sour stuffs of life? And in particular, what happens when he is exposed to the care*taker*—the human being who does the feeding, the diaper changing, the sheet smoothing, and much more?

Without human contact a baby's fate is seriously compromised. Psychiatrist René Spitz studied babies in a foundling home, set up after World War II outside the United States, where babies were given good diets and warm beds, but where the ratio of trained nurses to infants was only one to ten. At the end of two years—in contrast to an adequately staffed "nursery" in the United States—the foundling home babies were judged to be 45 percent below normal in general development. Mentally they were classified as low-grade morons. They were also strangely susceptible to every kind of minor disease and infection. In spite of sanitary conditions and adequate medical facilities, the mortality rate for these infants at the end of the two-year period was a shocking 37 percent.

There are pitiable cases of deliberate child abuse at home, of boys and girls fed and clothed, but locked in rooms or chained to bedposts. Such treatment also leaves indelible marks. If such children do reach psychiatric hospitals they are so deeply disturbed that they will suffer emotional, if not intellectual, impairment for the rest of their lives.

The same is true in species close to man. Dr. Harry Harlow of the University of Wisconsin has raised monkeys in isolation and given them "surrogate mothers"—wire screens covered with terry cloth—which the

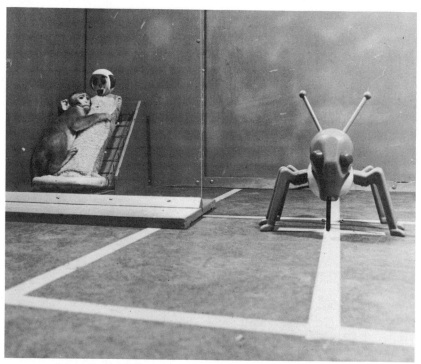

Monkeys deprived of contact with their real mother and provided with only a wire or cloth substitute exhibit extreme fear reactions to strange or foreign objects introduced into their environment.

2

monkeys can stroke, suck, or caress. In some cases these monkeys died. In others they grew up to be forever strange, frightened and nervous when introduced to their fellow monkeys, unable to exhibit normal sexual behavior or maternal care.

What parents can do for children is more dynamic than mere attention to physical needs. Parents handle children. A mother picks up her baby, she pets him, smiles at him, hums in his ears. She watches how he reacts to the bath water, the overhead light, the wool blanket she tucks around him. The baby will turn or kick or cry or scream or smile or blink, or he will not react—he will sleep through the noisy party, not hear the door slam, or notice the light turned on in the nursery. And so, by a process of mutual stimulation, a teasing of both their senses, mother and child will come to know each other. More than this, they will come to establish a two-way system of communication that is vital to the survival of the individual upon his entry into the world. The mother is the prime

source for stimulating a baby's senses, and hence his developing brain. Through her a baby comes to know the world, and by her he makes himself known to that world.

But the gulf between the two is so wide at first that it is a wonder that communication is ever established. At birth a baby's language of the senses is primitive. He speaks a kind of pidgin in comparison with his mother's fluent idiom.

She will rely heavily on what her eyes and ears tell her, the special sense organs that above all others will be educated through this experience. She will look at her newborn and perhaps see the whitish, waxy substance on his skin that protected him from the fluids of her uterus. She will see his limp and fragile body, his head much too big in comparison with his body, and elongated now from having been squeezed in its passage through the birth canal.

She will look at his face and see that his eyes may be open. She can examine every part of him, see him as a solid being that fills space and has weight, see the color of his hair and eyes, the pink of his lips, whereas he is color blind and sees only grays, blacks, and whites. He sees vague shapes, or flashes of light, but without meaning. His eyes can neither focus on nor follow a moving object. He is even farsighted since his eyeballs are foreshortened at birth. And what he sees is flat. He uses only one eye at a time, his eyes not yet working together to sight an object three-dimensionally.

If he cries she can hear and lift him up and press him to her breast. She may murmur soothing words which he may hear, but he cannot turn his head toward the sound, and needless to say, he will not comprehend. He lies flat on his back or stomach; his arms and legs are able to move, but only haphazardly. He cannot lift his head; much less can he manage the job of sitting, standing, or moving about.

His mother can amuse him with a rattle held in her hands. He can't yet manage that very human feat of opposing his thumb to his other fingers. He will close his fingers around the rattle if she presses it into his hand, but he can't hold on and it will fall.

These are extraordinary deficiencies, and they make a human baby more helpless than most other creatures at birth. The newborn fawn or colt can scramble to its feet and walk. The newborn guinea pig or monkey can cling tightly to its mother's body and hold fast as she makes her daily perambulations. Only in the next three-quarters of a year will a human infant gain some of these skills.

Yet he is not without resources. He can smell. Milk apparently smells good to him and if he can't use his eyes to find his mother's breast, his nose can help guide him. He can taste, too. Tests have shown

4

that even premature babies can tell the difference between sweet and salty flavors. His sense of balance is working; it might even have figured in positioning him in the uterus in the head-down posture that is normal before birth. And he seems to have an instinctive fear of falling.

The infant is sensitive to heat and cold, touch and pressure. He reacts to the way he is picked up, squalling when an angry or nervous mother is doing the handling, calming down almost at once when a relaxed grandmother takes over. Already his senses manage some neat trick of integration so that his over-all reaction to differences in touch, temperature, and pressure is one of either pain or pleasure.

Doctors at New York State Psychiatric Institute tell an even more dramatic story of such unconscious perception. They show medical students a photograph of a baby taken in the first year of life and ask their opinion. Unanimously the students agree that the baby looks sick, sad, and unhappy. Then they show the students a picture of the baby a year later. This time they all agree that whatever had been wrong has cleared up; the picture is of a healthy, happy baby. Finally the doctors reveal that it was the mother who was ill initially. The same day her baby was born an older child was killed in an automobile accident, an event which plunged the mother into a severe depression. It was only toward the end of the child's first year that she began the psychiatric treatments which helped her adjust to the tragedy and restored her to normal by the time the second picture was taken.

The baby's senses, dismally deficient in some areas, are remarkably acute in others. Why this should be has long been a matter of speculation and theory; only recently has it been a subject of direct observation and analysis. The reasons for this change are twofold. One has been the general leap forward in research that has come about by applying some of the techniques of electrical engineering and computer research to the study of the brain. These techniques recast the interpersonal dynamics of mother-child contact into the more abstract framework of energy transfers and information-processing systems.

Looked at this way a mother's role is that of an information filter between the world and the child. The world broadcasts, using heat, light, sound, chemical or mechanical energy to carry its message. The baby comes equipped to pick up those energies, albeit some channels are better than others at first, and in the process to generate messages of his own. His sense organs are the receivers. Technically they are also energy converters, transducers, so differentiated that some can absorb heat, others light, still others mechanical pressures, and convert these energies into the one form of energy the nervous system can use—electrical energy. It is no accident that these transducers are primed to pay special attention to sound energies that correspond to the human voice, to light reflected from a human face, to pressures from human hands.

The brain's action once it has processed this information will take the form of electrical impulses that go out to the body's muscles and glands. This time electrical energy will be converted to mechanical movements or chemical reactions.

Of course the analogy would be meaningless were it not for the other side of research—the increasingly detailed investigation of the single cells or cell groups that make up the sense organs, as well as the nerve cells, nerve fibers, and supporting structures of the nervous system. The goal of this neurophysiological research is to explain how the sensory transducers transduce, how nerve fibers code and conduct electrical impulses, where they go in the brain, and how that organ is arranged to cope with signals coming and going at all times.

When the double approach of computer engineering and neurophysiology is combined with studies of growth and development, a dynamic element is introduced. Time becomes important. What a baby can or cannot do at any stage of its life reflects the state of development of the nervous system, its growth and maturation in time. Once this concept is understood something strange happens: the mystique surrounding birth itself vanishes.

Birth is an arbitrary event, a vertical cut in a horizontal time-line that continues from conception to death. Though no one is certain why it occurs precisely when it does, there is one good mechanical reason. The human brain, the most complex and elaborate structure to develop in the course of evolution, has already, in the course of nine months, grown so big that its container, the head, approaches the physical limits in size to which a woman can give birth.

At birth the brain is one-fourth adult size. It weighs about half a pound, about 7 percent of the baby's total weight. It is so soft it could take the shape of any container it was poured into. Yet in spite of its semi-solid state this mass of gray and white tissue is covered with wrinkles and folds and parts that bulge.

Structurally all the complex parts of the adult brain are there, though many are dwarfed and hidden by the pair of gray cerebral hemispheres on top and the glistening bulge of cerebellum behind. Functionally there is a profound difference. Many nerve cells and fibers are still growing; many parts of the brain have not been hooked up yet, either with each other or with various sense organs all over the body. Circuits which might take the working black and white visual signals from one part of the brain and interpret or store them elsewhere are just

6

beginning to be put down. The baby can see, though it cannot make sense out of what it sees. But circuits leading from transducer elements like the color cells in the eye have not been completed, and the baby is color blind. Circuits to and from the spinal cord, the slender stem on which the brain flowers, are still to be completed. By far the bulk of these are the ones that go out to control voluntary movements—hence a baby's general floundering.

Although these missing links underlie a baby's overt deficiencies, there are other lines in full operation at birth. Some of these circuits monitor vital life processes such as breathing, digesting food, and eliminating waste. Here the initial signals are triggered by transducer elements *inside* the body; sensing mechanisms which respond to changes in blood pressure, to mechanical stresses or strains on lungs or stomach or bladder walls. They inform the brain and spinal cord of what is happening to the "inner man" at every instant of life.

Of greater interest, however, are those nerve connections existing at birth that step into the outside world; indeed they need contact from the world to reveal themselves. Their function explains why, if a rattle is put in a baby's hand he tries to grasp it; why he blinks if a light shines in his eyes; why he may blink and try to move away if his bottle crashes to the floor, but why, if the nipple of the bottle is applied to his lips, he will turn his head toward it and will suck.

These complex patterns of behavior represent hereditary networks built into the nervous system, reflexes common to all human beings at birth. In the simpler cases the design is usually described as a simple reflex arc: a sensory input signal, a nervous system connection, and a "motor" output—a signal going out to a muscle or gland. The circuit is automatic, requiring no thought, no act of decision. It has been programmed into the machinery like the push-button controls on a washing machine or TV set. Historically this is why reflexes have been called simple, but simple is a dangerous word ever to apply to the nervous system. No reflex is self-contained. Even the simplest reflex may involve hundreds of nerve and muscle fibers, nor does it go unnoticed in other parts of the nervous system.

The feature that all reflexes have in common and which explains their automatic nature is that they are protective, life-preserving. You don't have time to think in an emergency. You must act. If a car backfires you still blink your eyes. If a pin pricks your hand, it hurts, and you pull it away, just as the baby does. These and other reflexes such as coughing, sneezing, gagging, vomiting, and yawning are reactions of the nervous system to threats to your body, actions to keep you out of trouble or pain.

7

Other reflexes are equally important in life-sustaining activities such as searching for food and feeding. Grasping, swallowing, and sucking are also programmed into the machinery. Circuits like these last will fade with time. For part of the charm of the nervous system is a certain architectural flexibility. Form tends to follow function. When function ceases or is replaced by improved mechanisms, form may disappear. So at some point in infancy the baby no longer grasps everything put into its hand, or tries to put it in its mouth and suck it.

Nor can the baby swim, though had his body been immersed in water in the first few months of life, his arms and legs would have made movements to keep him afloat, a reflex which may have had its origins in the liquid environment of the uterus itself. For the uterus too is a world, a dark, wet, insulated world in which, as the embryo grows, its developing nervous system reacts. Conventionally birth is taken as the starting point of experience. In reality it is just an arbitrary point in a continuum that begins with the earliest flowering of the senses in embryo. Tracing these prenatal lines of development now will reveal fundamental clues to the future behavior of the individual.

The Beginning of Life

Life starts with a single fertilized egg, a single cell of soft, colorless, living material enclosed in a transparent membrane—smaller in size than the period which ends this sentence. Before long, however, that small object divides in two, and then each again divides in two, and so on. A mass of tiny cells form and in due time, a different shape is assumed. The small dot becomes a comma, a crescent shape with a blob at one end. This is true whether the egg was fertilized in man or mouse, monkey or giraffe, for all mammals develop along similar lines in the beginning. From one cell they develop into many—cells of different kinds that so begin to group themselves that the embryo body falls into three tube, or cordlike, structures. One is a tube that starts at the mouth and ends at the anus. The lining of this tube will give rise to the linings of all the parts of the body that have to do with eating, breathing, digesting, assimilating food, and eliminating waste.

Another is a cordlike structure that will attract to it cells which will eventually form the framework of the body. The cells will grow into the budding bones that form the skeleton, as well as muscles and blood vessels.

Finally there is a third structure, a tube which lies above these other two and very close to the back of the embryo. This is the neural tube, a special development of the tissue that forms the skin itself. Out of this will grow the two great information-processing and integrating structures that form the central nervous system—the brain and spinal cord. The clusters of cells gathering along both sides of the tube toward the back will give rise to nerves that lead into the tube as well as out to the sense organs of the body. These nerves will unite with other cable-like structures streaming out from both sides of the tube on the front side destined to reach muscles and glands.

If you take a thin strip of paper and turn the long sides in toward each other you can make a tube. That's how the neural tube begins to form early in life—about the third week after conception—when the embryo is barely six-hundredths of an inch long. The tube starts to close around the neck region first, then toward the head, then toward the tail. By the twenty-fifth day the tube is completely closed. The head part, which is thicker, will grow into the brain. The tail part is more cylindrical. It will form the spinal cord. This order of growth is the first important clue to the order of behavioral development in man. The nervous system governing behavior develops from the neck up and the neck down.

While this is going on other changes are taking place in the embryo. Some cells are migrating toward the framing cord that lies under the neural tube. Eventually these cells will come around to circle the neural tube and form the bony spinal column that will both protect and support the spinal cord. The bones forming in the head will be doing the same thing for the brain. So vital are these structures—the spinal cord and the brain—that in their final form they will lie suspended in a fluid pool that will lubricate, nourish, and help make them shock-resistant. They will be encased in three thin but tough membranes, and, finally, guarded by armor, the skull and spinal bones themselves.

Visualizing the development of the central nervous system and the other tubelike structures before birth is important in gaining an understanding of man's anatomy. Man's fundamental shape is that of a cylinder. The brain and by far the most important sensing gear are at the top. Down the center runs the spinal column, a major highway with entrances and exits placed on either side all along its length to serve the nerves passing to or from the periphery of the body. This must be borne in mind because it is easy to forget that man is split into two halves. There are thirty-one pairs of spinal nerves lined up on either side of the spinal cord, and twelve pairs of cranial nerves of the brain itself: two optic nerves, two auditory nerves, and so on. Nearly all the complex internal parts of the brain and spinal cord also show this duality, coming in pairs which have the symmetry of a butterfly or the inkblot patterns psychologists are so fond of. One of the few exceptions is a structure

9

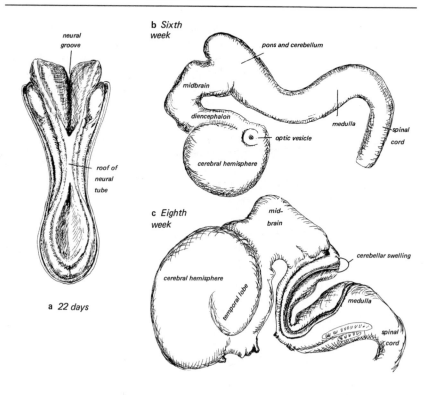

deep in the center of the brain called the pineal gland. Because it was unique René Descartes, the seventeenth-century philosopher who also conceived of the notion of a reflex, thought the pineal gland might be the seat of the soul.

While at birth not all the intricate parts of this system are working, the over-all pattern is visible and the parts themselves are assembled astonishingly early in the life of the embryo. By the twenty-fifth day of life, when a woman may not even know she is pregnant, the embryo heart has already formed and started to beat. Several days later it will actually pump blood manufactured in the liver.

At about this time the foreparts of the brain start to swell and put forth tiny stalks from which the eyes will develop. The ears will follow about a week later; the external flaps forming from little folds that are embryologically related to gill slits, their inner parts forming from tissue lining the mouth, and the eardrum and middle ear structures developing from tissue in between. The nose begins to jut out during the fifth week while, in the next fortnight cheeks and lips swell enough to give contours to the face. By the end of the second month the embryo has become a fetus, a

10

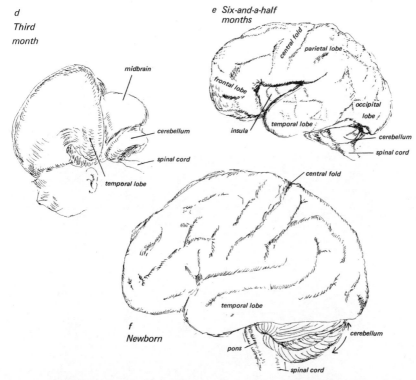

Some of the stages in the development of the nervous system in embryo through to birth. Drawing A shows the whole embryo; drawings B, C, E, and F show the brain and part of the spinal cord; drawing D shows facial development at an intermediate stage.

miniature human being, almost all of whose organs have appeared, even though it is only about an inch long.

The striking feature of this rapid growth and organ development is its functional significance. Not only are the parts of the vehicle assembled quickly, they are tried out. This is a second clue to behavioral development. Nature works efficiently; the engine, the steering, the distribution, and transmission systems are all working before the upholstery is added or the final paint job dry.

This had made sense to embryologists when they looked at the heart and blood systems, the liver, kidneys, and other organs involved in the growth and maintenance of the fetus. The question remained whether or not the nervous system could function. Could it sense anything? And if so: What? When? How?

The answers to these questions have come for the most part from

11

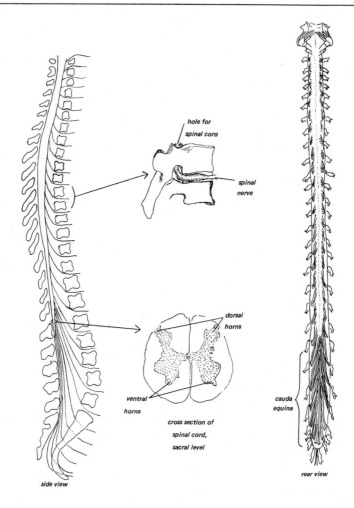

hole for
spinal cord

spinal
nerve

dorsal
horns

ventral
horns

cross section of
spinal cord,
sacral level

cauda
equina

rear view

side view

The spinal cord lies within the vertebral canal extending from the base of the skull to the lower border of the first lumbar vertebra in the adult. It is cylindrical in shape, swelling to spindlelike enlargements in the cervical (neck) and lumbar regions. These portions of the cord innervate the upper and lower extremities, respectively. The lower end of the cord tapers into a cone, and the lowest spinal nerves to branch off at this point travel some length before emerging through the intervertebral spaces. This part of the cord is known as the cauda equina, or horse's tail. Details show the structure of the intervertebral spaces and a cross section of the cord typical of the lower part. The gray matter (stippled area) has a butterfly shape, the farthest dorsal and ventral parts being known as the (dorsal and ventral) horns.

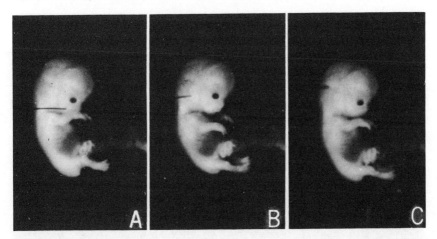

Three prints from a motion picture showing very early reflex activity occurring at the late embryo stage. The length of the embryo from crown to rump is just over 1 inch. Print A shows the position of the embryo before it has moved. Print B illustrates reflex movement: a bending away from the side touched, a backward and downward motion of the upper extremities, and a slight rotation of the rump. Print C shows the position after the reflex has been completed.

the painstaking researches of the late embryologist and anatomist Dr. Davenport Hooker. He and his colleagues at the University of Pittsburgh examined some 150 embryos and fetuses over the course of twenty-five years, infants whose premature delivery came about as the result of spontaneous abortions or surgery to save the life of the mother. For a brief time these very premature babies were alive, and their state of development could be observed.

Hooker found that the nervous system was no different from other systems of the body. No sooner are its parts connected than it can react—crudely, at first, but then with increasing refinement. At the extraordinarily tender age of seven and one-half weeks—the late embryo stage—the neck can bend to one side in response to stroking the mouth or the sides of the nose with a single human hair. The reflex movement is always away from the stimulus, as though to avoid the touch.

In a week's time the response spreads to include movements of the upper trunk and shoulders, and still later reaches the lower trunk, legs, and feet. By twelve weeks there have been refinements in the movements. The head can now rotate gracefully to one side and the arms move inward, but the response is still very generalized.

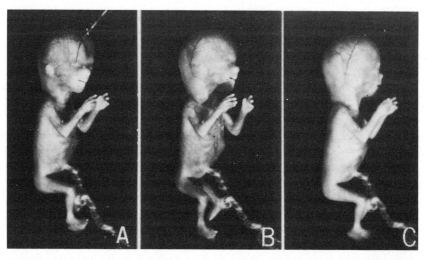

At approximately three months the fetus (now about 3.5 inches long from crown to rump) exhibits local reflexes. Shown here are one involving the eyelids and another producing an elevation in the angle of the mouth. At the same time the head bends to the side and the face turns away from the side of the face touched. Head and trunk also move backward. Print A shows the position when the eyelids were touched, before movement began. Print B illustrates the tightening of the closed lids, producing a squintlike movement, and shows the corner of the mouth lifted, the face turned away, and the back straightened. Print C shows additional turning away of the face and backward bending of the head.

By the thirteenth or fourteenth week however, there is a significant change in behavior. No longer do touches on various parts of the face bring about movements from unrelated or distant parts of the body. Instead local responses take over. Stroking the bottom lip now causes the mouth to open, and during the next two months there will be a step-by-step progression to lips protruding, to pursing, and finally at twenty-nine weeks to a vigorous sucking. In the meantime inspiratory gasps, swallowing, tongue movements, and lip-curling responses will have been established and tried out. For the baby will use the amniotic fluid bathing him to practice with. The fluid also may have some nutritious value in the stomach or lubricating value in the lungs.

As early as ten and one-half weeks the fetus will have begun to make spontaneous movements. In response to a stroking of the palm the fingers will start to close. At about eighteen and one-half weeks the hand can hold a glass rod, and by twenty-seven weeks the grasp is strong enough to support the whole body, though it is confined to one hand at a time. (Stimulating the right hand while the left is holding an object causes the object to be released.)

Dr. Hooker has speculated that some of the stages of reflex development that occur before birth may parallel ancestral habits. Thus the strong grasp at twenty-seven weeks, which is not present at birth, may relate to functions used by tree-living ancestors. The swimming reflex might relate to some stage of development of a sea-dwelling ancestor.

Dr. Hooker also noted another principle of development: when the nervous system is threatened by exhaustion of its oxygen supply, it is the last acquired reflex which is the first to be lost. This is true down to the earliest, most generalized response. In illness or shock in postnatal life also, only the more primitive reflexes may remain.

At many stages of development, follow-up microscopic studies of nerve tissue were made by Dr. Hooker's co-workers, including Dr. Tryphena Humphrey, now at the University of Alabama's Medical Center. Dr. Humphrey pointed out that the earliest neck-bending reflex at seven and one-half weeks was signaled by branches of the fifth cranial nerve located about the region of the mouth. Fibers from this area enter the brain and group into a bundle which grows down into the spinal cord. When the fibers reach the upper cord level they can make contact through other nerve cells or neurons with cells which can trigger the contractions of the neck muscles, and the reflex arc is completed. When movements of the upper trunk are first observed, the fibers of this nerve

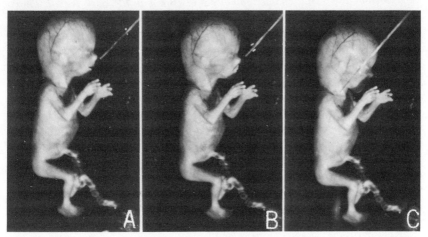

Also at about three months the fetus shows reflex mouth closure and swallowing. Print A shows the fetal position at the time the upper lip was touched; print B illustrates mouth closure; print C shows the forward bending of the head that accompanied swallowing. (Shadows obscure the movement of the Adam's apple that indicates swallowing.)

15

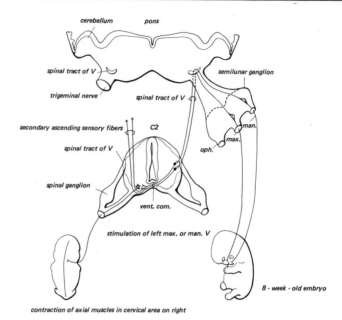

cerebellum pons

spinal tract of V

trigeminal nerve spinal tract of V

semilunar ganglion

secondary ascending sensory fibers C2

man.

max.

spinal tract of V oph.

spinal ganglion

vent. com.

stimulation of left max. or man. V

8 - week - old embryo

contraction of axial muscles in cervical area on right

Diagram illustrating the pathway of an early reflex arc. Beginning at lower right, branches of the fifth cranial nerve around the mouth of the embryo send impulses into the brain at the pons level. The fibers move down into the cord (spinal tract of V) and contact spinal cord neurons in the neck region. These in turn excite nerve cells whose fibers signal the contraction of head and neck muscles, completing the reflex arc.

have grown further in the spinal cord. Thus the anatomical evidence was found to back up what the eye observed.

If these observations are combined with evidence drawn from studies of evolution and comparative anatomy a detailed picture of development emerges. An infant first senses the world through tactile stimulation of his face around the mouth and nose area. The experience is somehow unpleasant, for the reflex is to turn away. Later on, touching this same oral area will inspire a new set of special reflexes that are concerned with keeping alive rather than avoiding danger.

The order of development mirrors the initial neck up, neck down closure of the neural tube. The earliest sensations are felt in the lower part of the face. This extends up to the eye level and then down to trunk, limbs, and feet.

This order, and the role the earliest reflexes play, help explain why local senses—touch, temperature, pressure, pain—take precedence over

16

the distance senses—vision and hearing—in early development. The local senses are stimulated by intimate contacts and are immediately concerned with threats to survival or with life-sustaining activities. Smell, though technically considered one of the distance senses, functionally figures in the first group because of its relation to food.

This developmental hierarchy of the senses will determine the order of the chapters to follow. The earliest, most general, local senses will be described first, while vision and hearing will be discussed last. This progression will also, bit by bit, reveal something of the order that exists within the brain itself. For it, too, as it rests atop the spinal cord, has developed from the ground up. The structures near the base represent an early ascent in the scale of evolution, a thickening of the neural tube and an elaboration of special centers that serve the same purposes whether in man, frogs, snakes, or fish: this is why the collection of parts

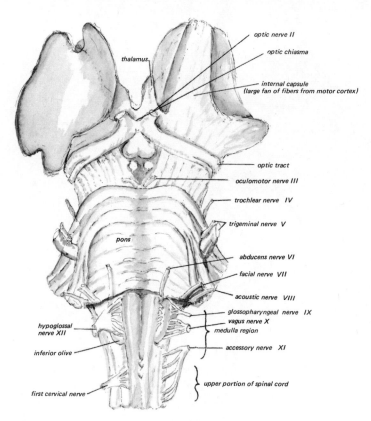

Ventral view of the brain stem showing the major divisions and some of the cranial nerves and pathways.

17

is sometimes called man's reptilian brain. The bulk of these structures constitutes the brain stem which in man is largely hidden beneath the canopy of the cerebrum and cerebellum. Moving upward and forward from the cord (for the brain mass now bends at an angle to the spinal cord), the main divisions of the brain stem are the medulla, the pons (literally, bridge), the midbrain, and the diencephalon ("between" brain). In addition the reptilian brain includes the cerebellum and several cortical structures including the olfactory lobes and certain clusters of nerve cells called the basal ganglia. These ganglia are among the

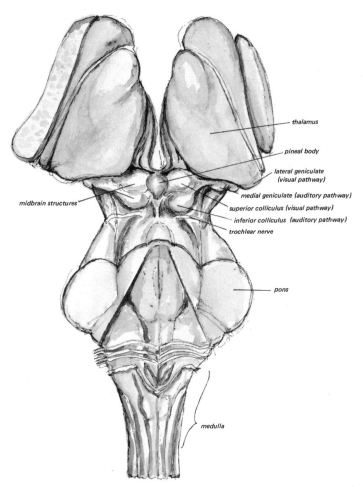

Dorsal view of the brain stem showing major divisions and important sensory relay areas.

18

oldest parts of the forebrain or telencephalon (endbrain) to evolve, and in lower animals they are largely responsible for stereotyped patterns of motion. They control the way a fish swims, a snake crawls, and a bird flies. In man these structures survive and play an auxiliary role in motion, but the telencephalon is dominated by the more recently evolved neocortex with more sophisticated sensory, motor, and integrating areas. It is this new brain which has been elaborated into the familiar folds and convolutions typical of the brain surface in man. They are the means by which nature has chosen to expand the surface area without further enlarging the dimensions of the skull.

Each successively higher section of the brain stem represents a more complex and elaborate body of nerve cells and nerve fibers which communicates with and exerts some influence over lower parts. Some of the nerve fibers belong to the twelve pairs of cranial nerves entering or exiting from the brain. These are the brain's counterpart of the spinal nerves issuing from the spinal cord. Some of these are highly specialized nerves controlling particular kinds of eye movements; some are sensory in nature, like the olfactory, auditory, or optic nerves. Others may be concerned with visceral responses, swallowing, coughing, sneezing, digesting food, and so on.

Each division of the brain stem also contains streams of nerve fibers on their way up to higher brain centers or descending from such centers. Sometimes these fibers continue without interruption through segment after segment of brain stem. Sometimes they communicate with clusters of nerve cells (nuclei) at a particular level. These nuclei are the relay stations handling incoming impulses and transmitting new signals. At the medulla level, for example, are certain centers that control respiration, digestion, and vomiting. At the midbrain are important relay stations for auditory and visual signals. But the key structure involved in the transmission of sensory information is undoubtedly the thalamus, the major subdivision of the diencephalon. Impulses coming in from every sense system of the body except the olfactory ultimately are projected to the thalamus before being conveyed to the cortex. In addition to serving this primary function in data processing the thalamus also helps regulate the level of cortical activity and hence determines a person's state of wakefulness.

Above the brain stem, surrounding it like a ring which gives the group of structures the name limbic lobe, sometimes called man's "lower mammalian brain," are nuclei and fiber pathways which mark a higher stage of evolution. Here are the olfactory centers, as well as cells or fiber pathways, which when stimulated can alter blood pressure, heart rate, respiration, sexual activity—in short they signal the physiological con-

19

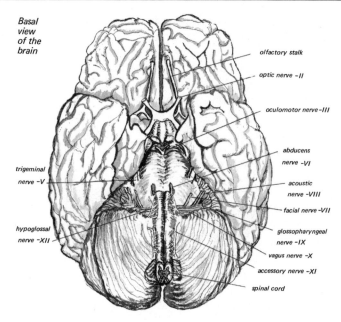

Basal view of the brain

olfactory stalk

optic nerve –II

oculomotor nerve–III

abducens nerve –VI

trigeminal nerve –V

acoustic nerve –VIII

facial nerve –VII

hypoglossal nerve –XII

glossopharyngeal nerve –IX

vagus nerve –X

accessory nerve –XI

spinal cord

All but one of the twelve pairs of cranial nerves exit from the ventral, or basal, surface of the brain. The exception is the trochlear nerve (IV), which exits from the dorsal side; this is the nerve which allows rotation of the eyeball outward and downward. Following is a list of the cranial nerves with a brief description of their major functions:

Cranial Nerve	Designation	Function
I	Olfactory	Subserves sense of smell
II	Optic	Subserves sense of vision
III	Oculomotor	Elevates lid, controls vertical and converging movements of eyeball, participates in lateral eye movements, contracts pupil, alters convexity of lens
IV	Trochlear	Rotates eyeball downward and outward
V	Trigeminal	Controls jaw movements and supplies touch, pain, and temperature innervation to face
VI	Abducens	Turns eyeball outward
VII	Facial	Controls facial movements, supplies taste fibers to anterior two-thirds of tongue, innervates salivary glands and mucous membranes in mouth
VIII	Acoustic	Subserves hearing and balance
IX	Glossopharyngeal	Supplies taste fibers to posterior third of tongue
X	Vagus	Controls many visceral activities, including respiration, blood pressure, digestion
XI	Accessory	Controls certain movements of head and larynx
XII	Hypoglossal	Controls tongue muscles

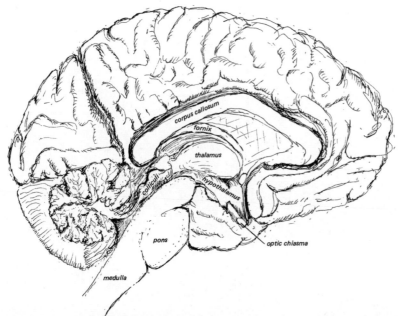

A view of the left side of the brain sectioned down the middle reveals the structure of the main divisions of the brain stem, the "old" brain, which is normally almost completely covered by the cerebral hemispheres. The brain stem is usually divided in four parts, beginning with the lowest, the medulla, atop the spinal cord; next the pons; then the midbrain—a small section containing four rounded bodies called the colliculi; and finally the diencephalon, containing the all-important thalamus, the major relay station for sensory impulses coming in from all parts of the body. Underneath the thalamus is the hypothalamus, which controls many glandular functions; regulates temperature, hunger, and thirst; and is involved in many complex circuits relating to the emotional aspects of behavior.

comitants of emotions. At the same time they convey the emotional message itself. These still more elaborate, specialized brain parts essentially color experience. They tell you whether a given sensation feels good or bad, pleasant or painful.

For the developing baby this information will count very much in determining behavior. He will come to associate the breast or the bottle with relieving the pain of hunger and releasing pleasurable feelings of satisfaction. His body will relax, he may smile, and there may even be some sexual response. For the pleasure of eating creates an aura of well-being. A male child may have an erection during feeding.

At first the pains of hunger or thirst or the pleasures of eating or being held are only felt as coming after the event. But their power lies in

21

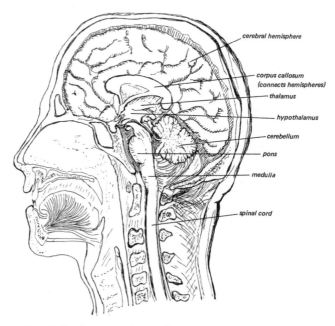

A cross section of the brain in the skull.

the fact that associations are made so the pain or pleasure is signaled before the event, and this helps shape the course of events. The baby smiles just at the sight of the bottle. This makes the mother happy, so she is more relaxed and holds him more easily, or he cries "ahead of time" in order that the bottle be brought.

Here again the engineers have a word for it: feedback. In terms of machines it means that some of the energy the machine produces is fed back into the system to control the machine itself. The classic nineteenth-century example is the steam governor on a locomotive. When the jet of steam produced in the boiler rises to a certain point it forces open certain valves which, through other connections, close down on the amount of coal fed into the boiler. With less coal coming in, the amount of steam produced drops and eventually the valves close again (just from the force of gravity).

In terms of sense energy, feedback means that some of the energies of pain and pleasure will be discharged into areas of the brain which will either try to cut down pain or promote whatever is making the baby feel good.

At birth these highly charged feelings, the hereditary reflexes and random spontaneous activities, are man's resources for coming to grips with the world. In time some reflexes will be modified, others pushed

22

into the background by the overwhelming barrage of stimuli he learns to attend to. Pain and pleasure will grow into the variety of human emotions such as fear, anger, love, and hate. Reflex and chance movements will evolve into voluntary control. He will learn not to blink when the doctor wants to put drops in his eyes; nor gag when swallowing a pill. He can grit his teeth to control the pain when a hypodermic needle is stuck in his arm and hold his temper if the needle breaks. Indeed, if yoga is practiced, conscious control may even touch the involuntary inner processes so that a person can start or stop his stomach's contractions, or so temper his breathing that he appears to be in a state of "suspended animation."

Not everyone will travel as far as the master Yogi on the road from involuntary reflex to absolute control, of course, but we all will go part of

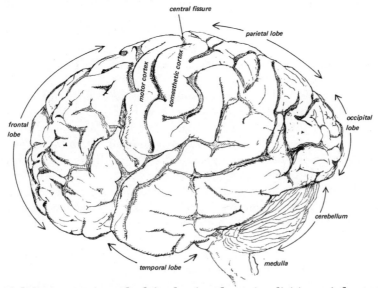

An adult brain seen from the left, showing the major divisions of the cortex into lobes. The region immediately behind the central fissure is the primary receiving area for sensory signals from the body, the somesthetic cortex. Nearby regions in the parietal lobe are considered important association areas for the senses, and figure in intellectual activity. The primary visual receiving area lies in the occipital lobe; primary auditory centers lie in the temporal lobe. Just in front of the central fissure is the primary motor cortex. Signals from this part of the cortex govern voluntary movements. The frontal lobe is generally assumed to contain the sites involved in reasoning or imaginative thinking. These distinctions should be interpreted in the broadest possible sense, however, for all parts of the cortex are linked with each other and lower regions. Oftentimes major parts can be destroyed with little noticeable loss of function.

23

the way. And the nervous system will undergo profound changes en route. It will make literally millions of cross-links between the senses, record particular traces of patterns which will be vague at first, and then become part of an almost ineradicable memory code. In such a way does man's emotional and intellectual life—all the attributes wrapped up in the elusive word "mind"—develop. It is as though life itself makes the difference. *Vive la différence,* indeed, for the act of living imposes a world upon an individual. It imposes the contacts, the concrete objects of sensory experience which start the links in the nervous system going. In time the external world is endowed with meaning. It holds its own in a dialogue the individual maintains between himself and everything he comes to regard as non-self.

Charting the exact lines of this progress belongs to the realm of pediatrics, psychology, and child development and not strictly to the story of the senses alone. Acute observers, such as the eminent psychologist Jean Piaget who has painstakingly noted the day-by-day changes in a number of children—and his own three in particular—come to conclusions which in many ways are consistent with Dr. Hooker's observations.

Piaget, too, sees at first a tendency to generalize and improve a reflex, then a narrowing down accompanied by a change in purpose. The sucking reflex is first extended to many objects besides the nipple and is improved in practice. Then the thumb is singled out to be sucked, and takes on a special meaning, a pleasurable feeling, different from sucking for reasons of hunger.

All the time this is going on, the eyes are beginning to focus and work together, and sooner or later they catch sight of the thumb. And now something very like a game develops. "Find the thumb" can be frustrating when the thumb disappears, but it is satisfying later when the baby learns to coordinate hand and eye, finally learning that he can control his hands to bring objects into view.

The ears and eyes are also combining their reactions. Here Piaget points to the special privilege of the human face, for it is a source of simultaneous excitement to both senses.

The pioneering that Hooker and Piaget have done in pre- and postnatal behavior is now being amplified and extended in many parts of this country. The National Institutes of Health have set up perinatal studies in which 50,000 mothers-to-be will be followed from the time of their baby's birth through the first five years of the life of their children. Well-baby clinics (clinics that do not treat overtly sick children; injections, vaccinations, and periodic check-ups can be given in such places) have been established in a number of cities to help provide pediatricians and

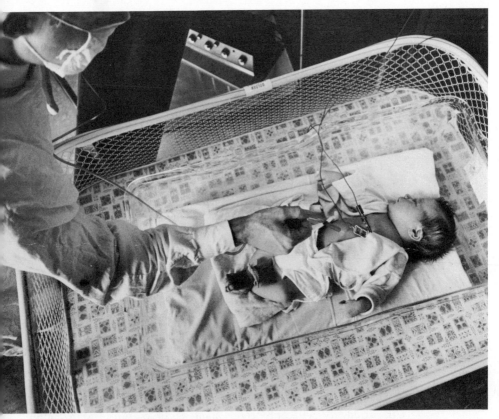

A physician from Albert Einstein College of Medicine in New York City tests a newborn's reactions to a small puff of air applied to the chest as part of a research program to measure sensory discrimination abilities during the earliest period of life.

psychologists with data in deciding what makes some mothers good and their children healthy and happy.

Sensory testing programs like those conducted at the Albert Einstein College of Medicine in New York are trying to measure newborn babies' sensory capabilities more accurately, looking for correlations between alert, attentive, easily stimulated children and intelligence. Typical questions might be: Was the baby born awake? Was he the first to be aroused when the door of the hospital nursery was opened or the light switched on?

These determinations, if made in a large enough sample, may also show some correlation between sensitivity and creativity, between hearing ability, say, and musical talent. In this way science may get some clue in understanding how such child prodigies as Mozart or Haydn came to develop their skills; some of the "wonder" will be taken out of *Wunderkind.*

Equally important will be the early detection of sensory deficiency. It seems absurd to think that children are placed in retarded classes or fail in school because they cannot see or hear normally; that a difficult personality may be a child's reaction to the impatience or anger of adults who fail to understand that he is literally unable to see the point or pay attention to the question.

Even more poignant are the occasional stories of children who grow up with congenitally perfect eyes or ears, but little chance to exercise them. One such boy, suffering from cerebral palsy, was the eldest of three children brought up by blind parents. Psychological testers in two hospitals had declared him mentally retarded. His mother refused to accept the 44 I.Q. noted on the hospital referral form, however, and took him to a school for handicapped children. There it was soon evident that he was far from subnormal. What had fooled the testers was his shy, touch-oriented behavior. He had never learned the proper use of his eyes, but imitated his parents' way of feeling objects to know the world.

The sad truth remains that the communication system is not easy to establish. Flat on his back with his independent eyes and free-moving hands and feet, the baby has no consciousness of space, or dimension, or extension. Incredibly, he does not know he is a separate being.

This discovery will only come some eight or nine months after birth, about the time, interestingly, when mouth, palate, tongue, and larynx are in position for him to mimic his first word. This is something of a time of crisis. It will be followed by the discovery that the world is a place of depth, with objects that can be crawled around, with doors and armchairs behind which people disappear. This is a very strange and magical time when a baby begins to discover himself as a self—an entity separate from the outside world.

II

The Sense of Self

If you had to think about walking down a flight of steps the chances are you'd falter. You'd be slow about it, and your movements would be jerky. You'd stop to consider what your toes were doing, why your weight was unbalanced, what you should be doing with your hands. You might look down at the full flight below and panic. How in the world could you manage all those steps? It's hard to remember, but there must have been a first time. There must also have been a first time when you took a step, or stood up; the first time you turned over in your crib; the first time you opened your eyes.

It's hard to remember these things for a very good reason: 99 percent of the time such movements take place at a subconscious level. All these activities, voluntary and involuntary, depend for their smooth operation on signals from several types of organs coordinated by a special part of the brain below the cerebral cortex.

It is the combination of these signals that gives you an indefinable sense of familiarity with your body, a sense of weight and position, a feeling that your limbs are well balanced. These qualities of the body

27

are so much a part of "youness" that their control, like the control of breathing, is an activity you are aware of only when it is jeopardized.

Yet just being bedridden for a short time can upset the normal control. You may remember the first day you got up from a sickbed. You felt dizzy and a walk was a self-conscious adventure in which you relied on the strong arm of a nurse or a friend, or else you reached out for the comforting support of furniture. You probably spread your feet farther apart than you would normally to gain better anchorage. Scientists are hard at work to see that the same sort of debility does not afflict astronauts confined to the weightless atmosphere of space capsules. They too have little chance to exercise their arms and legs and can suffer a similar wasting of the tissues.

Again disease can strike your limbs or nervous system directly and bring on more severe problems. Parkinson's disease, multiple sclerosis, St. Vitus' dance (chorea), and palsy are some disorders of the nervous system that seriously disturb movement. Syphilis, too, can cause nerve damage that upsets balance and leads to the shuffled, unsteady gait of locomotor ataxia. Arthritis, bursitis, rheumatism, and other bone and joint diseases can be equally troublesome. In all these instances you must pay attention to a part of your body you learned to ignore because it worked automatically.

Yet at birth you had no consciousness of yourself or your body. The knowledge that you are you gradually develops in the first year of life, culminating in what psychiatrists call the "eight-month identity crisis." For with the knowledge of self comes fear. It is at this time that a baby's crying may take on a new meaning. His mother has left the room, and suddenly the experience of being alone is shattering. Fortunately at this time nature comes to aid that loneliness, for now a baby begins to be self-propelled. He can crawl around and explore the world. Gradually he acquires the locomotive skills which can be the means of being able to move toward others, as well as the means of moving away, to avoid or escape danger. In terms of survival both reactions are vital, but the act of motion toward things takes on a special importance for the child. It becomes a magnificent aid to understanding and communication, not only with the strange world of three-dimensional objects, but with the dynamic world of living people.

What a child thinks about himself or the world at this stage is not known. Indeed it may not be valid to use the word "thinks" in the usual sense at all. Only a child's behavior can be observed. Again, in a way that fits Piaget's concept of the need for stimulation, an infant seems driven toward exploration and activity. To be sure, the activity is very generalized. A baby crawls with its whole body. Its movements are awkward and redundant. But with time, precision comes. With time there comes a fine control over the parts of the body especially suited for upright posture and walking. Eventually these voluntary acts will be coordinated with signals from sense organs all over the body.

"Sono io!" the Italian says, "proprio io!", he exclaims. The scene is animated. The signore has been locked out of his house on a cold night. There is a sense of wounded dignity, injured pride. "It is I," the Italian says, "really me," he adds emphatically. But the "really" does not do justice to the "proprio," and the idiom eludes translation. Proprio stems from the Latin proprius—one's own. When the Italian says proprio he is passionately declaiming his identity—his selfhood. In English the root exists only in such extensions of oneself as "property" or "proper name" and in the word "proprioception" which the English neurophysiologist Sir Charles Sherrington coined to describe the sense of self.

"Proprioceptors" are sense organs that tell you where you are in space, whether you are moving or standing still, whether hands and feet feel light or heavy, balanced or unbalanced. Another word used in this connection is kinesthesis, with its adjective, kinesthetic, from the Greek verb kinein, to move.

The body depends on two main systems of proprioception. One involves receptors that are spread out in muscles and joints and related tissue. The other is confined to special organs in the inner ear. Both systems are very old in terms of evolution. The inner ear receptors have taken over a major chore in keeping the body balanced. They are particularly responsive to changes in the position of the head. They also sense the passive motion of the body when it is subject to the changes of speed of a car or train. They record G-forces (gravity forces), giving you the sense of rapid climbing or descent that can make you feel dizzy in an elevator.

The body receptors are responsible for tracking the position of the body at rest and when self-propelled. Both systems combine forces with the eyes, for these too also survey position and movement. All feed some of their signals into a common coordinating center in the cerebellum, a large globe of tissue in the brain at the back of the head, jutting out from under the cerebral hemispheres. (The inner ear organs and the eyes will be treated later when the special senses are discussed.)

The body proprioceptors belong with the systems of touch and temperature as the oldest general senses to develop in animals and the earliest to mature in humans. Proprioceptive reflexes have been noted before birth, almost as early as the first touch responses that have been observed in human embryos. The reflexes are automatic, unconscious adjustments of muscles in the limbs, remarkable evidence that as soon as nature enables movement, it makes sure some part of the brain knows where those movements are being directed, even if the fetus isn't yet conscious of motion.

What Is It to Move?

Indeed a baby could hardly be expected to know what it is to move, even through the first years of life, because the concept of motion is by no means simple—nor is an understanding of the mechanics of human motion. Locomotion is an ability man shares with many organisms, but the techniques employed vary. Tiny sea organisms swim by means of the fine movements of hairs, or cilia, that fringe their bodies. Scallops jet-propel their way in water, expelling gulps of water in one direction and streaming off in the opposite. The particular technique higher forms use is more complex. It depends on having joints and "articulated members" (bones). This technique of motion is common to many species. One of the largest zoological families, a group which includes insects, spiders, lobsters, and crabs, is designated *arthropoda*, jointed-footed creatures.

The peculiar thing about joints, which link bones together, is that they are virtually empty spaces, or rather, cuffs or capsules filled with lubricating fluid. It is the shape of the cuff and the bone ends inside that counts. These shapes determine how much and what kinds of movements are possible.

The actual movers, however, are not the bones but muscles attached across them and through and about the joints. The muscles of the skeleton are like bundles of string. Given the "word," the strings hitch up and bones move, swinging in or out, or up or down or around a joint. Beneath the tender, enshrouding flesh man is nothing but a marionette on strings.

The bone's motion is always a rotation, measured in degrees. Your forearm bones, for example, swing through a 90-degree arc when you put on a hat. They rotate around the hingelike axis of your elbow joint. Your wrist bones may turn through a half circle (180 degrees), when you open a door. They swivel around the wrist joint.

What you see looks like straight-line motion. When you reach out to shake hands with someone your arm moves straight forward. This neat act results from two rotations—one around the shoulder joint, which allows the arm to swing forward, the other around the elbow, which allows an extension of the forearm.

The appropriate muscles in each case are hitched up, or con-tracted. That's all muscles do. Yet when a basketball player springs up and drops a ball in the basket, or a ballet dancer leaps across the stage, it appears that every part of their bodies is stretched and extended, just the opposite of a contraction. There is no contradiction, however, for by contracting certain muscles you can straighten out a limb. At the same time certain other muscles will be passively stretched. Muscle tissue is elastic enough to bear such strains—up to a point. You can see the principle at work by pulling a bowstring. Pulling back shortens or contracts the distance between the top and bottom of the bow, but the effect is to stretch out the bow. So it is with your limbs. Muscles which straighten out bones by contracting are called "extensor" muscles. Typical examples are the muscles that control the tough fibrous tissue, the tendons, which run down to the fingers along the back of the hands. If you brace yourself against the wall with your palms flat out you contract all those backs-of-finger controlling muscles.

Muscles whose contractions bend the limbs in toward each other or toward the center of the body—for example, when bringing the hands to the face, or putting the thumb and index finger together to hold a pencil—are "flexors." But motion is almost never purely flexor or extensor. Your muscles normally pay homage to a Law of Action and Reaction: for every extensor action there tends to be an equal and opposite flexor reaction, and vice versa. A small war builds up in every move you make, and the outcome, the final movement, is the dynamic balancing of opposing muscle forces.

Muscles, of course, do not initiate the skirmishes. The controls rest with the nerves, coming and going in and out of the brain and spinal cord. The signal to contract ultimately comes from special nerve cells near the front of the spinal cord, called motor cells. The fine fibers that trail out from these cells branch at their endpoints to make contact with the fine strands of muscle. The electrical impulses the motor fibers carry trigger the release of minute amounts of a chemical which starts the muscle contracting.

The greater the number of motor signals sent out, or the more frequently the impulses move down the fibers, the more will muscles contract and stay contracted. When the motor nerves stop firing, the muscle recovers.

The muscles are clearly at the end of the line, dutifully carrying out orders issued from central headquarters. Fortunately that's only half the story. They get a chance to fight back, or at least to protest against being overworked, stretched, or strained. Some of this signaling is unconscious. Your body adjusts to stresses and strains without your realizing it. Other signals arouse conscious proprioception-conveying information that reaches the highest centers of the cortex. These nerve impulses almost instantly let you know that you've raised your hand, twisted to

31

the right, or stepped off a curb. Both sets of signals depend on sensing mechanisms in muscles, in the sheathes around them or over bones, and in the tissues that make up ligaments, tendons, and joints.

These sensing mechanisms are tied to nerve cells that act in a way just opposite to the direction of activity of the motor cells. They carry electrical impulses *into* the spinal cord and toward the brain. The traffic is ever thus: motor cells send electrical impulses along fibers *out* to either muscles or glands, while sensing or sensory cells feed signals into the central nervous system. The traffic in any one fiber is always one way.

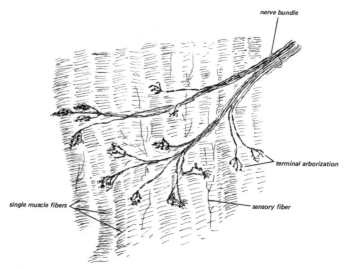

Motor endings in skeletal muscle. A single motor nerve fiber from the spinal cord may branch near its termination in the muscle and supply more than one muscle fiber. Each sub-branch then divides near its end point, loses its sheath, and branches into several twigs—its terminal "arborization." The junction with the muscle fiber is called a motor endplate.

Geographically the cell bodies of the sensory cells lie in clusters called ganglions clumped next to the spinal cord or inside the brain. Only their long fibers form the nerves that reach the periphery of the body. Often the fibers branch at their endpoints like the motor fibers and come into intimate contact with surrounding tissue. But many times a fiber enters a special end organ or receptor, such as a taste bud, which responds to certain kinds of energy, translates this to electrical energy, and passes it on to the nerve ending. The proprioceptors generally fall into this category.

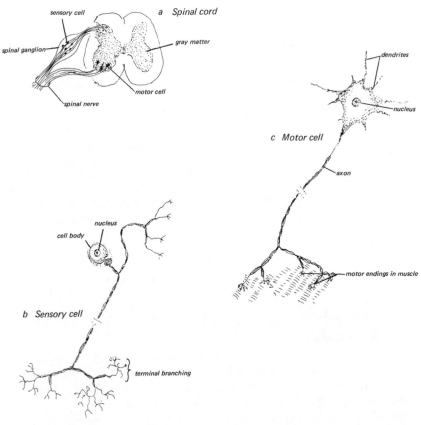

(A) Cross section of spinal cord to show the distribution of sensory fibers at back of cord and motor fibers at front. Sensory cell bodies lie outside the cord in clusters called ganglions. Motor cells lie in the gray matter of the cord and send out fibers (axons) which join the peripheral processes of the ganglion cells to form a mixed spinal nerve.

(B) A typical sensory cell of a spinal ganglion. The cell is ovoid in shape, usually emitting one process, and hence is called a unipolar cell. The process coils tightly near the cell body, then straightens and divides at a T intersection, one part going into the cord toward the back and subsequently dividing several more times. The other, peripheral process becomes part of a spinal nerve destined to innervate skin, connective tissue, joints, etc.

(C) A typical motor cell has several short processes (dendrites) through which it can communicate with other cells in the spinal cord, and one peripheral process, the axon, which emerges from the lower part of the cell, tapers into a thin thread, and then usually acquires a fatty sheath.

33

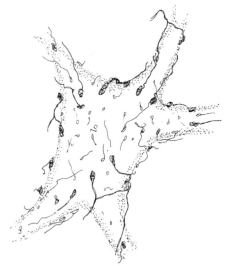

A typical motor cell of the anterior spinal cord (ventral horn region) may synapse with several hundred cells. The larger endings on the cell terminate in small bulblike expansions containing a neurofibrillar loop. Smaller endings are ring shaped. The junctions may occur throughout the body of the cell or on the dendritic processes.

Joint Sensors

Ruffini Endings

The most important position-and-motion sensors in man are shaped like microscopic firecrackers studding the fibrous strands that make up a joint capsule. Inside each cylinder are bundles of connective tissue interlaced with the knobby, branched endings of one or a pair of nerve fibers. These cylinder-wrapped nerve endings (named after an Italian anatomist, Angelo Ruffini, who died in 1929) respond to mechanical deformations of the tissue of the joint. But each responds according to its fashion. That fashion depends on the angle the joint moves through, which, in turn means, what part of the capsule cover is deformed. A typical Ruffini ending has earmarked a portion of arc, usually no more than 10 or 15 degrees wide, to which it responds. No matter how the joint is moved—whether by a fast snap of the fingers or a gentle motion—if the joint passes through the favored region with sufficient deformation of the tissue over a certain time interval, the nerve ending inside will become excited, firing impulses to the brain. If you hold the joint in this position for a while the nerve fiber will settle down to transmitting a steady frequency, just as if you had tuned in to a radio station. Ruffini endings broadcast at the feeble rate of 10 or 20 impulses a second. During the course of movement—for example, when you swing your knee back and forth as you walk—whole sequences of Ruffinis are being tuned in and out. How fast this happens, how many fibers come into play, and which ones maintain activity when you come to rest tell the whole story of the movement and the position of the knee.

It doesn't make any difference to the nerve ending whether the knee joint is swung to or fro in the course of passing through the receptor's excitatory angle. This might cause confusion (are you coming or going?) but the brain prevents this. It appears that the signals that

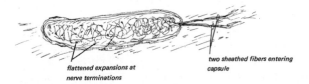

flattened expansions at
nerve terminations

two sheathed fibers entering
capsule

The Ruffini corpuscle found in joint capsules. A smaller version in skin may act as a receptor for warmth.

are finally relayed to the cortex contact one of a pair of cells. Signaling one cell means the joint has moved back to front, signaling a nearby partner means just the opposite.

It is comforting to think that some Ruffini nerve endings are firing all the time; that they neither fatigue very much nor habituate, i.e., stop sending signals after a while. Probably this explains why when you wake up in the morning it's the bedding that is knotted and not you. All during your sleep the brain has been receiving signals of the positions of your arms and legs. No doubt some of the kinesthetic dreams people have, of falling or kicking or climbing, may involve some of the inputs from these faithful sensors, and may even be a way of waking a person when his position is awkward.

Pacinian Corpuscles

At the same time the Ruffini endings note joint positions and movements, other receptors inform the brain of stresses and strains on muscles. Principal among these are the Pacinian corpuscles. These are pressure receptors, which were first observed by a student working in the anatomy laboratory of Abraham Vater at the University of Wittenberg in 1741. Almost a century later, Filippo Pacini described the corpuscles in greater detail to the Societá Medici-Fisica in Florence, and the corpuscles were named after him.

A Pacinian corpuscle looks like a miniature onion, not a microscopic onion, just a tiny, one-twenty-fifth-inch-diameter bulb made up of layer upon layer of delicate tissue wrapping. If the wrappings were peeled away a fine nerve ending would be exposed at the heart of the bulb. This is the naked terminal of a sensory fiber that develops a thicker

35

sheath and trails out of the corpuscle, eventually to enter a larger nerve bundle.

The corpuscle is extremely mushy, almost liquid. Slight pressure on it from any angle deforms its shape and in turn the shape of the nerve terminal inside. The terminal is oval in cross section, and some investigators believe this contributes to sensitivity because the same pressure when applied to an oval cylinder will deform it more than when applied to a round one.

Dr. Werner R. Loewenstein of the College of Physicians and Surgeons of Columbia University has shown that the electric current generated in the corpuscle originates at sites along the fine nerve terminal. If this "generator potential" builds up enough it triggers an impulse down the thicker part of the fiber, like a fuse detonating TNT. The explosion shows up as one or more bursts of electric activity that look like vertical lines on an oscilloscope; these are called spikes.

Pacinian corpuscles are found around joint capsules, in the tissue covering muscles and tendons, in the linings of the lungs and other visceral organs, in blood vessel walls, and also in the deeper layers of skin. Placed in this way they can respond to pressure and tension changes that occur externally as well as internally, as limbs or the various internal masses of the body move over or against each other.

When stimulated, Pacinian bodies are quick to react and fire a strong volley of impulses. But the signals fade fast. They are like "on" switches, signifying a change in status. If the change is maintained, the corpuscle adjusts to the new status; the nerve is no longer stimulated—it adapts.

When you get up, your body undergoes sudden pressure changes.

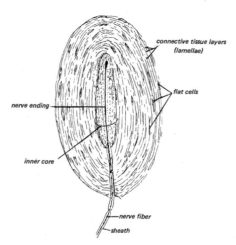

The Pacinian corpuscle. The naked nerve fiber at the core of the corpuscle is supported by an inner core of tissue, which is in turn surrounded by many thin connective tissue layers. In and between the layers are numerous flat cells, blood vessels, and fibrous material. Pacinian corpuscles continue to grow during life, attaining lengths close to one-quarter of an inch in some cases.

Your inner organs shift position; your stomach or bladder may feel more distended because of the sensory signals now arriving in the brain. When you take a step forward Pacinian corpuscles under the tendons in your toes signal the acute strains to which you subject your feet. But once you adopt a new stance the Pacinian corpuscles sign off, ready to go on again only when new pressure changes demand their attention.

Other Endings

The Ruffini endings and Pacinian corpuscles probably contribute most to the sense of your body, but a number of other endings also react to mechanical deformations or pressures. Some of these lie in the joint capsule or in nearby ligament endings, where they may supplement the Ruffini organs, indicating joint angles and behaving similarly as slow-adapting receptors. Others lie at the junction between muscles and tendons. Sometimes they appear to be distributed along the lines of stress. The supposition is that they act as force or strain gauges. Still other endings, sometimes encapsulated, sometimes loose, are found in the tissue that cover bones, the periosteum, as well as in the fine wrappings over muscles, tendons, and ligaments. Many of these endings may be pressure indicators, but some probably register pain as well.

The density of these sensory endings as well as the ratio of motor nerves to muscle fibers varies throughout the body. Generally an area that is rich in its supply of nerves to contract muscles is equally well endowed with sensors. Thus the muscle that allows you to flex your thumb and oppose it to the other fingers enjoys the ratio of close to 1 nerve fiber for each muscle fiber as compared to ratios of 1 to 100 or more in other parts of the body. The nearby joints at the knuckle of the thumb and of the index finger are so sensitive you can detect a difference in thickness of only six-thousandths of an inch between two stacks of paper if each is held in turn. The joint sensors will have noted the tiny variation in angle.

Some of the larger joints of the body, like the shoulder and hip, are extremely sensitive. So are the wrist and elbow. One of the pioneer German investigators of the nineteenth century, A. Goldscheider, discovered that movement of the shoulder joint by as little as one-quarter of a degree is detectable. In contrast, the ankle must move through more than 1 degree before the receptors respond.

To the Brain

The impulses triggered by proprioceptors are carried by some of the fastest conducting nerves in the body, with velocities between 200

37

and 300 feet per second. The fibers come into the spinal cord and ascend in thick bundles at the back of the cord, the dorsal columns. The fibers reach the medulla at the base of the brain where they contact particular clusters of nerve cells. (The region of contact is called a synapse, a microscopic space between the tip of a fiber and either the membrane of the body of a nerve cell or one of its fiber extensions. At this junction the nerve impulse jumps across the gap to stimulate, or "synapse with," the second cell.) After one more relay in the thalamus the final fibers in the system reach the highest level of the cortex.

It is at the cortical level that awareness of movements comes, and through such awareness, association of certain gestures and positions in learning complex skills such as riding a bicycle, typing by touch, or playing the piano. Moreover, once mastered, such kinesthetic abilities seem to leave an indelible trace on the nervous system. You may not have been on a bike in twenty years yet you would have little difficulty if you were to ride one tomorrow. Other skills with continuous practice become more and more automatic. Normally neither the executive secretary nor the concert artist need look at the keys of his instrument. But a concert pianist tells the story of an audition in his younger days when he found he was uncharacteristically striking wrong notes. A setback to his career was averted when it was discovered that the piano he was using was one especially designed for Joseph Hoffman, a gifted soloist whose hands were surprisingly small. The keys were narrower than standard.

The kind of kinesthetic learning possible in ordinary circumstances has recently been extended to include learning how to control at will individual motor nerves in the hand and limbs. To do this a microelectrode is inserted into the muscles of the thumb, for example, and connected to an oscilloscope to give a visual display of nerve activity. At the same time the signals may also be fed into sound equipment to emerge as a series of noises. The investigator first asks the volunteer to move his thumb. This causes a flurry of discharges which appear as clusters of spikes or splutters of sound. The investigator may then indicate a particular impulse pattern or sound and ask the volunteer to concentrate on that alone. Amazingly the combination of visual or auditory feedbacks works so well that within fifteen minutes a fair number of people can be trained to fire a particular motor nerve on demand. Both Russian and Canadian investigators have explored the possibility of using such knowledge in connection with artificial limbs. Amputees might gain much finer control over more subtly designed electromechanical devices if they could use the intact nerves above the stump as triggers. The Russians have in fact successfully built such a model hand.

38

Muscle "Tone"

While many proprioceptors are involved in pathways relaying conscious awareness of the body's position and movements, others monitor muscle and tendon activity in ways which may never rise to consciousness. However "silent" these partners are, their contribution to the over-all efficiency and economy of the nervous system is enormous. Among other things they are in part responsible for man's ability to stand erect against the forces of gravity—to become, in Aristotle's classic phrase, "a featherless biped."

One of the chief concerns of these sensors is in maintaining that slight degree of contraction in muscles that the Greeks likened to the taut strings of a musical instrument, and so named "tonus." Such tonic contractions accomplish several useful things:

(1) Fast Reaction Time: In a state of slight contraction your muscles are ready to serve you quickly in an emergency. There is no need to warm up the muscle motors; they are idling all the time. What's more, part of the energy used for these "maintenance contractions" is dissipated in heat which helps regulate body temperature. In repose, this is barely noticeable, but the combination of the heat of contraction with work done—during a strenuous game of tennis or a lively frug—makes you well aware of the heat liberated. And you make good use of this by hopping from one foot to another while waiting for a bus on a cold day in winter.

(2) Reflex Postural Contractions: A posture expert has calculated that about 80 percent of the time when standing we do not assume an "ideal" balanced position. We lean on one foot, raise a hip, tilt forward or backward, and move our arms every which way. All the while the nervous system must perform a delicate juggling task to keep the body balanced. Walking itself has been described as a series of "arrested falls." Since it took man a few million years to achieve upright posture, it is not surprising that the nervous system's accomplishments in this realm are complex.

Looked at mechanically man is a very precariously balanced construction of globes, pipe stems, and rectangular solids, each with different weights and centers of gravity. The knees have a built-in bend. When you stand up the flexors at the front of the bend ought to give way to gravity, continue to flex and topple you over. The reason they don't is that the nervous system supplies the antagonist extensor muscles at the backs of your legs with signals to contract and ways of maintaining the contraction with the aid of the silent sensors. The back muscles are called "antigravity" muscles for this reason.

39

(3) The Knee Jerk: The third task that falls to the lot of the muscle and tendon sensors is a protective one; they signal an alarm when a muscle or tendon is stretched. When you submit your crossed leg to the physician's rubber hammer he is testing just such a reaction. The hammer blow passively stretches your knee (patellar) tendon. The sensory fibers ° cry out and relay directly to motor cells in the cord to bring on the contractions that make your leg fly out.

The lack of the knee jerk reflex is usually a sure sign of nerve damage. Again syphilis may be responsible for this by attacking the large cell bodies of the sensory fibers, preventing the alarm signals from getting through, but there are many other causes as well. Another clinical indication of malfunction of these sensors is called a "positive Romberg sign." In this test a person with his feet close together can stand normally with his eyes open, but tends to sway when the eyes are shut. The visual proprioceptive clues maintain balance in the absence of muscle and joint senses, but when they are eliminated the body becomes unstable.

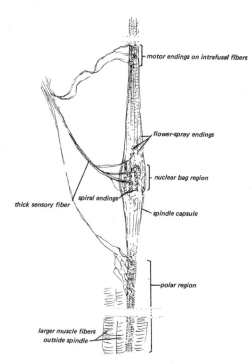

Diagram of a muscle spindle. The thin fibers of the spindle run parallel to the main muscle fibers and are striated toward the ends (the polar regions). The central area, thick with cell nuclei, is not contractile and is innervated by large sensory nerve fibers which spiral around the muscle fiber in ribbonlike fashion. Secondary sensory fibers may spread farther up and down the spindle in flower spray endings. The usual length of the polar segments of the fiber relative to the bag region would be three to four times the length shown here.

° These fibers are the thickest, fastest-conducting nerves in the nervous system, relaying impulses at rates over 300 feet per second.

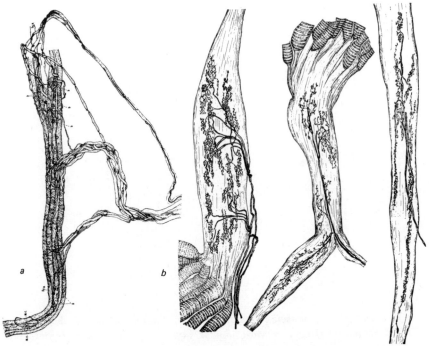

(A) A drawing of a muscle spindle showing the ribbonlike spirals of the sensory fibers in the center

(B) A drawing showing the flower spray endings of a tendon spindle.

Muscle and Tendon Sensors

The mechanisms underlying these complex activities are muscle spindles and tendon organs. Typically muscle spindles are found in the most active muscles aligned parallel to the long fiber strands. The long spindle-shaped capsule encloses a set of fine muscle fibers called intrafusal fibers, which taper at both ends. The fat midsection contains a cluster of muscle cell nuclei and so is called a nuclear bag. One sensory nerve fiber wraps around the bag in a spiral while two others grab hold of sections on either side of it. These adjacent endings (and similar endings in the tendon organs) branch to form very beautiful "flower spray" endings.

When a muscle is stretched the muscle fibers outside the spindle exert a pull on it. This pull deforms the nuclear bag and starts signals in the sensory fiber enwrapping it, which in turn trigger the reflex arc. Trains of motor signals are sent out to contract the muscle and counter

41

Typical stretch reflex

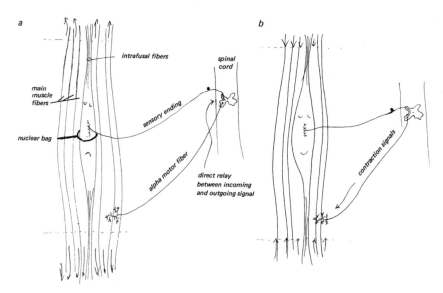

(A) *Pulling on large muscle fibers also pulls on the nuclear bag of the spindle. This deformation triggers sensory signals into the spinal cord to initiate the reflex arc.*
(B) *A sensory cell relays directly with a large motor cell in the ventral horn. It signals contractions in large muscle fibers, relaxing tension on the bag.*

the stretch. Such motor signals come from large "alpha" motor cells at the front of the cord and cause contractions of many muscle fibers in the neighborhood of the spindle. As soon as they begin to contract the tension on the bag eases and quiets the alarm signals.

The Gamma Loop

This circuit describes a typical stretch reflex which occurs in the knee and elsewhere in the body. It also describes the kind of internecine warfare that is set up during a voluntary act like threading a needle. When the thumb and index finger muscles are flexed to hold the needle the extensor muscles on the opposite sides of the fingers are automatically stretched. The needle would never be threaded if these signals were allowed to trigger stretch reflexes all the time. Fortunately multiple systems of nerve control are at work to prevent this.

To some extent the muscle spindle and tendon organs act in opposite ways, responding to stretches and contractions, respectively.

**Fooling the spindle:
The gamma loop**

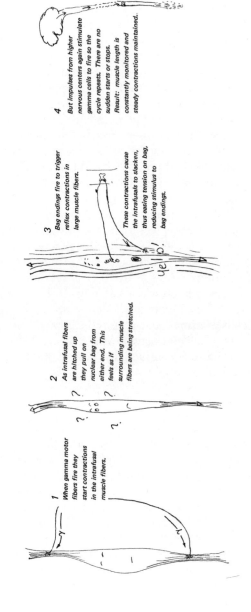

1
When gamma motor fibers fire they start contractions in the intrafusal muscle fibers.

2
As intrafusal fibers are hitched up they pull on nuclear bag from either end. This feels as if surrounding muscle fibers are being stretched.

3
Bag endings fire to trigger reflex contractions in large muscle fibers.

These contractions cause the intrafusals to slacken, thus easing tension on bag, reducing stimulus to bag endings.

yelp!

4
But impulses from higher nervous centers again stimulate gamma cells to fire so the cycle repeats. There are no sudden starts or stops. Result: muscle length is constantly monitored and steady contractions maintained.

Modifying these responses, however, are a variety of facilitatory or inhibitory signals originating in the spinal cord or higher up in the brain. These signals can enhance or depress the peripheral activity. It now appears that such descending signals are used to manipulate spindles in order to maintain steady contractions in muscles. This is a game in which the spindles are fooled into thinking the muscle is being stretched when it isn't. To do this the nervous system makes use of special motor nerves which go out to the intrafusal muscle fibers. These stem from small "gamma" motor cells in the spinal cord whose impulse firing rates can be increased or slowed down by the brain. Under certain conditions the gamma cells' output rises enough to cause the intrafusal fibers to contract. As they do they stretch the nuclear bag, exactly as though they were ropes tied to the poles at each end of the spindle and were suddenly being hitched up. This has the same effect on the nuclear bag as if the muscle itself were being stretched, so again, the alarm signals from the spiral endings are tripped, and signals are triggered to the large motor fibers that can contract the surrounding muscle. Each time the main muscle fibers contract, the intrafusals slacken slightly. But now the brain renews its signals to the gamma motor cells and the cycle is kept going smoothly. The net result of this intricate interplay is that the spiral endings' firing pattern is a sensitive indicator of the relative lenths of muscle fibers inside and outside the spindle.

The efficiency of the method shows up in energy terms. The gamma motor cells are small and require little fuel to fire, but they start the larger contractions. Their activity is a delicate, low-energy means of controlling major muscle contractions, smoothing them, and keeping them within reasonable limits.

The Master Coordinator

The intricate workings of the gamma loop and the complexities inherent in ordinary voluntary movements involve signals from the highest centers of the cortex, as well as reflex circuits through the spinal cord. Between the two, however, there is a major modifier of muscle activity, the arbiter between intention and deed. This function is performed by the cerebellum, a section of the brain that looks and acts very differently from all other parts. Even its external convolutions are not at all like those of the cerebral hemispheres above it, but are more dense and more regularly spaced. When split down the middle this paired organ presents a handsome leaflike pattern the ancients called the *arbor vitae*, the tree of life.

The cerebellum's purpose was unknown until a few years ago, for

44

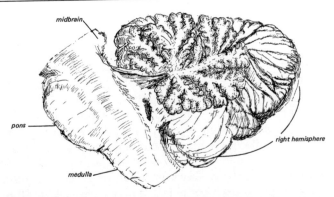

Section through the midline of the cerebellum showing the arbor vitae, *or tree-of-life, pattern. This part is known technically as the vermis.*

unlike many other parts of the brain it is not necessary to life. Living without the cerebellum is not easy at first, but the nervous system can partially compensate for its loss. Now it seems clear that the reason for this is that the cerebellum does not initiate activity on its own, but coordinates activities of other parts.

For example the cerebellum receives a duplicate signal every time the brain initiates a voluntary motor act and it also gets a signal from the sensing organs in muscle and in related tissue. It compares the two—input and output—and then issues modifying commands. It may curb the voluntary impulses of the brain if these place too much stress on the limbs, or it might amplify the signals if the muscle's response is too weak. These changes occur continuously while the movements are being made. Thus the cerebellum operates as a major feedback mechanism, constantly modifying the output of the system of which it is a part, preventing excesses and working toward a smooth performance.

How the cerebellum manages this is not completely understood. There are enormous possibilities for altering signals. An incoming nerve fiber may relay with a cell which can synapse with hundreds of other cells, each in contact with hundreds more. Some of the most interesting work in neurophysiology today is being done to determine just what this vast communications network accomplishes. The Nobel laureate Sir John Eccles believes that an intricate system of facilitation and inhibition is at work here, a system which achieves exquisite precision and economy in the over-all operation of the nervous system.

Other investigators point out that cerebellar cells have a peculiar high frequency, small-height wave form which may be the electrical key to understanding the way the cerebellum changes signals.

In any case it seems clear that if the muscle spindles get out of hand the cerebellum can send out signals which either inhibit them or else amplify the signals going out to opposing muscles. Again the nervous system can achieve its ends by two ways: active inhibition of one set of signals, or facilitation of opposing signals—by dynamiting the enemy directly, or supplying the allies with more ammunition.

When the cerebellum is not functioning properly a person typically exhibits a constellation of symptoms. Usually there is a kind of "drunken" gait. Similarly the other symptoms are what one might expect to occur in the absence of smooth control and coordination: jerkiness of movement, possibly a sway, a lack of finesse in measuring distances. If the hand is put out to reach an object it may overreach it. More drastic symptoms have been observed in animals. A cat without a cerebellum may walk directly into a wall and persist in its motions even after it has hit its head.

But a person, or a cat, can still walk and in time may relearn certain acts with a fair amount of skill. The major motor pathways are intact. What is lacking is smoothness and efficiency. The graceful gesture has regressed to an awkward groping. Economy of motion has given way to wholesale energy-wasteful acts, a state of affairs very much like the first months of life. In the baby's case, however, it is not cerebellar malfunction we observe, but the normal course of development, where the circuits controlling the smooth operations of standing and walking are just being laid down.

Moreover as the baby concentrates on crawling he may not hear or see the rattle his mother holds out to him. For the coordination and integration of motion with the other senses have to be learned. Now it appears that these too are under cerebellar control. Through other complex circuits the cerebellum directs muscle movements in response to what interests the sense organs. It regulates neck muscles so that you move your head smoothly toward a sound you hear at one side of you, or look up to see who said hello. It sees to it that you don't bury your nose in the rose you want to smell.

In the beginning these complex integrations take time, but once established, again they become so automatic you don't think about them. If someone asked you to walk across a four-foot plank placed on the living room rug you'd shrug your shoulders and do it. You'd look at the plank, initiate a plan which would be modified appropriately by the cerebellum, and accomplish the feat neatly. But is this sensory-motor integration always a good thing? The cerebellum is the great synthesizer, the "secretary of the cortex," but is it possible that at times too much information can be dangerous? How would you cope with the

46

plank-walking task if your eyes saw that the plank was stretched across twin mountain peaks? If your life depended on it, you might be better off if your eyes had been shut. For now vision, and with it memory and fear, impose confusion on the fine mechanisms of the cerebellum. You hesitate and tremble. Having seen, you cannot "unsee" the problem. You need even more reassurance, more sensory cues. You yearn for something to grab hold of, something to touch. . . . But that is another chapter.

III

What's in a Touch

It is literally very difficult to lose the sense of touch, even the slightest touch—a mosquito landing on your skin, or a raindrop, or cigarette ash. The times that touch disappears, when the dentist has plied your gums with Novacain or your arm or foot has fallen asleep, leave part of you feeling strangely foreign to yourself. So does the parlor trick of taking your index finger, joining it with someone else's, and then feeling the pair with the fingers of your other hand. The stunt makes you laugh, the feeling is so bizarre. You can see the fingers and watch your hand's strokings, but it is as if your finger were no longer a part of your body.

Such experiences point to the fundamental nature of the sense of touch. It is taken so much for granted that it is missed only when it's gone, when drugs, or a lowered blood supply (the reason your limbs fall asleep), or the brain's confusion (as in the parlor trick) disturb its function. Sad to say there are serious conditions in which the loss of touch is permanent: when nerves are damaged or diseased, or when surgery performed to relieve severe pain sacrifices the sense of touch as well.

For most people, however, touch is a friend to rely on. Without the more specialized senses one can still get along by touch, as Helen Keller and others have shown. We frequently prove it to ourselves. In a strange house at night we may grope for a light switch, feeling the edges of furniture, or the flat, smooth surfaces of walls; a current of air on our cheeks may tell us we're near an open window or door. Or we may walk along the beach on a moonless night with a quiet surf and feel the crunch of sand beneath our feet. If it becomes damp or wet we know we've strayed too close to the water. Sticking our big toe forward we may come up against the hard surface of a rock, or a smooth piece of well-worn driftwood. Heading away from the water we may encounter the feathery strokes of grasses and seaweed. In this way, we develop a touch map of the landscape, a terrain in which space is measured by its smoothness or roughness, its sharp or soft edges, its metallic, papery, wet, or dry qualities. We may even sense life in the quick, vibratory pulses of a bird in a nest, or the wings of an insect brushing against the face. In so doing we come to understand a little what the world must be like for many animals, for the mole channeling through earth, the maggot boring through rotting vegetation, or the moth extending its feelers in the dark.

Some creatures have developed elaborate touch mechanisms. The mole's snout, for example, contains special cells connected to lever-like rods that can sense variations in the soil that might signal the presence of an earthworm several inches away. A cat's whiskers can also act as long-distance ("teletactile") receptors, reacting to minute air pressures stirred by distant movements, perhaps by a mouse.

The skin over a duck's bill can sense water vibrations; a woodpecker, after it has drummed a tree trunk, may use its tongue to feel reverberations that indicate hollow spaces where insects live.

The Common Denominator Sense

All these acts are special ways of learning about the world through touching it. At lower levels of life both touching and being touched are more generalized. The amoeba may simply engulf the food particle that has grazed against it; the paramecium may turn and swim away from the foreign body that has displaced its fine hairs. What is interesting is that no matter where one looks in the order of life there is a sense of touch. All creatures great or small react to being poked or prodded, pressed or caressed.

At the primeval level, the makings of life could be said to depend on touch. The groups of atoms which accumulated in the soupy seas of the primordial earth had to be within a "chemical touching" distance if they were to coalesce to form molecular bonds. The French biologist Jean Rostand, in his charming book *Bestiaire d'Amour*, says "we are led to wonder whether there is not an 'internal propensity toward union' in even the apparently insentient and inert molecule." Then he goes on to explain why, in lower forms like the sea urchin and starfish, where fertilization takes place outside the body, great masses of sperm and egg are deposited in the water. It is to increase the chances that a few will come within touching distance for reactions to take place.

Basic associations like these relate touch to man's emotional or visceral life, as opposed to the loftier spheres of intellect. This relationship is borne out developmentally, since it is known, through the work of Davenport Hooker and others, that touch is the earliest sense to mature, already manifesting itself in the late embryo stage and coming into its own long before eyes, ears, and higher brain centers are in good working order. At birth, touch figures in feeding, in exploring the world, and in reacting to it, for the baby's emotional development depends in part on how it is picked up, handled, and held.

Very early in life vision and hearing take over; the hand becomes the handmaiden of the eye, and the written and spoken word become the dominant modes of sensory communication. Touch still retains its influence, however. Language, for all its abstraction, is steeped in touch metaphors. Emotions are "feelings." One speaks of being "touched" or of someone being "touchy." Personalities are smooth or thorny, oily or prickly.

An example of the importance of touch used with striking effect occurs in the description of a character in *The Notebooks of Malte Laurids Brigge*, by the German poet Rainer Maria Rilke: *

There is a portrait of him at Dijon. But even so one knows that he was squat, square, defiant, and desperate. Only his hands, perhaps, one would not have thought of. They are excessively warm hands, that continually want to cool themselves and involuntarily lay themselves on any cold object, outspread, with air between the fingers. Into those hands the blood could shoot, as it mounts to a person's head, and when clenched, they were indeed like the heads of madmen, raging with fancies.

Society today tends to downgrade the sense of touch, equating it with manual as opposed to mental skills. In so doing society ignores the

---

* Trans. by M. D. Herter Norton. New York: W. W. Norton & Company, Inc., 1949.

extent to which the combination of touch and intellect constitutes the art of the pianist or surgeon, sculptor or mechanic, inventor or magician —not to mention the few individuals, the safecracker, pickpocket, or card shark, who have misdirected their talents.

Heredity probably plays a role in producing talent. Just how great a role and how much training improves the raw material is not easy to determine. Not all concert pianists have greater than octave spans; apprentice pickpockets are known to acquire their skill from professionals (sometimes while both are in jail). Harry Houdini, the magician, practiced constantly. He is presumed to have learned his first tricks at the age of sixteen from a fellow worker in a necktie factory.

The interesting feature of the varied careers represented by concert pianist, pickpocket, and escape artist is that in every case touch was encouraged. The sense was stimulated, trained, and so disciplined that the brain, guided by and guiding the skin sensors, could master new tricks, direct magnificently smooth motions, and discriminate exceedingly fine details.

In this way a cooperation was built between cells scattered all over the body and interpreting mechanisms in the brain. How such an alliance starts and how far it can go are fascinating questions. They concern the nervous system's degree of specialization and its resourcefulness, its ability to adapt, to associate, and to learn.

We are educated by touch in the first years of life. In turn we educate touch. We compare skin sensations with sights and sounds and smells and tastes to build a unified picture of the world. At first there are confusions between the senses and lags in growth, so that for a time the eyes and hands don't work together: the right hand literally may not know what the left hand is doing; the chest may react to a touch while the leg, touched at the same time, won't. All this is in keeping with the direction and rate of growth in the nervous system, but at reasonable intervals skills mature. At twelve years of age most of the adult patterns of sensation have been established and taken for granted, to such a degree that we may not realize how intricately varied the patterns are.

The fingertips are more sensitive than the back; the lips more than the top of the head; the elbows more than the shins. Some parts of the body are ticklish. We may itch or we may favor certain parts of our body in making judgments. A cook tests the candy syrup by trying to roll it into a soft ball between her fingertips; a carpenter runs his thumb over the beveled edge he's been shaping to pick up the rough spots; a counterman feels the weight of coins in his palm and spots a slug instantly. The list is endless.

Not only can we feel the texture of objects, grade fabrics, sandpaper, wood, judge the ripeness of fruit, or the freshness of bread, but we can run our fingers over type and identify letters. (This is what makes Braille, a system that uses raised dots for letters and punctuation, a successful reading method for the blind.) We can read messages spelled out on skin and feel the vibrations from the stem of a tuning fork placed on a forearm.

It is easy to locate the places where we've been touched. A woman feels the run in her stocking, a man can instantly feel the razor touch that pulls a single hair, and each can put a hand out to touch the spot without having to look.

A person can tell when he's been touched in more than one place simultaneously, if, for instance, he is grabbed at once by the shoulder and lapels. In one parlor trick, someone takes a pair of dividers, or a child's compass, and using different radii, applies the points to another's skin. The game is to decide when you've been touched with one or both points without looking. Here a man's judgment may be less accurate than he thinks. On the back, for example, the dividers have to be a minimum of 2.5 inches apart before most people can feel two distinct touches; if closer together they feel like one.

Tests like this reveal the rich diversity that underlies what seems like a continuous wrapper—the skin. Yet neither in its most superficial layers nor at its depths is the container homogeneous. On the outside it is completely dead; there are no nerve endings and hence no feeling. This is the coat that is easily shed, the one that forms part of the ring around the tub after you bathe. Then there are the inner layers of

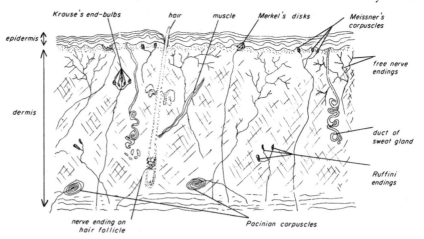

Schematic diagram of a cross section of skin to show cutaneous nerve endings and other epidermal and dermal structures.

epidermis, and below that, the dermis. These vary in thickness, the epidermal layers from one two-hundredth to one twentieth inch thick, and the dermis from one fiftieth to one eighth of an inch.

Feeling only starts at the inner layers of the epidermis. Generally speaking the thinner the skin the more sensitive it is. This is one of the reasons safecrackers have been known to sandpaper their skin. This gives the touch receptors in the little ridges that form fingerprints a chance to get even closer to the surface.

These are just some among many structures that populate the underworld of skin. The region is like a jungle, filled with swamps and streams, attenuated roots, spider webs, and bulbous plants, sometimes clustered, sometimes lying apart.

To figure out the precise meaning of the tangle, investigators of the nervous system explore the skin, probing it with fine recording electrodes and stimulating surface spots with a variety of touches, as well as cold- or heat- or pain-inducing stimuli. The activity is as fascinating at the microcosmic level as the most ambitious pioneering of space. Surprisingly, even at this late stage of scientific development, new receptors still show up, discoveries that swell the knowledge about the nervous system's already impressive store of equipment.

Generally speaking the touch receptors can be divided into two groups: those which are complex multicellular organs, capsules, or corpuscles, incorporating nerve endings inside them; and free endings—naked nerve terminals which may spread and branch in lacy patterns, or else wind around certain cells like string around one's finger.

Capsule Endings

Pacinian Corpuscles. The biggest and best known receptors are the thick Pacinian corpuscles, the onion-shaped pressure sensors that exist around joints and tendons and in linings of visceral organs or blood vessels, as well as in the skin. They are responsible for telling the brain not only what is pressing from outside, but what happens when joints move or organs change their shape and positions as you eat, get up, stretch, and move around.

In the skin the Pacinian corpuscles lie deep in the dermal layers, but they can be aroused by pressures that may deform the surface skin by as little as two-ten thousandths of an inch in a tenth of a second.

Prof. T. A. Quilliam of the University of London has observed reactions of isolated Pacinian corpuscles to the movements of people crossing the laboratory floor. This sensitivity may account for the typical crouching posture of a cat on the floor. In the cat the tissue that attaches

A group of human finger Pacinian corpuscles together with an artery. The central core of each corpuscle contains the nerve ending. The bulk of the corpuscle consists of a series of thin layers (lamellae) separated from each other by interlamellar spaces. × 72.

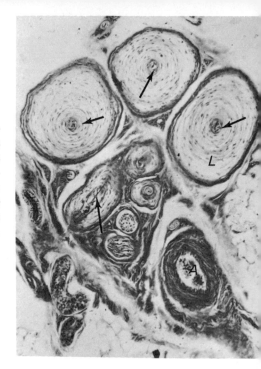

Distribution of Pacinian corpuscles (P) in the skin and subcutaneous tissue of the finger pad of a child, showing their relationship to blood vessels (arrows). S = sweat glands. × 40.

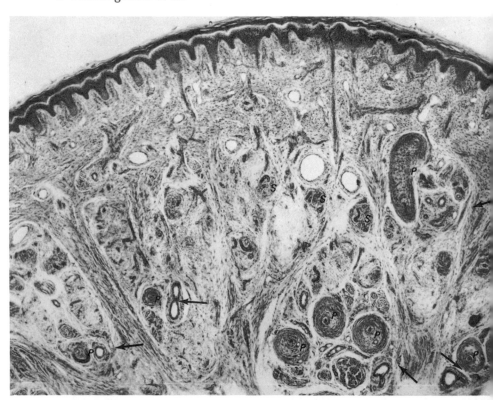

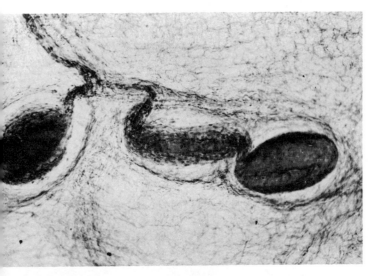

Pacinian corpuscles in the mesentery of a cat. × *120.*

the intestine to the abdominal wall, the mesentery, as well as the paws and leg joints, contain Pacinian corpuscles and these could pick up the vibrations of a mouse crossing the same floor.

Wherever they are found, Pacinian corpuscles generally behave the same way. They are the fastest-reacting receptors in the body; an electrical change in the corpuscle occurs in less than one-fifth of a thousandth of a second. Because they are also associated with the thickest, fastest-conducting nerve fibers in the skin, they get their message to the brain in short order. As soon as they transmit it they sign off. The skin over the bills of ducks and other water birds contains a structure similar to the Pacinian corpuscle called the Herbst corpuscle. It too is a many layered "onion," though thicker, stiffer, and more curved, presumed to act as a detector of water-borne vibrations. It is a Herbst corpuscle in the woodpecker's tongue which locates insect hiding places.

Quilliam suggests that the many layers that make up these receptors may be a way of tuning them to certain vibration frequencies. In experiments with cats, for example, he has found that Pacinian corpuscles respond well to frequencies of about 400 vibrations per second, but show little or no response below 50 or above 600.

The "Eimer organ" of the mole's snout is another Pacinian-like corpuscle that overlies a rodlike attachment that extends from the epidermis into the dermis. Quilliam thinks that this arrangement creates a

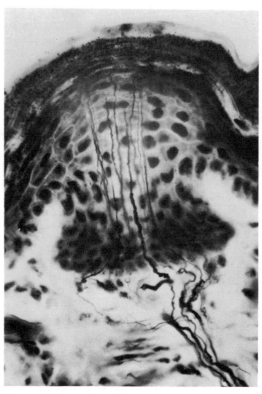

Eimer organ from the external nose of the mole (Talpa europaea). × 600.

channel for vibrations that would otherwise be absorbed and lost in the soft tissue. This way the mole may get continuous information about the soil while digging through it and so be alerted to what lies ahead.

Meissner's Corpuscles. The border between the epidermis and dermis undulates like the waves of a gentle sea. Swelling the waves under certain parts of the body are microscopic egg-shaped corpuscles with much thinner wrappings than the Pacinian bodies. These are Meissner's corpuscles, found in abundance on the fingertips and palms, toes and soles, on lips and tongue, and in sexual areas—around the nipples, clitoris, and penis.

Their presence is the main reason for heightened sensitivity in these areas, for Meissner's corpuscles are optimal feelers. The naked nerve terminal ending inside a single corpuscle loops and branches to form a mass of intertwined fibers arranged in planes parallel to the skin surface.

The capsule itself is made up of several fine wrappings of elastic

Meissner's corpuscles lie in the undulating border region between the dermal and epidermal layers; they are found in the convex portions, or papillae. A group of four Merkel's disks (arrows) lie on the deeper side of the intermediate, or sweat, ridge. × 180.

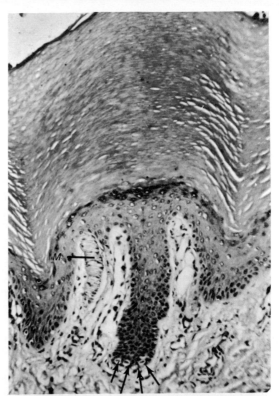

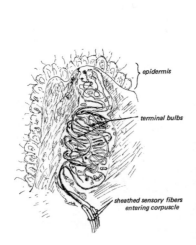

epidermis

terminal bulbs

sheathed sensory fibers entering corpuscle

Simplified drawing of a Meissner's corpuscle in the upper dermal layer of skin.

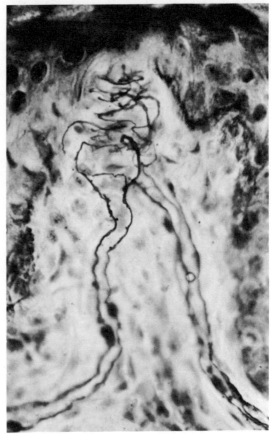

Meissner's corpuscle in the dermal papilla of the skin of the human finger. × 600.

connective tissue. This rubbery quality probably accounts for the close match between the point of skin touched and the portion of the corpuscle excited. It's as though the receptor were composed of separate coils like an innerspring mattress; one can be depressed without disturbing the others. Such specificity goes a long way in explaining how we can judge so accurately where a pin touches a finger.

Likewise the area of skin above the corpuscle where a pinprick or other tactile stimulus may be applied and cause a change in electrical activity in the nerve ending below is also very small. This patch of skin is known as the receptive field of the unit, a term of widespread use in the study of the nervous system. (For example the receptive field of a rod or cone in the retina of the eye may encompass a few degrees of arc in the visual field; the receptive field of a cortical cell may be a small area at the tip of the tongue.) The receptive fields for Meissner corpuscles are so small they are referred to as touch "spots." In one experiment a nerve fiber presumed to come from a Meissner receptor in a fingertip ridge responded to a pressure of 20 milligrams (the weight of a fly) applied

Electron micrograph showing a longitudinal section of the superficial part of a Meissner corpuscle. The laminar cells (lighter bands) are separated from one another by an intercellular substance (darker bands) and interleaved with nerve endings (N). E = epidermis. × 3600.

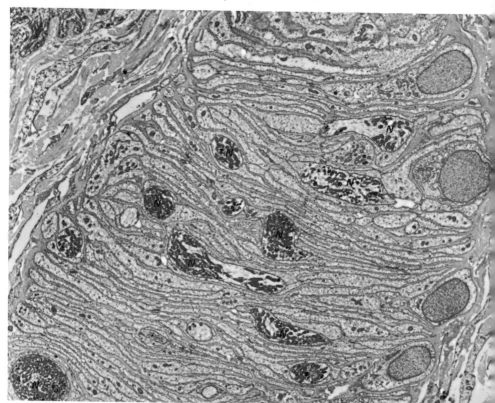

to a point exactly in the center of the ridge. If the stimulus was moved as little as eight-thousandths of an inch in either direction along the ridge, or into the valley on either side, the force had to be ten times stronger to excite the fiber.

Merkel's Disks. Some investigators think that the parallel arrangement of fibers within the Meissner corpuscle makes them ideal receptors for perpendicular touches. These same investigators point to another organ, the Merkel's disk, which lies like a flat, oval saucer at the base of some parts of the epidermis. Here the array of fibers may be specialized to react to tangential touches.

Other thin capsules surrounding nerve endings include the small, round Golgi-Mazzoni corpuscles, thought to be pressure receptors, and the genital corpuscles of Krause. These are relatively large bits of tissue (up to 0.004 inch in breadth and 0.016 inch in length) that are found in and around male and female sexual organs.

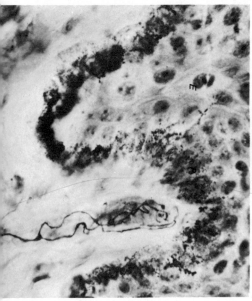

Genital corpuscle from glans penis (human). × 600.

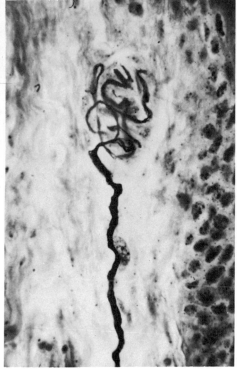

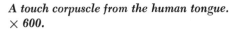

A touch corpuscle from the human tongue. × 600.

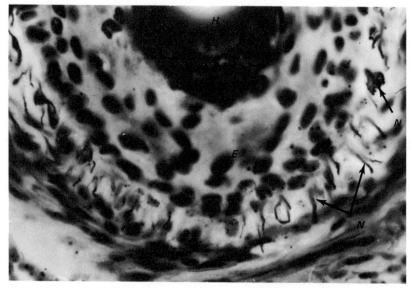

Transverse section of a human hair showing nerve endings (N) arranged around the epithelial root sheath (E). H = keratinized shaft of hair. × 600.

Free Endings

The other class of touch receptors includes a major group of endings associated with hair, perhaps the most obvious feelers of all. Hair is a special kind of growth peculiar to mammals (though related to a reptile's scales). Each hair is rooted in a follicle in the dermal layer of skin which is usually wrapped around with a nerve ending, or is associated with a nest of nerve endings nearby.

Hairs are among the most sensitive touchers the body has, and generally the hairy parts of the body are more sensitive than smooth hairless areas, mainly because hairy skin is thinner. A single hair can respond to mechanical deformations of its tip, as well as to major pushes or pulls. It can also respond to depressions of the skin around it which do not even touch the hair. In either case, the alarm goes off. The mechanical disturbance upsets the distribution of charged atomic particles, or ions, in and around the nerve ending. This upset starts the buildup of an electric potential which, when it reaches a certain threshold level, triggers a nerve impulse down the fiber toward the central nervous system.

It is important to distinguish between the nerve ending, the last piece of fiber naked and uninsulated, and the thicker fiber wrapped in a

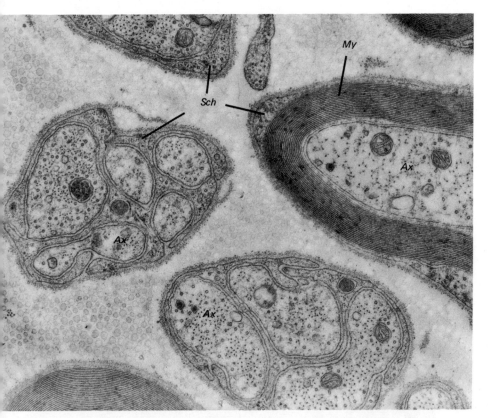

Electron micrograph of a cross section of sensory myelinated and nonmyelinated nerve fibers of the skin at the tip of a rat's ear. Ax = axon or branches of axon. Sch = Schwann cell cytoplasm. My = myelin lamellae of a myelinated axon. × 32000.

fatty insulating sheath called myelin, which extends back to the spinal cord. The myelinated fiber is like a mouse trap (coiled spring) that has been set; its naked nerve ending waits for a mouse to nibble at the cheese. If it nibbles enough, down goes the spring.

The remarkable feature of these hair endings is their sensitivity. It takes very little to spring the trap. Recent investigations which "comb" the hairs, differentiating between fine "down" hairs and coarser "guard" hairs, and examine their varied types of innervation have shown a wide range of receptive fields and sensitivities. The prize goes to certain fine myelinated fibers associated with down hairs. These can be excited by a displacement of a hair tip by as little as 0.00004 inch. The experiments were made on rabbits, cats, and monkeys, all mammals with skin receptors and sensitivities similar to man's.

In addition to the free endings around hair, there are also nerve

61

terminals which are the end-processes of fibers that have divided and branched repeatedly to form exceedingly fine webs in the dermal layer of skin. A good many of these fibers remain thin and uninsulated all the way back to the spinal cord and brain. In recent years they have become the subject of much attention because they seem capable of a wide variety of activity, and for this reason, have sparked a lively controversy about the nature of all cutaneous sensation.

The question is simply whether each kind of touch, or pressure, or vibration, as well as sensations of heat and cold and pain, must necessarily be related to a specific receptor organ. Does each have to have its

Intraepidermal free nerve endings in the hairless area of a pig's nose. × *600.*

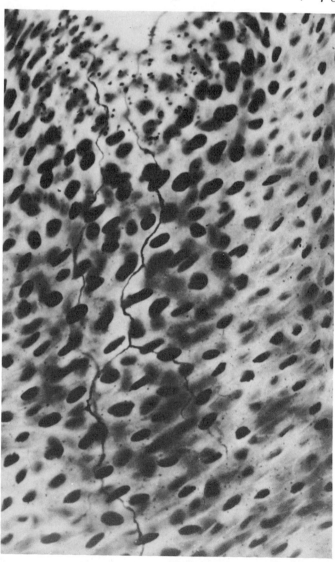

own special "eye" or "ear" in the skin? Or do these fine networks of fibers found all over the body send changing patterns of activity to the brain which sometimes mean touch, sometimes heat, sometimes cold, sometimes pain—depending on how the signals are arranged in time and in space.

Some advocates of the pattern theory go so far as to deny that well-defined structures like the Pacinian corpuscles are specialized. Others regard them as special cases of adaptation that make them suited for certain kinds of stimuli but not exclusively so, and not without simultaneous stimulation of the web fibers as well. This milder version is held by a group of workers at Oxford University headed by Graham Weddell. They base their claim on finding that there are parts of the body (like the skin of the ear, which contains fine nerve endings but few corpuscles) where all qualities of touch, temperature, and pain can be sensed with accuracy.

The controversy has arisen in the last decade when techniques enabled investigators to look at skin in greater detail and record activity from thinner nerves. The traditional view was stated at the end of the nineteenth century by a German, M. von Frey, who also bequeathed to research a set of hairs, von Frey hairs, graded according to stiffness and used in skin tests. During von Frey's lifetime Pacinian corpuscles, which are visible to the naked eye, and other well-formed receptors all but glared up at the investigator. Later, during the twenties and thirties, when the first electrical recordings from sensory nerves were made by Lord Adrian, Yngve Zotterman, and others, it was again the thicker myelinated fibers, often associated with special receptors, that were easier to tease out of a nerve bundle and study. This is not to say that the fine fibers were not observed in von Frey's time. They were, and he fitted them into his scheme as pain-specific endings.

Technology has run apace, however. Today still finer dissections and recordings are possible which suggest degrees of specialization among the gossamer strands as well. Such has been the work of a group of researchers at the University of Edinburgh, including Ainsley Iggo and A. R. Muir; and of W. W. Douglas and J. M. Ritchie at Albert Einstein College of Medicine in New York.

Iggo and his co-workers were able to track down individual unmyelinated fibers that travel in bundles of fifteen or twenty in thicker nerve cables. It is impossible to separate one from the rest of the bundle without injuring it, but by using electrical stimulation single fibers can be identified by their distinct trademarks: the height of the impulse spikes, and the speed with which the fiber conducts the spikes. (This is related to the diameter of the fiber.) Tagging the fibers this way, Iggo then followed through to the skin surface to see what natural stimuli could excite them.

He found a high degree of selectivity. Some fibers responded only to temperature changes; others only to mechanical deformations of skin or hair. Among the touch fibers were some innervating hair follicles which were so sensitive they could be excited by movements of the tips only slightly larger than the movements which excited prize myelinated fibers innervating down hairs. The sensitivity range extended to other touch fibers that required forces of several grams to set into action. None of these fibers responded to heating, cooling, or applying painful chemicals or other noxious stimuli to the skin.

On the other hand a few unmyelinated fibers responded both to touch and to cooling. Generally these were slow-adapting fibers that would increase their rate of firing when skin temperature was dropped suddenly by 20 or 30 degrees F.

The Iggo Corpuscle. When Iggo extended his survey to myelinated fibers as well, he also found a slow-adapting, touch-and-cold receptor in hairy skin. The patch of surface skin forms a distinctive small dome over the unit which is known informally as the Iggo corpuscle. This "new" receptor had been observed in human skin in 1904 by Felix Pinkus, but until Iggo dissected it, it was an unknown quantity. The dome covers a group of Merkel's disks lined up along the base of the epidermis, each supplied with a branch of a single myelinated nerve fiber. The receptive field for these units is so small they can be considered touch "spots"; they are so sensitive they can respond to a touch of less than one-thousandth of an ounce, about the weight of a mosquito. They seem exquisitely designed to respond to touches in skin between hairs, for they are oblivious to hair movements unless the hair gets pushed over onto the hump itself.

If Iggo's findings had matched every fiber with a unique sensation, it would have been a hard blow for the pattern theory. As it is, there seem to be a small but not to be dismissed number of fibers, slow-adapting ones in particular, which can signal more than one kind of sensation.†

This has led other well-known investigators in the field, among them Vernon Mountcastle of the Johns Hopkins University School of Medicine in Baltimore, Maryland, and Jerzy E. Rose at the University of Wisconsin, to reopen a theoretical discussion begun several generations ago by Henry Head, an English neurologist. Head theorized that there were two kinds of sensibility in man: one was a primitive "proto-

---

† Though Iggo suggests that in these cases as well, the effect may be due to some chemical change in the receptor electrical generating mechanism that occurs in slow-adapting units and is not directly due to the temperature stimulus.

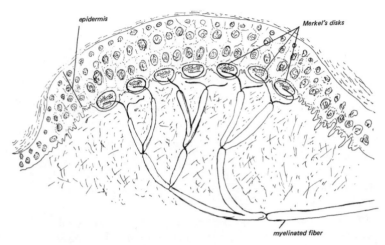

The Iggo corpuscle. A single myelinated nerve fiber branches to supply a series of Merkel's disks along the base of the epidermis. The branches lose their sheath before entering the disks.

pathic" system; the other was a later product of evolution and adaptation, an "epicritical" system. Knowing you've been touched, somewhere, somehow, would be a protopathic phenomenon, while fine discriminations —your ability to grade velvets or sandpapers, or feel a tuning fork's vibrations—would be epicritical.

Mountcastle and Rose have suggested that if the nervous system does distinguish two kinds of touch, it would make sense for the older division to be characterized by the smaller, less specific nerve terminals, while the epicritical system would come with specially designed end organs and streamlined nerve fibers. If the nerve pathways that take touch signals from the skin to the brain broke down into similar crude or refined routes, the situation would resolve itself nicely.

Tantalizingly, this is almost what happens. There *are* two main pathways that carry touch signals to the brain. One is a pair grouped with the kinesthetic or proprioceptive system in large tracts that line the rear of the spinal cord, the dorsal columns. The other pair, mixed with fibers relaying temperature and pain, lie on either side of the spinal cord, toward the front, the spinothalamic tracts.

The dorsal columns are by far the better known route, and lend support to one-half of the theory, for if this part of the spinal cord is crushed or cut, there is a loss of the vibration sense, two-point discrimination, and generally the more complex patterns of touch over parts of the body.

65

The spinothalamic tracts are more elusive. No one is certain where the fibers come from, how much they interact with cells and fibers of the other system, or whether or not single fibers carry different messages at different times, sometimes signaling touch, sometimes pain. Even the results of crushes or cuts of this part of the cord are not conclusive. There may be some loss of sensitivity to touch, temperature, and pain, and fewer touch spots on the skin, but the chief characteristics that show up are strange: there is a loss of the sensation of tickle and a serious disturbance in touch involved in sexual excitement—phenomena hardly suited to primitive pathways and raw nerve endings.

Decoding Signals

On the other hand what you call tickling (or what the brain decodes as a tickling) may be an interaction of simpler sensations, touch plus pain, both of which would be carried in the spinothalamic system.

The same may be true for other complex qualities of touch described by a single word. "Hardness" or "softness" may be a combination of surface touches and deeper kinesthetic responses in joints or tendons. (Here the dorsal columns carry both kinds of fibers.) "Wetness" may be a trio of touch, temperature, and pressure—involving both sets of pathways. Such an analysis becomes all the more intriguing with the realization that one doesn't have to *get* wet to *feel* wet. A woman's hands sheathed in rubber gloves as she washes dishes still feel wet.

The way the fiber bundles are coupled together with chances to interact in relay stations on the way to the brain may thus have important implications in interpreting complex tactile sensations. The pattern of coding in these cases depends on the sum of activity in whole groups of fibers, not just on signals coming in on a single channel.

Localization

Still another item of information that appears to be built into the structure of the nervous system is our ability to localize very readily what part of the skin has been touched. The brain could keep track of this if the peripheral nerves entered the spinal cord or came into the brain from the face and head regions in an orderly fashion, and if this order were preserved to the highest centers of cortex.

Certainly one would expect some order at the point of entry of the nerves considering the cylindrical arrangement of the body in embryo. Since the spinal nerves come off in pairs at each rung of the vertebral ladder, it would seem reasonable that the branches of these nerves supplying the skin would stay within the modest bounds of their original rungs.

This is exactly what happens, and if there were no other evidence for it, doctors could point to the painful skin disease shingles (*herpes zoster*). The disease is caused by a virus which attacks the larger sensory nerve cells in a ganglion next to the spinal cord at a specific level. These are the very cells whose fibers spread to a patch of skin as cutaneous nerves. Since the red spots of shingles appear neatly aligned like a belt, usually around the chest or abdomen (a symptom so characteristic that the name of the disease itself derives from cinch or girdle), the obvious deduction is that the spinal nerves segment the body in an orderly way. Of course the adult is no longer the tube he was in embryo. As arms and legs grew out from the torso they carried the spinal nerves with them. If a horizontally striped sock is put on a doll, the stripes at the arm level get pulled and stretched over broader areas, but the general order of stripes is preserved. Of course the nervous system has some "insurance" built into it in that a stripe at any one level contains threads from the stripes above and below. Still, the exact distribution of each spinal nerve can be worked out, an area which is called a dermatome.

The ordering from dermatome to dermatome is beautifully preserved all the way up to the cortex in the touch pathways, especially in the dorsal columns where at each level new fibers coming in tend to align themselves in layers to the side of the existing, more centrally located fibers. The arrangement is rigorously maintained as the fibers cross from one side of the cord to the other and relay with cells in the thalamus, which send new fibers up to the cortex. There a whole map of the body appears as a strip an inch or so wide just behind the center crosswise fold of the brain, all sensations from the left side of the body or face appearing on the right hemisphere, and vice versa (with allowance for some fibers from both pathways, from facial nerves, and other less well-known pathways, which may not cross over but stay on the same side of the brain).

The arrangement in the brain strip makes it possible to tie a single cortical cell to a surface spot of skin, its receptive field. Sometimes the field is no bigger than a point, a touch spot on the little finger, perhaps. Sometimes it may represent several square inches of back. Generally speaking adjacent cortical cells have overlapping fields, so that a small zone of activity lights up when a peripheral point is touched. But each cell has its favored region of excitement, usually toward the center of its field, grading to weaker responses toward the edge and finally, just outside the field, it may even be surrounded by sidebands or a halo of inhibition. A touch on the skin corresponding to this zone will prevent

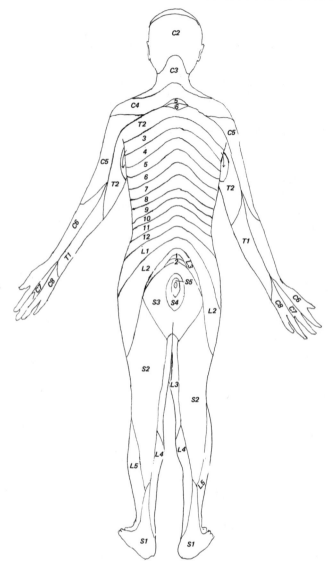

A map of dermatomes on the dorsal surface of the body. Letters and numbers refer to spinal nerves innervating the area. C = cervical, T = thoracic, L = lumbar, S = sacral.

the cell from firing. Thus a variety of interactions between neighboring cells is possible, which not only may sharpen your ability to localize touch, but may figure in identifying shapes and contours of surfaces.

68

The Homunculus

As a result of the varied densities and sensitivities of nerve endings in skin, the brain's picture of the self is not a perfect mirror image but a fun house distortion. You have a big face with a large mouth, big hands with huge thumbs, big feet and toes, but a small trunk—an image that Wilder Penfield of the Montreal Neurological Institute styled the "homunculus," or dwarf. Similar distorted body images have been mapped on the cortexes of rabbits and cats and monkeys, the monkey's approaching a distortion pattern like man's.

While the strip region, known as the somesthetic cortex, is the primary target area for general body sensation (including proprioception, pain, and temperature) it is not the only part of the brain involved. Regions nearby are important in interpretations of touch. Some of these areas receive signals directly from the primary area, and seem to function as a dictionary that gives meaning to words spelled out at the somesthetic cortex. Sometimes these secondary areas receive direct inputs from other relay stations lower down in the brain; sometimes they correlate general body sensations with other parts of the cortex concerned with the special senses or with motor pathways.

If electrical probes are applied to the primary area alone, people feel only vague tinglings or "funny feelings" in their arms or legs, nothing like normal sensations.

On the other hand, if there is brain damage further back in parts of the parietal lobe, a person may still be able to feel objects but cannot identify them without looking. A wristwatch, a child's jack, a book of matches, are just nameless weights and pressures. This condition is equivalent to the kinds of aphasias that occur in relation to other senses. In visual aphasia for example, a person's sight is intact, but he may no longer be able to recognize objects or read print. Auditory or speech aphasias involve difficulties in attaching meaning to sounds or in naming everyday objects when pointed out.

Evidently what goes on at the cortical level is an intricate decoding process which is only complete after many parts compare notes. Efforts made to crack the code so far have involved studying the way individual cortical cells in the primary strip behave when the stimulus is changed in frequency, intensity, or position.

Changes in the frequency or intensity of a touch in a single place can bring about a number of events: a cell may become very excited and try to keep up with the changes until it becomes fatigued. On the other hand, if the activity keeps up at a steady rate, it may become habituated or adapted, and turn off.

69

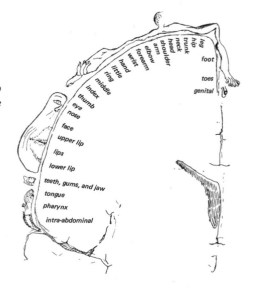

The sensory homunculus: a map of the body as it appears on the somesthetic cortex.

This is very characteristic of the sense of touch. No matter what may be said of newer or older divisions of the system, the sense itself is a very old and very alerting "on" system. What touches you is instantly attention-getting. Your life may depend on it—if it's a lion's paw. Or your future—if it's the "touch of your hand on mine." Or your business—if you shake hands with a stranger—a gesture so rich in content that it has become an international communication, common to almost all societies.

No sooner does the cortex receive the signals of these contacts than it comes to a decision. You leap from the lion, smile at the lover, or decide that this fellow with the clammy hand is not going to get a contract with your firm, and the cortical cells turn off. Even if the contact had persisted the cortical cells would have turned off because in this case they tend to follow the peripheral touch receptors' general lack of concern for steady-as-you-go information. This is most fortunate, else all day long you'd be plagued with feeling your clothing, or the chair you're sitting on, the rings on your fingers, or the wallet in the pocket of your trousers.

On the other hand, if those steady contacts change some way, or more important, change position—suppose a stocking runs or an ant crawls up your shirt sleeve—then there is a burst of activity in the brain. It is an escalation over and above what a single touch on your shoulder causes, for of all the events which stir you, none is so exciting as motion. This kind of complex cortical activity has yet to be deciphered. For now whole populations of brain cells are turning on and off in a variety of

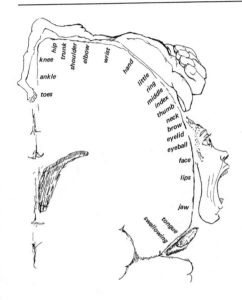

The motor homunculus. The motor innervation of the body shows a comparable distortion of the body, which is mapped on the cortex immediately forward of the central fissure. The somesthetic cortex is immediately behind the central fissure.

sequences and patterns that add up to vast amounts of information pouring in and out.

Unconsciously you make use of this phenomenon in reverse when you run your fingers over surfaces, for now you yourself trigger variations, exciting different receptors at different rates and different times. Unless you do this you may be stymied. Try to grade sandpaper sometime without rubbing it (and without looking). Trying to judge two samples, one fine, one extra fine, by merely resting your fingertips on them won't work, because the particles of sand are so close they defy your two-point discrimination limits.

But supplying the cortex with this extra information, scanning the surface and feeding in instantaneous changes in mechanical deformations and pressures on your skin, enables the cortex to solve the problem. It reads the message from the noisy mixture of on-off beatings of the skin just as an operator deciphers the dots, dashes, and spaces of Morse Code.

Hearing With the Skin

Hearing with skin—this analogy has struck more than one investigator of tactile sensation and led to one of the most interesting potentials for touch: the possibility of a skin language in which letters of the alphabet would be associated with certain frequencies of vibration at certain strengths lasting for a certain length of time and applied at certain points on the body—in all, a four-dimensional code which would be worked out within physiological limits:

(1) Frequency. Just as Quilliam's cat could "hear" some frequencies better than others, so humans too can judge certain vibrations accurately—up to about 70 cycles per second. Above this, judgment is affected by how strong the vibrations are. Like high notes on a piano they need to be louder in order to be appreciated.

(2) Duration. The length of a burst of vibrations can be judged reasonably well. For the purposes of a code the limits could range from about a tenth of a second up to two seconds—an interval in which time periods can be distinguished with accuracy.

(3) Intensity. We can note sufficient changes in the strength of a signal to be useful in a code.

(4) Location. Skin language excels over the spoken word. We hear with our ears, but skin hearing can extend to the 23 square feet of body surface of the average male (15 square feet in a woman). What's more, the same vibration on the chest could mean something different on the back.

For maximum usefulness the vibrations should be applied to more than one part of the body at a time. This is possible, bearing in mind the limits of two-point discrimination: you may not be able to separate two close-together vibratory bursts. Also there is a problem of localization under certain conditions. If a set of vibrators is attached to a person's chest and back he can distinguish one from another only if their bursts are varied in time or frequency of vibration. If all the vibrators fire identical bursts simultaneously he feels only a poorly localized single vibration.

On the other hand if there are small time differences between bursts and the vibrators are fired in sequence, something even stranger happens—there is a perception of movement comparable to the "phi" phenomenon in vision, the term psychologists use to describe the impression one gets of lights moving around a theater marquee when all that is occurring is that individual bulbs are turning on and off in sequence. The equivalent vibrational sensation creates a unique feeling of being caught up in a swirl of movement.

In spite of these "sensational" sensations a number of researchers, including Drs. Frank A. Geldard and W. C. Howell at the University of Virginia, worked out skin languages and trained people to use them. In one test sentences could be transmitted at the rate of 35 words per minute with 90 percent accuracy. The same timing between letters and words was used as in the International Morse Code: 0.005 second between letters and 0.1 second between words. The average five-letter word takes less than one-tenth of a second to transmit.

The importance of such a system to the blind or deaf is obvious. Less obvious is its potential as a means of long-distance communication in space, where sound may be unusable. This applies to "inner space" as well, the term now fashionable to apply to deep water research. The exotic gas mixtures divers breathe, in particular combinations of helium and oxygen, have freakish effects on the human voice, producing a high-pitched Mickey Mouse sort of gibberish. Given a choice of attending to Mickey Mouse or a whirlwind of meaning around the chest, most divers would opt for the whirlwind.

IV

Two Kinds of Temperature

Anyone stuck in the shower when the hot water's gone off abruptly knows the shock of exposing flesh to sudden cold. In seconds the warm, pleasant feeling passes into shivers, the fingers turn blue, and the teeth chatter. Frantically you turn the faucets off and grab for a towel. You put on your warmest robe and slippers and if you're still feeling chilled you have a cup of coffee or maybe some whiskey. Whatever else cold has meant to you it has made you move. You don't take it lying down.

If you did it might mean that it was already too late, that your body's processes had slowed and were fast coming to a halt. One by one your nerves would numb. You would no longer be able to see and hear. Eventually your heart would stop. This can befall any animal. Though such a fate may seem as remote as the old "conquest of the Pole" movies, in which the hero comes upon the frozen bodies of men and huskies curled up as though they were asleep, there have been enough severe blizzards in the last few years to serve as grim reminders of how vulnerable men and animals are.

These are extremes of course. The nervous system's capacity to sense cold and take steps against it are remarkable; so is the body's ability to recover in an emergency. In many cases frostbitten limbs and frozen ears can thaw and be restored to life as good as ever. Scientists have been able to make use of this power to "tame" cold to save lives. In "hypothermic" surgery a person's body is chilled, or the blood is passed through a cooling chamber and then recirculated, to reduce the temperature from the normal 98.6 degrees Fahrenheit to about 77 degrees. At this level one is unconscious and insensible to all feeling, including pain. Respiration must be maintained artificially, and the lungs are supplied with pure oxygen. But the body's tissues, especially the highly active nerve cells, are quiescent and make few demands on the body's resources. In this way complex time-consuming operations can be performed with greater safety. There is less shock and blood loss and no aftermath of reactions to anesthetic drugs.

Obviously an understanding of the body's reactions to cold is not without useful applications. As knowledge proceeds and the subtler details unfold it is possible that cooling techniques could make longdistance space travel practical. A visit to Mars by a hybernating astronaut is not a science-fiction fantasy, but conceivably the best solution to the problems of logistics and boredom that might attend the trip. Hybernation also temporarily renders animals immune to the effects of radiation. If this proves true for humans, then travelers exposed to brief rains of intense radioactivity might at least be able to prolong the wait for medical treatment.

Some amount of excess cold can do good. The same is not true of heat, unfortunately. The body's ability to endure ordeal by fire is sharply limited by the proteins in cells. Beyond 10 degrees of normal, proteins start to break down. Like the goose you get cooked. This is why high fevers are so dangerous. Years ago doctors occasionally experimented with inducing mild states of fever knowing that this would recruit the body's major defense mechanisms. In this way they tried to lick stubborn infections elsewhere in the body. But with the advent of the major antibiotic drugs the idea of fighting fire with fire has gone out of fashion.

Given the narrow limits of bearable heat, and the only slightly wider margin for cold, it is not surprising that the creatures of the earth tend to abound in the warmer belts. A record of existing mammals and reptiles compiled by Otto Rahn in 1939 revealed that there were 2,076 mammalian species and 2,785 kinds of reptiles living in the tropics, as against 948 species of mammals and 335 of reptiles living farther north and south. True, some of these differences relate to shorter generation times in warm climates and, consequently, greater chances for evolutionary changes to develop. Numbers of these species can also thrive in other regions, once they get there. But getting there comes later. Life on earth seems to have arisen at or near the equator.

In time the most highly developed species, birds and mammals, acquired the ability to maintain a constant body temperature independent of the environment. This was the boon to the greatest population explosion ever: the "warm-blooded" animals and birds spread to the four corners of the globe. An Eskimo can live in Florida or an Arab in Peru. Barn swallows winter in Brazil, bobolinks in Venezuela, and the Arctic tern makes the longest trek ever, wintering at the South Pole.

"Cold-blooded" animals on the other hand usually stay in one place and have to rely largely on the heat of the sun to keep them active. The lizard basking in the desert, as well as the fly buzzing around the kitchen window screen, are happiest at those seasons and times of day when the sun warms the earth to temperature ranges in which their systems can work. These intervals vary from species to species but are never very wide. On cloudy or overcast days a chameleon may lie dormant, even in mid-August. An ant will slow its pace when the thermometer's down, and, according to the noted entomologist Vincent Dethier, the best way to anesthetize a fly is to put it in the freezer for a few moments. When winter comes the only choice for these creatures is the long sleep of hibernation or the longer sleep of death.

Because it is just as important for cold-blooded animals to know how hot or cold it is, perhaps even more important since all they can do is take refuge, it is not surprising that some of them, as well as warm-blooded animals, have elaborate temperature-regulating and temperature-sensing mechanisms. Bees have developed a highly efficient insulating mechanism in clustering and the pair of conical pits near a rattlesnake's eyes are a remarkable sensory device. Lining these pits are cells which can pick up invisible heat rays—infrared radiation—given off by all warm objects. Rattlesnakes and other pit vipers may squint in the sun; they are deaf to sounds; but they can poise and strike a warm target when the pits are excited. What's more, the position of the pits when they are most excited is coordinated with the snake's striking stance.

It is now generally believed that mosquitoes, moths, and several other species of insects have infrared detectors, too. This would account for the blood-suckers' unerring ability to single out a sleeping body in a bedroom or a horse in a stable. It may also account for the difference in people's "insect-proneness." If you generate more heat than your friends you are probably the prime target for bites when you're out together walking in the woods.

Infrared sensors in the more benign insects may serve as species or sex detectors, each species having its own wavelength band.

76

Man lacks such natural sensors but has been able to manufacture them: A Sidewinder missile makes use of an infrared detector to seek out enemy aircraft or missiles by their heated vapor trails.

Instead of infrared sensors human beings come equipped with a multiplicity of nerve endings that respond to conducted heat more than the heat of radiation. Whether the nerve terminal in every case is connected with a specific receptor—an end organ thermometer—is as moot a point for temperature as it is for touch. Two receptors, the Krause end-bulb and the Ruffini end organ (a smaller version than the Ruffini ending in joints), have been implicated, but there are many parts

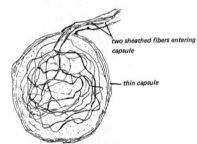

A drawing of a Krause end-bulb from the conjunctiva of the eye.

two sheathed fibers entering capsule

thin capsule

of the body where one can sense warmth or cold without these structures. Some of the naked nerve terminals in such areas may be temperature specific, as Ainsley Iggo has found. Others may be more generalized, responding to pressure or pain and usually to cold as well. Such endings may account for the strange paradox in which cold objects feel heavier than warm ones of the same weight.

This last observation points to a peculiar phenomenon of man's temperature sensibility. The thermometers (or nerve endings) do not behave like tubes of mercury or alcohol that expand when heated or contract when cooled, and so readily record temperatures covering a wide range. Instead some endings respond to cold and falling temperatures; others to heat and increasing warmth. The scales often overlap, and there are a number of situations in which both kinds of endings may be excited, but it would seem that the nervous system was doing its best to distinguish between the two.

The thermometers are found in different places under the skin and this underlines the distinction. If a fine pointed steel probe cooled about 30 degrees below normal skin temperature (about 90 degrees) is applied to your skin you either feel the cold or not. Measuring your reaction times when you do feel cold and comparing those times with the kind of nerve endings that exist below, researchers have concurred that cold fibers lie high up in the skin, about 0.007 inch below the surface. Placed here not only will they sense cold more quickly, but there will be less interference from the warming effects of blood vessels which are more concentrated below.

The heaviest batteries of cold receptors lie in exposed areas like the face, with emphasis on the tip of the nose, the eyelids, lips, and forehead. Parts of the chest and abdomen and sexual sites are also highly sensitive. It's always easier to get your feet wet than the rest of your body when you bathe in the ocean or a pool.

The same kind of test with a warm probe shows that warm spots are even fewer and farther between. They lie deeper in skin, about 0.012 inch below the surface. You have slightly greater sensitivity to warmth on the hairy parts of your head, around your knee caps, and on your tongue.

There is some agreement that the areas with the most cold spots have the greatest number of Krause end-bulbs. Equally, warm spots match the distribution of Ruffini organs.

Unlike the majority of touch endings, the fast "on" switches that signal changes of state, temperature sensors needle the brain with more frequent reports. Your forehead will feel cold after you've applied an ice bag and the temperature at the receptor level has reached a new low state.

Similarly when you're driving on a sunny summer day with your left arm resting on the open window edge, the skin warms up and stays warm so that at some point the underskin temperature is a constant. But the endings will still fire faithfully away to the brain.

From these observations it appears that the body's thermometers do two things: they report a change in temperature as it happens, as well as new highs or lows. Between sudden changes and the final states that temperature induces at the receptor level the behavior of an individual fiber will depend on a number of things: its original condition, its range and sensitivity, how quickly heat is transferred through the skin, and how extreme the final state induced by the thermal change may be.

Suppose your forearm skin was at the neutral temperature (about 90 degrees) and you put an ice cube on your wrist. This dramatic change brings a fast reaction from the cold fibers. Heat moves out quickly, the cold fibers are excited and may "over-react"—firing away at rates over 100 impulses per second. The actual temperature drop need only be a degree or so, and yet you will feel cold. Repeating the experiment with a hot compress shows the same behavior except that warm fibers take longer to react and never attain as high rates of firing as the cold fibers.

If, on the other hand, a woman has just dabbed her wrist with a drop of perfume or tested the baby's mild bath water with her elbow, the rate of heat exchange will be slower and the receptors more sluggish. A bigger difference in temperature may be recorded at the receptor level before she feels anything.

These are nuances of course. The actual experiments show changes in temperature of the order of hundredths or thousandths of a degree per second. The point is that the receptors respond to such nuances.

The more the temperature of the hot or cold source diverges from neutral the longer it takes for temperature changes under the skin to play themselves out. As they do the rate of change slows and may stop altogether. The fiber adapts to a new level, firing away at a rate which is correlated to that temperature as long as it is maintained. Experiments that measure these effects use special tubes with water flowing through at constant temperatures.

Whether or not you take notice of the sensation depends on what the final temperature is. Close to neutral, even if the fiber pulses signals at a steady rate, the brain may ignore them. Further out, the likelihood of awareness mounts, and below 68 degrees or above 104 degrees constant sensations appear.

If the warm or cold source is removed something else happens. The sensation lessens immediately, but, interestingly, it doesn't disappear. Your wrist stays cool for some time after you remove the ice cube even though the skin is now warming up. This is because the temperature changes are still in chilly enough ranges to keep the cold fibers excited, perhaps changing their discharge rates, yet are too low to trigger the warm fibers. The colder your wrist was to begin with, the longer the sensation lasts.

The hot compress experiment displays a similar aftereffect. As your skin begins to cool, its temperature may be beyond the upper limits of sensitivity of cold fibers, but still well within the range of warm fibers. Again the warm sensation persists.

Now suppose you don't gentle the skin, but subject it to a sudden jump in temperature when it has been cooled or an immersion into cold when it had been adapted to warmth. Anyone with separate hot and cold water faucets that feed into a common basin has done this time and time again. You feel the hot water with your left hand and the cold with your right, and some portion of each hand grows adjusted to the highs and lows before you put both hands into the lukewarm water. Now the hot hand feels cold, and the frigid hand, warm. This too can be explained anatomically: the cold fibers that had adapted to a cold state are momentarily stunned, or inhibited, by the sudden immersion into a lukewarm temperature. They cease to fire, while at the same time warm fibers suddenly turn on. The reverse happens when the warm-adapted hand is put in the same water: the warm fibers are stopped while the cold fibers turn on. A few moments later some warm fibers and some cold fibers again become active so that soon both hands adjust to a common experience of "lukewarm."

Paradoxical Hot and Cold

The normal range of sensitivity of cold fibers is between 50 and 104 degrees F. At the high end of the scale a fiber reacts weakly, firing only about one impulse per second. As temperatures lower the fiber gets more excited, and typically may have a peak of activity between 65 and 85 degrees. The scale for warm fibers is between 68 and 117 degrees with a tendency to increase the steady rate of discharge as temperature climbs to 117 degrees. At still higher temperatures there is a sharp drop-off.

Curiously both types of fibers can be excited at points outside their scales. A cold fiber is silent between 104 and 113 degrees. But then it suddenly starts to discharge again and continues to fire at still higher temperatures close to the threshold for pain (about 122 degrees). When this happens in a part of the body that is poorly supplied with warm fibers you feel cold, a paradoxical sensation since you are really being warmed.

The comparable effect for warm fibers, a freakish ability to fire at low temperatures, is less well documented. Warm fibers do respond to sudden cooling, but the response is brief and may be masked by cold fiber activity in the neighborhood. Still you may occasionally have washed your hands in water pumped from an icy well and felt a burning sensation. The illusion can also be encouraged with a little psychological hokus-pokus: the blindfolded fraternity pledgee may believe the sliver of dry ice (frozen carbon dioxide) touching his back is really a hot poker. (It helps a little if there's a sizzling sound like bacon frying in the background.)

More marked effects occur in some neurological disorders in which a person may lose the sensation of cold altogether, while still sensing warmth. In such cases ice cubes placed on the skin will feel warm.

What's Hot?

Sometimes partial nerve losses occur in which persons can sense some degrees of cold or warmth but nothing hot. At first glance this seems to contradict common sense. You would think that disruptions of nerve

80

pathways would affect fine discriminations first, and leave strong sensations alone. But the problem here focuses on what "hot" is. Many investigators feel that it is a distinct quality in its own right, not "strong warmth." Again, while the sensation is described in a single word it may be a combination of cold and warmth, and at higher temperatures, pain sensations as well. It would then follow that anything cutting out signals from some of these nerves would affect your over-all perception of heat.

Sensitivity and awareness of temperature change dramatically when the whole body is subjected to sudden variations, as when you dive into a pool or take a steam bath. The massive stimulation so increases your sensitivity that it takes only an over-all exposure to heat that warms your skin 3 or 4 degrees for you to feel distinctly warm. An even smaller drop of 1 or 2 degrees from neutral skin temperature is enough to make you feel chilly.

Under these conditions you are much more aware of the body's activity to combat the changes and bring you back to normal. Some of these are conscious attempts on your part: to keep warm you tread water rather than stand idly in the waves, or rub your hands and massage your ears to increase blood circulation and stimulate heat from muscle activity. To cool off you may rinse your hands and face in cold water, or drink iced drinks. But your major weapons are supplied by a completely automatic defense system, one more richly endowed in birds and mammals than in cold-blooded animals.

The Autonomic Nervous System

The autonomic nervous system consists of groups of nerve cells and fibers that are partly inside the central nervous system and partly outside in glands and muscles, particularly ones which are concerned with involuntary or visceral activities. Most of the time we are not aware of the juggling game these nerves play. Some can make the heart beat faster, some can slow it down; some can cause more digestive juices to flow, some less. Normally both sets of nerves are always at work striving for a happy medium. But in an emergency one or the other set may take over. Your eyes may pop, or your hair stand on end, your hands turn cold and clammy, or your mouth dry.

Changes like that are often associated with emotional states, such as being upset, or frightened, or surprised. To some extent they can occur in frogs or snakes or other cold-blooded creatures. But the system's extra salvation to warm-blooded animals is its ability to come to your rescue in a temperature crisis. When the temperature climbs the autonomic nervous system turns on the sweat glands in your skin. It may also make your face flush. When it's cold the system makes you shiver, get goose pimples, or turn blue.

Sweating cools you because the warm air around you is robbed of its heat as the sweat evaporates. The same thing happens when you walk by a building under construction. The atmosphere feels air-conditioned because the "sweating" concrete or plaster takes heat from the surrounding air in the process of drying.

When your face flushes it's a visible sign that the blood vessels under your skin are expanding, or dilating. The autonomic nervous system relaxes the smooth muscle walls of the vessels, opening the faucets wide so more blood heat can be conducted or radiated out.

Reactions to cold do just the opposite. Goose pimples mean that muscles in your skin are contracting, so less of you is exposed. Shivering generates extra heat from those same muscles. Blue lips or fingertips are signs that peripheral blood vessels are constricting, and blood is being shunted away from the surface to keep the inner fires burning.

As soon as you're back to normal the system automatically turns off the distress forces. The question is how does it—or you—know what normal is.

Defenses Against Heat

Probably it uses two methods, one conscious and voluntary, the other unconscious and automatic. The unconscious one involves a thermostat, an indicator built into your heating system that sets off an alarm when body temperature climbs. This is the key to warm-blooded animals' successful revolt against a hostile hot environment. Each warm-blooded species has a small temperature range which is optimal for survival, and each individual within the species has his thermostat set at a particular point within that range. For human beings the point, which is probably prescribed by heredity, could be anywhere between 97 and 99 degrees F. As soon as the thermostat climbs above that point the autonomic nervous system gets to work to counter the change.

For some time scientists speculated where the thermostat might be. Traditional places for taking the temperature like the mouth or rectum were possibilities, as were certain parts of skin, the ones most rich in temperature fibers.

But an even stronger case could be made out for a place deep inside the body. Here the control mechanism would be immune to constant swings back and forth as one stepped from a cool arbor into a hot sun, or sat becalmed in a sailboat and then was wafted by a cool breeze. Why shouldn't the body follow the logic we use in heating our homes? The thermostat isn't in the exterior walls, but in the living room, the place most insulated from transient changes, and the spot we're most anxious to have comfortable at all times.

The autonomic nervous system's living room is in the brain itself. The thermostat lies in the heart of the very tissue most in need of stable operating conditions, while at the same time most immune to the passing fancies of wind or weather.

The site is in the hypothalamus, in an area discovered in 1884 by a pair of medical students at the University of Berlin, E. Aronsohn and J. Sachs. They found that when they damaged this part of the brain animals became feverish. Amusingly the word hypothalamus itself means "under the bedroom" (hypo means under; thalamus is the Greek word for inner chamber, usually bedchamber). It was the Roman physician Galen (A.D. 131–201) who gave this name to the clusters of gray cells, and possibly adjacent parts, near the base of the brain, just above the place where the optic nerves from each eye come and meet at a crossroad.

The way receptor cells in the thermostat sense temperature is probably chemical in nature rather than a process that involves the direct exchange of heat energy. Scientists had to reject that more obvious idea, both for the hypothalamic receptor mechanism as well as for the temperature sensors in the skin, when they discovered nerve fibers could discharge regularly even when there was no temperature difference between the two sides of the receptor layer.

Support for a chemical trigger for the nerves' action also comes from the known effects of substances like menthol. Even a small dilution of menthol applied to the tongue after it has been warmed deliberately to quiet the cold fibers' activity, immediately starts them firing. A mint julep and a mentholated cigarette really are cool. It would be interesting to study other familiar taste sensations, like the heat of hot tamales or chili, or the cool of cucumbers, to see if they also may involve chemical effects on temperature fibers.

Brain Fevers

More recently a London neurophysiologist Dr. W. S. Feldberg has suggested that the temperature receptors in the hypothalamus depend on the amounts of three nervous system chemicals found there. Two of them, adrenaline and noradrenaline, act to lower temperature; the third, serotonin, raises it. Dr. Feldberg thinks that in some infectious diseases bacterial action may trigger the release of serotonin in the hypothalamus and bring on feverish symptoms. The high fevers that occasionally accompany brain injury may similarly be the result of throwing the delicate balance of chemicals out of kilter. When Dr. Feldberg, experimenting with guinea pigs, injected varying amounts of the substances into the front part of the hypothalamus (the specific site of the thermostat receptors), he was able to raise or lower temperatures.

Anesthetics generally lower temperature, possibly because they may stimulate the release of the two kinds of adrenaline in the brain. Normally the autonomic nervous system controls the release of these hormones from the adrenal glands above the kidneys. From there they pass into the bloodstream directly and become part of the body's defense system in emergencies, which we generally associate with a heated state. Indeed, by priming the heart to beat faster and stimulating muscles to greater activity adrenaline generally increases the body's metabolism rate and thus helps to generate heat. There is no contradiction however because what passes into the bloodstream in the body is often forbidden admittance to the nerve cells of the brain. A delicate system of fibers and supporting cells around brain tissue, called the blood-brain barrier, can filter the blood and prevent unwanted chemicals from coming into contact with nerve cells. The thermostat will be protected from adrenaline's effects.

Aspirin is still another chemical compound which can lower a high temperature but has no effect on normal temperature. How it works is still unknown.

Cold Hands . . . Warm Heart?

The adrenaline emergency reaction raises an interesting question about the body's extremities in relation to the brain. If you've eaten ice cream on a hot day you may cool off inside while your skin is still absorbing heat from the air. If you drink hot soup on a cold day you might begin to sweat even though your skin felt cold. It was to settle which information, the inside or the outside, was more important to the nervous system and which governed its reaction that a number of investigators built an elaborate body chamber in which both temperatures could be varied.

The chamber is called a gradient calorimeter. Working models of it were tested by Charlotte Kitzinger at the Naval Medical Research Institute in Bethesda, Maryland, and later a full-scale model was built under the direction of Richard B. Huebscher at the Laboratory of the American Society of Heating and Ventilating Engineers in Cleveland, Ohio. A volunteer lies down inside the chamber on a kind of slinglike stretcher, free from contact with the walls, which are lined with thousands of tiny heat-sensing elements.

During an experiment the amount of heat flow to or from the

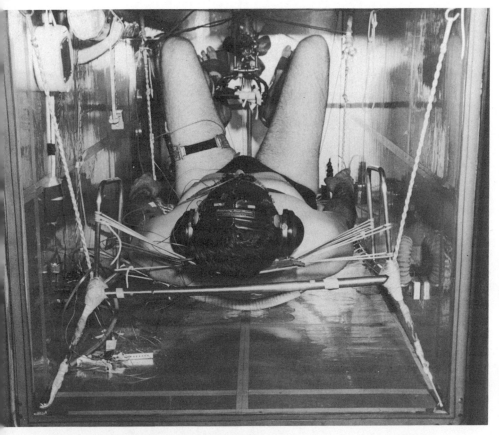

Interior view of the gradient calorimeter used in temperature experiments at the Naval Medical Research Institute. Subject lies on metal screens in a light frame suspended on nylon strings. Gradient layers are covered with anodized aluminum foil, giving interior a shining appearance.

volunteer's body can be accurately measured and the rate of blood flow in the skin calculated (to indicate how much the blood vessels have dilated or constricted). Humidity indicators measure the amount of sweat evaporated into the air.

In his time in the box the volunteer might be exposed to almost intolerable heat or unbearable cold. He might eat ice cream or hot soup, rest, or do strenuous exercises.

In this way all possible combinations of internal-external temperatures could be studied: hot-hot, hot-cold, cold-hot, and cold-cold. In every case the experiments showed that it was the subject's internal temperature that mattered. When the subject gulped mouthfuls of sherbet his temperature dropped—even while the air around him was desert hot. The thermostat turned off his sweating. Then his skin temperature actually rose as the rapidly drying skin could now be heated by radiation and conduction from the hot environment.

One of the unexpected results of these experiments was the discovery that rectal temperature does not accurately reflect either skin or brain temperature. Indeed the principal investigators, Dr. T. H. Benzinger and his group in Bethesda, all but despaired of proving anything by the calorimeter when they used rectal thermometers. It was only when they placed a thermometer for measuring internal temperature against the eardrum, a few inches away from the hypothalamus, that they got meaningful results. This finding could have widespread applications: the oral or rectal thermometer in use in homes and hospitals might be discarded in favor of the more accurate readings obtained from an eardrum instrument.

An X ray of thermocouples in various locations in the head. The subject, Dr. Benzinger himself, was seeking the best site for taking internal temperature.

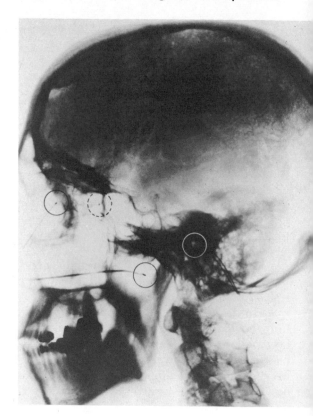

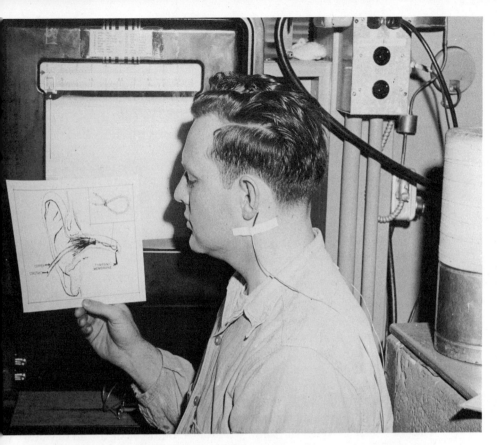

The final choice of a suitable location for measuring internal temperature was at the eardrum.

The eardrum thermometer is a thermocouple of constantan and copper wires. (One end of the double wire loop is placed against the surface whose temperature is to be measured; the other end is kept at a lower temperature. The difference in temperature at the two junctions causes an electric current to flow which is proportional to the temperature difference.) The bristles are to keep the thermometer in position against the eardrum.

The calorimeter experiments buoy the argument that the hypothalamus is principally concerned with protecting the body against overheating, and only incidentally concerned with cold states. It might exert inhibitory effects—turning off signals to sweat glands, for example. A few researchers have looked further back in the hypothalamus in search of other receptor cells which might specifically respond to cooling, and trigger some heat-generating activity in the body's cells, but the prevailing opinion is that low points on your temperature scale are handled by your skin receptors and relayed to parts of your brain that can link conscious perception with autonomic nervous centers.

Certainly the abundance of cold spots compared to warm endings in the skin, their greater sensitivity and faster reaction time, suggest that the division of labor is a fair one. The nerves bearing cold and warm signals come into the spinal cord, ascend as part of the spinothalamic tracts, and reach the somesthetic cortex—that body-image region in the middle of the brain that also is the major endstation for sensations of touch, pressure, and pain. Here, or in nearby areas, or possibly earlier even in a relay station in the thalamus itself, there is conscious awareness of cold. With awareness comes the ability to take action. You can put on a sweater or a coat, or you can go indoors. You can drink the coffee or the shot of whiskey to warm you up. (The alcohol temporarily dilates peripheral blood vessels creating a warm tingling feeling in your limbs. The effect is brief, however, and if you stayed outdoors on a cold day and kept on drinking you'd end up cooling the blood by constantly exposing the dilated peripheral vessels to the chilly environment.)

On the other hand there's not much you can do about warmth. There's a limit to the amount of clothing you can take off, the number of cold showers you can take, or iced liquids you can drink. If you're not careful, you may so cool your body internally that when you emerge into a hot, humid atmosphere you may find your hypothalamic thermostat has turned off the sweat glands and you may suffer all the more. Perhaps your best bet is to do what the natives in the tropics do—drink tea or hot food to increase sweating and stay out of the noonday sun. Take a siesta instead. Your body temperature generally falls as you sleep,° and your dreams may provide the proper antidote to the inferno around you.

° Your thermostat, like other biological clocks that regulate body activities, goes through daily cycles. You are normally cooler first thing in the morning and warm up during the day. Strangely lowest temperatures occur at about 4 A.M.—whether you're sound asleep or working the night shift.

V

A Blurred Pattern of Pain

The sense of pain is embarrassing to science. It is unspecific, subjective, and culturally conditioned. Pain impulses seem to be triggered by a ragged rat's nest of raw nerve endings distributed all over the body. The sensations they trigger may be sharp or dull, precisely localized or far removed from the source. Pain may be real or imagined; it may come in flashes or in aches. Some pain impulses are weak, easily lost, readily forgotten. They meander at feeble horse-and-buggy rates up to the brain. Others come fast and strong, rivaling the airplane velocities with which kinesthetic signals are triggered. When disease strikes the spinal cord the pain sense may be the first to go. In other diseases, pain is so viciously persistent that only severing nerve fibers will bring relief.

Pain is an important sense. No matter where or how it strikes, it signals an emergency. The agent of pain—the sting, the pinprick, the touch of a hot iron—tells you to take action quickly. Indeed the reaction in these instances is programmed into your nervous system as a reflex. You don't voluntarily withdraw your hand from the hot iron. It would take too much time. Instead the incoming sensory signals make a short

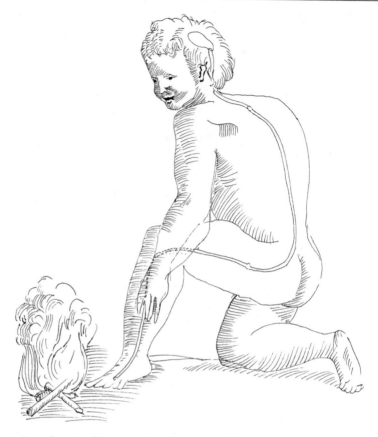

Illustration showing Descartes' concept of pain signaling an alarm in the brain. He wrote: "If for example fire comes near the foot, the minute particles of fire, which as you know move with great velocity, have the power to set in motion the spot of the skin of the foot which they touch, and by this means pulling upon the delicate thread which is attached to the spot of the skin, they open up at the same instant the pore against which the delicate thread ends, just as by pulling at one end of a rope one makes to strike at the same instant a bell which hangs at the other end."

circuit through the spinal cord and connect with intermediary cells, which in turn contact the motor cells whose fibers contract the muscles that move your hand back. At the same time, duplicate signals are relayed to higher centers in the brain. Only then do you feel pain and say "Ouch!"

This is one type of familiar emergency you cope with successfully.

90

You learned from it, too, for a small child, lacking experience, doesn't know that fire is hot or matches can burn. (In a few rare instances individuals are born insensible to pain. For them life presents endless hazards that they must learn about intellectually.)

But if heat and fire were all that the body were able to cope with, the human race would probably not have survived the misfortunes of earthly existence. The pain response is triggered by a vast catalog of harmful agents, and the signaling that goes on is more than the simple reflex arc and conscious sensation. Pain is intimately tied to that other network of nerves in the body, the autonomic nervous system, whose function is to conserve the body, to keep it intact, balance its chemical equations, watch temperature, regulate blood flow. Pain rings a general alarm. It arouses all the body's defenses and emergency equipment.

Suppose you step off the curb and sprain your ankle. You will feel pain, perhaps a sharp sensation, followed by a steady, burning feeling. But this is only part of your body's reaction. If there had been a camera observing you, it might have recorded your eyes growing larger, your face flushing, your whole body turning slightly pink. If a camera could have photographed the inside of your body, it would have recorded still other changes.

Some of these you were conscious of—your heart beating faster or your armpits moistening with sweat. Other internal changes you could only be aware of indirectly. The liver, for example, the prime organ for storing energy in the form of the sugar glycogen, releases this fuel to meet the emergency. The blood now pounding through your heart at a faster rate is also pumping through the arteries at greater pressure because the walls of the arteries contract; cinching in the tubes to press the oxygen-rich blood faster to the point where it's needed—your ankle. There just the opposite change in blood vessels takes place. They dilate so that the injured area is bathed in a rich blood supply, bringing to the sore spot the fuel and oxygen needed to start the repair process and also helping to wash away the waste products and the damaged tissue. The extra blood causes the redness of the sprain. Aiding and abetting these good works are the adrenal glands. Nerves stimulate them to release adrenaline, a chemical which can independently produce many of these changes and sustain them over a period. Adrenaline also has a direct effect on muscles, literally giving them a "shot in the arm" to erase the effect of fatigue in the emergency.

The blood which has been shunted to the sprain area has left a deficit in your gut. Digestion temporarily slows or even stops in the crisis. Gastric juices stop flowing. The smooth muscles of the intestine relax so that peristalsis—the rhythmic contractile movements that push food forward in the alimentary canal—cease. Food stays in your stomach until the emergency is over.

The part of the autonomic nervous system that carries out these emergency measures is the sympathetic division. It works in a whole-body way, producing flushing, sweating, dilatation of pupils, and major changes in blood pressure and digestion.

These same reactions also describe what happens to you physically in states of high emotion, when you are intensely angry or afraid, for example. Nor is this autonomic nervous system link of emotion and pain the only one, for in the higher centers of the brain, in parts associated with conscious thoughts and feelings, pathways and centers are inter-mingled that give the "affective" or emotional quality to pain. This is what colors pain, making it in some ways the most interesting of the senses, though the least measurable. Pain is both a thing in itself and also a "painful emotion."

Mingled with pain there may be fear, ultimately the fear of dying. There may be anger—How could I be so stupid!—or frustration—you skinned your knee but still didn't make the touchdown. There may even be passion or ecstacy. Most schools of psychology believe there is a close relationship between pain and pleasure in masochistic-sadistic personal-ities.

Anthropologists contribute their observations to support the im-portance of cultural or group attitudes toward pain: consider the fire-walkers of Samoa; the circumcision rites at puberty of the Trobriand Islanders; the ordeals by nails, fire, nauseant drugs, and beatings which are widespread in human experience. In the cultures where the rites are standard, few die or suffer permanent damage as a result of the cere-mony.

A similar ability to endure pain often accompanies acts of great heroism. A fireman rescues a child at the cost of searing his own flesh. A ragged refugee mother walks miles in ice and snow carrying her baby. A soldier wounded in battle drags another back to safety. All these cases demonstrate seemingly superhuman efforts directed away from the call of duty to one's own body.

In a sense they are negative events: instead of resting, taking cover, binding up the wound, or in the case of tribal rites, instead of hitting back at the individual in charge, individuals willingly submit. Moreover they often don't feel any pain. Dr. Henry K. Beecher of Harvard University in a study of 150 American soldiers wounded at the battle of Anzio, Italy, in World War II found that only one out of three asked for morphine or other drugs. The majority denied any feelings of pain at all. Yet when Beecher made a later survey in peacetime of 150 men who had undergone surgery involving less trauma than that caused by the injuries of the wounded soldiers, over 80 percent pleaded for drugs to relieve severe pain. As the noted authority Dr. E. K. Livingston of the University of Oregon Medical School has asked, "Can you call a pain a pain if it's not felt?"

Attention and Inhibition

What makes the difference between these extremes is probably a drama played out in the higher centers of the brain. The negative display, the ability to endure or deny suffering, may indeed be a negativity on the part of the brain, an actual outpouring of inhibitory signals that control pain signals all along the line. Sometimes particular masses of cells in the lower parts of the cortex or in the thalamus seem to be involved, sometimes parts or pathways higher up. It is not easy to specify "this part" or "these cells" as sources of the signals because pain signals ramify so widely in the brain and often exhibit erratic behavior. Attention and inhibition are key words. If in a crisis your attention is overwhelmingly directed toward something other than tissue damage you may be able to ignore pain. The sensation may only be postponed, however. When the crisis is over, your mind may turn toward your body again. Often you may be mercifully spared "the worst." Even a third degree burn has its peak, after which the body will be less sensitive because the nerve endings themselves have been destroyed and signals cannot get through.

Concentration and distraction operate when circumstances are not so dire or life-threatening. Dr. Livingston, who likes to fish, tells of the time he felt a heavy strike on his line and saw a large salmon break the water. In the struggle that followed he crossed from boat to boat—in a chain that stretched between two sandspits. Finally he had to get out onto the beach itself before he was able to land the fish. Only then did he notice blood dripping down his trouser leg, reddening his sneakers. There was a bad gash down his leg. Further examination revealed skin scraped off three knuckles, a friction burn on his right thumb, and two massive bruises on his left thigh. All had been ignored, unnoticed, unfelt.

Distraction and Attitude

The philosophy of distraction directs some of the attempts to mitigate dental surgery. Sounds of "white noise" (mixtures of all frequencies of sound) or sweet music, and even records that tell the patient to "relax

. . . feel the muscles in your toes relax . . . relax in your feet . . . your ankles . . ." have been known to help. Sounds of the sea give psychological aid to some women in childbirth.

What pain means to you also determines your emotional attitude and reaction. To a native boy circumcision rites may mean, "Today I am a man," and the vaunt to ego dominates the cruel treatment.° A woman in childbirth may be calm and relaxed, or panicky and fearful, depending on how her feelings about having a baby were nurtured.

In American culture childbirth is generally viewed as a serious and painful matter. Yet anthropologists can point to other cultures where birth is a minor interruption in the day's work. The woman comes in from the fields, gives birth with no visible distress, and soon returns to the fields. Her husband in the meantime has taken to his bed, moaned and groaned as though in agony, and after his wife has left, stays in bed with the baby to recover from his ordeal.

Attitude probably accounts for the differences between the war-wounded and the surgical patient. For one the injury may be the "million-dollar" wound, the passport to safety, away from the constant threat of death or mutilation in battle. For the surgery patient, perhaps an automobile accident victim, just the opposite reasoning prevails. Life, tranquil a moment before, now presents him with a multitude of fears and threats ranging from the immediate concern for life and loved ones to time and money gone down the drain.

Too fearful a concern for pain may exacerbate it, making recovery slower and more arduous. This is true of childbirth, as well as serious illnesses like heart disease or cancer. Hypnosis has been known to help some individuals, never by eliminating the pain altogether (which could be dangerous), but by mitigating the person's attitude toward it. Several cases reported by a Canadian physician involve the projection of a pain from cancer in an internal organ to pain in a hand or forearm. Such a change often enables the person to bring a degree of detachment to the illness and even allows him to work. Certainly it lessens the dependence on drugs.

The parts of the brain that figure in attitude and attention in a sense are the alpha and omega of the system. They are at the end of the line, making associations, recalling past experiences and behavior, yet insofar as they are constantly directing traffic all along the line they are

---

° Some social psychologists in America think that the injury- or death-inviting games like "chicken," in which teen-age drivers aim their cars at each other at full speed, take their hands off the wheel, and wait to see who will be the first to weaken and avert a crash, are perverse forms of initiation rites created by the children themselves in a culture which no longer officially recognizes the transition into adulthood.

present even at the beginning, almost at the presentation of whatever tortuous or tormenting thing becomes the pain "stimulus." How the brain can be both "with it" and on "top of the situation" is a lesson in neurophysiology. It will help to trace the course of events chronologically.

The Triggers

The number of things that can cause pain is so large it may hurt just to think about them. A pinprick, bee sting, mosquito bite; a dab of iodine, household ammonia, lye; a swollen gland, a pimple, a blister; a full stomach or bladder, a torn ligament or broken rib, an inflamed joint—anything that swells, smarts, or twists your insides, anything that burns, bites, or cuts your outside. Loud sounds or bright lights can hurt. So can abrasions, tickles, itches; a tap on your back when you're sunburned; a slap, rap, or a squeeze of your fingertips caught in a door or window. All manner of intense mechanical, light, heat, sound, or chemical energies can afflict your skin. Your insides can suffer from an acid stomach, heartburn, sore throat, earache, chest pains, cramps, rheumatism, neuralgias, as well as a variety of mental states of anxiety or fear that bring on headaches, tension, nausea, dizziness, and assorted miseries.

Sometimes your body seems to conspire against you. After you've burned or cut yourself there is painful swelling and blistering. The wounds discharge waste substances into the bloodstream that cause more pain. Bacterial or viral toxins and other foreign matter can do the same. But the body itself releases chemicals, histamine from cells in connective tissue, or serotonin from cells in the bloodstream, which do some good by dilating blood vessels in the infected area. But in small doses histamine makes you itch; in larger amounts both histamine and serotonin cause pain. Interestingly the pain is not unlike that caused by the venoms of deadly snakes and jellyfish, sea urchins, and the Portuguese man-of-war. Even such harmless chemicals as potassium, a normal constituent of cells, can, on release from damaged tissues, relentlessly trigger pain.

"Neurokinins," "bradykinins," and "blister fluids" are other substances recently discovered as pain causers, proteinlike substances produced by the body, sometimes to keep the alarm mechanism in operation so the body can heal faster but sometimes for apparently no good reason. Again some venoms may trigger the production or increase the amounts of these substances by contributing proteins and proteinlike molecules. The venom of the stonefish, one of the deadliest fish in the world, is also rich in proteins.

Squeezing a limb and strangling the blood supply can hurt, too. This condition, called ischemia, leads to deprivations of oxygen and fuel to nerves and muscles. When this happens the cell membrane walls may change in permeability and again let potassium seep out which brings on pain.

It was the discovery of this phenomenon that led to the analysis of a strange poisoning that afflicted fishermen off the coast of the Malay peninsula. An English investigator Dr. H. A. Reid found that the highly toxic bite of the sea snake *Enhydrina schistosa* could go unnoticed except for the initial prick but within an hour would induce agonizing muscular pain in parts distant from the bite. The clue that provided the answer was that the urine turned red. Analysis showed the color came from myoglobin, the pigment that makes all meat, or skeletal muscle, red. If muscle tissue was being savaged so severely that the large (and non-pain-causing) molecules of myoglobin were being released, obviously the smaller molecules of potassium and possibly other pain-causing substances were on the loose as well.

The pain of gout, too, has now been diagnosed as chemical in origin. The disease, which usually afflicts knee or foot joints, derives its name from the French for drop or swallow because it was thought that something ingested settled in the lower parts of the body, causing trouble. This idea wasn't so far from wrong, for it appears now that gout sufferers have difficulty metabolizing uric acid. To test this idea two stalwart British investigators, Drs. J. S. Faires and D. J. McCarty, injected sodium urate crystals into their own knee joints and waited. Within two hours they suffered excruciating pain and an acute inflammation. Both men had walked about freely after their initial injection, and they theorized that the body weight on the needlelike crystals broke them up in a way that provoked the formation of kinins, the pain-causing substances. Floating in the plasma, the liquid part of the blood, the kinins in turn affected the permeability of the walls of capillaries, allowing plasma to escape into the joint itself to cause more swelling and pain.

Visceral Pain

Many but not all of the things that hurt your hide hurt your inside. Dr. Livingston describes the first time he was called upon to assist in an operation that required the reopening of a colostomy, a surgical procedure by which the colon is diverted from its normal course and an

96

artificial opening made for it on the body surface. He was horrified to see that the patient had been prepared with only a local anesthetic while a red hot poker was readied and then thrust into the colon. But there was no pain. Burning and cutting the intestines has no effect.

It is difficult to describe internal pain. Perhaps the artist has an advantage. "This is where it hurts," Albrecht Dürer indicated in this self-portrait he sent to his doctor.

Only certain kinds of internal damage can be felt: e.g., stretching or twisting the walls of the gut or other hollow organs or the effect of acid leaking through onto the stomach wall as in the case of a stomach ulcer. Other chemical invasions via bacteria, or viruses, or venoms, or

97

poisons also cause distress. Often visceral pain occurs because nerves in the delicate tissue linings of blood vessels or vital organs are aroused while the tissue itself is impervious. The pain of pleurisy—which can make lung movements so unpleasant that hiccups or sneezes are inhibited—occurs partly because the infected pleural linings of the lungs are so rich in nerve endings. So are the membranes that surround the brain and spinal cord. This accounts for some of the pain of meningitis. Yet these central mines of nerve tissue are themselves insensitive to pain. Brain surgery can be performed under a local anesthetic (needed to make the initial incision painless).

Anything that compromises circulation internally can be painful for the same reasons as restrictions in a limb or little finger. The chest pain of *angina pectoris*, for example, comes from ischemia, in this case constriction of the coronary arteries supplying heart muscle. Again the potassium or other cell products released would trigger pain.

Migraine headache, on the other hand, results from an initial phase of just the opposite state—too great an expansion of the arterial vessels that ring the head. In seeking the cause for this dilatation the late Dr. Harold Wolff of New York discovered a proteinlike molecule in the plasma similar to the other kinins. He called it neurokinin because he thought it was produced by the nervous system itself. Drugs which constrict head arteries are often prescribed for migraine, but their effectiveness is mitigated because the condition itself is tricky. In later stages of migraine the arterial walls may constrict again and cause ischemic pain.

Tightenings and knottings of neck and head muscles are the basis of tension headaches that are apt to worsen because as your head feels more miserable, the more rigidly you are apt to hold it, and this results in more tension on neck muscles and more pain—a good example of a vicious circle in operation. Almost the best thing to do is "go soak your head." A soothing bath or gentle massage may do as much as anything to relax the muscles.

It is strange but true that the vital organs of the body are less well supplied with nerve endings than the skin. Possibly because the skin is the first line of defense, the nervous system puts much of its ammunition there.

Referred Pain

This factor may also account for the anomaly of referred pain. The real trouble spot may be internal but the pain is noticed superficially. Thus an incipient heart attack may be felt in the left armpit or down the left arm.

Appendicitis may cause heat and reddening of the skin on the opposite side of the abdominal area. Liver and gall bladder disturbances may be felt in the shoulder.

Some investigators think this happens because the weaker visceral signals are discharging into the same pool of nerve cells in the central nervous system that receive signals from skin. Others have further elaborated that if in turn there is a discharge of sympathetic nerve fibers in the neighborhood (for reasons of stress), blood vessels in the skin may be constricted. If this goes on for a time, the same kind of peripheral malnutrition can take place and pain signals coming from skin will be legitimate.

Pain When There Is No Pain

The most plaguing pains of all are those that defy common sense. The pain of an amputated member for example, the so-called phantom limb pain, has at various times been deemed magical, hysterical, or neurotic in origin. Today physicians know that this is a very real pain present in many amputation cases. Usually it fades, but about 5 percent of the time the condition persists and may be a problem for years. Often the person has a mental image of a grotesquely foreshortened ghost limb, in a tense or awkward position. In the case of an amputated hand the fist may be envisioned as being clenched or the fingers bent uncomfortably.

Damage to peripheral nerves also brings on a strange complex of pain symptoms. There may be an absence of pain or a weakened sense, hypalgesia, at first, followed by a most disagreeable burning sensation, causalgia. Parts of the skin in such areas may then become hyperalgesic— so sensitive that a gentle touch or a wisp of breeze cause agonizingly painful seizures. (You experience hyperalgesia in a minor way when someone touches your sunburned back.)

Sometimes pain in these affected areas (and also in phantom limbs) can be triggered by a touch, or heat, applied in a remote part of the body, a "trigger" zone. Again pain can occur with no apparent cause in the affected area or elsewhere.

Pain Signaling

Any theory which hopes to relate stimuli to nervous system behavior must take into account these pathological conditions as well as the catalog of ordinary pain causers. Clearly the sources of pain seem infinite. But nerve endings are finite. To find out which of them react, when, how, and why, is no simple matter. If the disputes about specific receptors or fiber endings vs. patterns of impulses for touch, temperature, and pressure are heated enough, the problem of pain endings is an even more burning one.

The question put simply is whether you hurt when somebody steps on your toes because the heavy pressure excites lots of nerve endings that are firing in a pattern the brain interprets as pain, or because distinct pain receivers have been excited, presumably because their higher thresholds have now been reached or passed. Does a needle prick hurt because the needle struck the receptive field of a pain ending, or because the non-specific ending underneath is stimulated now by a particular intensity applied to a minuscule spot? In this case it sends a signal which the brain reads as pain. In milder circumstances it would send a signal that would mean only a light touch.

Tests of sensitivity are not conclusive. Some investigators find pain spots where the pressure of a pinpoint hurts while the same pressure on the skin an inch away feels like a touch. Others do not find such spots and maintain that intensity is all that matters.

Temperature variations raise the same questions: as warmth passes into heat into burning sensations, is it because at the highest temperature pain endings are summoned, or is it the pattern—perhaps a barrage

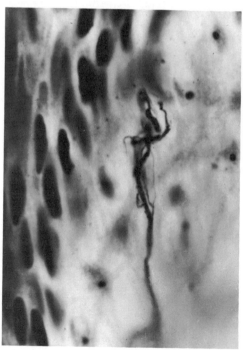

A free nerve ending in human finger skin. Its many branches stem from a single fiber. It might be a pain receptor; it might subserve a number of senses. × 1200.

of fast volleys from myriad all-purpose nerve endings in the neighborhood—that counts?

Slightly different arguments pertain to the pains of bright lights and loud sounds. In the case of the special senses there are reflex muscles that act under duress to protect you. In sudden brightness the eyes close down to pinpoints. This happens so fast that the muscles controlling the action go into spasms and nerve endings inside them fire alarms to the brain. Similarly eardrum and middle ear muscles may clamp down under the pressures of loud sounds. These painful contractions are to your eye and ear muscles what labor pains are to the uterus. But there may also be "pure" pain endings in the cornea or middle ear structures that react as well.

There is much to be said for both pattern and specificity theories. The strength of the specificity theory lies in its delineation of a division

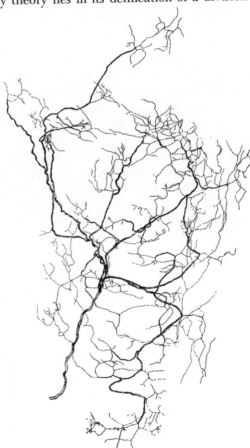

Drawing of a free sensory nerve termination with multiple fine branches in the epithelium of the urethra of a cat.

101

of labor at the periphery, with particular fibers for particular purposes. A number of clinical and experimental tests do suggest that the myelinated fibers of smallest diameter, the "A gamma" and "A delta" fibers, and some portion of the even finer unmyelinated "C" fibers are involved in pain sensations. They are most populous in at least one important pathway to the brain, the spinothalamic tracts. Cutting some or all the fibers in these tracts can eliminate pain in parts of the body, but not always, and even if successful, not always permanently.

A Pain Is Not a Pain Is a Pain . . .

The difficulty is that the spinothalamic tracts are only one among several pathways signaling pain. Furthermore what seems particularly true for pain is that specificity for the nerve ending or pathway does not guarantee the brain's specificity. It may read a "pain" signal as something else if it chooses, or else ignore it completely. How else can the war-wounded reaction be explained? This has a counterpart in animal experiments: Pavlov's dogs first yelped and howled when an electric shock was administered to them prior to being fed. Later they seemed to ignore the shock and salivated in anticipation of the morsel. In short, pain does not seem to be a simple system with a single pain center as an end station for incoming signals, where pain is always read as pain. It is instead an amalgam of many centers and pathways out of which comes some final judgment or interpretation of the stimulus.

The pattern theorists would assent to this. They plump for the brain's mastery at subtle summations, of weighings and balancings, of feedbacks and facilitations. They may err in assuming that such subtlety need extend back to the skin itself. While one theory may be too simplistic and shed little light on the complicated pathological conditions of pain, the other may exaggerate the complexity, gloomily pointing to the failures of pain surgery, the "tractomies" that sever nerve fibers, or the destructions of cell groups in the brain itself, while overlooking the number of successes.

The Gate Theory

An ingenious way to extract the best from both theories and build them into a synthesis has been suggested by Dr. Ronald Melzack of McGill University in Montreal and Dr. Patrick Wall of the Massachusetts Institute of Technology. The kernel of their theory is that fibers signaling pain as well as other body sensations come into the cord and sooner or later enter the horn-shaped gray matter at either side of the rear of the

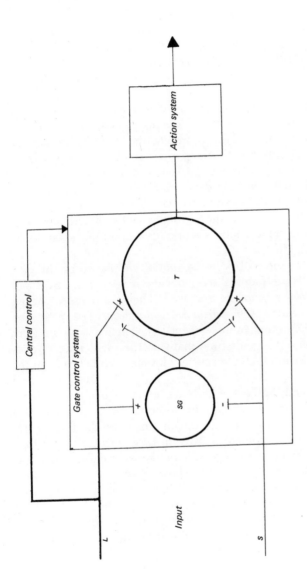

Schematic diagram of the gate theory. L = large-diameter fibers; S = small-diameter fibers. The fibers project to the substantia gelatinosa (SG) and first central transmission (T) cells. The inhibitory effect exerted by SG cells on the T cells is increased by activity in L fibers and decreased by activity in S fibers. The central control trigger is represented by a line running from the large-fiber systems to the central control mechanism. These mechanisms in turn project back to the gate system. The T cells project to the entry cells of the action system. + = excitation; − = inhibition.

cord. Here in the "dorsal horns" there is a pool of small nerve cells which act like a gate or a lock of a canal. Certain kinds of incoming signals tend to open the lock, so that it fills with signals which in turn amplify activity in a nearby pool of larger cells which operate as transmission ("T") cells. At a critical level the T cells trigger an action system which signals pain to the brain and sets off a chain of responses. Other fibers inhibit the gate cells, closing the lock and suppressing activity in the T cells so that the action system is only weakly triggered, or perhaps not at all.

Melzack and Wall hypothesize that the gate openers are the small A and C fiber signals associated with the branching, naked nerve terminals spread throughout the body. These represent the majority of sensory nerve endings. The closers are the larger fast-conducting fibers associated with touch, pressure, or other special receptors in the body, and fibers from the brain itself, reaching down via feedback circuits. For the descending system to work the brain must quickly learn what has happened in time to suppress the gate cells and forestall the T-cell action system. The net result of these three controls working at cross purposes determines the response to pain.

The beauty of the model lies in the subtle role played by the gate cells. These small cells are found throughout the length of the cord and have a counterpart in the brain stem as well. They are densely packed together in a mass called the *substantia gelatinosa*. The cells can communicate with each other from segment to segment via an adjacent pathway, Lissauer's tract. Signals from many of the smaller nerve endings in the body come into the gate cells at all times and hence keep the gate partially open.

What Melzack and Wall call T cells are larger cells of several types surrounding the *substantia gelatinosa*. In the usual textbook account of pain pathways, the fibers carrying pain signals come into the spinal cord, split, go up or down for a segment or two (in Lissauer's tract) and then enter the dorsal horns and contact cells of the *substantia gelatinosa*. These cells then relay to the T cells whose fibers give rise to long pathways to the brain. Melzack and Wall suggest that many kinds of fibers contact both gate cells and T cells, and the way the T cells behave is not so much a function of direct inputs to them, but of the complex interactions of inputs and feedbacks on the *substantia gelatinosa* cells.

Action Systems

The action system triggered by the T cells is complex. Again, the best-known pathways, the spinothalamic (ST) tracts, are assumed to derive from

104

them. These tracts cross to the opposite side of the cord and send long fibers to the thalamus. There new fibers arise going to higher brain centers.

But, in addition, the ST tracts send out fibers that form another system carrying pain signals. It is a broad tangle of cells with short fibers that carry a variety of signals up to the reticular formation of the brain stem. Pain relayed through this diffuse, ambling pathway is assumed to be associated with aftersensations: slow, burning feelings as opposed to sharp pricks.

By the time all these signals have found their way to the brain they encounter analogous systems bringing in pain signals from the face and head. There is a considerable amount of mingling and meshing, and many fibers will end up either in the reticular formation or in a region called the central gray matter. Others will continue to regions of the thalamus. From there (or other relay stations) new fibers spread to the cortex. They do not go just to the body-image somesthetic area, or regions close by, but to the frontal lobes and to clusters of cells and pathways that constitute the most primitive cortex, the lower ring of structures and pathways, the limbic lobe.

Connections here will contribute importantly to pathways originally outlined by James Papez in the thirties as ones deeply involved with the emotional aspects of behavior, including the psychic element of pain.

Many of these parts have figured in operations performed to eliminate pain. A small cellular mass in the thalamus can be destroyed in animals and produce what overtly appears to be indifference to pain. A cat so treated will not react to a sharp pin jab, and a monkey will play with burning matches with no sign of pain. Higher up, the operation of frontal lobotomy in which either parts of the frontal lobes are removed, or the fiber connections to the rest of the brain severed, has been successful in some cases of severe pain in man. Usually the person is still aware of the pain, but is no longer disturbed by it. The emotional *Sturm und Drang*, the excessive anxiety and demands on the body that such pain creates, disappear. Unfortunately frontal lobotomy may also alter the personality. As Dr. William H. Sweet of Harvard Medical School remarks, "the price paid for such relief includes inability to experience keen pleasure as well, i.e., there is a flattening of all affect and the development of a more or less apathetic state." There is no guarantee that the pain relief will be permanent either.

More recently Dr. Paul MacLean of the National Institute of Neurological Diseases and Blindness has been experimenting with certain portions of the limbic lobe. A shock to a forceps-shaped group of fibers called the fornix inhibits and delays reactions to painful stimuli applied to the face for as long as two minutes. Removal of certain cell groups toward the front and side of the limbic lobe results in bizarre behavior and complete indifference to pain.

In some cases of the very painful facial neuralgia, *tic douloureux,* fibers from the trigeminal nerve (the fifth cranial nerve) have been severed, again with some success, but often with a loss of temperature and touch sensation in the face.

Most authorities agree that these methods are only partial solutions to the complex problem of intractable pain. Melzack and Wall further suggest that the reason they may not be foolproof or permanent is that the gate system can find other routes or change the balance of signals to reintroduce pain. The good side of that coin, however, is that there should be still other means of changing the balance to cut down on pain.

For example, if the gate opens because of a lot of small fiber activity, it can be closed again by a resurgence of activity in large fibers. When you rub a sprain or lightly scratch, stroke, or massage a painful area of skin you excite these large fibers. This flood of activity works two ways: though it stimulates T cells directly, it closes the gate behind them, and the over-all effect affords temporary relief. Keeping it up for long will alter the signals, this time because the large fibers adapt. Again if the pain was very great, the extra stimulation to T cells may make matters worse before they improve. This could also happen if you scratch too hard or too deep.

Here's how Melzack and Wall describe this intricate interplay:

If the stimulus intensity is increased, more receptor-fiber units are recruited and the firing frequency of active units is increased. The resultant positive and negative effects of the large-fiber and small-fiber inputs tend to counteract each other, and therefore the output of the T cells rises slowly. If stimulation is prolonged, the large fibers begin to adapt, producing a relative increase in small-fiber activity. As a result, the gate is opened further, and the output of the T cells rises more steeply. If the large-fiber steady background activity is artificially raised at this time by vibration or scratching (a maneuver that overcomes the tendency of the large fibers to adapt), the output of the cells decreases.

In other words scratch, but not too often and not too hard.

The complex interactions involving the total number and kinds of fibers, their firing frequencies, and states of adaptation takes time to evaluate. This interval explains how the brain itself has time to feed back to the system. If there is a sufficient delay while the T cells take their census, then the census can be tampered with by signals from fibers descending from higher cortical centers. This activity would have been triggered initially by systems that simultaneously feed into the gate system and rush quickly to the brain. This is exactly the role played by the large-fiber system of the dorsal columns (relaying touch, pressure, and kinesthetic senses), and presumably by still another fast-acting pathway originating in the dorsal horns. Such systems can modulate gate activity at the same time their main lines are expressing signals to the brain. They act as "central control triggers" according to Wall and Melzack and offer an anatomical explanation of how prior events can color your reaction to pain, how the brain is on top of the situation while it is happening.

Suppose you cut your finger while washing a glass. As soon as the brain gets the precise information from the fast systems that convey the nature and location of the stimulus, you not only can say "ouch" but you can look down, turn your head, pick up your finger to examine it, turn the cold water faucet on to rinse the wound, compare this situation to the time you cut your thumb when slicing bread, remember if you have a supply of Band-Aids in the bathroom, figure out how long you are going to have to wear the Band-Aid, and, if you're a woman, whether you can wear a sleek pair of gloves you just bought.

The time delays and multiple inputs into the gate system can also explain some of the confusions and anomalies associated with pathological conditions:

(1) Hyperalgesias: In peripheral nerve damage hyperalgesia could result from loss of more of the thicker nerves than the thin ones. The resulting lack of equilibrium would allow the gate to be filled gradually from the slower conducting fibers, with no brake or check. Even small fibers conducting touch or pressure signals might contribute to the sum and hence be the neutral source for noxious feelings.

(2) Spontaneous pain: This condition again would be due to the unchecked flow of impulses from slow fibers (remember that many do fire spontaneously or continuously). At random times the gate would receive sufficient stimulus to activate the T cells.

(3) Referred pain, spread of pain, and trigger points at some distance from the site of damage: These phenomena could be explained in two ways. The gate cells themselves receive inputs from both sides of the cord and for several segments up or down. If intense enough these could activate T cells. Also the T cells' receptive fields may be out of commission in the damaged peripheral area, so that their normal dominance over inputs from remote parts of the body is not operating.

(4) Varying hypalgesias and hyperalgesias: Inhibition from the brain may be prevented in the case of brain injury or disease. Removing

this damper to the T system could result in severe pain. On the other hand brain injuries or tumors change with time and could also cause too much inhibition leading to states of lessened pain sense or even analgesia. (Onslaughts like the sudden, severe onset of heart attack pain can be understood as an overwhelming barrage to the system that occurs before any central nervous system inhibition can be tripped.)

Feeling No Pain

Melzack and Wall point to the potential that gate theory holds for the treatment of pain by methods that are substantially different from drugs and surgery. Strong analgesics depress central nervous system activity so drastically they either induce sleep or alter the personality dramatically.

This is true of morphine and other opiate derivatives, or the synthetics that mimic their effects, like Demerol. The mode of action of these drugs is still little understood. One theory is that they block synaptic transmission in the central nervous system. The chemical evidence suggests that the molecules must attach to sites on cells in very special ways. Only one configuration of the morphine molecule is an analgesic. Its mirror image isomer is ineffective. The same "handedness" is shown by all the morphinelike drugs on the market. Novocain, procaine, and other cocaine derivatives are effective as local anesthetics because they block the transmission of peripheral nerve impulses. Aspirin, too, may block peripheral transmission, but only in certain nerve endings mediating chemical causes of pain. Alcohol too acts as a central nervous system depressant. The kick it gives at first is a kind of double negative for it depresses inhibitory mechanisms. Enough of it will eventually knock you out.

Melzack and Wall propose a study of chemical agents that could selectively change the activity of cells of the *substantia gelatinosa*. Fortunately these cells are sufficiently different from others in the nervous system to offer the hope that a drug could work on them exclusively and avoid the wholesale effects the most potent drugs have.

"Magic"

Again there is the placebo effect to contend with. Placebos are harmless sugar or salt solutions which can be injected or given in pill form. They can ameliorate pain in some people some of the time, presumably because the wish to believe in their efficacy is strong. It would seem that each of us comes equipped with a personal and cultural attitude that

forms our individual armament against pain. Such personal idiosyncrasies are of considerable importance in the course of treatment of
illness and in the communication between doctors and patients.

One anatomy professor summed it up nicely by imagining an English doctor treating an Italian patient. On entering the room of the hospital the English doctor hears moans, groans, and sees a weeping family
in worshipful attendance. The answer to the doctor's inevitable "How are
you feeling?" is simply a higher order of moans, groans, and sympathetic
wails. The Englishman might well assume the man was *in extremis* and
consider what drastic treatment might be necessary. Were an Italian
doctor to visit a sick Englishman the situation would be equally misleading. The quiet calm figure in bed might answer, "Quite all right" to
the doctor's query, when in fact he was in severe pain. So each culture
employs a form of magic: the Mediterranean believes that screaming
helps. The stoic stiff-upper-lipped Anglo-Saxon believes just the opposite.

Perhaps these clichés are less true today with the greater amount
of travel and cultural exchange. What may be more true, however, is our
increasing awareness of pain and of pain relievers. Anyone who has
watched television can appreciate the economic importance of aspirin,
tranquilizers, sedatives, and multipurpose pain relievers. Americans
consume an estimated 16 billion pure aspirin tablets every year. These
and aspirin in combination with other drugs represented a $350 million
business in 1963.

There's no doubt that drugs do help, even if their subtle ways are
only partially understood. But it almost seems as if nature were playing
a cops-and-robbers game with man. No matter what new super analgesic
man invents to trap pain, there are always some pains that get away.

At work here are many of the psychological factors already discussed, factors which might have started affecting us in the womb, and
have continually developed to produce our present attitudes toward
pain, attitudes that are subject to change, to suggestion, to hypnosis, and
to the less dramatic changes of mood from day to day and month to
month. Perhaps it is in the sense of pain that human variability shows up
most clearly, both between man and man and within the life of every
man.

VI

Your Nose Is a Camera

Zoologists often remark on the amazing sensitivity of the proboscis–snout–trunk–antennae—whatever goes as a nose—in creatures other than man. The male silkworm moth can scent a mate seven miles away. The salmon smells his way to the stream of his birth hundreds of miles away. Moving up the scale, there are marvelous tales of the successes of the truffle-sniffing pig, the man-tracking bloodhound, or the honey-seeking bear. What is rarely mentioned is that man, too, has a perfectly respectable sense of smell. Each nostril contains thousands of tiny receptors spread out to form a penny-stamp-sized screen. Now it appears that these screens pick up different scents in different places. The result, blended in the brain, is an intricate odor snapshot of the world.

So indelible is this picture that were you to smell an odor tomorrow that you hadn't smelled for twenty years, the chances are that it would not only be instantly recognized, but that it would trigger a whole flood of memories and emotional associations.

This link of odor to emotion and memory has been a favorite source of inspiration for writers from Biblical times to such twentieth-century authors as Colette or Marcel Proust, whose voluminous *Re-membrance of Things Past* seems at times to be an exquisite compilation of smell reveries: °

I would turn to and fro between the prayer-desk and the stamped velvet armchairs, each one always draped in its crocheted antimacassar, while the fire, baking like a pie the appetizing smells with which the air of the room was thickly clotted, which the dewy and sunny freshness of the morning had already "raised" and started to "set," puffed them and glazed them into an invisible though not impalpable country cake, an immense puff-pastry, in which, barely waiting to savor the crustier, more delicate, more respectable, but also drier smells of the cupboard, the chest-of-drawers, and the patterned wallpaper I always returned with an unconfessed gluttony to bury myself in the nondescript, resinous, dull, indigestible, and fruity smell of the flowered quilt.

When we ourselves are alone or wandering something very like the writer's reveries may stir in us. Walk past a movie house in a small town and suddenly that whiff of stale air takes you back to the time you used to line up on Saturday mornings to catch the latest chapter in a serial. Enter a hospital corridor and feel yourself getting moist-palmed and nervous at the smell of ether.

There are school smells and army smells, laboratory smells and church smells, all of which will evoke deep memories. There are local smells: the coffee-roasting smell most New Yorkers will recognize as coming from downtown on days when the wind is right; the smell of a cheap saloon around the corner; of a large city's Chinatown.

And there are travel smells: the clover smell as you ride the highways through Indiana or Iowa; the sage smell of the far west. There is the briny smell of seaports everywhere, be they San Francisco or Marseilles. And the spice market smells of Marrakesh or Madras, Guadalajara or Istanbul, assailing your nostrils with cinnamon or coriander, nutmeg, rosemary or thyme—smells that serve as a reminder of how much the world owes to the original spice seekers.

Travel in particular seems to titillate the sense of smell. The old ladies who tend their charcoal braziers along church steps in Guatemala City produce a more memorable souvenir—of acrid smoke and tortillas boiling in oil—than the churches themselves. So, in their way, do the pizza vendors of Naples or the candy and pastry sellers of the Middle East.

° Marcel Proust. *Swann's Way.* New York: Random House, 1956, pp. 69–70.

111

The strength of these aromatic memories ultimately stems from their visceral connections in the nervous system. We tend to ignore these aspects today because our travels are undertaken for pleasure and at our leisure. Originally, however, travel for all species capable of locomotion—for early man, as well as for nomadic cultures still extant—was an urgent necessity motivated for life-preserving purposes. One traveled in search of food. Smell was the first "distance" sense developed to aid that search. The primeval fish with a "nose" no longer had to swim aimlessly or wait passively for a food particle to brush against him. He could travel to his dinner, guided by chemical clues—certain molecules detached from their source and dissolved in sea water. These were not food particles that came into contact with the body and excited a generalized chemical sense. They were simply specks, traces of substances that excited new mechanisms altogether. This marked the divorce of smell from taste. From now on taste would become associated with what was put in the mouth. Smell was the preliminary investigator. We sniff before taking the plunge.

But a fish doesn't stop at sniffing for food. He sniffs to find out if there may be a shark around, or possibly a mate.

Thus the sense of smell came to serve species-preserving as well as life-preserving functions. So successful was it in coping with these vital needs that in time the small lump of olfactory tissue atop the fish's nerve cord grew into a brain. The cerebral hemispheres were originally buds from the olfactory stalks. En route, other senses developed, and in man, they came to preempt brain space. Man's frontal lobes, his highly developed sensory-motor areas, his capacity for reason, imagination, and memory, in combination with the greatly enlarged auditory and visual centers, far exceed olfaction in importance. Man has become a microsmatic (small smelling) animal.

In anatomical terms the sense of smell has literally been pushed aside in the brain. The olfactory areas are creased and folded, turned in towards the midline or tucked under the temporal lobes. Many of the original substructures no longer subserve the sense directly, but have become part of the emotional-visceral brain, the limbic lobe. (Alternately it is known as the rhinencephalon or smell brain, a name that preserves the original olfactory link.)

Secondary olfactory impulses reach limbic structures along with inputs from other senses or brain parts. These inputs trigger reactions that relate to survival. They elicit emotions such as fear or anger, pain or pleasure, along with their physiological analogues controlled by the autonomic nervous system. Some inputs will lead to reactions of the parasympathetic half of the autonomic nervous system concerned with

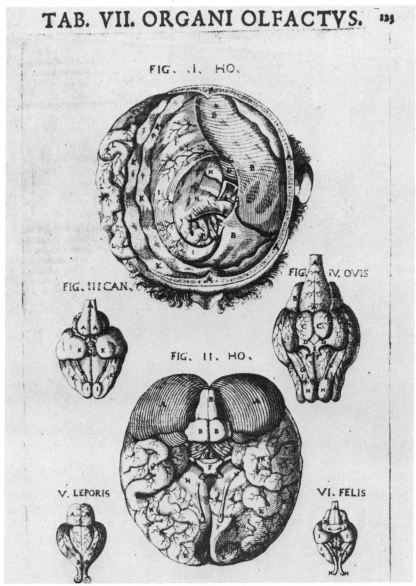

TAB. VII. ORGANI OLFACTVS. 123

FIG. .I. HO.

FIG. III CAN.

FIG. IV. OVIS

FIG. II. HO.

V. LEPORIS

VI. FELIS

A sixteenth-century anatomist named Casserio pioneered in studies of comparative neurology and wrote extensively about the senses. Fig. I is his drawing of the human brain, viewed from above. The remaining figures compare the olfactory bulbs and related centers of man (II), dog (III), sheep (IV), rabbit (V), and cat (VI). These views are of the base of the brain, with ventral parts at the bottom, dorsal parts at the top of each drawing.

113

vegetative processes, such as the release of saliva or gastric juices. This is why your mouth waters when you smell baking bread. Other inputs will release sympathetic responses, raising blood pressure, stimulating sweating, or triggering sexual behavior.

The anatomical situation is different in macrosmatic animals. Dogs, pigs, rats, rabbits, deer, and elephants—in general the quadruped mammals, whose heads (or whose trunk, in the case of the elephant) hang close to the ground where the moisture-loving and heavier smell molecules tend to congregate—all have large, well-developed olfactory lobes. The same is true for many snakes, fish, and insects.

The dog's sense of smell is renowned, of course. Any dog can identify his master, even if he is one of identical twins, by smelling any object he has touched or stepped on. Special breeds like bloodhounds can follow a track two days old, even after a heavy wind and rainstorm. Pigs can burrow six inches under the soil of an oak tree to ferret out a truffle. Bears, who are fossil relatives of dogs, are not so easy to observe. But one surprised fisherman recently found himself adopted by a black bear. "Bosco's phenomenal sense of smell amazed me. Trudging along behind me, he would suddenly sniff the air, and make a beeline for a big, succulent mushroom 200 yards away, to a flat rock across the river under which chipmunks had warehoused their winter seed supply, to a berry patch two ridges over." †

Among insects it is the wasps, bees, moths, and ants that rate high. One species of *elphiates* wasp lays eggs on the larva of the wood-wasp buried well under the bark of pine or fir trees. Apparently this degree of smell-insulation is no deterrent to the wasp's antennae.

The silkworm moth probably takes the prize for odor detection. The males who fly upwind seven miles following the come-hither scent of the female (who, incidentally, is odor-blind to it) are responding to infinitesimal amounts. Chemists at the United States Agricultural Service in Beltsville, Maryland, found that a similar substance which they were able to synthesize in the European gypsy moth was detectable in amounts as small as 0.000,000,000,000,004 ounce.

The change that distinguishes man from these highly olfactory-oriented species occurred in the course of evolution. Man's ancestors moved from sea to land, and then to trees. It was here that vision and hearing took over as the prime distance senses. Monkeys are not as good sniffers as rats or rabbits. Birds on the whole are worse. Most vultures are not attracted to carrion by smell, but make use of their astonishingly

† Robert Franklin Leslie. "The Bear Who Came to Supper," *Reader's Digest*, December, 1964.

good eyesight. (Even here there are exceptions, however. Tests have shown that the olfactory nerve of the turkey vulture responds very effectively to odors; also shore birds apparently have highly developed olfactory apparatus.)

Of course man's ancestors didn't stay in the trees. They came down to earth where they could once again benefit from a rich store of odors. But by this time there was no backtracking in the brain. Vision and hearing had risen to their positions of dominance. These senses, combined with man's upright posture, which cut off the quantity of stimuli that could arouse the smell areas, permanently dwarfed the importance of smell.

So man exists today, between the birds and four-footed beasts, far superior to the whales and porpoises that have no sense of smell at all, but still inferior to many others.

For man the sense is non-intellectual. We have great difficulty in describing smells—except as similes with other smells. But perhaps that very degree of weakness in the intellectual quality of smell explains why its emotional impact is so profound. Smell can conjure up the past or quicken the present; it can nauseate or excite, repel or entice us.

Not everything in life smells. Whatever smells has to broadcast. The source must be volatile—evaporating molecules into the atmosphere. This automatically eliminates iron, steel, and many other common materials (provided they are clean), because at room temperature they are not volatile. On the other hand the requirement is not very strong. Musk and vanilla, though not especially volatile, are two of the most powerful odors known to man—musk is detectable in quantities as little as 0.000,-000,000,000,032 ounce, and vanilla when it is present at a level of two millionths of a milligram per cubic millimeter of air. Heating of course increases the rate of evaporation. This is one reason why cabbage cooked is smellier than cabbage cold.

Once broadcast, the smell molecules must reach the receiver. In the human nose this is the square inch patch of skin, yellowish in color, that lies at the upper part of each nostril—the olfactory epithelium. Reception isn't automatic because the same bulging of the brain that pushed the smell centers back under also made the airways of the nose take a hairpin turn. Human noses stick out like no other mammals'—a fact that makes them objects of wit, ridicule, or charm. The airways they enclose make a sharp downturn toward the lungs, a fact which makes breathing difficult and smelling more so. Normally when you breathe, the air barely touches the olfactory surface. It rushes on below it. At most, according to the Dutch investigators Hessel de Vries and Minze Stuiver who made a statistical analysis of the dynamics involved, only 2

115

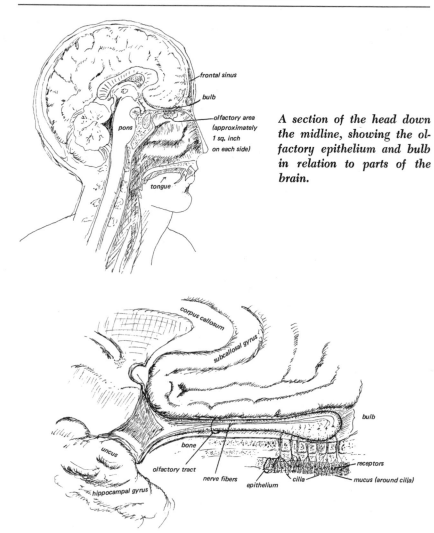

A section of the head down the midline, showing the olfactory epithelium and bulb in relation to parts of the brain.

A semischematic drawing showing the arrangement of cilia, epithelium, and bulb in greater detail. Fibers from the receptor cells pierce the cribriform plate of the ethmoid bone of the skull on their way to the olfactory bulb.

percent of the air reaches the smell area. Sniffing improves matters. When you consciously sniff you draw air up over the olfactory surface to allow maximum exposure.

Dogs, rabbits, and other good smellers have more efficient arrangements. The air makes a straight run back to the lungs. Blood-

116

hounds even have heavy pouches—those folds of skin which give them their dour look—which trap the air for a time and thus reinforce the stimulation to the olfactory nerve.

Still some molecules obviously get through to the human receiver, if only to meet several more hurdles. One is that the molecules must to some extent be soluble in the saltwatery mucus that lines the nose (shades of the old sea within us). Another is that they probably also need to be dissolvable in the fat and watery solution that makes up the lining of the olfactory cells. In a word, the receiver is sticky and the molecules must be in a form to penetrate the muck and come in contact with the receiving cells.

Even this is no guarantee that you will smell something. For the three requirements—volatility, water, and fat solubility—are, as the logician says, "necessary but not sufficient conditions." They explain in part why some things don't smell, but they don't begin to account for all the things that do, or for the peculiar quirks of certain odors.

Some smells change as you smell them. Nitrobenzene at the first whiff smells like bitter almonds but ends up smelling like tar.

Some smells change when diluted. A heavy essence of skunk odor (essentially ethyl mercaptan) can make a dog vomit. But a faint trace flavors the air with a slightly gamey, not unpleasant aroma, at least for humans. Extracts from the anal or perineal glands of the musk deer or civet cat evoke shudders. Yet in precious drops they contribute to the pleasure and lasting power of expensive perfumes.

Other smells stay the same. Gasoline is gasoline is gasoline whether by the drop or the tankful, and so powerful is its odor that it can blunt your nose to other scents for some time after—a fact that more than one courtroom lawyer has used to confute a witness' testimony.

Ether, camphor, and oil of cloves are all potent smell-dullers. Some smells cancel each other when mixed: Peruvian balsam neutralizes iodoform. Other smells can be masked: a fact the multimillion dollar deodorant industry makes use of, as did the burglar who warded off watchdogs by playing with his pet bitch in heat before going out on a job. (Apparently his doggy smell so entranced female as well as male watchdogs that they overlooked his strange human scent.)

Like chemicals often smell unalike while unlike chemicals may smell the same. Hydrogen sulphide smells like rotten eggs. Nail polish smells like banana oil. Certain poison gases smell like fields of clover. Cyanide, like nitrobenzene, as all mystery fans know, smells like bitter almonds.

Add to this confusion the potential for smell the nose possesses— that new, quite smellable smells are being produced in laboratories, perfumeries, or in the discharge stacks of factories all over the world—and you begin to understand why smell theories have a hard time satisfying the logician's precise conditions.

Earlier theorists proposed lists of basic smells whose mixes would produce all other smells—in the same way that primary colors can make all colors. The eighteenth-century Swedish naturalist Carolus Linnaeus thought some such scheme might help in classifying plants. A century and a half later, German psychologist H. Henning proposed six kinds of scents: flowery, fruity, resinous, burnt, putrid, and spicy. He was followed in 1925 by a physiologist, H. Zwaardemaker, who changed some of these categories and added three more, including "nauseous"—decaying meat and feces—no doubt forgetting that for some people the higher the goose hangs the better they like it and that babies show no repugnance, but often fascination with fecal matter.

More recent theories probe the chemistry of smell molecules, trying to classify smells according to the way their associated molecules absorb infrared radiation, or in terms of their electric charge, their shape, their ability to act as catalysts, and so on. Even the yellow pigment that colors the olfactory area has been implicated.

Many of these ideas are attractive. Many give partial explanations. Industrial chemists have contributed a few working details: add a branch to a straight chain of carbon atoms in a perfume molecule and you increase the potency. Chains of four to eight or more carbon atoms in certain alcohols are associated with strong odors. (When the female silkworm's essence was analyzed by the Nobel prize winner Adolph Butenandt of the Max Planck Institute for Biochemistry in Munich it was found to be an alcohol with 16 carbon atoms per molecule.) Still no one could come up with a general theory. Smells just don't lend themselves to the neat analytic measurements that sound and light do. There are no smellicycles or smellivolts.

The situation stayed this way until John E. Amoore of the Western Regional Research Laboratory of the United States Department of Agriculture at Albany, California, and James W. Johnston, Jr., and Martin Rubin, at Georgetown University in Washington, D.C., proposed a theory which has passed an impressive number of tests. Strangely enough this new theory, the stereochemical theory of odor, is a modern version of one put forth 2,000 years ago by the Greek poet, Lucretius, and suggested again in 1949 by a Scot, R. W. Moncrieff.

Recently several modifications of the theory have been proposed as new data have appeared, but in essence the idea is simply that the nose acts like a prospector's pan, sieving the air for molecules. The pan's holes come in a few basic shapes and sizes. If a molecule of the right shape falls into the right hole, the connection is made and a message is sent from that part of the pan. If a great many different shapes find their respective holes a great many messages get sent and the brain decodes them so that sometimes the smells blend—like red and white mixed into pink—and sometimes they remain distinct—like a candy cane striped with red and white.

The "pan" is the olfactory epithelium. (Think of the one-inch-square screen magnified many times.) The "holes" are the strategic sites on nerve endings in the area. These holes come in several varieties—the "primaries" of smell—camphorlike, musky, floral, pepperminty, etherlike, pungent, and putrid.

Amoore arrived at these conclusions by systematically sorting the smells of 600 odorous organic compounds (compounds containing carbon) according to the number of times a particular smell was mentioned. If there were primaries, he reasoned, they ought to show up time and time again. In this way he singled out camphor (more than 100 mentions), and so on.

But it remained to investigate what all these camphor brothers and sisters looked like. This was done by means of X-ray diffraction, infrared spectroscopy, electron beam probes—all sophisticated techniques that essentially get molecules to take their own structural snapshot according to the way they reflect or absorb high-energy rays. Thus it happened

Camphor-like
spherical

Musky
disk-shaped

Floral
disk plus flexible tail

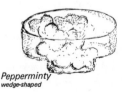

Pepperminty
wedge-shaped

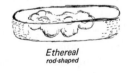

Ethereal
rod-shaped

Five of Amoore's primary smell categories depend on the shape and size of the molecule—stereochemical properties. Two other primaries, pungent and putrid odors, depend on positive and negative electric charge properties, respectively.

119

that many smell-alike chemicals composed of many kinds of atoms began to show the same over-all shape. Camphor-smelling compounds were roughly globular, and, equally important, of the same diameter, about two and eight-tenths millionths of an inch.

"Musk" was a larger disk shape; floral odors were kite shaped, a kind of disk with a tail; peppermint was wedge shaped, with a group of atoms near the point of the wedge that could form a particular kind of chemical bond at the receptor site. Ether molecules were small rod shapes.

"Pungent" and "putrid" were of another class. Here the smell didn't depend on the shape of the molecule but on its electrical state. Pungent molecules lacked electrons (negatively charged particles) at their outermost boundaries. Like magnets seeking a pin they would be strongly attracted to the electrons of neighboring atoms. Putrid molecules were just the opposite. Electron-rich, they would seek out the cores of nearby atoms that were positively charged.

Armed with this tentative smell "palette," Amoore and his colleagues went about "painting." They enlisted the aid of expert smellers (including bees and frogs), lab technicians who could help synthesize test compounds, and an instrument called an olfactometer which measures the amount of a substance discharged into a controlled column of air which the volunteers would breathe.

First they tried to predict odors. Mix up a compound that is kite shaped. Will it smell flowery? Actually what they did was something that was more sophisticated. They realized that their basic shapes were not independent—a rod-shaped molecule might fit into a rod-shaped hole one way but it might also fit in a wedge shape or a kite shape if the molecule were turned on one side or another. In fact such a complex molecule might account for a complex odor—a "fruity" blend of the three primaries.

So the experimenters decided to monkey with the structure. They would try to change a single atom at one part of the molecule and substitute a couple of atoms whose shapes would now stick out a bit more to prevent the molecule's fitting the kite- or wedge-shaped slots, but still, via shorter branches, be able to slip into the rod shape. According to the theory such a compound would smell ethery.

Rubin synthesized both compounds and the results checked out perfectly: the panel said the first one smelled fruity, the second like ether.

Successive tests showed that the theory could be used to synthesize some of nature's complex smells. Even the Cedars of Lebanon scent, of Song of Solomon fame, yielded to a structural analysis that sug-

120

Ambiguous or complex odors can occur, according to Amoore's theory, when a single chemical molecule can fit more than one primary site. The molecular shape above represents acetyltetrabromide, which is described as smelling like camphor and ether. Left-hand position of molecule would fit a spherical, i.e., camphoraceous, site; right-hand configuration of molecule (turned on its side) would fit a rodlike ethereal site.

gested four of Amoore's primaries: camphor, mint, floral, and musk. After eighty-six tries he was able to produce a blend that satisfied the experts.

To see if unlike chemicals whose size and shape are similar would smell alike, the experimenters tested five disk-shaped compounds on their panel of experts, carefully scrambling them among a host of others. Again the group singled out the five from the rest as smelling musky, and then had great difficulty distinguishing any differences in smell among the five.

Amoore's theory is intuitively appealing, and when it was first announced it gained widespread support. Chemists and neurophysiologists were quick to point out, however (along with Amoore himself), that as long as experiments conducted to test the theory were psychophysical in nature—depending on the responses of people or animals—they couldn't confirm the truth of the theory at the molecular level. It wasn't possible to say for certain that the olfactory receptors did contain molecular sites of specified shapes and that these trapped appropriate molecules. Only chemical studies of the membrane could confirm the hypothesis and these are not yet possible. The neurophysiologist's technique of recording the activity of single cells or fibers might have offered some support if it could be shown that single receptors responded to one and only one type of odor.

Unfortunately this didn't happen. Specifically, Robert T. Gesteland (now at Northwestern University) with J. Y. Lettvin and W. H. Pitts at the Massachusetts Institute of Technology studied the cell-by-cell reactions to odors introduced into the frog's olfactory epithelium. The electrical responses they picked up were highly complex and elaborate. Activity in a single fiber of the olfactory nerve may be depressed by some odors, excited by others, show intermediate levels of activity to still others or to mixtures of odors, or be completely unaffected by the

121

stimulus. These experiments suggest that there are many kinds of molecular traps on each cell but how many, what kind, and whether they are specifically stereochemical in nature cannot be said. Furthermore, comparing the activity from nerve fiber to nerve fiber, the three investigators were forced to conclude that the more odors tested the less likely was it that any two fibers would behave the same way. In other words it might be possible to find fibers A and B which were both excited to the same degree by camphor and depressed by mint. But if you tried a third scent, say musk, fiber A would react differently from fiber B.

So rich is the field of odors and so individual the behavior of single fibers that Lettvin and Gesteland now suggest that the number of "primary" odors may have to be increased considerably. (To some extent Amoore himself concedes that some of his primaries may have to be split into subcategories, and others added.) Moreover, Gesteland and Lettvin speculate that each olfactory receptor takes an over-all view of the odor world, or as they put it, odor space. Instead of the olfactory epithelium reacting as a simple camera film recording parts of the scene in different places, it is as if each "grain" of the film records its characteristic picture of the total odor space, and all these images are integrated in the brain.

From Nose to Brain

The technique which Gesteland developed for taking the electrical pulse of a single olfactory cell was an impressive achievement for these cells are not only small, but unlike the cells of many other sense systems of the body, the unit is both the receiver (transducing the chemical energy) and also the transmitter—the first nerve cell of a chain that will relay electrical impulses to the brain. It's as though the cell had two arms, one reaching out to the periphery, the other reaching back to the brain. The peripheral arm is actually a rodlike structure swollen at the tip and fringed with fine hairlike filaments, or cilia.

It is tempting to think that these cilia act like fingers feeling for stimuli. As they stick into the mucous lining of the nose they are free to move as air is drawn in, but they may also be able to move independently. In either case they would present a vastly increased surface area of "holes" for Amoore's primary smell molecules to cling to. Lloyd M. Beidler of the Physiology Division of Florida State University has calculated this for the rabbit, whose 100 million olfactory rods contain cilia which vary both in number and in thickness. (This factor again suggests selectivity.) Assuming an average cilium diameter of six millionths of an inch, a length of four thousandths of an inch, and 13

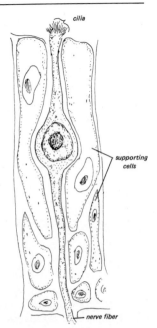

An olfactory receptor cell.

cilia per rod (man has more cilia per rod, but the cilia are shorter—four to eight hundred-thousandths of an inch), this works out to a surface area about the size of a sheet of typewriter paper. If this assumption is correct, the cilia and rods would seem like microminiature versions of an insect's feathery antennae. Man and other higher forms of life might just have put their antennae inside.

Wherever the receptor sites are, they are remarkably powerful transducers. De Vries and Stuiver have calculated that at most 8, and probably only 1 molecule of the right sort needs to find its home site on a cell to set that cell firing. And only 40 cells need to cooperate to trigger a conscious sensation. That's on the order of 320 molecules—provided they hit the right places. The 0.000,000,000,000,032 ounce of musk we can detect contains about 1.6 million molecules.‡

This degree of elegant sensitivity and structure continues into the brain itself. The other "arms" of the first nerve cells are the fibers Gesteland tested which combine to form the two olfactory nerves. These move almost straight up to a pair of thin tubes of tissue about an inch

‡ As sensitive "noses" this puts us roughly in the same league with moths. Scientists at the United States Agricultural Service at Beltsville, Maryland, found that male gypsy moths were sensitive to the female odor substance when present in amounts on the order of 200,000 molecules—one-eighth as many as our threshold for musk.

Olfactory fibers

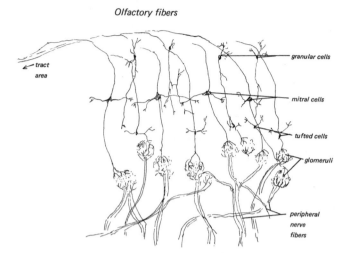

The olfactory bulb is a layered structure. Incoming receptor cell fibers, which form the olfactory nerve, ramify widely, coming into contact with processes from the large "mitral" (miter-shaped) or small tufted cells in fiber clusters called glomeruli. Axons from mitral or tufted cells continue upward toward the brain as fibers of the olfactory tract. Small granular cells at the highest level may modify activity in cells lower down. In addition to the fibers from one nostril streaming to or from the brain, large numbers of fibers in the tracts cross from one nostril to the other.

long, the olfactory bulbs, that lie at the base of each cerebral hemisphere. Here the incoming pulses converge on "mitral" cells—large nerve cells that look like a bishop's miter. From this depot the impulses continue to the smell centers of the cerebrum itself, taking two main routes, one toward the midline, one toward the side of each hemisphere in a curving branch.

This whole pathway is only about three or four inches long, but it is extremely complex. The smell fibers are among the most gossamerlike in the body. The fibers of the first cells in the pathway are not even wrapped in the fatty sheath typical of many nerves of the body. This makes them slow conductors—the impulses move at about 1 yard per second. On the other hand what they lose in speed of conduction they make up for in information-carrying capacity. Without their overcoats, a great many more fibers can be packed in the same space, each conveying a special bit of information to the brain.

And of course the more information gathered from the outside, the more sophisticated the brain's interpretations and instructions for action can become. To fill in the outline sketched earlier, some of the tiny smell

124

fibers from one nostril branch and loop back to connect with the other nostril. Some ultimately will reach the hypothalamus with its appetite and pleasure centers, as well as its areas governing various hormone secretions throughout the body. Some stay within the confines of the limbic lobe passing via the forceps-shaped bundle of fibers, the fornix, through the hippocampus (a sea-horse-shaped area), or into the amygdala (almond shaped). These sites when stimulated elicit fear or rage reactions or their opposites. Smell fibers also contribute to circuits which loop up to the highest centers of the cerebral cortex and back down to lower areas of the brain stem. Because of its evolutionary history the olfactory system differs from all other sense systems of the body. It starts high, at the cerebral level, and descends to the thalamus, the hypothalamus, the midbrain and medulla regions, and so on.

That the connections are widespread shows up sometimes as a result of an operation or as a symptom. People whose pituitary glands have been removed sometimes complain that they no longer can smell anything. People with certain kinds of brain tumors or epilepsy may have nasal hallucinations called uncinate fits, imagining themselves smelling of, or being enveloped in odors, often foul or medicinal. One butcher complained that he could smell the stench of the slaughterhouse. A woman reported that everything smelled of iodine.

This kind of phenomenon probably stems from local irritation or

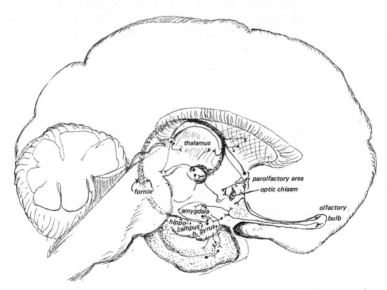

A section of the brain down the midline, showing some of the synaptic connections made by olfactory fibers.

destruction of tissue associated with the recognition of smells.§ But the effects can be complex. Virtually no area of the brain is isolated. A loss of tissue in one part may be compensated for and go unnoticed. But it may also be an integral part of a network, a circuit that starts with the original stimulus and ends with conscious action like picking up your fork and eating strawberry shortcake, or hurrying from a concert hall when the air-conditioning system fails and the atmosphere becomes fetid.

Sometimes of course the action is unconscious, in the form of reflex pathways present at birth. Babies seem to like mother's milk, for example. In the first few hours or days after birth they are as much guided by smell as touch in finding the breast.

In lower animals, especially those with minimal development of the other senses, one would expect to find that such built-in smell pathways are dominant. It's hard to imagine, for example, that the minnow "learns" to avoid the carp, its arch enemy. For not only do animal behavior studies show that the minnow freezes in place like a toreador dropped by a bull (in both cases the enemy responds to a moving target), but if the minnow is attacked it releases a substance into the water which acts as an early warning system to alert the rest of the school.

Minnows are an interesting example of a species that uses smell as a defense detection system against a sight-guided enemy. Cats and mice are another. Mice smell cats, and this explains the scrupulous whisker-rubbing and body-washing activity of cats. It is an attempt at deodorizing. While cats do have a sense of smell, they primarily depend on their eyes to spot mice.

Sight-guided man probably deserves special mention in the list of predators. He is the greatest predator of all, and almost any animal that can smell at all reacts violently to the human scent. Scores of small woodland animals take to their burrows at the first whiff of *Homo sapiens*. Even the rattlesnake may be deterred by the cowboy's old trick of encircling his sleeping bag with his lariat, impregnated as it would be with the smell of the owner. Elephants will panic, gorillas beat their chests if they are confronted by human beings (non-aggressive and avoidance acts). The exceptions are the few domesticated animals trained to abide us, and the few who can and do prey upon us: insects and other parasites, sharks, grizzly bears, some of the bigger cats, or rhinoceroses—who will charge if the faintest trace of man aggravates their nostrils. Lorus and Margery Milne in their book *The Senses of*

§ But occasionally nasal hallucinations accompany mental disorders where there is no apparent tissue damage.

Animals and Men tell a chilling tale of how, on one African journey, their guides never took their eyes off a group of rhinos grazing 200 yards away, stopping every few moments to test the breeze lest it change and the party get downwind of the rhinos.

Scents and Counterscents

But more often than not the cat-and-mouse game in nature is played between species that both use smell. Here nature plays no favorites. The shark can smell the octopus, and the octopus can smell the shark. Survival depends on which is more effective in improving detection abilities or in developing countermeasures. It's now known that the octopus' inky camouflage contains a shark repellent. Obviously the skunk is not alone in malodorous warfare. The millipede goes these animals one better. When threatened, or when hunting, it can trigger the opening of a duct to mix two ingredients, harmless when separate, but when combined form cyanide gas—about as effective a means of chemical warfare as any army labs may have developed.

One interesting fact these examples reveal is the universality of the world of natural smells. One species can smell another. Some species, like bees, can be trained to accept or reject a variety of scents human noses know. Gesteland's frogs reacted to eight different scents—five of which matched Amoore's primary odors in man.

Within each species there are of course variations in smell talents. An animal born with a bigger nose may have a gross physical advantage. A great deal depends on use, training, association, and so on. There is variation within the individual as well. Under stress the sympathetic nervous system may directly affect the olfactory cells, making them more sensitive, or it may indirectly work to alter the blood flow in the olfactory area in such a way as to expand the surface—very much as our pupils dilate when we're angry or afraid. The nostrils may flare, also, admitting more air, which is consciously sniffed.

Daily cycles of smell responsiveness have also been observed. You may be able to smell things just as keenly when you get up as you do in the late morning and late afternoon. But at those times you may be more susceptible; coffee breaks may have a legitimate foundation.

Sensitivity also depends on certain characteristics of the stimulus: how fast is it moving across the smell area; how long does it last. A quick whiff of a substance may trigger a greater response than a slow one. A long-lasting continuously smelled odor may stimulate the cells to fire for a while at a steady rate but then dwindle down to nothing. Adaptation has taken place. A fine thing if you happen to be a garbage

127

collector, or work in a fish factory, but one that requires caution if you're a coal miner. (The canaries caged in mines are kept there to signal the presence of marsh gas. The miners' noses may react at first but not enough to arouse a conscious sensation. After a while the system will have adapted to it, but the canaries, while unable to smell the gas, will be the first to succumb.)

Living in an urban society today, it is difficult to measure just how much use we make of our noses. We are no longer hunters stalking game, wary of an approaching jaguar. On the contrary we are more likely to be prey to the smogs and hazes of an outrageous industrial production, or conditioned by advertising which more and more insists that everything in nature be deodorized—whether it's man, his cat, his dog, his bathroom, or his kitchen—and then reodorized by synthetics— pine scents for bathrooms; leather odors for plastic upholstery; charcoal essence for steaks. It is as if all natural smells were inherently evil. We live in a society in which one can say that a woman is a lady of taste but never of smell, as Roy Bedichek comments in *The Sense of Smell.*

On the other hand the perfume industry carries on the tradition of love potions and philtres from ages past. Whether their promises have any physiological base is debatable. The area is laden with psychological overtones and associations.

On the side of the believers is the fact that perfumes often contain substances which play a vital role in the sexual behavior of other mammals, initiating mating, for example. Even more striking than these immediate behavioral reactions are the possibilities of long-range effects. Drs. A. S. Parkes and H. M. Bruce of the Division of Experimental Biology of the National Institute of Medical Research in London have shown in an extraordinary series of experiments that the fertility of female mice may be seriously disturbed, if, after mating, they are kept in the same cage, not with the male they mated with, but with another male of the same or a different strain. The animals do not even have to come in contact with each other—the "strange" male may be caged in the female's box. But what would normally be a highly probable pregnancy does not take place. Something in the odor of the strange male inhibits the production of the hormones necessary to aid the implantation of the fertilized egg in the mouse's uterus. One theoretical interpretation of this is that smell operates as a natural means of birth control, inhibiting a population increase if animals are thrown together and there is likely to be a food shortage.

To extrapolate from an example of how smells can affect the sexual life of mice would, of course, be misleading if the theory based on such data were applied directly to man. Yet it points to the need for much deeper investigation. The sense of smell is so stressed in folklore that science has reacted against its study—ignoring or neglecting its importance.

Instead of having to tolerate the tales of Don Juans who boast that they can smell when a woman is "receptive," it would be interesting to find out if the various cyclical changes in women do have minute but detectable olfactory effects. It appears that there may be sexual differences in human as well as animal smell abilities. Women are more sensitive than men to a mixture of cholesterol and a derivative of the male sex hormone testosterone. And the female hormone estrogen apparently has to be present in the blood in order for a person to smell a particular chemical related to the civet cat extract used in certain perfumes. So children and men and women past reproductive age—can't smell it. Some workers have suggested, however, that these statistics may reflect the fact that women are much more vocal about smells than men.

What these findings suggest is that there's much more to our noses than anyone ever thought. But if we don't watch out, we may lose these gifts through propaganda or neglect. As the Milnes point out, in an age that developed contact lenses, we don't even need our noses to support eyeglasses. Yet use and training can improve our skills considerably. The human nose still has greater discriminatory powers than any instrument designed to analyze odors. Some individuals have capitalized on this—the tea and coffee blenders, the perfumers, the proverbial sniffers of the wine-bottle corks.

And at least one individual in our time had no choice but to develop her sense of smell. Her record more than any other should be convincing evidence that the potential is there, and that this much neglected sense holds charms and powers undreamt of. Here is how Helen Keller describes her feelings: ‖

Smell is a potent wizard that transports us across thousands of miles and all the years we have lived. The odors of fruits waft me to my southern home, to my childhood frolics in the peach orchard. Other odors, instantaneous and fleeting, cause my heart to dilate joyously or contract with remembered grief. Even as I think of smells, my nose is full of scents that start awake sweet memories of summers gone and ripening fields far away.

‖ Helen Keller. "Sense and Sensibility," *The Century Magazine*, LXXV (February, 1908), 573–77.

VII

Concerning Taste There Is Dispute

Judging from the current abundance of cookbooks, magazine recipes, and television culinary shows it would seem that America was embarking on a new gastronomical era. At this rate the second half of the twentieth century might see gustatory pleasures elevated to heights sufficient to invoke the spirit of Jean Anthelme Brillat-Savarin, who personified taste as *Gasterea*, the tenth muse. Along with the enthusiasts, however, are some doubters who dismiss the sense as a poor second to olfaction. They point out that a cold in the nose which stuns the sense of smell inhibits taste as well. They go so far as to suggest that taste makes a very insignificant contribution to the satisfactions of eating. "Taste is 90 percent smell," they conclude, "all you really can taste of a steak is whether it's salty or not."

The implausible, uncomfortable fact of the matter is that much of what they say is technically true. Taste is an unusual sense which doesn't conform to simple rules. It is mixed-up with sensations of temperature, texture, and smell.

Yet it is a sense in its own right, one of the body's two main channels of chemical information. In its origins it was linked with smell, but the two separated early to become as distinct in higher organisms as the nose is from the mouth. For, barring the adaptations of some insects, and a more generalized distribution of taste receptors in water-dwelling animals (taste buds were first observed in fish skin), the sense of taste usually occurs in relation to the mouth, and its history is intimately related to that organ.

The mouth appeared early in the evolutionary process. The one-celled paramecium has a mouth, as do worms, bugs, and all more complex organisms. In the developmental process, too, the mouth is precocious, making its debut in the human embryo at three weeks. In terms of design the mouth is an excellent example of nature's architectural specialization. The simplest forms of life, such as algae, are like houses without doors. The mouth is a door, the main door to the body through which food, drink, and air pass, all the necessities of life. In its essence the mouth is a hole, an opening to the tube which becomes esophagus, stomach, gut, rectum, and finally anus.

But the mouth grew to be more than this. As animal life evolved the mouth became the vehicle for ingenious substructures, for the female digger wasp's drill for depositing eggs, the mosquito's saws and syringes for drawing blood, the beaver's gnawing teeth, the balleen whale's plankton net—and for most creatures, and man in particular, the tongue.

It is the tongue which has become the most important substructure in the mouth. With it man accomplishes two prime talents—he can talk and he can taste. Strangely enough, the two activities have more in common than a simple sharing of the same muscle. We think of speech as one of the crowning achievements of man's intellectual growth, of his adaptation to communal living. Taste, on the other hand, seems strictly visceral, unrelated to the brain's highest centers. But in a very important way it is related, for of all the senses taste is the one most involved with conscious behavior. Vision and hearing, smell and touch can all occur without active participation on the part of the individual.

But tasting implies attention and coordinated activity, and such attention and coordination was especially important for our anxious forebears whose waking hours were dominated by the search for food. Taste continues to be the prime guide in food acceptability. Food may look all right but whether you swallow it or not depends on the judgment of your tongue. Even the most hardened "Greasy Spoon" habitué will complain if his hamburger is burned or the coffee cold.

The act of judgment is implicit in the word itself: Taste is presumed to come from the Latin *taxare*, a verb which means to touch sharply, an intensive form of *tangere*, to touch, but it also means to appraise, to estimate, or to judge. *Tasto*, the noun in Italian, means a trial or touch, as well as taste. So the sense of taste is a means of testing the environment in an intense intimate way, more final in its consequences than any of the other senses. Taste *is* the final arbiter of what is to be admitted to the body.

This dual role may account for much of the controversy between food lovers and those who disdain the pleasures of the table. For the abstemious the idea that gourmands spend hours in conscious deliberation over what is fuel for their bellies smacks too much of craven animal nature. The excesses of gourmandism bring to mind the picture of epicene guests reclining at a Roman banquet or Henry VIII slavering over a joint of beef. Not for nothing is gluttony deemed one of the seven deadly sins, the only one specifically linked to one sense.

Yet in the light of recent experiments it appears that gourmands, if not gluttons, are on the side of the angels after all. And it is better to educate the palate to the delectations of *sauce béarnaise* or Perigord truffles than to consider the mouth only a way station between table and gut. "By setting up favorable conditions for digestion the flavor factors in food play a role in nutrition comparable to those of vitamins and hormones," comments California Institute of Technology biochemist A. J. Haagen-Smit.

Dramatic proof of this comes from a number of observations of tube-fed persons. Among these is a classic case in the annals of medicine, the story of Tom, an Irishman who at fifty-seven was studied by Drs. Stewart Wolf and Harold Wolff at New York Hospital. Tom was a valuable test subject for the study of the effects of drugs or emotional states on digestion.

In 1895, when he was nine years old, Tom had drunk some burning hot clam chowder that had closed his esophagus. After the accident a tube was surgically implanted in his stomach to allow direct feeding. But Tom didn't gain weight normally. No matter how good the food looked or smelled before it was placed in the tube, he remained poorly nourished and felt hungry.

The idea came to him, however, that he would feel happier if he could taste the food before it was put into the tube. This marked the turning point. He gained weight, his appetite felt satisfied, and he lived a reasonably normal life.

A more recent case reported by Drs. Henry Janowitz and Franklin Hollander at Mt. Sinai Hospital in New York City involved a woman who also had learned the habit of chewing and expectorating her food before an intragastric feeding. The doctors tested several menus on her: one was a nutritious but bland cereal product, the second a typical hospital ward meal, and the third a meal of the patient's choosing. In each case the doctors measured the effects of the sham meal (the food was not introduced into the stomach tube) on salivary and gastric secretions. They found enormous differences in stimulating power, graded from the cereal to the self-selected meal. The pleasurable choice resulted in an over-all doubling of the amount of juices, a tripling of the peak flow rate, and a greatly increased time period—two hours—in which secretions were active.

These and similar cases are especially interesting in the light of proposed plans for space travel. Vitamin pills and tube-squeezed food may suffice for short-term orbital jaunts, but astronauts on planetary voyages may have to depend on something more pleasurable and substantial than processed algae or food concentrates. The same admonition applies to army K rations or the various meal-in-one dietary aids in vogue today.

Obviously something important happens to you in the act of tasting, something that directly affects your capacity to break down food and derive the maximum benefit from it. Of course the act itself climaxes a chain of events. Consider what happens when a steak is taken from the broiler: you hear it sizzling, you see the fat crisp and dripping in the pan, the juices forming a concoction of brown-red richness at the sides, you smell the fumes of grill or charcoal, of meat and fat. Already your mouth has started to water and your tongue moves in anticipation of the first bite. Sight, sound, and smell alone can trigger parasympathetic nerve signals so that the salivary glands are prepared for their initial part in digestion, supplying the enzyme that breaks down starch. The signals will be further enhanced (or inhibited) as soon as the first bite is taken. At that moment two more senses, temperature and touch, will add to the complex of sensations. You have only to think of mealy cold potatoes, of steak too leathery to chew, or custard which has separated into lumps swimming in a thin gruel to realize how significant these qualities are in the over-all flavor of food.

Still there remains the taste itself, the "savor" part of flavor. Reasoning by analogy with the sense of smell, one might suspect the existence of a fundamental group of tastes, the "primaries" whose mixtures created an endless variety of sensations. This is the case, only instead of a theoretical seven or more primary tastes the fundamental group is surprisingly small. Studies in man reveal that we respond to only four qualities: salt, sour, sweet, and bitter. And the difference in taste between ripe or rotten peaches, lemonade that is too sweet or tart, soup that is too bland or highly seasoned, lies in the varying concentrations and combinations of these four tastes, and where they strike your tongue.

133

Where the Taste Buds Are

At first glance the spongy spatula in your mouth appears to be the same all over. Actually, it developed in two parts: a front two-thirds, which is the body, and a rear third, the root. Both parts of the tongue grew out from side and central swellings of embryo tissue which fused down the middle and then joined front and back along a V-shaped ridge. You can see the ridge if you stick your tongue out. You can also see the midline furrow. This cleft automatically deepens in the sucking reflex; you used it when you first drank milk. By sticking your finger on the tip of your tongue even now you can feel the ridge deepen.

If you've been eating salted peanuts or using your fingers to lick a whipped cream or syrup ladle you'll also pick up these flavors at the edge of your tongue, because you will have stimulated taste buds there. But had you put your finger under your tongue or across the center

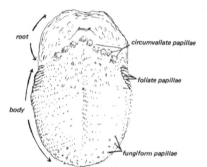

The upper surface of the tongue, showing the positions of the papillae associated with the taste buds. The taste buds in the root of the tongue are innervated by the glossopharyngeal nerve (the ninth cranial nerve); those in the body of the tongue are innervated by branches of the fifth (trigeminal) and seventh (facial) cranial nerves.

top, you would have tasted little or nothing, for there are virtually no taste buds there. The tongue is sensitive to taste at the tip, the sides, and along a ridge at the back that parallels the V-separation between body and root.

The location of the taste buds makes sense when you consider what happens when you eat. You bite the food at the tip of your tongue and grind it up at the sides, using molars to propel the food into the extremes of the mouth (the "vestibule"). Muscles in the cheek then bounce the food back again and the process is repeated, providing a constantly changing stimulus to just those areas rich in nerve endings. As food gets pushed back in the mouth prior to swallowing, a third array of taste receptors are ready to act. The rear guard is of great importance.

As early as the sixteenth century the Italian anatomist Malpighi had realized that these tasting spots on the tongue occurred in relation to the little swellings, or papillae, that give the tongue its spongy surface. These swellings vary. At the tip and around the front of

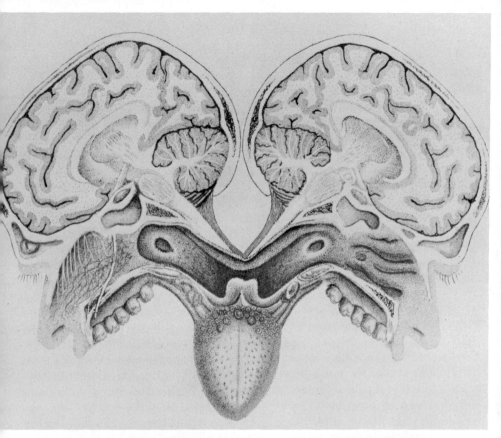

A nineteenth-century Italian anatomist, Paolo Mascagni, showed the relation-
ships between the tongue and the two halves of the brain in this arresting
manner.

A human taste bud from the top of a
fungiform papilla. The fine dark lines
are nerve endings among the supporting cells. × 1200.

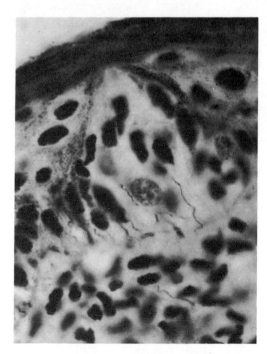

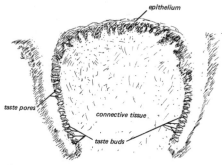

epithelium

taste pores

connective tissue

taste buds

A circumvallate papilla.

the tongue are tiny mushroom-shaped, or fungiform, papillae whose upper surfaces are dotted with taste buds. Farther back on each side there is a set of about a half-dozen grooves, the foliate papillae. Here the taste buds are sunk into the trenches carved by grooves. Still further back in the root is a V-shaped row of from eight to fifteen large circular swellings, the circumvallate papillae. Here again the taste buds line the trenches.

About a hundred years ago the German anatomist Georg Meissner (for whom the touch receptor was named) and zoologist Rudolf Wagner carried the anatomy of taste a step further and stripped the buds down to their basic units, the taste cells. It is these cells, four ten-thousandths of an inch long and half that broad, lying close together like petals in groups of ten or twelve, that give the bud its name. In any one cluster several cells point up fine hairs into the watery spaces around the papillae. These may be the active sensing cells, the other cells serving as supports, though some observers think that the cells are all alike, and look different because they are at different stages of development.

The taste cells are among the most dynamic in the body. We are born with taste buds around the hard and soft palate, the pharynx and epiglottis regions, as well as on the tongue. Many of these wear out as we grow older. Some, like those at the tip, "continually insulted by various strong agents in the food," according to Florida State University physiologist Lloyd M. Beidler, may wear out and be replaced every two weeks. Those at the root die more slowly, with less chance of resurrection. The adult has about 10,000 taste buds, a population which stays relatively stable until he is about forty-five. Then there is a gradual decline, and with it, a loss of sensitivity. The jaded palate is a physiological fact as is the heightened sensitivity (sometimes read as conservatism) of children. What tastes like pap to Pop may be ambrosia to a child, and vice versa.

Beidler suggests that the variations in the life spans of taste cells in different parts of the mouth may in part explain variations in sensitivity: The tip of your tongue is more sensitive to sweet tastes, the sides to sour,

136

and the back to bitter. A number of substances, including saccharin, the sugar substitute, actually change flavor as they move from front to rear, acquiring a bitter aftertaste. The salt-sensitive taste buds are more uniformly distributed, with some emphasis on the front edge.

These sensitivities are not cut and dried, however. They are more like the colored tiles in a mosaic that appears bluer here or redder there but is never purely one color anywhere. Even the tiles themselves, the taste buds, are not always pure. Some may react exclusively to salt or to sour, but others respond to combinations of two, three, or all four tastes. Moreover that versatility extends to the cellular level. Microelectrode tests suggest that the surface of an individual taste cell may be designed to pick different kinds of stimuli in different places.

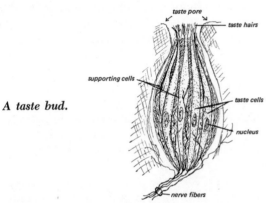

A *taste bud.*

Just exactly what that design may be as yet eludes taste researchers. As in the case of smell, scientists have tried every sort of chemical measure to fit the taste to the taster—size, shape, and weight of the molecule, chemical group, electric charge and bonding properties, and other characteristics derived from these. A criterion that works for one category may not apply to another, while within each category there are usually exceptions to the rule.

Sour = Acid

Take sour for example. When you pucker up your face when sucking a lemon, you think "sour." But a chemist probably thinks "acid," citric acid in this case. Of all the subjective taste sensations sour is certainly one that is objectively linked to a chemical concept: acidity. An acid is a substance containing hydrogen, which dissociates in solution into a number of free positively charged particles, cations (cat'-i-ons), or more simply, ions. The more dissociation the stronger the acid and the sourer the taste. Indeed hydrochloric, sulfuric, nitric, and other strong inorganic acids (ones which do not contain carbon) were originally noted by alchemists as substances having in common a strong sour taste. Yet their sourness is not very different from the taste of vinegar, or lemon juice, or other weakly dissociated organic acids. At the level when the difference between a vinegar solution and water is barely detectable, the concentration of hydrogen ions is actually less than that of a hydrochloric acid solution subjected to the same threshold test.

Though researchers feel sure they have their hands on the essential ingredient in the sour reaction, they readily admit that the details have yet to be spelled out. Rates of acid adsorption onto membranes or penetration into the taste cells may be important. It is also possible that as ions combine with substances at particular sites on the cell surface new ions may be released from solution. This characteristic might distinguish organic from inorganic acids and explain why the organic varieties are as effective as they are, and also why their effects last longer. Saliva, too, is a factor. It is mildly alkaline and acts as a buffering agent, tending to resist changes in ion concentration when acids are introduced into the mouth. The degree of alkalinity varies from person to person and hence introduces differences. Variations in the size and length of side chains in the acid molecule may explain some exceptions to the rule: why some amino acids (the building blocks of proteins) taste sweet, or picric acid bitter.

However these nuances may be worked out, there is fair agreement on how sensitivity to different sour substances varies. Of four commonly tested organic acids most people judge tartaric acid (the ingredient of baking powder) as the most sour, followed either by lactic acid (found in sour milk) or acetic acid (vinegar), and in fourth place, citric acid. In one test conducted by Rose Marie Pangborn of the Department of Food Science and Technology of the University of California at Davis, an adult panel could detect a sour flavor 70 percent of the time when the concentration of tartaric acid was as low as 0.00022 percent. At the same level of correct judgments the concentrations for the other acids were 0.00038 percent for lactic, 0.0006 percent for acetic, and 0.0008 percent for citric. Interestingly, at concentrations well above threshold, citric acid was always judged less sour, while the other three subjectively seem to lose their differences in intensity, being rated as equally sour.

Sweetness Is All

Sweetness in its own way presents a problem of organic vs. inorganic substances. If you started to list some of the things that taste sweet you might come up with fruits, sugar, honey, maple syrup, the cola drinks, rum, alcohol, liqueurs, and synthetic sweeteners. Chemists could contribute whole families of sweet-tasting compounds: the aldehydes, which include formaldehyde and the flavors from almonds, cinnamon, and vanilla; the esters, including some common fruit extracts like n-amyl acetate (banana), octyl acetate (orange), ethyl butyrate (pineapple), used in artificial flavorings; the amides, urea, the ingredient of urine is the most familiar of these, and so on. The element common to all these groups as well as the foods and drinks is the element carbon. They are all organic substances, an interesting phenomenon perhaps, but hardly a touchstone for sweetness. For there are also inorganic substances that taste sweet. The salts of heavy metals like lead or beryllium tend to taste sweet. So, eerily enough, does a very dilute solution of ordinary table salt.

Given such a mixed bag of sweets scientists tend to look for some over-all stereochemical or physical quality of the molecules to explain the stimulating ability. As in the case of recent researches into smell, the shape, volume, and weight of the molecule are considered likely factors. Investigators know, for example, that there are cases of right- and left-handedness, where compound X tastes sweet, but X', its molecular mirror image, is virtually tasteless. Ordinary table sugar, sucrose, is like this. You could get along with half the sugar in your coffee if you knew which half you could taste.

Saccharin, too, is beginning to arouse new interest. This molecule was discovered by accident in 1879 by a pair of chemists working on coal tar derivatives. It is two to three hundred times sweeter than sucrose, yet a change at one place in the molecule eliminates its taste altogether. Other simple substitutions can alter the flavor, making it taste bitter or soapy.

Recently saccharin's shape has undergone extensive study by K. Okaya of IBM who has made use of the high-powered methods of X-ray crystallography combined with the resources of a computer to analyze the results. These showed that the double-ring structure of the molecule—a six-carbon ring called a benzene ring, joined to a five-atom ring—is unusual in two ways: (1) the benzene ring is compressed and slightly unstable and (2) the five-atom ring lies flat instead of assuming the buckled shape most five-atom rings do. This is because the atoms usually make large angles with each other at the corners. Saccharin contains a sulfur atom, however, and this makes a small enough angle to allow the ring to lie flat.

The dramatic changes in saccharin's taste show up primarily as a result of tampering with the five-atom ring. It is here that the shielding of a nitrogen atom by a methyl group (one carbon linked with three hydrogen atoms) succeeds in making saccharin tasteless.

Whether or not saccharin will provide the evidence for a stereo-chemical theory, that a "key" molecule will fit into the "lock" of a certain receptor site, awaits further investigation.

But in the meantime scientists have other resources. There is a long and distinguished history of work with animals and natural stimuli in the chemical senses. Some of the earliest electrophysiological recordings of all were those of Lord Adrian and C. Ludwig of Cambridge University in the thirties, tapping the brains of catfish in response to olfactory stimuli. Observational work goes back even further.

Over forty years ago D. E. Minnich of the University of Minnesota noticed that when he applied certain sugar solutions to the sensory hairs on the feet of butterflies or the mouth parts of flies they extended their proboscises as a preliminary to feeding. The entomologist Vincent Dethier at the University of Pennsylvania has continued this work in his studies of the blowfly, a pest with a decided "sweet tooth." Dethier compiled a kind of gourmet guide for the blowfly, a long list of apparently succulent offerings. He was also able to reconstruct the architecture of the hair shafts from a series of microscopic sections. He showed that each shaft contains the fine filamentous extensions of a pair of taste cells at the base. A third cell at the base turned out to be a touch receptor responding to hair movements.

Now Edward Hodgson of Columbia University, J. Y. Lettvin of the Massachusetts Institute of Technology, and Kenneth D. Roeder of Tufts University have extended Dethier's work, recording from the individual cells in the hair base when the filaments are bathed in test solutions. This required the designing of glass tubes that were so fine that they could slip over a single hair, filling them with water with a trace of salt in it to act as a medium for conducting electricity, and then by means of silver wires, connecting the tube to an amplifier and an oscilloscope and back around again to a neutral part of the fly's head to complete the circuit. The ingenious setup allows the solution in the tube to be both test solution and the means of picking up electric currents, as the scant trace of salt does not interfere with the major responses of the cells.

Fortunately for Hodgson and his colleagues each of the pair of taste cells had a distinct pattern of broadcasting—one produced impulses with a constant amplitude of about 300 millionths of a volt; the others, 200 millionths of a volt. The larger (L) pulses generally were associated with a variety of flavors that were unattractive to the fly. The smaller (S) pulses were typically produced when certain attractive sugar solutions were applied.

It was when Hodgson began juggling the test solutions more closely to see which produced the strongest and weakest responses that the question of molecular architecture came up. In one striking series of tests four alcohols of identical atomic make-up but different shapes were introduced to the hair cells. Normally the fly's response to alcohols was unfavorable and a series of (L) impulses would be produced. This was true for three out of the four alcohols in question, but the fourth, inositol, produced strong S-type signals. It has a ring-shaped structure radically different from the others, much more like the sugars that strongly stimulated the fly.

Hodgson suggests that the mode of action of the S-receptors involves enzymes, whose specificity to shape (the lock-and-key theory) is notorious. The L-receptor may involve some less stereochemically specific mechanism, perhaps some kind of ion bonding to the cell surface. Such a mechanism has been adduced for salt receptors in mammals.

Bitter

Much of what has been said about sweet applies equally well to bitter. The catalog of bitter tastes is voluminous. No one chemical group or physical characteristic has sole claim to the sensation, although there is some association with the element nitrogen. Some of the bitterest tastes of all come from alkaloids—plant-derived nitrogenous compounds that include caffeine, nicotine, strychnine, and quinine.

What is especially interesting about the bitter taste is its behavioral significance. While you may feel positively disposed, or at least neutral, toward sweet, sour, or salty things, you are apt to reject bitter tastes as unpleasant. This phenomenon is widespread in the animal kingdom, as though evolving nervous systems had come to associate the quality with what was dangerous—with poisons, or with the actions of certain bacteria in spoiling food. Significantly, man's threshold for bitter is lower than for any of the other taste qualities, as if the body were primed to reject the least bit of bitter that could titillate taste buds in the circumvallate papillae—whose purpose would then seem to be to act as a last ditch stand against destruction.

Of course not everything bitter is bad for you. But more often than not you have learned to like the taste of olives or endive, of certain aperitifs, or of nicotine. Even tea and coffee were suspect when they were first introduced, and many of their strongest fans today would not think of drinking them without the ameliorating effects of sugar and cream.

Salt

Judging by their names alone, the four tastes run the gamut from vagueness to precision. "Sweet" and "bitter" suffer an embarrassing generality. "Sour" is associated with acidity. "Salt" turns out to be nearly a tautologous description: salty things contain soluble salts—crystalline compounds which dissociate in solution into positively charged cations and negative anions. Salts can be formed from acids by replacing some or all of the acid hydrogen with a metal. Thus ordinary table salt, sodium chloride, could be thought of as the salt of hydrochloric acid, with the metal sodium replacing the hydrogen.

But what subtle characteristic of salts affects the taste buds is not clear. Equal concentrations of different salts don't taste equally salty. Worse, when such solutions are made to match the saltiness of a standard solution of table salt, they always have an added flavor which distinguishes them from "pure" saltiness.

Researchers have tried to evaluate the relative importance of cations and anions in determining flavor. Typically they have run tests in which first the cation may be held constant, comparing threshold values and flavor qualities of say, sodium chloride, sodium bromide, and sodium acetate. Then they do the same for a standard anion, comparing ammonium chloride with calcium chloride and so on.

Tentatively there is some suggestion that the cation plays the predominant role, while the anion may exert a slightly inhibitory effect. The next step is to try to deduce what general laws may be working here: what is the relation between cation mobility and saltiness, between ionic weight and saltiness. At what point does sheer bigness or heaviness interfere with reactions so that, for example, salts of a heavy metal like mercury taste metallic, while some beryllium and lead salts taste sweet.

Sauce for the Goose, Sauce for the Gander

A reasonable question to ask in any discussion of the senses is what special purpose is served by the ability to detect certain qualities of the environment. Is man the better off for being able to savor the sweet, the salt, the sour, or the bitter? If the sensations neatly matched man's biological needs, the answer would be yes. In terms of evolutionary selection and adaptation it would mean that he had acquired food-scanning equipment appropriate to survival.

Man's basic needs are not very different from other animals however. The carbohydrates, fats, proteins, vitamins, minerals, and water that are vital to human existence are, in different forms and proportions, vital to other species as well. Since they too have evolved similar sensors and spectra of taste it would seem all the more reasonable to expect some association between sensation and need.

A taste for sugar and salt would clearly fill the dietary bill for some carbohydrates and minerals. Sour substances may be involved in more subtle biochemistry like maintaining the body's ion balance. They also may have acquired value as satisfying thirst, or promoting digestion through their stimulating effects on the salivary glands. (You can make a person's mouth water by sucking a lemon in front of him.) In the course of human history sour flavors may also have come to be associated with powerful hidden ingredients. Lemons and limes were eaten as scurvy preventatives long before vitamin C was isolated.

Bitter would fit the evolutionary scheme as the avoidance factor, enabling animals to filter out life-destroying from life-promoting substances.

The distinction seems especially fine in the case of the nitrogen element. Animals apparently can detect its bitter end in poisonous waste products, while at the same time accepting it as an element common to the amino acids of proteins.

Of course the acceptability of proteins may not depend on the nitrogen atom at all. Knowing how important they are in building and repairing body tissue, some researchers have recently explored the possibility that specific amino acid or protein receptors exist. Hodgson found that the freshwater scavenger crayfish *Cambarus* showed positive feeding responses to glutamic acid and glycine, both likely to be present as breakdown products in decaying fish. Varieties of jellyfish also show feeding behavior in relation to amino compounds.

Among higher species the rat has been tested. Investigators found that bathing the rat's tongue with certain amino acids produced a set of nerve spikes which built up slowly and maintained their firing rate for some time. This was in marked contrast to the high frequency bursts typical of the reaction to sugar or salt.

Such findings are particularly interesting in the case of the rat because it means that a mammal may have amino acid receptors, and that mammal is very close to man in tastes and biological needs. The groups of essential amino acids, those which must be obtained from the environment and cannot be synthesized in the body, are almost identical

143

in the two species, a link that may explain the conspicuous success of rats in their association with man throughout a long and plague-ridden history. If anything rats may be even more finicky in their feeding habits since they cannot vomit. They are notoriously difficult pests to control because they are suspicious of new foods and only cautiously sample bait.° The best rat poisons today owe their success to the fact that the rat can't taste them.

In comparison with rats, animals that might be thought to be higher up in the evolutionary scale display different, and in some cases, less discriminating taste habits. The cat shows little or no response to sugar. Calves, lambs, chickens, and pigeons also seem to lack a "sweet tooth," while dogs, pigs, hamsters, and monkeys not only respond to sugar, but in most cases react to saccharin as well.

These species' likes and dislikes should not be taken to mean that each animal has carefully eliminated the negative and accentuated the positive in its diet. The chance factors in evolution insure that at any one stage there is usually a residue of useless skills or information passed on from generation to generation, while something profitable may never be acquired. What makes the difference between success or failure of a species is the whole armamentarium of sense and sensibility, the variety of skills and their integration in dealing with the environment.

The Relation of Need to Behavior

Mistakes in the choice of food do have more disastrous consequences than errors of vision or hearing, however. The fact that species around us have been here for considerable eons bears witness that in the choice of food, the forces of caution and choice have operated reasonably well. Moreover, a number of experiments offer strong evidence that many animals do know what's good for them when placed in situations of deprivation or self-selection.

The need for salt is a good example of this. The laziest cow as well as the fleetest of deer will find its way to a salt lick to build up a supply of mineral salts not obtainable from plants or grasses. Carnivorous animals may not have this problem but they too show distinct preferences, thresholds of taste, and rejection levels. Rats have a low sodium to potassium ratio in their bloodstreams. They are extremely sensitive to sodium chloride, show a distinct preference for a mildly salt solution over water, and have a low cut-off point. Cats and dogs are less sensi-

---

° The noted animal behaviorist Konrad Lorenz reports that if the leader of a rat pack rejects some unknown food it will often deliberately urinate or defecate on it as a warning to other rats.

tive, tolerate higher amounts, and maintain correspondingly higher sodium to potassium levels.

Controlling the salt level in the bloodstream is one of the functions of the adrenal glands in mammals. If they are diseased or destroyed, great amounts of salt are excreted from the body in urine, and unless additional salt is supplied, the animal will die. Some years ago Curt Richter at the Johns Hopkins University School of Medicine showed that adrenalectomized rats fed a normal diet would die in a week or two. Given access to salt, however, they invariably would take sufficient amounts to be able to lead reasonably normal lives.

He found the same was true for rats deprived of calcium when the controlling parathyroid glands were removed, and for rats made diabetic after removal of the pancreas. Diabetic rats also drank quantities of water to aid in eliminating the sugar they were not able to metabolize. Further, if they were given a choice of foods rich in fats, proteins, or sugars as basic components of their diet, they all but eliminated sugar.

The guiding role of taste in this behavior was established when Richter performed the same experiments in rats whose taste nerves had been severed. Then all self-regulating ability was lost. Richter also found that in some cases the metabolic disorder sharpened taste: the salt threshold in adrenalectomized rats was fifteen times lower than in normal rats.

As a final test of self-regulation Richter raised two groups of rats, one on a normal laboratory feed, the other given access to the basic nutrients and water in more or less pure forms. At the end of the experiment both groups appeared equal in health and development. The difference was that the self-regulating rats had eaten 36 percent less food to attain the same state.

Self-Regulation in Man

The heyday of nutritional behavior experiments was in the twenties and thirties when the roles of vitamins, hormones, and glands were exciting medical attention. It was during this time that C. M. Davis studied human infants and concluded that they too displayed innate abilities to select what was essential from a wide assortment of natural foods. A child with a marked vitamin D deficiency would even choose to drink large quantities of cod-liver oil.

Davis did much to dispel the myths about the vitamin-rich oil. He found that children up to about five generally liked its taste, but their zest for it tapered off the older they got, no matter what their previous experience had been. He speculated that the early preference was correlated with the greater needs for vitamins A and D during the rapid growth period of infancy.

Davis also cited examples of physiological cravings: children with a parathyroid deficiency sometimes would eat chalk or plaster as a source of calcium. He thought too that the bizarre practices of clay- and dirt-eating that are found among the world's poorest and hungriest people also derived from needs for minerals or trace elements.

Adults with various glandular deficiencies also show physiological cravings. Adrenal disfunctions can lead to a craving for salt. But so can an excess depletion of salt through perspiration or excretion of liquids in hot weather or after heavy exertion. The Mexican habit of taking tequila with salt and lemon may very well be a cultural adaptation that recognizes this need. Many tourists too find themselves reaching unaccustomedly for the saltcellar when they're in a hot climate, lacing their food with a much more liberal dose than they would at home.

Having a Taste for Water

The adrenal glands not only work to retain salt when the body needs it, but they also sound an alarm when there is an oversupply. It is by this roundabout route that you become thirsty. When you eat peanuts, or popcorn, or other salty tidbits during the cocktail hour you want to have another drink not because you're dehydrated, but because the body needs the water to dilute the extra salt. A sailor cast adrift can't afford to slake his thirst with sea water. Its salt will only make him more thirsty.

Such an indirect arrangement seems surprising considering how important water is for survival. The average person could get along without food for two weeks or more, but lack of water would carry him off in eight or ten days. Yet frogs, toads, cats, dogs, and even monkeys apparently have distinct water taste receptors. Man and rats do not. The charms of branch water, or the sweet, pleasant taste you may associate with your local supply, is either the contribution of minerals or additives or else an aftereffect sometimes experienced after tasting something sour. If anything, pure distilled water placed on the tongue has a depressing effect: Yngve Zotterman of the Department of Physiology, Veterinärhögskolan, Sweden, found it lowered the resting activity of taste fibers in the human subjects he tested.

Hypothalamic Control

The circuitry that controls the operations of the adrenal glands and kidneys is a complex one involving the autonomic nervous system, hormones, nerve secretions, and the pituitary gland, all under the influence of the hypothalamus at the base of the brain. If blood filtering through the kidneys is comparatively dilute, a hormone released by the adrenal glands acts to retain salt and release the excess water. Opposing this action is an antidiuretic hormone. This is released by the pituitary gland in just the opposite situation: when excess salt should be dumped from the blood and as much water retained.

Thus the hypothalamus is something of a master juggler, constantly getting feedback signals from visceral organs and in turn stimulating or inhibiting the appropriate glands.

These operations go on automatically at all times, usually with little awareness on your part. In more extreme situations—if you've missed a meal and your stomach starts growling, or if for some reason the water-salt regulating system is strained—the hypothalamus initiates conscious food- and drink-seeking behavior. Such activity is in response to the balance of signals originating in specific hunger and thirst centers within the hypothalamus. If certain cells in the hunger center are destroyed, for example, an animal will be driven to eat and become obese. Lesions in an adjacent area will have just the opposite effect: they can produce complete apathy to food and lead to emaciation. The amphetamine-containing weight-reducing drugs are thought to work by affecting this area of the hypothalamus.

A similar reciprocity exists in the thirst center: lesions in one area can lead to polydipsia, or excessive drinking; lesions nearby can mean that you can literally lead a horse to water but you cannot make him drink.

These hypothalamic functions are impressive additions to an already distinguished list of activities that marks this brain cell mass as one deeply concerned with regulating many aspects of man's emotional and visceral life. At the same time it is capable of relating these states to higher centers of thought and behavior. When the hypothalamus signals the cortex that you're hungry you stop what you're doing, go to the kitchen, and raid the refrigerator.

Taste Circuitry

How pleasant or unpleasant that raid turns out to be will again involve hypothalamic reactions and other "old brain" centers. But now we can also trace the direct course of taste fibers when they have been stimulated. For the hypothalamus cannot tell you exactly what food you've eaten, when you last ate it, what memories that occasion stirs, and whether the taste was better then or now.

147

These are cortical funtions dependent on the ultimate end stations of signals originating in the tongue. The fibers innervating the taste cells are bundled into two major nerves: the chorda tympani branch of the facial nerve for the body of the tongue and the lingual branch of the glossopharyngeal nerve for the root. These nerves go to the medulla where new fibers arise and pass to the thalamus. Very little convergence takes place at either of these relay stations, which suggests that the pattern of impulses is carefully preserved all the way to the cortex. There the thalamic fibers end in an area close to the somesthetic band, but farther toward the midline of the brain. If you sliced across the brain at about the ear level, the coronal or crown-shaped cross section would show a small island of gray surrounded by the white fiber tracts of nerves passing to and from the cortex. This insula, or areas very close to it, is thought to be the center of taste. When it is damaged, taste hallucinations and losses of sensation can occur.

The nerves carrying taste sensations carry temperature, pain, and touch impulses as well, and while microelectrodes can generally distinguish impulses at the receptor level, the problem gets complicated the higher up you go. Even at the taste bud level, a single nerve fiber may branch out so that one part goes to a taste cell, but others may innervate surrounding touch or temperature receptors.

Compounding this complexity at the periphery is the fact that foods and drinks do not come served up in the isolated purities of laboratory tests with ever-constant temperatures. The taste of food is profoundly affected by a set of parameters the lab technician calls chemical reactions and what you call cooking. Herein lies the magic of food, the charm which usually makes it impossible to analyze taste completely and reconstruct the parts into a flavor "whole."

The tricks of the good cook are being attended to seriously in the laboratory. In carefully controlled experiments trained panels of judges do find that a pinch of salt added to a sweet mixture intensifies the sweetness, while a trace of sugar enhances saltiness (though not to the same degree). Beyond a certain point of course the reaction changes, and salt will mask sweetness and sweet salt.

Both salt and sugar reduce the sourness of acids (else lemonade would be undrinkable). But the reciprocal effects are not so clear-cut. Some years ago F. W. Fabian and H. B. Blum of the Michigan Agricultural Experiment Station at East Lansing found that most acids increase the saltiness of table salt; that hydrochloric and acetic acid had no effect on sucrose, but that other acids increased its sweetness. The sweetness of the fruit sugar fructose on the other hand was reduced by most acids (except hydrochloric and citric, which had no effect).

Time, Temperature, and Texture

Methodically mixing pairs of tastes and seeing the result of the blend is a synthetic way of studying taste. Analytic approaches have also been tried, starting with a blend and trying to break it down. The taste pyramid conceived by the German investigator H. Henning is a model for this approach. He placed the four taste qualities at the vertices of a pyramid and then plotted flavors at various intermediate points in relation to these. In this scheme sodium bicarbonate lies on the line connecting salt and bitter. Flavors involving three qualities would fit on one of the faces, and blends of all four would lie at points inside the pyramid.

But analysis falls short of the mark in instances where the combination of two flavors has a greater intensity than either alone. Glucose is less sweet than sucrose but when they are mixed the combination is sweeter than the simple addition of their individual sweetnesses. This is because judgment of intensity is not always a simple (linear) function. You may like a faint bitter taste, but just a tiny bit more is enough to make you dislike it intensely.

Interactions can occur over a period of time as well as simultaneously. If you've just eaten something sour you may tolerate more sour substances you might have rejected at first. Equally, something sour may ruin the taste of food in another category. Most wine drinkers know the folly of eating an oil-and-vinegar-dressed salad before tasting the wine.

Temperature independently affects taste judgments. Salt and bitter both are reduced in intensity when heated. Sugar and sour are enhanced. It's a wise cook who knows when to sugar the candy or salt the stew.

The shape and texture of food also contribute to the pleasures or displeasures of eating. Ernst R. Pariser of the Technological Laboratory of the Department of Interior's Bureau of Commercial Fisheries recalls being given a large crystal of rock salt as a child and finding it very pleasant when he popped the whole thing in his mouth, much more than a pinch of granulated table salt. Similarly a panel of subjects he tested greatly enjoyed sucking a small lump of 100 percent sucrose, but complained of the sickeningly sweet taste of a 50 percent sucrose solution.

Pariser suggests that these results have to do with the amount of flavor dissolved in the saliva at any moment. In the case of the rock salt or the sugar lump the taster can regulate this and swallow at the moment he is satisfied. No such control is possible in the case of the salt granules or the syrupy solution and their instantaneous impact is unpleasant.

A Code for Taste

The flexibility of taste cells in response to such changing qualities of the stimulus, their ability to alter the impulse frequency, fire sooner or later, adapt more quickly or slowly, and preserve this information on the way to the cortex suggests a fairly elaborate coding system, one that can explain why there can be so much more to taste than simple sums of sweet, salt, sour, or bitter.

One of the most distinguished researchers in taste physiology, Carl Pfaffman of Brown University, has suggested how intricate such a code might be. Again it was the rat that inspired the analysis. Pfaffman noted two single fibers:

The two fibers A and B respond to both sodium chloride and sucrose, but A is more reactive to sodium chloride and B is more reactive to sucrose. At all concentrations of sodium chloride, the frequencies in A are higher than that in B, at all concentrations of sucrose, B is greater than A. Such a two-fiber system, therefore, signals sodium chloride when A is greater than B and sucrose when B is greater than A. Thus different information may be conveyed by the same nerve fiber depending upon the activity in a second parallel fiber.

Imagine this kind of functionally dependent relationship extended to many fibers and not just two, and the subtlety of taste will become apparent.

Taste Habits

The decoding and spreading of signals from the cortex to other parts of the brain accounts not only for the possibility of recognizing foods, but for the ability to make the various associations of memory and experience that determine likes and dislikes. These are often so deeply rooted in folklore and custom that it sometimes seems a miracle that individuals ever venture to try anything new. Thoughts of the stranger in North Africa offered the delicacy of sheep's eye, the South American Indians' communal consumption of drugs mixed with spittle, the Malaysian habit of eating raw meat stuffed into bamboo rods that have been inserted into earth and left for two years are singularly unappealing to Americans. Yet the typically American habits of eating corn on the cob, spreading masses of peanut butter on bread or devouring watermelon on a summer day can evoke raised eyebrows from even the most cultured and traveled Europeans. A vast majority of the world's peoples would think a cheeseburger an astonishing concoction.

Such cultural conservatism starts in the cradle, for in spite of what a baby might do in the laboratory, the average child grows up shaped by its parents' choices and opinions. If they make faces at baby foods the baby may end up disliking the food and crying. Occasionally manufacturers even cater to the less sensitive adult taste and oversalt the products. The gimmick may increase sales, but it is of no use, and in fact can be harmful to the baby.

Food habits are reinforced in homogeneous cultures where there are long-established traditions or religious taboos. If the country is poor, malnutrition can become accepted as part of the way of life.

This is why distributing surplus foods or designing programs to feed the world's poor and hungry is so vastly complicated. Scientists at the Instituto de Nutrición de Centro America y Panama (INCAP) in Guatemala City labored for several years to produce a cheap protein concentrate from cottonseed that was easy to prepare and looked and tasted like a popular corn-flavored but not very nutritious Indian beverage.

United States Department of Interior researchers are equally concerned that fish flour, the protein-rich white powder that is extracted from whole fish grinds, can be the basic ingredient of a variety of attractive foods—breads, cakes, cookies—adapted to the food preferences of the consumer.

Starvation simply does not lure people from basic taste conservatism. Hungry children raised on corn flour reject soybeans. Cow's milk may be revolting to desert nomads used to camel's milk.

Shellfish is a classic example of a food which divides the world. It also has considerable economic significance. Professor Ritchie Calder of the University of Edinburgh points out that the waters surrounding the Indian state of Kerala abound in lobsters and prawns, while the backwaters teem with frogs. The Indians wouldn't think of eating any of these but export large quantities to grace the tables of New York and Paris restaurants. In turn they use the money to buy power equipment for the boats they use to catch the fish they do like to eat.

One cannot help but wonder who was the first brave soul to eat certain foods, to discover that lobster had to be alive immediately before being cooked, or that an oyster was delectable when raw. The wonder grows as we think back in time to the discovery of fire and the vast enrichment to man's food stores this meant. Not only were there the immediate gains of the chemical effects of heat—the coagulating of proteins and melting of fats in broiling a steak or the dissolving of connective tissue in stewing—but the long-term gains of food storage: preserving fruits through boiling jellies and jams, or smoking fish and meat. With the beginning of agriculture man took another giant step forward, discovering the effects of yeast, baking soda, and tartaric acid in making bread, or the process of fermenting fruits and grain in making wines and spirits. In more recent times one is struck by the improbability of someone's conceiving of the complex picking, drying, and roasting processes that make coffee possible.

Of course a lot more courage is displayed and many a cultural inhibition lost when the rumor goes out that eating such and such a food restores the complexion, increases brain power, or works as an aphrodisiac. Not surprisingly this field is riddled with myth and superstition. Writers as distinguished as Norman Douglas and Brillat-Savarin have contributed to the literature, Douglas with his *Venus in the Kitchen*, Brillat-Savarin with the classic *The Physiology of Taste*. Brillat-Savarin was convinced that fish were sexually stimulating because they contained large amounts of phosphorus and other "hot" or "inflammable" ingredients. Truffles, he declared to be the food of love, while cordials—mixtures of wine and sugar—he touted for their restorative purposes or for their use on wedding nights.

Much attention is being paid today to the biochemistry of the nervous system and the roles played by various naturally occurring amine compounds and of ribonucleic acid, RNA. This substance, well known for its role in carrying out the protein-building instructions coded in the genes of every cell has recently been implicated as the molecule involved in memory. If these experiments were verified, it would be amusing if people turned again to rich sources of RNA and protein to improve their minds. The lowly yeasts and fishes would once more be elevated to high place.

Of course almost any food you eat is fuel for the highly active nervous system. That some food may also alter behavior can often be explained in terms of a drug effect. Alcohol is a fine example. So are the hallucinogenic mushrooms, the leaves of the cocaine plant, or the hemp product, hashish. While many of these drugs are extracted and purified to be taken straight, there are lots of places in the world where their effects are diluted either by eating the less processed raw material or by mixing with food or candy.

Drugs in their own right can in turn exert observable effects on taste. Chewing the leaves of the Indian plant *gymnema sylvestre* reduces sensitivity to sweet and bitter, but leaves salt and sour unaffected. Cocaine and nicotine depress most taste sensations. The Sudanese plant *Bumelia dulcifica* is said to change sweet and bitter to sour. And a plant found in Ghana, *syncipalium mirabilis*, has long been consumed by the natives upon arising since it tends to sweeten everything eaten during the day.

All taste effects of course show individual differences. Some are even genetic: particular chemical compounds containing phenylthiocarbamide, PTC, taste bitter to most people, but have no taste at all to some. This appears to be inherited (carried by a recessive gene), and the failure to taste is assumed to occur at the receptor level. But usually, and interestingly, individual likes and dislikes are not particularly marked by individual changes in sensitivity in the tongue. Even in the case of physiological needs the alteration in behavior seems to come primarily from the brain. This is also true in the case of the healthy pregnant woman: her cravings are not the result of changes in the taste buds.

That an altered psyche may have profound effects on taste has shown up recently in a study of the side effects of a particular tranquilizing drug used to treat schizophrenics. The problem of determining the ideal dosage that will eliminate side effects is often handled through trial and error. In this case however the researchers Roland Fischer, Walter Knopp, Frances Griffin, and James Beck of the Ohio State University College of Medicine were able to show a correlation of taste sensitivity with dosage. All the women patients tested had below normal taste sensitivities to quinine, but when the group was divided into the more and the less sensitive, it was found that the more sensitive were also more drug reactive: smaller doses could bring about side effects.

One interesting observation of this experiment was that of the general reduction in sensitivity in all the patients, confirming a view of schizophrenia as a disorder characterized by a diminished input of sensory information. Certainly there seems no question that such a decline, even in the case of taste, would be a loss, not as profound perhaps as becoming short of sight or hard of hearing, but one that would sharply reduce the more immediate pleasurable aspects of life, graying the world to a depressing degree. Indeed one has only to turn to Brillat-Savarin once more for a classic description of the unfortunates in whom taste is diminished or absent:

Those . . . from whom nature has withheld the legacy of taste, have long faces, and long eyes and noses, whatever their height there is something elongated in their proportions. Their hair is dark and unglossy, and they are never plump; it was they who invented trousers.

VIII

The Auditory Code

The mechanics of human hearing can be summed up in a single sentence, albeit a sprawling one. Sounds set up vibrations in air that beat against the thin skin of the eardrum, which pushes against a chain of tiny bones that presses fluid in the inner ear against one membrane, which in turn pushes fluid against a second membrane, which sets up shearing forces across a third membrane, which pulls on tiny hair cells, which trigger electrical impulses in nearby nerve cells, which travel to the brain, which interprets them, and you hear. A remarkable device: Rube Goldberg couldn't have done better.

This elaborate machinery for handling sound is the product of evolutionary adaptation, a relatively recent product compared with the development of the other senses. While the design may appear esthetically awkward, it is technically a triumph—a dazzling display of engineering subtlety.

The human ear can detect sounds as soft as the proverbial pin drop, as well as boiler shrieks 100 trillion times as loud. Man can dance to the thump of a jazz double bass, as well as to a piper's pipe seven octaves higher. Yet neither that range nor those dynamics include the most intimate of body sounds. You are normally deaf to your heart's beat, your joints' creaking, your stomach's peristaltic movements, your eyelids' opening and closing several times a minute. To some extent you can also blot out unpleasant or continuous external sounds: traffic noise, an air conditioner's whine, the clatter of typewriters, and the ringing of phones in an office. You can also tune in selectively: overhear a conversation at a cocktail party while making polite chitchat, or wake in the middle of the night to a baby's crying, but sleep through the sound of a neighbor's record player.

By nurturing these talents you may acquire the perception of the conductor who can single out the erring note in the third movement of the Mahler Ninth, or the skill of a scientist who can tell what part of the brain he's tapping by listening to brain wave patterns played through sound equipment.

Part of the conductor's skill lies in pinpointing the source of sound. You, too, can locate a sound by virtue of the difference in time of arrival of sound waves at each ear—even though the difference is of the order of thousandths of a second. Slight differences in loudness, independently, will accomplish the same feat. If you were in total darkness you could develop the skills of the blind, using the echoes of a tapping cane to give shape to your surroundings.

You can't buy high fidelity equipment that good. Microphones can pick up sounds and change them to electrical signals. Amplifiers can magnify them, and loudspeakers play them back to you, but never the same way your two ears hear. The telephones, television sets, radios, and phonographs in use today often fail in range. Often they distort sound, flattening low notes or sharpening highs; sometimes they strain the juice out of music completely, losing just those harmonic undertones and overtones that give instruments their special qualities. Stereo equipment with its paired amplifiers and speakers comes closer to the high marks set by human ears, but even it pales in contrast to the instantaneous adjustments, modulations, and balances achieved by the ear-brain hook-up.

Yet for all this engineering grace there is something awkward about the ears' development. Man's ancestors evolved from a watery environment to an airy one, so we shouldn't be surprised to learn that we still hear in water. But this is just what complicates auditory engineering. Normally the fluids of the inner ear have to be stirred if a sound is to be signaled to the brain. Stirring that water in just the right way to preserve the quality of the original airborne sound is the work of nature's genius.

155

Sounds in Air

How does a sound begin? Something, somewhere, disturbs the air causing molecules in motion in the immediate neighborhood to swing back
and forth rapidly. Visualize what would happen if you were to inflate a
balloon with a bicycle pump. As the balloon skin swells, it pushes
against the air molecules immediately in contact with it. These molecules in turn press against the ones nearest them, so that ever-larger
spheres of compression move out from the surface of the balloon. If the
pump piston is now drawn back, the balloon starts to deflate. As it
shrinks, the shell of air around it becomes rarefied, and nearby air rushes
in to fill the partial vacuum. This creates a second rarefied zone which
will again be filled by the surrounding layer of air, so it appears that a
set of rarefied shells moves out from the balloon.

This is a slow-motion picture of sound. Indeed if you pumped fast
enough, maybe 25 or 30 cycles per second, the successive waves of
compression-rarefaction, compression-rarefaction, fall within hearing
range and you would hear an extremely low-pitched foghorn sound.

Each molecule nudged by its neighbor moves very little, vibrating a short distance around its original position, but the disturbance—the
sound—spreads out in space in all directions. Molecules must be present
to propagate the waves: sound cannot travel in a vacuum (nor for that
matter in the near vacuum of outer space). And the molecules must be
able to come together and bounce apart again. The medium has to be
elastic.

This physical picture of sound is easy to relate to the familiar S-
shaped (sine curves) or more complex wave forms of physics textbooks or

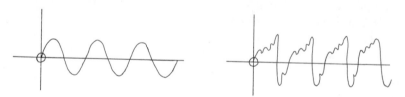

electronics manuals if we make a mathematical jump. We can think of
the three-dimensional compressional movements as though they were
restricted to one dimension, and then map the population of molecules
as it changes with time. Of course physicists carry the analysis further by
showing that the path of a particle set in motion by a tuning fork, or
other simple tone-making device can be described as simple sine or cosine
waves.

These translations are useful because they elucidate certain prop-

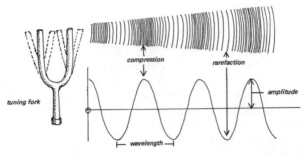

A simple sound in air can be translated into a smooth curve shape.

erties of sound. The mathematical picture shows at once that the sound waves of a simple prolonged tone are periodic: after a fixed length of time the wave pattern repeats itself. The wavelength or the distance between successive peaks (or troughs) is a constant, as is the frequency, or the number of waves that pass a given point in a given time. Usually time is measured in seconds, so frequency is given in waves (or vibrations, or cycles) per second (cps).

Subjectively we perceive frequency as pitch: the greater the frequency the higher it sounds. And so good is our perception that within certain regions of the adult hearing range (about 15 to 15,000 cycles) we can detect the difference between notes only two or three cycles apart. Acuteness in the high frequency range falls off with age. The drop was a regular 80 cycles every six months for one group of individuals in their forties tested over a period of five years, a fact they found most depressing.

The bigness of sound shows up as the height or amplitude of the peaks on the curve. The more "ample" the peak the farther the molecule traveled in its vibratory path and the greater the energy of its motion. This is usually measured in terms of the pressure of the sound source.

The human ear perceives amplitude or intensity as loudness. Again both the limits of audibility and man's perception of just noticeable differences in the loudness of tones are extraordinary. At the absolute threshold of hearing sound pressures are on the order of 0.0001 dyne ° per square centimeter. Ordinary atmospheric pressure at sea level—the weight of a column of air on the body surface—is approximately 15 pounds per square inch. This is equivalent to a million dynes per square centimeter, or ten *billion* times the pressure of the barest audible sound.

Because sound pressures are so infinitesimal and yet range considerably, it is more convenient to measure intensity in ratios, noting that

° One dyne is the force which will accelerate one gram of mass at the rate of one centimeter per second every second.

157

one sound is so many times more powerful than another. The decibel and bel scales are based on such ratios. A sound ten times more intense than another at the same frequency differs from it by one bel; a decibel (db) is 1/10 bel. The decibel scale starts at an arbitrary reference point, a "0" db, which does not indicate the absence of sound, but the minimum sound level in quiet surroundings. The usual reference level taken is about twice the absolute threshold pressure, or 0.0002 dyne per centimeter squared.

Intensities given on the decibel scale can be physically measured in the laboratory. Loudness, on the other hand, is a quality of perception that varies from individual to individual. In experiments with human subjects psychologists frequently use a special loudness scale whose units are "phones" or "sones." Comparisons of the two scales are of course possible and the intensity levels of familiar sounds can be measured. A whisper is about 20 db, or a hundred times as loud as 0 db; normal conversation is 60 db, a million times as loud, while the noise of a jet take-off is of the order of 160 db—10^{16} or 10 quadrillion times the zero level.

Normally the human ear experiences different sensations of loudness throughout the hearing range. Low frequency sounds, for example, the base notes of a piano or organ, seem to get much louder with increases in intensity. On the other hand the distortion you experience when you turn on the radio at full volume is a high frequency one. The mechanical shortcomings of microphones and recording equipment are such that loud high frequency tones mask low tones.

The ability to perceive just noticeable differences in the loudness of tones at the same frequency is best in the same region of human hearing range where the finest frequency changes are perceived—around 2,000 cps. Here you can distinguish which of a pair of tones is louder when the difference between them may be of the order of one decibel.

Because the speed of sound is constant in a given medium, high and low frequency sounds reach the ears at the same time. This means that high frequency waves must be associated with short wavelengths and low frequencies with long waves since both have to cover the same distance in the same time. This fact is expressed in the equation:

$$\text{Frequency} \times \text{wavelength} = \text{velocity}$$

The speed of sound in air is about 1,100 feet per second. In a thunderstorm lightning is virtually instantaneously visible, but the sound it creates reaches us more slowly. We count the seconds before we hear the thunder to judge how far away the storm center is—5 seconds would be approximately a mile.

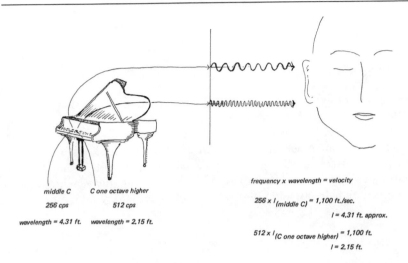

frequency x wavelength = velocity

middle C   C one octave higher

256 cps   512 cps

$256 \times l_{(middle\ C)} = 1,100\ ft./sec.$

wavelength = 4.31 ft.   wavelength = 2.15 ft.

$l = 4.31\ ft.\ approx.$

$512 \times l_{(C\ one\ octave\ higher)} = 1,100\ ft.$

$l = 2.15\ ft.$

The sound of course is normally not so loud as it would be at the center of the storm because the original energy of the vibrating molecules in the first small shells moving out from the source gets spread out across larger and larger spheres. The wave picture will show a characteristic drop in amplitude called damping. Eventually sound dies altogether, its energy absorbed as heat by the molecules.

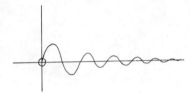

Perhaps it is not too farfetched to say that you are occasionally aware of this excess thermal energy when you listen to a noisy discussion or declare the speaker's words to be "a lot of hot air."

Normally sounds don't die a natural death because the atmosphere is so filled with objects for the waves to hit. When this happens the energy may be absorbed (the drapes and carpets of a room do this), it may be bounced back from surfaces, producing echoes, or some—usually less than 1 percent—will pass through to travel in the new medium. When this occurs the waves usually change speed and direction just as light rays do when they pass from air to a glass of water.

When sound waves strike the ear any of these things can happen. The reason that the sound is not lost in penetrating the ear tissue is due largely to the extraordinary design of the outer parts. The complex arrangement is really a stunningly effective way of delivering nearly as much sound energy to the fluids of the inner ear as came in. It avoids the 99 percent loss due to reflection.

The Outer Ear

The process begins with the external ear, whose shell-like shape helps a little in separating front from rear sounds. It acts as a funnel, catching sounds and channeling them inward, but not to a great degree, not as much as the horseshoe bat, for instance, who wriggles his long, pointed ears to focus sound efficiently. If your ears were cut off or muffled you could still hear well. After all women in head-hugging cloches, motorcyclists with helmets, and skiers with headbands manage all right.

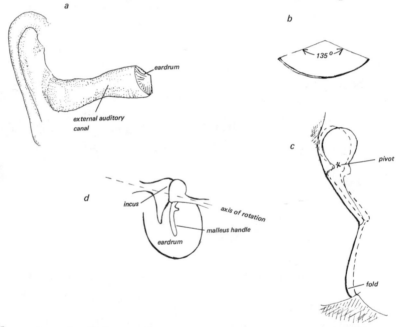

The eardrum is a light membrane in the shape of a cone approximately 135 degrees at the apex. In place, the eardrum diagonally closes off the external canal. Set in motion, the eardrum moves backward as though pivoted on an axis near its upper rim. Note the fold near the lower rim; this enables the eardrum to move backward rigidly without strain. Two of the ossicles of the middle ear, the malleus and the incus, are aligned so that they and the eardrum rotate as a unit around a common axis. The comparatively large heads of the bones act as counterweights to their long processes, keeping the center of gravity of the system close to the center of rotation. Thus the bones are not easily rattled by cephalic movements.

A one-fourth-inch-wide canal extends from the bowl-like opening of the ear for a little over an inch, ending in a fine membrane that is covered on the outside with a thin skin. This is the eardrum, the tympanic membrane. It is a broad flat cone about one-half inch across at the base, one-fourth inch high and 135 degrees at its apex angle. It sits at an angle of about 30 degrees to the canal which widens en route.

The eardrum is the body's microphone. It doesn't change sound waves to electric signals, but it behaves like the larger cones of microphones and loudspeakers: it moves as a rigid whole when sound waves strike it, vibrating at exactly the same frequency as the sound. By virtue of its resiliency it can spring back quickly to its resting state. It has been calculated that the membrane moves as little as the diameter of the smallest atom, hydrogen, roughly a billionth of a centimeter: 0.000,000,000,4 inch at the threshold of hearing. This in itself might not be remarkable; what makes it so is that the infinitesimal movement is transmitted through the ear and ultimately detected as sound.

Technically the eardrum's adroitness is aided by a little fold on its lower rim. This gives it the leeway to move as a rigid whole without straining.

As the eardrum moves in and out, producing miniatures of the bicycle–balloon skin oscillations, it starts movements in a set of tiny bones, the ossicles, which are the main inhabitants of the middle ear, a one-half-inch-wide cavity, still air-filled, between the outer and inner ear.

Middle Ear Mechanics

The three bones, the malleus (hammer), the incus (anvil), and the stapes (stirrup) are the three smallest bones of the body, the stapes weighing only four ten-thousandths of an ounce. Yet their small size belies their powerful function, which is to carry sound waves across the barrier from air to water.†

The hammer's handle, the manubrium, sits on the upper part of the eardrum's back along a radius that runs from the apex to the upper rim. When the eardrum moves, the hammer's handle moves with it, and so

---

† The middle ear is sealed in by the eardrum. Air pressure differences would build up within it if it did not have some other connection with the outside world. This is provided by a cartilaginous canal, the Eustachian tube, which extends from the middle ear into the throat and automatically opens when you swallow. This is why you swallow a few times when you go through a tunnel or take off in a plane or even suffer a fast elevator ride. Your middle ear can then adjust to the rapid pressure changes going on outside.

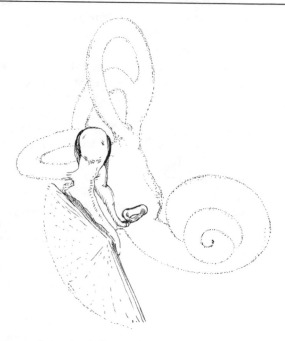

The handle (manubrium) of the malleus rests on the eardrum. The head of the malleus articulates with the body of the incus, which in turn communicates with the head of the stapes. The footplate of the stapes rests on the oval window of the cochlea.

closely does the hammer's ball-shaped head fit the cuplike anvil socket that this too moves as though all three were one, finally delivering a mechanical blow to the head of the stirrup which drives its footplate against a small membranous surface, the oval window, of the inner ear.

A closer inspection reveals even more the remarkable ingenuity of this arrangement. The added weight of the hammer handle on the eardrum makes the drum sway in its motions, rotating on an axis that is roughly tangent to its upper rim. Ligaments holding the malleus and incus in place restrict their movements to rotations around this same axis, too. Their weight, in turn, is distributed so that they can balance at a point very close to the center of rotation. This makes them look misshapen with lumpy heads and longish handles, but the result is that they don't rattle when you turn your head. Their position also helps cut out unwanted body sounds which can bypass the middle ear and travel directly to the inner ear along the bones of the skeleton.

Further, two tiny muscles, one for the malleus and one for the stapes, tighten up reflexively when loud sounds (strong pressures) hit

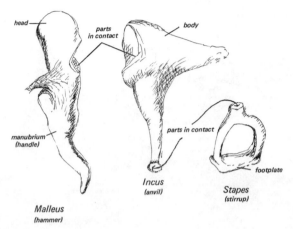

head

parts in contact

body

manubrium (handle)

parts in contact

footplate

Incus (anvil)

Stapes (stirrup)

Malleus (hammer)

The bones of the middle ear, separated to show their complex shapes and areas of contact.

the ear. This restrains the bones' movements and helps prevent the transmission of harmful blows that could damage the inner ear.

Though the ossicles work like a chain of levers, their combined efforts produce an effect more like a hydraulic press. The lever action reduces the amplitude of the sound waves a little, but the main job the bones accomplish is delivering the pressure originally applied to the whole eardrum surface to the tiny surface of the oval window, only one-twentieth as large. The net result is a twenty-two-fold increase in pressure.

The situation is comparable to the difference between the surface area of a man's rubber heel and a lady's spike heel: his won't make a dent in the floor because his weight is spread over a few square inches, but the heel of a woman of the same weight concentrates force over a fraction of a square inch.

This increase in pressure is what brings off the trick of letting sound energy pass from air to water. Technically the sound waves have the added power to match the greater "impedance" of the water molecules.

Inside the Inner Ear

The footplate of the stapes sits neatly on the oval window surface attached to it by a ligament around the rim. The ligament allows the stapes to move more freely at the front than at the back, so when pressure is applied to the bone it doesn't push the window in uniformly.

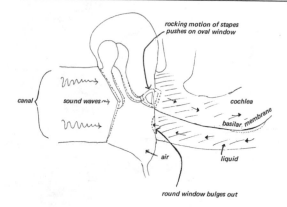

This illustration shows the action of the eardrum and ossicles when sound waves hit the ear. When the drum moves in (dotted lines), the ossicles translate the motion to the footplate of the stapes, resting on the oval window. The ligament fixing the stapes to the window is more firmly attached at one end than at the other, so that the footplate rocks in the window like a pendulum. Almost at once the pressure wave circulates through the cochlea and causes the round window to bulge out. The action of the ossicular chain and the reduction in area from the eardrum to the stapes' footplate results in a 22-fold increase in the pressure of the sound waves when they reach the oval window.

The "heel" moves very little, while the "toe" presses in making the oval window swing in like a door on a hinge. This swinging or rocking movement starts the vibratory movements in the fluids, which will eventually be perceived as sound in the brain.

Between that start and that perception lies a gulf that has occupied the attention of physicists as well as biologists for well over a hundred years. For the inner ear has everything working against the chance to conduct a careful scientific analysis. It is tiny. Your hi-fi equipment is packed into a fluid-filled snail-shaped shell, the cochlea, half an inch across at its base, about an inch away from the oval window, and rising only a quarter of an inch to its apex. It is also hidden. Your hi-fi system is literally built into the temporal bones of the skull. This gives it fine protection and insulation, of course, but makes it a nuisance to investigate.

Even after accomplishing the tedious task of removing the bone with jeweler's tools a more delicate job awaits the scientist. For the cochlea is not just fluid-filled. Through it winds a soft wormlike tube, the cochlear duct, coiling the full two and three-fourths turns of the shell, separating each turn into top and bottom ramps except at the very top where the tube ends. This soft membranous tube, itself fluid-filled, holds the organ of Corti (named after an Italian anatomist, the Marchese Alfonso Corti, who discovered it as late as 1851), the structure that contains the all-important sensing hair cells and the auditory nerve endings. So complex and yet so obscure is this sensing mechanism that Georg von Békésy, who won the Nobel Prize in 1962 for his researches on hearing, tells the story of a biologist friend beginning to do work on the ear who remarked that it took him "over a month to find the organ of Corti."

From the moment of Corti's discovery, however, it was clear that what happened to the organ was crucial, and sooner or later every theory of hearing would have to describe its functions in detail. It was easy enough to say that movements in the cochlear fluids triggered by the footplate of the stapes jiggled the cochlear duct, and that these

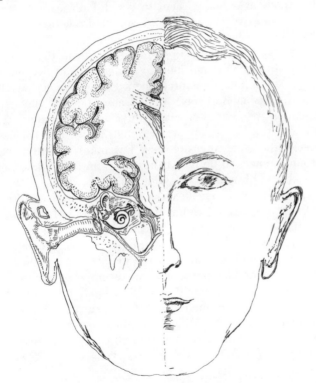

The approximate sizes and positions of the internal parts of the ear in the head. The cross section of cortex immediately above the inner ear structures is a portion of the temporal lobe. Auditory fibers eventually reach this part of the brain after a circuitous route.

jiggles were felt along the surface of the organ of Corti by the hair cells. This mechanical action would be the immediate stimulus to the cells just as though they were touch or pressure receptors on the skin or in other parts of the body. The crux of the matter was what were these jiggles really like. Very early on it appeared that sounds at certain frequencies only jiggled certain cells. If the cochlea was damaged toward the base, the high notes were cut out; if toward the apex, the low notes were eliminated.

Nowadays much more is known of the inner ear's detecting skills: if you transmit complex sounds to it, be they the full harmonies of a symphony, the more restricted range (800 to 2,000 cycles per second) of conversation, or the random jumble of frequencies that constitutes noise, the cochlea can pick out the dominant notes (composed of one or more sounds of pure frequencies or tones). It can add frequencies to produce combination tones or subtract them to get difference tones—those you hear as beats when two close notes are sounded together. If you try to simplify its job by playing a pure frequency to it, it seems able to complicate things all by itself, supplying multiples of that frequency to produce harmonics (whole multiples of a fundamental frequency) of its own. (To give the hi-fi manufacturers their due one would have to admit that the ear distorts sounds, too.) At the same time the cochlea notices how loud sounds are. The interplay of these two, pitch and intensity, is not simple, and the ear is not perfect: high notes may be masked by middle ones of the same intensity; very low notes as well as very high ones need more power to be heard than tones in the middle range, but by and large the cochlea manages, and manages very well.

The small size of the cochlea, the difficulty of making direct observations in living animals, as well as the uncertainties of drawing conclusions about tissue once it has been dissected have created severe difficulties for researchers. All theories of hearing that have evolved since the time of Corti have had to wait until the methods, the microscopy, and measuring equipment had improved. As recently as twenty-five years ago the English neurophysiologist A. F. Rawdon-Smith could write that there had been no physical model built of the ear that did not bear out the theories of the builder—and there were many builders.

Issues are not completely resolved today, but at least scientists have a better idea of what the cochlea looks like.

A Wedge-Shaped Worm

The worm which winds through the spiral turns of the snail shell is more wedge shaped than round. If uncoiled it would be about one and one-

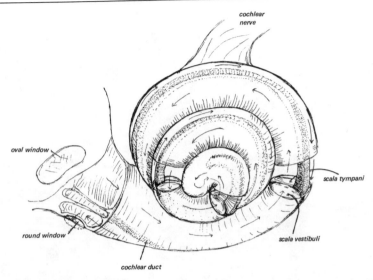

The human cochlea, partially cut away to show the wedge-shaped cochlear duct between the scala vestibuli and the scala tympani. The duct ends at the apex of the cochlea, leaving a small space where the scalae meet.

half inches long. Its flat top surface is formed by a fine double-layered membrane called Reissner's membrane. Its curving outer face is made up of a blood-rich tissue, the *stria vascularis*, which lines a ligament that follows the bony, curving wall of the shell, and hence is called the spiral ligament. The duct's bottom surface is formed by the basilar membrane, a fibrous, moist carpet which attaches to the spiral ligament at its outer edge and to a bony shelf jutting out from the central core of the shell on the inside. This floor, with the duct riding on it, effectively divides each turn of the snail shell into two ramps—an upper scala vestibuli (scala means staircase) and a lower scala tympani—both of which contain perilymph, a water-and-salt solution very much like cerebrospinal fluid. The cochlear duct itself contains endolymph, more viscous than the perilymph and differing from it in salt content. This portion of it is called scala media. It takes up most of the duct, bathing the minuscule portion of it which is the organ of Corti.

A House of Cards on a Flying Carpet

The organ itself is a humpbacked conglomeration of cells that rides on the carpet of the basilar membrane as it flies through the turns of the cochlea. The hump is shaped by stacks of rod-shaped cells leaning in

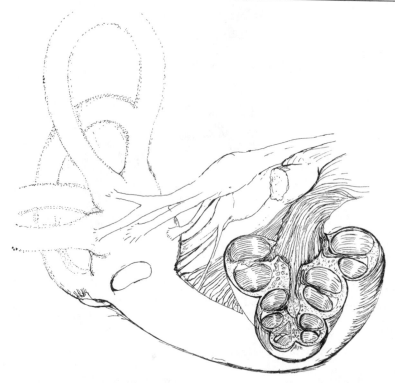

A view of the cochlea of the right ear, in place with the top removed. Note how the oval window leads into the widest basal turn of the shell. There are approximately two and three-quarter coils, which if stretched out would be close to two inches long. Each bony turn of the cochlea encloses the ramps of the scala vestibuli and scala tympani. Separating them is a shelf of bone and membrane, atop which lies the organ of Corti and the scala media of the cochlear duct.

The membranous cochlear duct winds through the bony shell. Attached to it are the auditory nerve fibers of the spiral ganglion.

toward each other as though the flying carpet had a house of cards built on it. Against this buttress stand the flasklike hair cells, their feet cushioned by cells on the basilar membrane, their bodies and hair stems caught in a stiff tangle of fibrous cells called the reticular lamina, and their fine hair tips grazed over by still another delicate surface, the tectorial membrane. This membrane is hinged along its inner edge to the limbus, a shelf that projects from the inner core. Toward the hinge, on the innermost side of the house of cards, stands one row of inner hair cells. Flanking the other side of the house are several more rows of outer hair cells, their number depending on the width of the basilar membrane—which, in confusing contradiction of the shape of the snail shell itself, starts out narrower at the base (so there are three rows of outer hair cells) and widens toward the apex (where there are five).

Tinker to Evers to Chance

When the footplate of the stapes kicks the oval window the compression is felt by the perilymph of scala vestibuli. It has no place to go but down, pushing Reissner's membrane. This in turn pushes the endolymph, and so bearing down on the basilar membrane, finally pushes the perilymph of scala tympani. Here there is an escape hatch—a tiny round window, membranous like the oval one above it, and like it, opening into the middle ear. When the compressional wave reaches the round window, it bellies out. The space is so small and the speed of sound so fast that a push in at the oval window is almost instantly accompanied by a push out at the round. The net effect on the cochlear duct is to push it down and bulge it slightly toward the round window.

That is still only a crude description of what happens when a sound wave disturbs the cochlea. It explains a little how the duct jiggles but it is not enough. In truth the presence of the duct, with its variation in thickness, mass, and elasticity, creates a more subtle stumbling block for sound. And since of all its structures the one most sensitive to movement, most varied in dimensions throughout its length, and most intimately associated with the organ of Corti is the basilar membrane, interest came to focus on it. To figure out how the basilar membrane responded to sound would be to deduce the selective behavior of the organ of Corti. The basilar membrane became the driving force for the organ, and hence for all theories of hearing. In retrospect they pay charming tribute to the mathematics, mechanics, and music of the nineteenth century—the century of Brahms and Beethoven, of Fourier and Morse, of Helmholtz and Bell.

For Hermann von Helmholtz, physicist, physiologist, writer on

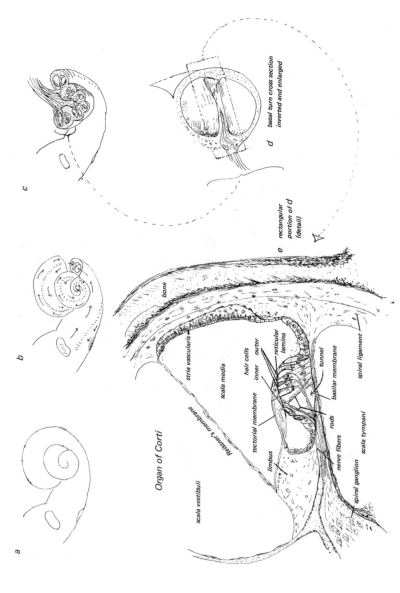

These drawings summarize the anatomy of the cochlea, culminating in the details of the organ of Corti, which forms only a minute part of the whole.

a

b

c

d   basal turn cross section
    inverted and enlarged

e   rectangular
    portion of d
    [detail]

Organ of Corti

scala vestibuli

Reissner's membrane

stria vascularis

scala media

tectorial membrane

limbus

hair cells
inner   outer

reticular
lamina

rods

nerve fibers

tunnel

basilar membrane

spiral ligament

spiral ganglion   scala tympani

bone

optics and vision as well as on sound and music, the basilar membrane was a piano whose fibers were tuned like the instrument's long, medium, and short strings so that they would resonate sympathetically when stimulated by tones of just the right frequency.

Resonance works like getting a push when you're on a swing. You've been swinging along at your own rate rising to a fixed height at each cycle. Along comes a friend who pushes just at the right moment, at the end of one cycle, and the swing arcs to new heights.

All bodies have a characteristic resonant frequency determined by their volume, mass, tension, and so on. These features are carefully built into the design of a piano or a violin's strings or the air-filled pipes of organs or horns. Ordinarily the oscillations are much too small to be seen or felt but when played upon by external forces they become evident. This is why a plate rattles when the air conditioner is turned on, or why you hear sounds of the sea when you hold a seashell to your ear (the shell's shape amplifies those random airborne noises that sound like waves). This is also why the Tacoma Narrows Bridge in the state of Washington collapsed a few decades ago. Sympathetic resonances started it vibrating violently. Resonant properties are at work in your outer and middle ear cavities too: they are in large measure responsible for the keenness of your hearing at the range of 800 to 6,000 cps that includes the human voice.

Helmholtz believed that either the transverse fibers of the basilar membrane or the humped arrangement above them resonated selectively. By a simple extension of this idea it seemed clear to him that complex sounds could be broken down in this way into simple combinations of pure tones. This was in line with the beautiful mathematical theory worked out by the French mathematician Fourier, who derived a theorem which says in effect that any complex periodic function can be reduced to sums or differences of simple harmonic (sine or cosine) waves. Helmholtz proposed that the ear was capable of such Fourier analysis.

Helmholtz used these ideas as a basis for a physiological theory of harmony, a latter-day variant on the harmony-of-the-spheres philosophy of the Greeks. The reason certain sound combinations sounded pleasing to the ear—consonances—could be explained by the ear's anatomy. The whole scale of Western music—the octave with the eighth note double in frequency over the first and the others arranged in ratios of three to two, four to three, etc.,—was clearly a consequence of the structure of the inner ear. All this was very beautiful to Helmholtz the mathematician and physicist, and, he supposed, equally so to the composer and the listener.

Helmholtz was a nineteenth-century scientist and philosopher living in the golden age of German musical composition. It was natural for him to try to relate or to explain the emotional impact of music in terms of the physiology of the body. He lectured at Bonn (Beethoven's birthplace), describing why the ear was sympathetic to the consonances and harmonies of music, and how this created a sense of well-being in the listener. Dissonances, on the other hand, jarring notes and discords, would evoke sadness or the negative passions.

Such neat syntheses of art and physiology are no longer possible in a world in which musicologists and anthropologists have made us aware of the many different scales or modes of music which have arisen among the world's peoples. Chinese operas and Zulu chants usually sound very strange to Western ears, yet neither the Chinese nor the Zulus possess an ear which is anatomically or neurologically different from ours.

Hearing à la Bell

Not long after Helmholtz proposed his resonance theory the telephone was invented and by 1886 a physicist, W. Rutherford, had proposed a telephone theory of hearing. In this the basilar membrane was supposed to undergo major bulges in and out, moving as a whole like the disk diaphragm in the mouthpiece of a telephone. The cochlea and organ of Corti would then mimic perfectly whatever sound waves were applied to it and pass the information to the brain for analysis there. Loudness, rather hard to explain in the Helmholtz theory, could be easily accommodated in terms of more excessive bulgings of the basilar membrane.

As time went on advancing techniques created embarrassments and then emendations of the theories, while still others came into being. J. R. Ewald suggested a complicated theory in which the basilar membrane might permit standing waves to be set up. These are waves that move back and forth in a chamber closed or confined at both ends, sometimes reinforcing, sometimes canceling each other. Waves you stir up in a bathtub can do this, so do waves set reverberating in a string fixed at both ends. These are the basis for the harmonic overtones produced by violins and other bowed or plucked instruments. Later on von Békésy, experimenting with a variety of materials, proposed that traveling waves might exist. These are the kind of waves that are produced if a cord is snapped that is fixed at one end.

A refinement that seemed to weight the odds heavily in favor of the telephone theory came in 1930 when E. G. Wever and C. W. Bray, working in the Princeton University Psychological Laboratory, discovered a dazzling talent of the cochlea. They were trying to measure electrical responses in the auditory nerve of a cat after stimulating the

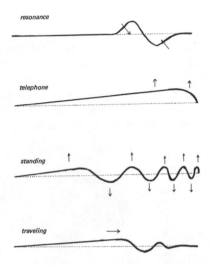

cat's ear with a variety of sounds. What they picked up from their electrodes and read out on the oscilloscope was an exact duplicate of the sound input—so perfect a record of the complex wave form, following it in frequency and amplitude, that a person looking at it could identify who had spoken or what sound had been used. The cochlea was a true microphone reacting exactly like the carbon mike of the telephone, transforming the instantaneous movements of the diaphragm into electrical voltage changes.

This seemed the crucial blow to the resonance theory of Helmholtz, but it was shown, by Lord Adrian and others in the early thirties, that whatever mimicry the cochlea was capable of, it wasn't passing it on to the nerve. Nerve fibers cannot send variable signals to the brain. A nerve cell that fires down its axon, if it fires at all, fires a spike that is always the same height, and its rate of firing is determined biologically. It has a fatigue, or refractory, time following the discharge of a signal in which it can't fire. This refractory period varies, but is of the order of a thousandth of a second, much too slow to transmit a high frequency sound wave of, say, 10,000 cycles per second.

Even this hurdle was cleared by a modification of the Wever-Bray theory in which the basilar membrane is still considered to respond as a whole to frequency. Instead of burdening one nerve cell with the impossible task of firing 10,000 times a second, a group of cells might respond to the first wave of a train, firing synchronously like a platoon of soldiers. A second group might respond to the second wave, a third to the third, or possibly even the first group, having had time to reload, would be ready to fire again in time to the third wave. The result would be regular volleys of impulses timed to give an exact duplicate of the frequency of the incoming sound.

A striking experiment by S. S. Stevens of Harvard University and Halowell Davis of the Central Institute for the Deaf in St. Louis, Missouri, supported this. At frequencies up to about 850 cycles, the auditory nerve showed a constant high amplitude wave form as though all the fibers were able to respond synchronously to every wave of the incoming signal. But at 850 cycles the amplitude dropped abruptly to

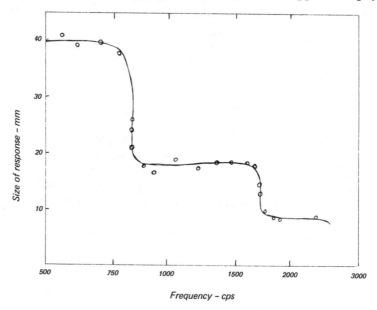

Frequency – cps

An experiment of S. S. Stevens and Halowell Davis in 1936 supported the volley principle. At frequencies up to about 850 cycles, the auditory nerve showed a high amplitude waveform, as though all fibers were responding synchronously to every wave of the incoming sound signal. The amplitude dropped by half in the region between 850 and 1,700 cycles, as though half the fibers were now firing to the first, third, fifth, etc., waves the other half to the second, fourth, sixth, etc. At 1,700 cycles another half drop came, as though the cells were now divided into three platoons.

half the height, as though now first and second platoons were at work with half the fibers firing in time to the first wave, the other half to the second. At 1,700 cycles another sudden half drop came, as though the cells were now divided into three groups. Above 3,000 cycles the response was no longer synchronized and no regular amplitude could be recorded.

Space vs. Time

So it was that the resonance and the telephone theories, each with experimental evidence in its favor, each holding excitements and charms for its adherents, came to polarize points of view on hearing in much the same way as the particle vs. wave theory of light had occupied the attention of physicists since Newton's time.

For the science of hearing, it was virtually a space-time controversy: resonance meant that the ear reacted according to a particular place or space on the basilar membrane; the telephone theory postulated that the ear could count frequencies—timing the nerve fiber's response to match the signal. The situation was to remain unresolved until someone could unravel the mysteries of cochlea.

That someone was von Békésy. He didn't probe the ear, or even build physical or anatomical models of it at first. What he did was to observe what happened when he took a piece of rubber and played with it—varying its thickness, its tension, its elasticity. Then he observed what happened if he punched it delicately. He discovered that each of the rival theories of hearing could fit the model if he tinkered with it in certain ways.

The resonance theory fitted a moderately thick membrane which bulged slightly when depressed, and produced, looking from top down, a series of elliptical waves spreading out from the disturbance. A slightly thicker membrane would bulge as a whole producing almost circular rings. This would be in accordance with the telephone theory. A thinner membrane fitting his own theory showed traveling waves, while an even thinner one produced standing waves à la Ewald.

The key question then was what were the true dimensions, technically the volume elasticity, of the basilar membrane.

Von Békésy managed to cut away the bone, put in transparent windows, and photograph the basilar membrane of a guinea pig ‡ with a stroboscope camera. This camera is fitted with a rotating disk with holes in it, which can be set in motion fast enough so that the lens shutter clicking just as light enters a single hole will arrest the motion of an object moving too fast for the eye to see. Von Békésy had to combine his camera with a microscope, of course, since the whole of the guinea pig's inner ear is, as he described it, "no bigger than a drop of water at the end of a medicine dropper," and he had to devise special cements to fix his lens in the watery fluids bathing the cochlea, but for the first time someone was able to see and to photograph the object of speculation.

‡ The guinea pig is a model animal for hearing research. Although its cochlea is smaller and has four turns to it, it is more accessible, not completely buried in bone.

175

What he saw confirmed his theory. Traveling waves move down the cochlea.

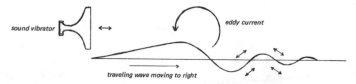

The initial movements are in phase with the movements at the oval window, but because the basilar membrane is narrower and thicker at the base end (100 times less elastic than at the apex) the movements act as a whip for the rest of the membrane, building up to a maximum wave peak, after which the waves are sharply damped. Von Békésy had feared that the action might be more complicated and that other kinds of waves might exist or interact. Instead he found almost pure traveling waves combined with small eddies in the fluid, currents of water turning in circles near the region of maximum amplitude. When he played upon the basilar membrane with high frequencies the peak region moved closer to the base end; lower frequencies peaked out toward the apex. Here, then, was direct evidence in favor of the space theorists.

But—and this was a very big but—the positions of the maximum peak were not sharp. The traveling waves grew to a gentle rounded peak.

Von Békésy reasoned that other mechanisms must be at work. One idea that immediately suggested itself was inhibition: the brain may be able to localize the peak sharply by cutting out signals from surrounding nerve cells. The same sort of phenomenon exists in touch endings in the skin and in the eye—else whatever we looked at closely would have a halo around it—so why not in the ear. This time von Békésy built a model cochlea which he placed against his own forearm as a nerve source. The model was a plastic tube filled with water and fitted with a membrane one foot long. It responded to vibrations with traveling waves and had a range of two octaves. To his surprise the area of skin that felt stimulated when he activated the model was only about an inch long—even though the waves moved throughout the model with very little difference in amplitude. At high frequencies the area of sensation moved toward the piston end, the vibration source; at low frequencies it moved away. Even more surprising was the degree of sensitivity of the model: it needed only two wave cycles to elicit a sharply localized response on the skin.

The verification of the traveling wave hypothesis has helped enormously in clearing up the problems inherent in middle and high frequency analysis. It does not rule out certain aspects of the volley theory

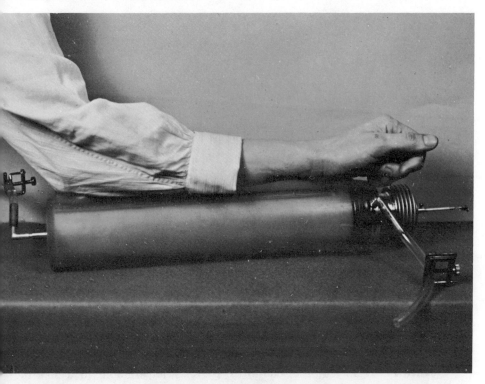

Von Békésy designed a model of the human cochlea which he tested against his own arm as a nerve supply. The vibratory sensations he felt were surprisingly localized, even though the traveling waves which moved down the model showed no sharp peak but rather a flat maximum. When the frequency of the vibratory stimulus was increased, the sensation moved down his arm toward the piston end of the model (at right); this represented the stapes footplate of the ear. At lower frequencies the area of sensation moved in the opposite direction.

for low and middle frequencies, however, as the Stevens-Davis experiment indicates.

Still more recently a third mechanism for frequency analysis of high frequency sound waves has shown up in Davis's "summating potential." The idea here is that beyond a certain point, about 10,000 cps, cells may no longer be able to react to individual vibrations, so complex and fast are they, but instead may respond to the general shape of their wave forms—what is known in mathematics as the "envelope."

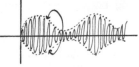

envelope

In the end the resolution of space and time theories was achieved, as it was in physics, through a combination of the two—holding on to both, and not finding it surprising that the ear carries on this duplex (or, if we add the summating potential, triplex) analytic theory.

One might well ask at this point why this degree of complication. The answer is probably phylogenetic. As animals evolved more complex nervous systems the tendency has been to pile the new developments on top of layers already established. Because hearing itself is a relatively new sense reaching its full development only in mammals, the application here is not so clear-cut, but the direction of development from low to high frequency is. In fish, in reptiles, and in some birds hearing is neither subtle nor extended (the top range is about 2,000 cycles), and the mechanism seems more closely related to vibratory, touch, and balance senses. The low frequency response in man may be a direct outgrowth of these. But if an extension to higher frequencies was to prove useful, new neurological equipment would have to evolve to handle it.

Halowell Davis in summing up this state of affairs points out that this overlay of new on old may confound man's understanding but is probably important to the brain in its analysis of auditory information. In the overlap region of 500 to 4,000 cycles, for example, in which the inner ear responds to stimuli both through volleys and according to place, the brain receives added information about the signal in terms of the time delay between the initial platoon volleys and the time it takes for a traveling wave to reach the peak region of the basilar membrane. That nature wastes nothing is a safe rule to follow.

Davis' reasoning introduces the next and most exciting phase of hearing research today: how information about sound is coded in the auditory nerve fibers and processed in the brain. It's as though science, having devoted a century to tracking down the first step—how the cochlea acts as a mechanical frequency analyzer—was now ready to tackle the rest of the course.

Initial Coding: By a Living Battery?

The functioning of the cochlea is still not perfectly understood. There are still unexplained subtleties in its operation, among them the initial translation of sound waves (mechanical vibrations) to electricity. The simplest explanation would be that the bending of the tips of the hair cells alters the cells' internal electric charge, and starts a flow of electricity directly into the uninsulated nerve fibers. These reach out from cell bodies in the core of the cochlea and grasp the hair cells by their roots. When the charge in the neuron builds up sufficiently it could then fire the all-or-none spike down the fiber it sends toward the brain as part of the collection that makes up the auditory nerve—the eighth cranial, or cochlear, nerve.

But because the nerve cells can often fire for some time after sounds have stopped, there is reason to believe that the real source of power may not be the hair cells—they lack the necessary juice—but the surrounding endolymph. Unlike all the other fluids which bathe the cells of the body, the endolymph in the cochlear duct has a high potential. Some authorities think it could be a living battery, constantly recharged by the bloodstream, that is simply tapped in selected spots by the hair cells and pumped to the favored neurons.

"Favored" implies another subtlety of cochlear action. A close look at the hair tips reveals that they don't all move in the same direction. When the basilar membrane starts vibrating, it gets stretched in two directions, crosswise and lengthwise. The crosswise stretch tugs the tectorial membrane the same way (it and the basilar membrane are hinged to the same bony core). But the reticular lamina in between feels a shearing force. Since this layer holds the necks of the hair cells, while the tectorial membrane touches their tops, the tips are caught and bent in a squeeze play. Those in the region of maximum movement are bent radially, out from the axis of the cochlea. But because the basilar membrane is a continuous strip (and the traveling wave has a flat maximum), other hair tips are bent longitudinally, an arrangement which Davis thinks may help sharpen the area of maximum stimulation. Perhaps only the nerve cells in touch with the radially bent hair cells are excited, while the others are inhibited.

From this point on the activity will be electrical, read off as so much potential picked up from groups of nerve fibers, or, by means of microelectrodes, from single cells or fibers. All this takes place against a changing background of brain activity.

Now the problem will be to find out what the brain does with auditory signals that enables a person to recognize "The Star-Spangled Banner" on the first "Oh-o-say," to feel the powerful crescendos of a Verdi aria, or on a more practical level to know that when one hears a mosquito's whine around the ankle one is in imminent danger of being bitten.

These basic measures of sound—frequency (pitch), intensity (loudness), and direction—must all be built into the pulses and pathways of nerve fibers in the brain, and ultimately fused into a sound "picture," just as colors, brightness, and shapes fuse into the images we see.

Indeed, comparing the two senses is exciting in the light of the most recent experiments. For the brain may show a beautiful symmetry

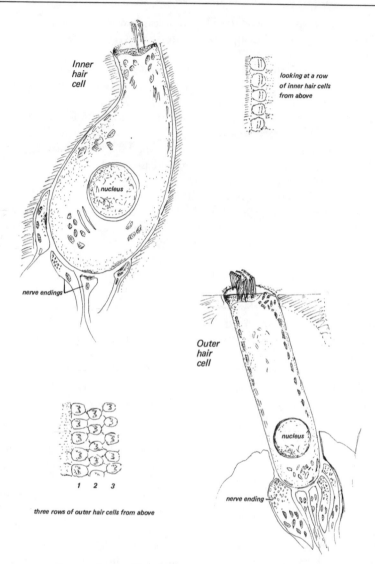

Inner hair cell

looking at a row
of inner hair cells
from above

nucleus

nerve endings

Outer hair cell

nucleus

nerve ending

1   2   3

three rows of outer hair cells from above

The inner and outer hair cells of the organ of Corti are different in structure and in hair arrangement. The flask-shaped inner cells have two rows of hairs arranged parallel to the long axis of the basilar membrane. The outer cells are more cylindrical in shape and have three rows of hairs that form a W pattern, when viewed from above. Investigators believe these variations may have functional significance. The inner hairs may be more suited to shearing movements in a radial direction; the W-shaped outer hairs may be sensitive to longitudinal and oblique as well as radial movements.

in its behavior: certain cells in its auditory centers noting how signals change in time, other cells in its visual centers noting how signals shift in space. But this is presumed to take place at the cortical level. A good many things happen to auditory signals before they get that far—probably more things than happen to any other incoming messages. No other sense system of the body makes as many stop-offs en route to the cortex, splits and branches so extensively as to supply information from each ear to both sides of the brain. The auditory system is also particularly richly supplied with feedback loops, circuits that can control its own activity at any stage.

Some of this geographical complexity may have occurred as a result of the late development of the sense of hearing. Harlow W. Ades of the School of Engineering at the University of Illinois suggests that

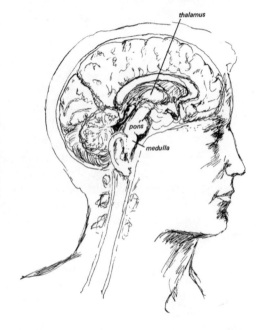

The auditory nerve enters the brain at the medulla level. From there the pathways ramify in the pons, midbrain, diencephalon, and temporal lobe of the cortex, anatomically near the external ear itself.

the pathways squeezed in where best they could in a brain already teeming with traffic. That might explain why simply following the "classic" pathways described by the great Spanish neurophysiologist Ramon y Cajal is like driving from Rome to Florence: the beeline distance isn't great, but the road wanders through many hill towns in between.

On the other hand it's safe to assume that the nervous system doesn't elaborate itself wantonly, and though the routes may be serpentine, their underlying complexity is undoubtedly there for a purpose.

181

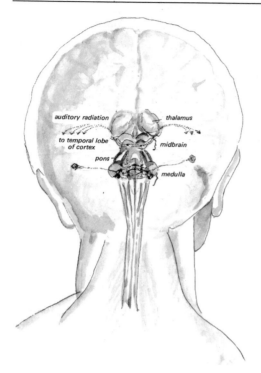

Some of the auditory path-ways as sketched from the rear. Fibers bearing impulses from one ear have a number of opportunities to make con-tact with relay stations on the opposite side of the head, so that by the time the cortex is reached each ear is repre-sented bilaterally. Not shown are the descending pathways, the multiple connections in the cerebellum or in the ret-icular formation (a complex web of nerve cells and fibers close to the midline of the brain).

The increase in relay stations, for example, may be a way of sorting information by providing short and long routes to the cortex. Some express messages will gain quick access to cortical cells, perhaps to be followed a fraction of a second later by a signal that has traveled a slower route. All of these factors may make a difference in the cortical cell's behavior.

Then too, hearing has at least one inherent problem that requires special handling. This is loudness, the measure of the strength or inten-sity of the sound stimulus. Usually the sense systems of the body respond to an increase in intensity—a brighter light, a stronger taste, a harder touch—by an increase in electrical activity, i.e., more cells firing more rapidly. In this way high frequencies of nerve impulses become associ-ated with high intensities of the stimulus. Alas for hearing, the frequency of firing in the nerve fiber has to some extent been pre-empted to tell us about pitch—the frequency of sound. Think of the platoons of cells firing in time to sounds between 15 and 4,000 cps. To code for loudness the auditory system may have had to put in extra cells and special routes and substations in the brain. Some of the cells may be back in the cochlea itself. These might be sluggish, high-threshold cells that would only respond to loud sounds, supernumeraries that help swell the chorus in the big scenes.

But not all sounds are matched in frequency by synchronous volleys of spikes. For higher tones there is also the frequency-according-to-place rule. This apparently applies to fibers inside the brain as well, especially in the early stages. In spite of their devious pathways, the fibers tend to follow the base to apex order of the first nerve cell fibers as they unreel from the cochlea to form the nerve. This would enable the brain to code pitch according to place, an arrangement called tonotopic ordering. Allowing for this kind of display while at the same time letting fibers branch and make contact with more than one cell at each relay station accounts for a good deal of the system's complexity.

So do projections of fibers into newly discovered areas or in directions away from the cortex, as in the feedback circuits. Here again hearing is special because it has two kinds of feedback. One that you may not be aware of is in control of all incoming sounds. The other you consciously or unconsciously make use of every time you open your mouth. Note how different hearing and vision are in this regard. Our faces and bodies are targets for other people's eyes, but only pale stimuli for our eyes. On the other hand we generate sounds. We speak and what we say is instantly monitored, heard as airborne sounds by our ears, and also conducted immediately to the inner ears by bones set into vibration by the vocal cords. (The reason recordings of our voices often sound disappointingly thin, compared to the sounds we hear when we speak, is that the bone-conducted sounds favor the sonorous low tones which the recorder can't pick up.)

Were it not for the ability to control the sound of our voices, we would have a hard time adjusting them to a noisy street corner or a quiet theater. We might even lose track of what we'd said. It would be extremely difficult for singers or musicians to keep on pitch while holding a note or correcting a faulty attack. No doubt much of the resentment that is unconsciously directed towards people who are hard of hearing stems from our having to speak "too loud," and in turn having to listen to voices that may be flat or monotonous, too soft or too loud, typical signs of the lack of this kind of feedback.

The situation is far worse for those born deaf. They have great difficulty learning to speak because they never hear sounds to mimic in the first place. When, with much effort they do learn, they forever lack the corrections and improvements that feedback permits.

This same feedback explains how you can show up a person who is shamming deafness. If you ask him to speak and at the same time play back to him a recording of his words delayed a few seconds in time, the person with normal hearing will soon be too confused to speak. The test is often used in settling insurance claims.

Some of these speech feedback circuits go through the cerebellum, that center of fine muscle control, to regulate the tensions on tongue and vocal cords. The cerebellum also figures in some feed-forward circuits, too, several of them not noted by Cajal. Some are involved in the reflexes of hearing, your automatic ability to turn your eyes, or your head, or even your whole body, toward the source of sound. Some are acquired habits: you learn to follow the drill sergeant's commands in the army, or do exercises to the "one-two, one-two" of a gym teacher, all through intricate connections between auditory, visual, and motor pathways co-ordinated in the cerebellum.

Still another sound-receiving station not noted by Cajal lies in the broad stream of tangled fibers that forms the reticular activating system. This system communicates with, and to some extent controls, the flow of information from all the sense systems of the body. In this way it contributes to the general state of arousal or alertness of an individual. Sound inputs here probably explain why you wake up when an alarm clock goes off.

As for the other kind of feedback, the control over what your ears are picking up elsewhere, as opposed to the sounds you yourself make, the auditory system again excels. It appears now that paralleling auditory fibers at every stage of ascent in the brain are descending tracts, fibers that can modify incoming activity.

One of the first to discover these fibers was Grant Rasmussen, Chief of the Section on Functional Neuroanatomy at the National Institute of Neurological Diseases and Blindness of the National Institutes of Health in Bethesda, Maryland. The original fiber tract he found in the cat, "Rasmussen's bundle," runs from the second relay station in the medulla, a cluster of cells called the (superior) olive (due to its rough approximation to the shape of an olive), down to the cochlea itself, where the slim bundle of 500 fibers ramifies so extensively that it can reach out to contact all the nerve cells in the cat's cochlea and possibly the hair cells as well.

Here may be the means for Davis's or von Békésy's inhibitory mechanism that makes it possible to pinpoint frequency so accurately. Here, too, may be the reason we have such sophisticated control over sound. We can inhibit the noise at a cocktail party and instead pay particular attention to what we want to hear.

An English engineer at the University of London, Colin Cherry, believes that the auditory system's ability to discriminate meaningful sounds against a noisy background may depend on the timing of the

184

inputs. Experimentally, he has shown that individuals can discern words or sentences piped into one ear while noise is piped into the other, as long as the word flow precedes the beginning of noise by a fraction of a second. He suggests that the meaningful message must precede the noise.

More recently Rasmussen and others have been able to fix the location of these feedback circuits in higher stations of the brain. They seem to cluster in the dorsal parts of the various cell groups, where they can reach out to control activity in the ventrally located cells. The caboose runs the train.

The Last Station

The foregoing description gives some idea of the kind of fine control the brain exercises over auditory signals from the moment a sound is heard. The evidence suggests that the brain depends on timing, inhibitory mechanisms, and on particular locations in the system in its act of perception.

It was this last point, particular locations, that was spotlighted when attention turned toward the final relay station of auditory signals in the cortex. Cortical research always begins when an area is discovered which responds differentially to certain kinds of stimuli. That was how D. Ferrier first found the auditory centers of a cat's brain in 1876. He stimulated certain parts of the cortex electrically and noticed that the cat's ears picked up. But the search for locations in the cortex has been carried on in a narrower sense: experimenters have combed the auditory areas for precise localizations of frequency, the tonotopic pattern. Harlow Ades and others think this tendency is in part the heritage of Helmholtz. Ever since the cochlea was likened to a piano there has been a deep, and probably excessive, concern for pure tones, and hence frequencies, to the exclusion of other qualities of sound.

The experimental history of the last generation or two has been rife with maps of the auditory cortex, and each map has tried to unfurl the cochlea in one way or another.

Unfortunately no two maps were alike. No matter what method was used, whether a study of the shapes and sizes of cells, direct electrical stimulation, severing fibers from other parts of the network to see the effect on the cortex, or using drugs like strychnine to suppress spontaneous brain activity and trigger special kinds of spikes, the results vary. Only the general auditory region in man has been agreed upon: an area in the temporal lobes of each hemisphere in and around a major infolding called the lateral fissure.

An experiment by Clinton Woolsey and E. M. Walzl in 1942 cleared up some of the confusion. They applied electrical stimulation to small groups of nerve cell fibers in the cochlea of the cat and observed where reactions showed up in the cortex. They found two tuning areas: a primary area, AI, in the form of a strip in which fibers from the basal turn of the cochlea were relayed to the anterior part of the strip while fibers at the apex found their way to the back; and an area AII, a smaller, less sensitive strip slightly forward and below AI, which showed the reverse order.

Subsequent studies changed the boundaries a little, added auxiliary territories, and introduced area EP, made up of the posterior parts of AI and AII and presumably functionally dependent on them. But Woolsey and Walzl's map and their terminology were both generally accepted to define the terrain of auditory cortex. Agreement on the tonotopic order within those boundaries however was not universal. Some investigators agreed in part, others introduced ideas of overlapping areas or extended the frequency range of cells in various subregions.

These theories led some investigators—a fair number of the distinguished map makers themselves—to suspect that the reason the cortex was proving so intractible with respect to frequency was that perhaps this was not its main concern. Certainly it was well known that the number of cells having other things to do with hearing besides frequency vastly increase as one ascends in the brain, so that by the time the cortex is reached, cells with responses solely dependent upon frequency and intensity are in the minority.

Furthermore subcortical studies had shown that tone-sensitive cells altered their behavior from station to station in ways that allowed for a good deal of information-processing. At the earliest brain station in the medulla, for example, the tone-sensitive cell generally shows a marked sensitivity to a particular frequency (its "characteristic" frequency) when the sound is barely audible. At increases in intensity the same cell frequently responds to lower tones as well.

At successively higher stations in the auditory pathways some investigators have found that the response interval (the "bandwidth" in radio language) of tone-sensitive cells narrows somewhat on the low-frequency side, but begins to extend upward so that a cell could now fire in response to louder and higher tones as well. At the cortex a cell would now be centered about its characteristic frequency but almost equally sensitive to other frequencies in a narrow interval. This arrangement at the cortical level would make it very hard to account for even average acuity in judging tones, much less the perfect pitch of some musicians.

Then in 1958 William Neff and his co-workers at the University of

Chicago reported the results of experiments in which they removed the auditory cortex in whole or in part from a variety of animals—dogs, monkeys, and cats, in particular—all animals with well-developed hearing. The cat's range extends to 70,000 cycles. The purpose was to see what effect this wholesale tissue removal would have on hearing. The answer was surprisingly little, at least as far as frequency was concerned. To be sure the cats needed retraining, but in time they learned to distinguish one tone from another. They had no problem judging loudness or softness either.

What they couldn't do, in spite of repeated attempts to train them, was to recognize patterns of tones; sequences of high-low-high could not be distinguished from low-high-low.

At about the same time a group of researchers that included Robert Galambos and colleagues at Yale, Yasuji Katsuki of Tokyo Medical and Dental University, and Ian C. Whitfield and Edward Evans of the Medical School of the University of Birmingham, England, began to implant microelectrodes into the brains of animals for the first time. Later they would work with them in unanesthetized, unrestrained

Microelectrodes implanted in the temporal lobe of a cat record single-cell activity as the cat listens to chirps, tones, and a variety of natural sounds in Evans' laboratory. The experimental use of microelectrodes in an unrestrained, unanesthetized animal proved far more revealing of cortical cell behavior than earlier techniques, leading to new hypotheses concerning auditory coding.

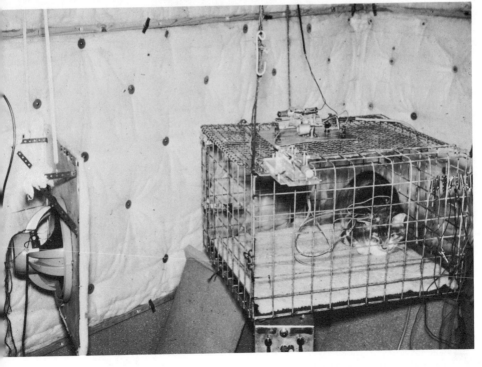

states, trying out more complicated types of sound stimuli. Not every experiment went all the way in simulating natural conditions, but little by little methods and equipment improved to free experiments from a variety of barriers to cortical recording: the deep anesthesia which suppresses much brain activity, and the rigid head-holding gear that prevents jostling the delicate microelectrodes as they probed the brain tissue. Finally the nature of the sounds themselves was refined. Researchers tried stimulating animals with natural sounds—chirps and clicks and scratchings, jangling keys and even kissing noises—to see what effect they would have on the animals.

Each step was a revelation. It was obvious that the cortex itself was less restrained. More cells came alive; more behaved in new, interesting ways. Galambos noted that only a general trend in frequency pattern could now be observed—low frequencies were concentrated in the posterior part of AI and high in the anterior, but there was a wide range of high and low frequency response between.

Then Evans and Whitfield published results of experiments with eighteen cats in which they were able to record the responses of 523 cortical cell units, primarily in AI. The cats were unrestrained, unanesthetized animals stimulated by a variety of sounds—pure tones, clicks (complex sounds of short duration), and changing tones—low to high, high to low, or else rhythmic rises and falls of a tone where the change was of the order of only 8 or 10 cycles in each undulation.

The results were impressive. Not only did a greater percentage of cells (85 percent of all units tested) respond than in earlier experiments with restrained or anesthetized cats, but of those responding more were excited by clicks or complex qualities of sound than by steady tones. Less than half the units responding to tones did so by simply turning on and staying on after the tone began and then stopping when the tone stopped. The majority were more specialized: Some turned on just at the beginning of the tone ("on" cells); others just at the end ("off" cells); others did both ("on-off" cells); some cells, previously active, became silent during the tone; some responded with a combination of these patterns; others only responded to a changing tone, a sweep up or down or a whole up-down-up cycle.

Moreover, these cells seemed partial to this latter kind of stimulus; i.e., tones whose frequency was changing. If they also responded to steady tones, the effect was usually less marked; the cells were less responsive or predictable and quick to adapt.

Also interesting was the fact that the cell's response interval sometimes broadened when a tone of changing frequency was introduced. While some cells were particularly active as the tone crossed the bound-

188

ary of their characteristic frequency interval, others proved responsive throughout as much as four octaves, indicating that their aim was not so much to select a particular frequency as to note in which direction of the scale the sound moved. David H. Hubel and Torsten Wiesel of Harvard had discovered a similar phenomenon with cells in the visual centers of the cortex: a concern for how lines or corners of figures may change position, i.e., move from left to right or up and down in the visual field regardless of their precise starting point.

What this suggests is that the cortex may be pre-eminently rich in cells that are not concerned with absolute qualities, but can discriminate relative changes; it can compare things rather than measure them against an arbitrary standard.

For hearing the comparison takes place in the dimension of time. At many subcortical stations cells can respond to certain qualities of sound which to some extent are independent of time, that is, they respond to a steady tone—the tuning fork that sounds in the air for several seconds. So a cat can learn to discriminate a high tone from a low one even when the top of its brain has been removed. Similarly prolonged loud and soft sounds can be distinguished. The cortex may be especially attuned to those accelerations in time, instantaneous changes of frequency, amplitude, and duration, wherever in the scale they occur. In short the cortex is paying attention just to those sounds which are not constant but varying all the time, and therefore, likely to be more interesting.

This could mean that the human brain is equipped with something akin to the sonar machinery presumed to be present in those mammals who use very sophisticated sound techniques for echo-location—the night-flying bats and the members of the whale and porpoise family. They transmit complex high and often varying frequency sounds and listen for the echoes these produce when they bounce back from objects, noting the variations in frequency and the time delays. Humans, cats, dogs, and other higher mammals may not actually transmit such signals but they may have this kind of FM (frequency modulated) receiver, capable of picking up sound signals that change every second.

This makes sense from the point of view of behavior. It is known that bats locate food by listening for echoes from tiny insects hit by their signals, while porpoises find their way in murky water in the same way. But it also makes sense to think of the highest centers of the cat's brain being tuned sharply to pick up the complex "FM" scrapes and chirps of mice, rather than the pure tones of a flute.

What is true for frequency may also be true for amplitude. Animals may be able to distinguish differences in loudness at substations of the brain, but the cortex may be necessary for continuously modulated amplitude. Your cortex may be an AM radio—amplitude modulated—as well.

Binaural Hearing

Still a third auditory talent that Neff's experiments suggest may only be possible with an intact cortex is the ability to locate a sound source instantly. Again if a sound stayed in one place and you were a cat without a cortex you might be able to turn your head, and by trial and error find out which ear felt the louder sound and what angle the head was making. Now it seems that particular cortical cells in each hemisphere are directional. Some fire only when the sound is on one side of the head, others when it is on the other, still others when the sound is on the midline, or when the cat is actually looking at and listening to the sound source.

These experiments point to the ability of the cortex to keep track of a moving sound source, monitoring the changes in position that occur in time. Neff and Colin Cherry (in his precedence experiments) have both suggested that this function of the cortex may be linked with a short-term memory.§

This is a powerful phenomenon which would go far to explain what otherwise seems an embarrassing amount of redundancy in the system: why both cortexes should be supplied with such great detail about what is going in each ear. So much is repeated that you could literally lose one side of your brain and not detect much difference in hearing acuity. With this double supply of information the cortex gives you stereo hearing. From an evolutionary point of view the stereo system is more efficient and faster. The gain in time is an aid to survival. You can quickly detect where food, friend, or foe may be and move one way or the other.

Unfortunately what is true at the brain's level does not extend to the receptor level: the redundancy of information received is still a function of both ears' good health. Hearing defects are far more common and are probably going to increase in a world growing noisier every day. At the moment there are 200,000 Americans who cannot hear the loudest

§ It is interesting to note that the temporal lobes on the whole have been implicated in long-term memory as well. In classic studies at the Montreal Neurological Institute Wilder Penfield found that when parts of the temporal lobe were stimulated in patients about to undergo brain surgery, they reported they were able to recall events that had happened long ago in almost perfect detail and sequential order.

conversation; they are technically deaf. Another 3 million are handicapped severely. And while it is true that every day brings new methods of surgery or drugs to alleviate or prevent some of the problems—especially those functional impairments or infections of the middle ear that are involved in the conductive stages of sound waves—the problem of sensory-neural or nerve deafness is less amenable, although some hearing aids can be of help in nerve deafness.

There is as yet no substitute for nature's solution of providing you with two ears. Indeed the virtue of the pair was noted 2,000 years ago by Epictetus the Stoic in an epigram science could affirm today: "God gave man two ears, but only one mouth, that he might hear twice as much as he speaks."

IX

A Euclidean World

Demonstrations of the balancing senses can seem bizarre: A professor holds a cat before a class. He lifts it in the air cradling it in his arms like a baby and then lets go. The cat lands on its feet and walks away. Next the professor opens the cage of a pigeon and twirls the bird around like a top. The bird suffers the indignity with aplomb, holding its head erect like a ballet dancer. Finally the investigator goes to a goldfish bowl. With an air of small boy mischief he flips a goldfish over on its side in the water. Almost at once the fish rights itself and swims away.

The class, having cheered the animals, waits to see what will happen next. But the professor is satisfied. He remarks, "You see the animals were never in any danger. They knew how to cope with the situation. And so, up to a point, would you."

The animals were reacting to strong forces—pushes or pulls that affected their position, motion, or direction in space. Man too can cope with such forces which are, technically, accelerations or decelerations. He has a pair of sense organs especially designed to respond to them. So automatically do these force detectors work that scientists were barely aware of their existence a century ago, and only today are working out the subtleties of their operations.

One of these detectors responds to gravity. It is the sense that tells you which way is up, or more directly, which way is down, for it senses the pull toward the center of the earth that makes all freely falling objects on the earth increase their speed by 32 feet a second during every second * of their drop. The same detector can sense straightforward (linear) changes in speed too. When you step on the gas pedal on a level country road or slow down at an intersection the change also registers on the gravity receptors.

The other force detector responds to angle changes when you're circling the floor in a night club, when a plane you're in banks for a turn, or when a boat starts to yaw, pitch, or roll. The same sense is at work when you nod your head "yes," shake it "no," or turn it to read a road sign when you're driving.

The job of these senses is not so much to report the exact measurements of the whirls, twirls, or G-forces you're feeling; they are not precise speedometers, tachometers, or accelerometers. Nor are they governors, mechanisms that automatically control speed or angle changes when they get out of hand. When you're on a Ferris wheel or riding in the back of a jeep, you have no means of control. Instead these force detectors do the next best thing: they try to compensate for the forces acting on you. They do all they can to keep your body balanced, your weight evenly distributed, your eyes focused on what you were looking at at the time the force disturbed you. In that sense they are balancing organs—striving to preserve your equilibrium in the face of change.

Balancing calls for fast timing and intricate muscle control, the earmarks of reflex activity. You probably neither think about nor notice that your knees straighten slightly when you go down in an elevator; that your left arm swings back as your right foot steps forward in walking; that your eyes slowly turn toward the rear as you survey the landscape from a train window, then quickly dart forward to take in the next bit of scenery as you move on.

The same kind of automation exists in other animals. A dog has never had to learn about bending its forepaws when you put his food dish in front of him. The familiar eating posture is a result of the dog's bending his head down, an act which trips signals to leg muscles that enable him to get closer to the food. The same trick works in reverse when he lifts his head to sniff what's in his master's hands. The forepaws automatically straighten to facilitate investigation.

---

* Usually abbreviated 32 ft/second^2.

In these cases the postural reflexes take their cues from the head, for this is the site of the balancing organs in mammals. You might surmise this if you could watch the cat's fall in slow motion. For what it does is to corkscrew through space. First the sensors indicate that the head is upside down, and reflexes are set in motion to right it. This stimulates neck muscles and neck-righting reflexes, followed by torso and hind part reflexes, the whole spiral completed with carefully controlled movements of legs and paws.

The cat of course is an exceptional animal, the apotheosis of balance, according to Dr. Werner Loewenstein of Columbia's College of Physicians and Surgeons. It owes at least a few of its nine lives to this talent, which is so extraordinary it can operate in pitch darkness. A blind cat[†] dropped down a well will still splash feet first. It is only when the balancing organs are removed that a cat suffers an unkind fate.

Man is not so instinctively adept at the art of balancing. The ballet dancer, the acrobat, and the high diver all have had to learn their skills. They use their eyes, or measure heights and distances ahead of time, so they can calculate their leaps, time their turns, and give themselves just enough of a push at the start to land in the right place at the right time. And in everyday activities it is so with the rest of us. We depend heavily on what our eyes and what the touch and pressure receptors in skin, limbs, and internal organs tell us about our body, so much so that the special skills of the balancing organs go unnoticed.

Steady States vs. Motion

Yet the balancing organs are part of our evolutionary heritage, and their location, in the inner ears on both sides of the head, bespeaks a tradition almost as old as locomotion itself. Consider for a moment the life of sea urchins, those quilled creatures that lurk at the bottom of the sea. Or the flowery sea anemones, barnacles, or the individual organisms that constitute corals. These are among the oldest forms of animal life, static forms in which the organism is attached to the same rock or anchored to the same piece of sandy bottom throughout its adult life. Behavior is clearly local. The anemone or urchin eats what drifts past it in the water. It may respond to light filtering through the water, or be chemically tuned to the presence of fellow organisms or of predators, but its total existence is quite unvaried. The Victorian mathematician E. A. Abbott [‡]

[†] But not a kitten. The righting reflex only matures after the kitten's eyes are open and the balancing organs have fully developed—after 33–36 days.

[‡] E. A. Abbott, *Flatland*. New York: Dover Publications, Inc., 1953.

amusingly described a comparable condition for points on a line: "[They are] forever cursed with the same neighbors and never able to step 'out of line.'" Naturally a strong wave may upset the urchin's roost and set it adrift a bit, but it soon settles down again.

In the next stage of evolution "roots" are given up and radical changes take place. The flower-round symmetries of urchins, anemones, and kindred species—marks of the sedentary life—give way to tentacles or fins, limb buds or feelers, that enable creatures to make their way in the water. A new symmetry develops, and with it a new order. A fish moves "forward" with a "head" end and "backs" up with a "tail," while the rest of it is distributed to "right" and "left." The front-back orientation becomes all important, determining the major saggital plane of the body. (Saggital comes from the Latin word for arrow; the concept is that if an arrow were shot through dead center from the rear to the head end it would make a vertical split down the middle.)

By the time evolution proceeds to the fish stage the head end has become the center of the various special sense organs used to explore the world and, along with them, a pair of organs that can monitor the body's position during that exploration.

When life moves to land and the streamlined shape of fish passes over into heads with separate necks, and dangling appendages, the balancing organs continue to attend to the position of the head, adding the complex circuitry that will guide the torso and loose hanging limbs.

These postural adjustments are of considerable importance in fleet-footed animals such as horses, giraffes, and deer, or in the sure-footed mountain goats and burros; they attain a state that is something close to perfection in the racing, leaping, and tree-climbing of cheetahs and ocelots, of jaguars, tigers, and other species of cats. But while the complex brains of such mammals may make them ideal for neurophysiological experiments, the real laurels for skilled maneuvers in space should be reserved for two older orders of life, fish and fowl.

The soaring flight of a tern or the crash dive of a shark are symbolic not only of superb evolutionary adaptation for motion, but a motion all the more impressive in its apparent defiance of gravity. Fish are heavier than water and ought to sink to the bottom. Birds have two feet and might be expected just to walk on the ground. Instead the two orders have developed ways of occupying new heights or depths in space, becoming creatures who truly live in three dimensions (as opposed to animals on the flat surface of the earth). Birds and fish are subject to frequent variations in the force of gravity. Individual species have favored levels, zones of activity where gravitational force, temperature, air or water currents, and available light are optimal. Staying within reasonable limits of that zone is important, and knowing which way they are straying, independent of any other sense, is essential. So the two balancing senses collaborate. The gravity organ becomes a kind of anchor, reeling out or pulling in so much line as the bird or fish changes level, or insuring the right end is up when it stands still. The rotary sense coordinates the flight or swim plan, supplying information and signaling compensatory reflexes as the creature wheels, dives, banks, or brakes in its daily excursions.

Euclid and Newton

What is fascinating is this: the way birds and fish as well as mammals detect positions or changes of position closely mirrors man's classical analysis of space. Euclid fashioned a solid geometry of points, lines, and mutually perpendicular planes usually drawn with the axes running up and down, right and left, and front and back. Descartes and Newton added algebra and calculus to the geometry so that any point in space could be located relative to the three axes, while the point's motion in a straight line or curve, subject to gravity or other forces, could be described in terms of simple equations. This is precisely the kind of information the inner ear organs are set up to supply. For all that each of our ultimate atoms may behave according to the twentieth-century theories of probability and relativity, the whole mass, bundled into the body's comparatively slow everyday motions, works in the classic modes of Euclidean geometry and Newtonian mechanics.

Spirit Levels

This seems intuitively clear from a gross observation of at least one of the inner ear structures, the semicircular canals. These three mutually perpendicular loops of bone stick out like miniature bicycle tires (about one-half inch in circumference) from a small baglike structure, the utricle. The tires contain fluid-filled inner tubes cushioned by a bath of fluid between tube and tire wall. William James called the canals the "spirit levels" of the body, for it appeared obvious to him that anytime you bob your head up or down, move it right or left, or roll it to one side, you were stirring the fluids in the appropriate inner tubes.

But "gross" and "obvious" are not fair descriptions of the canals, which are not only incredibly small—the diameter of the inner tube in a typical adult canal is of the order of a hundredth of an inch—but like the cochlea, the organ of hearing, the canals and utricle have been carved out of the petrous portion of the temporal bones of the skull. Getting to

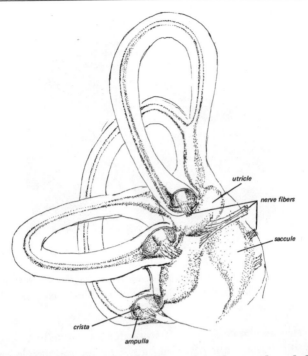

The vestibular organs are composed of the semicircular canals and the utricle and saccule. The membranous parts (stippled) are filled with fluid endolymph and are continuous with the cochlear duct. One end of each canal widens to form the ampulla, containing a crista (or crest), cupola, hair cells, and nerve endings. The posterior and superior canals unite at their nonampullary ends to form a common trunk before entering the utricle.

them entails wearing jeweler's loupes and using dental picks and drills. Indeed the elaborate maze of bone tunnels, tubes, and ducts that extends from canals to cochlea has been called the labyrinth and its midsection, containing saccule and utricle, the vestibule. The organs of balance themselves are called the labyrinthine or vestibular organs. The nerve fibers leading off from them constitute the vestibular nerve, the non-auditory branch of the eighth cranial nerve which terminates in the vestibular nuclei of the medulla.

Rocks in Your Head

For a clue to the gravity sense it is necessary to go beyond the canals and explore the utricle bag and a slightly smaller pear-shaped receptacle, the saccule, which is connected to the utricle on the side of the

197

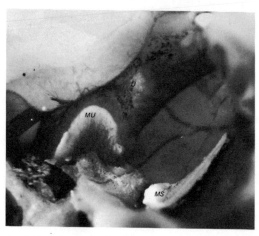

The exposed labyrinth of a guinea pig. The white areas show the maculae (MU and MS) of the utricle and saccule. The utricle (U) is cylindrical in shape and contains pigmented cells in the wall. At the far left is a part of the ampulla of a semicircular canal. The fine dark lines coursing through the utricular macula are nerve fibers.

vestibule toward the cochlea. At two oval-shaped swellings called maculae along the inner walls of these bags, one for the utricle, and one at right angles to it in the saccule, there are tiny "otoliths" of calcium carbonate, chalklike grains of material embedded in a delicate membranous mantle that rides over a layer of hair cells. Like an array of minuscule plumb bobs seeking the center of the earth, the otolith mantle slides over the hair cells as you move your head, deflecting different hair cells at different times with different intensities as you experience stronger or weaker gravitational forces.

Interaction

If you keep your head up and look straight forward the chances are that you are activating only the otolith organs. If you turn your head right or left you may excite only one pair of semicircular canals. But often all six canals and both sets of otolith organs may be stimulated—when you take off in a plane or accelerate uphill in a car, for example, or if you execute a flying three on an ice-skating rink. (In this last act there is, in addition to the rotational stimulus on the canals, the reaction of the gravity sensors to centrifugal forces.)

Because such complex interactions are more the rule than the exception, the individual specialities of each part of the labyrinth are often lost under a common heading, "the balancing sense" or "the sense of equilibrium." But the otolith organs and canals have distinct and complementary roles which need to be studied separately. Often this requires unique equipment and carefully controlled laboratory experiments. A volunteer may be blindfolded and rotated in specially designed chairs or tables, his head fixed in certain planes, his face shielded from drafts, and all sounds muffled lest the other senses cue what is happening. In animal experiments drugs, surgery, or direct electrical stimulation can be used to isolate the structures being tested.

Still the vestibular senses are peculiar compared to the others. When functioning properly you have little awareness of them. You have no idea where they are; you don't feel the pebbles sliding or the fluid in the canals sloshing back and forth; nor have you words or images or memories to describe a sensation of balance. What you feel are secondary effects, an amalgam of physical sensations which are usually the result of the reflex actions triggered by the organs, combined with visual or other sense impressions. Moreover the times when you are most aware of these physical effects are likely to be when the forces you're feeling produce in you a state of acute discomfort—of headache, vertigo, or nausea. Thus the irony is that your associations with the sense of balance are mostly associations with imbalance—times when you feel dizzy or afraid of falling, or else queasy.

Fortunately this state of affairs has recently been subject to change and accelerating forces. Jet and now space travel have made a deeper knowledge of vestibular structures and functions mandatory; they have also spurred research into drugs to handle undesirable side effects. International symposiums have been sponsored by the National Aeronautics and Space Administration as well as by private institutions, with the net result that there has been a greater gain in knowledge of these complex senses in the past ten years than in the preceding fifty.

Hits and Misses

The newer studies include the effects of days of weightlessness in space experienced by astronauts, the briefer moments of zero-gravity in planes flying "Keplerian" arcs, and a vast number of ground tests in special chambers or centrifuges. These, combined with some of the older studies of pilots in training at such places as Pensacola Naval Air Station in Florida suggest that man's judgments in unusual space conditions are at times eerily acute while at other times subject to wild distortions.

Thus groups of blindfolded pilots at Pensacola could detect the subtle changes from 1 to 2 G-forces (when a plane tilts and turns in a bank), first at a mild 10 degrees, then at a much steeper 60 degrees. Yet they floundered badly at guessing those very angles—the range was between 5 and 15 degrees. Their time judgments were off too; the first report of the sensation often came as long as 5 seconds after the turning had begun and persisted after it had stopped.

Even more humiliating is the experience most neophyte fliers have of flying upside down and not knowing it. This happens during night flying training. The instructor puts the plane through a series of maneuvers including a 180-degree turn and then asks the trainee to take over. The student may even interpret the city lights below to be stars.

Very slow accelerations may not be perceived at all. This situation can occur in elevators or in train stations when it is sometimes hard to know which train—yours or the one on the next track—is starting up or slowing down. Visual clues are not reliable in these circumstances because they depend on whether the observer is in motion.

Linear accelerations at stable air or ground levels are often associated with climbing; decelerations with descent, whether the subject is a pilot in training or a seasoned motorist driving on mountain roads at night or following the monotonous route of a tunnel. The blindfolded flight trainees experienced a sensation of tilting backwards at a 20- to 25-degree angle when the pilot applied slightly greater pressure on the stick (an acceleration equivalent to 0.1G), while a sensation like the beginning of a 15-degree dive accompanied a letup on the controls by the same amount. Again the tests showed that the sensory threshold was small: an accelerating force of only 2 percent of the force of gravity, or a deceleration of 8 percent of G was sufficient to arouse the subjects, even though the interpretation of the sensation was all wrong.

Sensory Conflicts

Most often vestibular cues work in harmony with visual or proprioceptive cues. Limb movements are coordinated with head positions, and reflex pathways control eye muscles to keep them fixed on a target while the body moves. This compensatory activity—a slow turning of the eyes *away* from the direction of the body's movement followed by a fast return *toward* the direction of movement—is called nystagmus, conventionally named according to the direction of the fast component. But there are times, usually under conditions of dim lighting or monotonous backgrounds, when eye and inner ear signals interfere, and eye movements give rise to illusions which dominate perception.

Thus staring at a fixed point against a dim background while you are being slowly whirled on a merry-go-round (or more drastically in a centrifuge) may impart a motion in the same direction to that point. This phenomenon, the so-called oculo-gyral illusion, has often been used as a measure of labyrinthine activity. It occurs at accelerations or decelerations of as little as 0.12 deg/second and as such it is a more sensitive indicator than body sensations or nystagmus which are only noticed when accelerations reach 1 or 2 degrees per second every second.

Staring at a single point under similar dark conditions, with or without body movement, can lead to the "autokinetic" phenomenon in which the point seems to wobble in random directions. This illusion explains why airplanes flying at night are illumined with bright and *flashing* red lights and why pilots are told to keep their eyes moving and avoid staring. Otherwise the results may be as disastrous as those Frank A. Geldard describes in *The Human Senses:*

In formation flying at night the pilot "flying wing" on a squadron leader will attempt to maintain a constant distance between planes by steadily fixating the light of his leader's wing tip. After a prolonged period of this the autokinetic phenomenon may supervene. The light ahead may appear to describe an arc as in a "wingover" or other radical change in the flight path; the hapless pilot makes rapid stick and rudder adjustments in an attempt to "follow," then finds himself either in a collision path with another aircraft or in a spin, recovery from which may be impossible.

Gravity Problems

More recent studies of the effects of the high G-forces that bracket intervals of weightlessness in space flight point to the need for considerable practice and training to improve performance and avoid illusions. At the same time they sound a warning of the potential damage to the organs that might result from prolonged conditions of stress, from the high intensity, low frequency sounds of the rocket at lift-off, from exposure to radiation in space, and from the abrupt changes that occur in the transition from suborbital to orbital flight.

The accumulated data from NASA's Manned Space Craft Center in Houston, Hollomon Air Force Base in New Mexico, Wright-Patterson Air Force Base in Ohio, and other NASA, air force, university, and industrial research centers suggest that the behavior of the otolith organs before and during the weightless state is not easy to predict. At 0 G, for example, the otolith organs seem to be in a state of sensory deprivation. They are "unloaded" and maintain only a minimal resting activity. "Tilting the normal individual then appears to have little, if any, effect," report Earl Miller and Ashton Graybiel of the United States Aerospace Medical Institute, in Pensacola. Furthermore, the decline in activity in the organs as the force of gravity shrinks toward zero is not proportional to the drop. At one-half G the compensatory eye movements, a rolling around their axes in the direction away from the tilt, were substantially less than half of what they were at 1 G. Still the absolute threshold of the organs is extremely low. They require only a fraction of the sea level force of gravity—three ten-thousandths of a G—to initiate a wave of excitement. The point is that the reflex eye movements that such a stimulus triggers are very weak. The authors conclude that the mild conditions of artificial gravity that have been proposed for space stations (usually by some means of rotation to induce centrifugal forces), as well as the weak gravitational field of the moon, would have such little effect on the organs that the environment would be virtually that of 0 gravity.

At the opposite extreme, subjecting humans or animals to hypergravic conditions either in launching space flight or in experiments using the extremely high accelerations and decelerations possible with rocket sleds or centrifuges, there is a danger of irreversibly damaging the vestibular organs. Donald Parker and Henning von Gierke of the Aerospace Medical Research Laboratory at Wright-Patterson Air Force Base, and Walter Covell of the Washington University School of Medicine, found that guinea pigs whirled in centrifuges for brief periods (14 to 20 seconds) and experiencing forces between 200 and 400 G's (more than fifty times the G-forces astronauts feel at lift-off or re-entry) suffered structural damage in direct proportion to the severity of the test. Normally guinea pigs are excellent swimmers but the most severely injured animals could no longer swim in straight lines. Instead they tended to swim in tight little circles. They no longer exhibited the righting reflex in free fall, either. In contrast, animals tested on rocket sleds and experiencing braking forces equal to 314 G's in one-hundredth of a second did not seem so affected in their behavior. Yet an examination of the organs later revealed considerable damage. In many cases the otoliths had been displaced from the membrane, while the sensory and supporting cells showed varying degrees of injury.

Canal Disturbances

While conditions of 0 G may have little effect on the otolith organs, movements of the pilot's head or attitude changes of the spacecraft will continue to excite the semicircular canals. How serious such stimulation may be in triggering nausea, vertigo, or other signs of motion sickness has been a major concern in the space program. So far neither Russian nor American astronauts have experienced much discomfort during orbital flight. However individuals vary greatly in their responses, not only in terms of symptoms of distress but in their abilities to make accurate judgments of spatial relations or of forces on the body. More tests will be needed for longer periods of time before final conclusions can be drawn. At present it would seem that weightlessness itself is an important factor adding to, rather than subtracting from, the stresses on the body. The problems of circulation, and of bone and muscle atrophy that the state imposes, may have direct effects on the autonomic nervous system. There is also reason to believe that a still greater danger lies in the abrupt transition between high and low G states—that the body's extraordinary ability to adapt to a new environment is a source of trouble when the body is forced to readjust rapidly again. You may not get sick in orbit but you might feel extremely uncomfortable when you step out of the capsule.

Again adaptation rates vary. Laboratory centrifuge tests suggest that the more quickly a person ceases to notice he is being whirled and feeling so many G forces, the harder and more unpleasant is the transition to normal. To establish general reference standards with regard to motion sickness a unique wave chamber was designed at the University of Rochester by G. Richard Wendt. The room was a vertical accelerator, a kind of elevator in which the height, frequency, degree of acceleration, and duration of wave forms could be regulated. While duration is important, it appears that frequency itself, plus the total amount of energy and the shape of the wave, are the major factors in producing nausea. Over half the officers tested became sick when subjected to 7-foot waves coming at a rate of twenty-two a minute. Slower rates affect some people, but faster ones are generally less effective. Only 7 percent became ill after exposure to 1-foot waves at 32 cycles per minute.

Some authorities argue that psychological factors weigh heavily in seasick proneness, that attitude, activities ("Keep busy and you won't notice the waves"), and past experience or training deeply color the reactions of the individual. Yet under normal earth surface conditions it is probably the inherent sensitivity of the labyrinthine organs themselves and, in particular, the canals that counts the most. Labyrinthine defective individuals rarely get seasick, and up to about the age of two, infants are usually good travelers because the organs have not reached full development. Past that point children may be more sensitive than adults, in keeping with the generally high state of health and performance attained by all the sense systems in youth. Nevertheless psychological factors do intrude. There's no denying that the sight of someone else being acutely seasick is distinctly unsettling to one's own viscera.

Excavating the Canals

That disputes about the causes and cures of motion sickness and seasickness persist is an indication of the degree of confusion and uncertainty that has surrounded the labyrinthine organs since their debut on the scientific scene. It was in 1824 that the distinguished French anatomist Marie Jean Pierre Flourens first described the canals of a pigeon in detail, noting that injury to them induced involuntary movements of the pigeon's eyes and head. He surmised that the canals figured importantly in balancing and postural reflexes, but it was over a century before experiments confirmed this and later speculations about their inner workings. As in the case of the cochlea no definitive answers could be given until fine examinations and close analyses of the structures in the natural state could be made.

One of the earliest observations was that when the head is held in a normal erect position the planes of the canals are not strictly horizontal or vertical. The canals that stick out farthest to the side of each ear (the exterior or lateral canals) are referred to as the horizontal canals, but actually lie in a plane tipped down toward the rear at about a 30-degree angle. The two remaining "vertical" canals are roughly at right angles to each other, like the corner walls of a room, but they also are askew. The one that juts toward the front of the head is higher than the rear-facing one, and it makes a 55-degree angle with the saggital, or midvertical, plane of the head. It is called the superior or frontal vertical

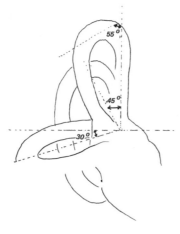

Approximate anatomical positions of the canals, showing the angles their planes make with the vertical (saggital) and horizontal planes of the head.

canal. The inferior or posterior vertical canal is set at about 45 degrees to the saggital plane.

The canals on either side are mirror images of each other reflected in the saggital plane, but their dips from true horizontal or vertical are such that the plane of the posterior canal on one side is parallel to the plane of the frontal canal on the other. So when the head turns it is these parallel rather than anatomical partners that work in tandem. The horizontal canals lie in approximately the same plane, so here anatomical and functional pairs match.

The ends of each canal fasten onto the utricle. The vertical canals share one such attachment, so the total number of junctions on each side is five rather than six. One ending of each canal swells into a hump called the ampulla. The hump is at the front for the horizontal and frontal canals and at the rear for the posterior canal. It is the ampulla which contains the nerve fibers and sensing structures.

Looked at in cross section the ampulla consists of a base layer

The anatomical placement of the canals is such that a rotation that affects the posterior vertical canal on one side will affect the superior vertical canal on the other: their planes are parallel. The horizontal canals also work as a pair.

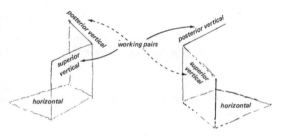

A cross section through the center of an ampulla to show the structure of the crista, which rises from the floor and is topped by the gelatinous mass of the cupola. Around the rim of the crista are hair cells whose cilia project upward into channels in the cupola mass. Nerve fibers supplying the hair cells clasp the base or sides of the cells, which are generally either flask shaped (particularly near the center of the crista) or cylindrical.

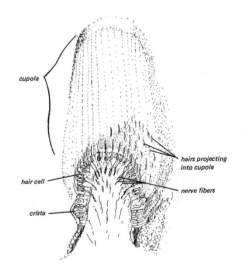

205

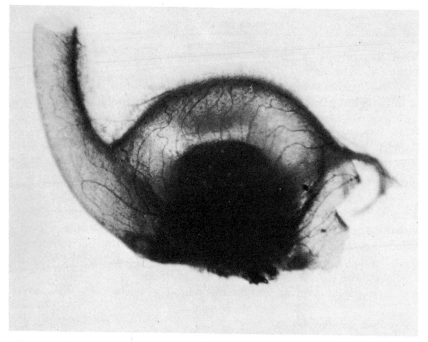

The ampulla of a semicircular canal in a guinea pig. The blood vessels form a rich network in the ampullary crista and along the wall.

Phase contrast photographs of sections of ampullary cristae from the squirrel monkey (left) and guinea pig (right). The density of sensory cells and thickness of epithelium appear to be more uniform in the guinea pig, in contrast to the thinner epithelial layer and less rich innervation at the peak of the monkey crista.

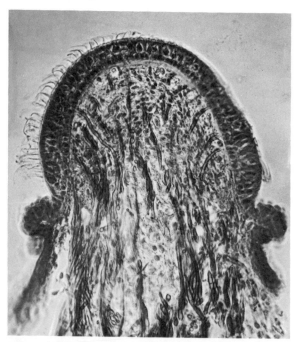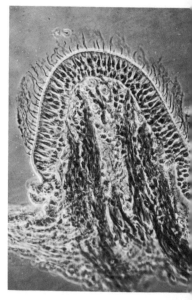

called the crista, or crest, which contains hair cells, supporting cells, and nerve endings, and above this, a cupola, a jellylike substance that forms a dome over the hair endings and extends almost to the roof of the ampulla. The hair cells and nerve endings are firmly rooted in the tube wall, while the cupola above is free to move.

The Swinging Pendulum

The current theory explaining how the canals work is credited to three nineteenth-century scientists, two Germans, Ernst Mach (that same Mach whose name is memorialized in designating multiples of the speed of sound in air) and J. Breuer, and an Englishman, A. Crum Brown. It is a hydrodynamic theory which assumes that the endolymph fluid that fills the tube can flow in such a way as to deflect the cupola. The cupola, being an elastic substance, can later return to its original position like a pendulum completing its swing.

Suppose you turn your head to the right. The theory states that both right and left horizontal canals will be affected by this rotation. The tube walls will follow the accelerations exactly, swinging around toward the rear or away from the ampulla in the right ear, and forward or toward the ampulla in the left ear. However the sudden motion of the rigid walls of each canal does not carry the endolymph inside with it. The fluid's movement lags behind and goes in the opposite direction. Wolfgang von Buddenbrock of the University of Mainz compares this to what happens when a little boy watches his sailboat move toward the opposite rim in a small tub. He wants the boat to sail toward him, so he picks up the tub and quickly turns it half way round only to see the boat still heading away from him, impelled by its inertial drag.

When this happens in the semicircular canal the endolymph pushes the cupola like a swinging door in the direction opposite to the rotation of the wall. The hairs sticking into the cupola are then pushed over or pulled back, and we assume that these mechanical events, like the shearing forces operating in the cochlea, are translated into changes in potential in the hair cells and electrical activity in the nerve fibers.

The theory was an ingenious and appealing one when it was first put forth but since no one had ever seen the canals in action, there were many naysayers. Even the scientists themselves had their doubts. They wondered if the endolymph in a tube of such a small diameter could really flow and later amended the theory in a variety of ways. But their original premise turned out to be right.

One of the earliest corroborations came from an "artificial" experiment by the German physiologist J. R. Ewald in 1874. He wanted to see whether or not the endolymph was the prime mover of the cupola so he devised a small "pneumatic hammer," a cylinder fitted with a movable piston. He then drilled two holes in a pigeon's semicircular canal. In the one farther away from the ampulla he put dental amalgam, damming up that end of the tube so no endolymph could escape. In the other he inserted his hammer. When the piston bore down on the canal the fluid moved, the cupola swung toward the ampullar end of the canal, and, what was most exciting, the pigeon's head and eyes moved toward the opposite side of the head—the typical compensatory reflex. When he pulled back on the piston the cupola moved in the reverse direction, and so did the pigeon's head.

One of the results of this experiment was to suggest still other artificial means of stimulating the canals. If movements of the endolymph were all that mattered, they might presumably be triggered by convection currents. Pouring hot water into the external ear cavity should alter the specific gravity of the endolymph making it rise in the vertical canals while cold water should make it fall. Indeed both temperature changes were effective and this experimental and clinical method is still used to test the integrity of the semicircular canals in one ear independently of the other.

Observations of canal action in more natural circumstances waited until the thirties and the experiments of W. Steinhausen and Gosta Dohlman, working with the pike and the codfish. (In general the canals of birds and fish are larger and more accessible than those of mammals.)

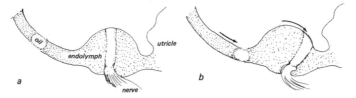

Dohlman injected a drop of oil into the canal of a codfish and then rotated the fish. At position a, before the rotation, the cupola was upright and at rest. When rotation began, the endolymph in the canal moved (position b), shifting the oil droplet and bending the cupola in the same direction.

In his experiments Steinhausen injected white ink to make the endolymph visible while Dohlman added an oil drop. When the fish were rotated around the appropriate axes the endolymph was seen to move and deflect the cupola in the direction opposite to the rotation, just as the theory predicted.

When rotation stops suddenly there is a backflow of endolymph which can reverse the direction of the cupola's bending. This is what accounts for the reversed motion you feel when you step off a merry-go-round or stop after a fast turn in a dance.

If you continue moving, however, so that the rate of rotation becomes constant, something else happens to the canals. The elastic cupola then slowly swings back to its original position, taking up to half a minute to complete its journey. Meanwhile the friction between the endolymph and the wall of the canal finally ensures that the fluid will "catch up" to the motion of the canal wall and start to move with it. The result is that the whole system comes to rest with respect to its constituent parts, no hairs are bent, no new signals are sent, and you feel nothing. This is why the response of the canals has been described as a reaction to *change* of motion rather than to motion per se.

Ewald's "Laws"

These experiments, combined with observations of such things as reversed nystagmus when rotation stops, suggest an interesting ability of the hair cells. They apparently can signal rotations in two directions, though not, as it turns out, with equal strength. It was Ewald who first observed this, and his statements of the phenomenon have come to be known as "Ewald's Laws." In the case of the horizontal canals he noted that when the right canal was rotated to the right, away from its ampulla, causing the endolymph in turn to move towards the ampulla, the sum of nerve impulses generated in the canal was greater than when at rest. In the left ear where just the opposite movements were going on, the total electrical activity was less than the resting level. In other words each canal showed a positive excitatory effect when rotated one way and a negative inhibitory effect when turned the reverse way. Just to confuse things, the direction for increased nerve activity in the vertical canals occurs when the endolymph moves away from the ampulla, while inhibition is associated with movements toward the ampulla.

In recent years a number of investigators have carried anatomical dissection further, using refined cell preservation techniques and electron microscopy in order to study the arrangement of the individual hair cells for possible clues to this preferential activity. The beautiful work of the Swedish investigators J. Wersäll and Hans Engström, Harlow Ades of the University of Illinois, and Heinrich H. Spoendlin of the University of Zurich suggests that just such an ordering does exist.

It now appears that each hair cell comes with a stack of about sixty or seventy stiff hairs, stereocilia, protruding into the cupola, or macular, space. They are arranged in size sequence like organ pipes, building up to one end of the cell where there is a special hair ending called a kino-

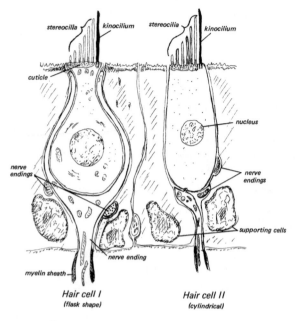

Vestibular sensory cells.

cilium, literally, a moving hair. The kinocilium has its counterpart in many cells found in nature; in one-celled organisms among protozoa, in cells that line the lungs or digestive tracts, in the hair cells found in the nose and eyes, and even in cells within the central nervous system.

Wherever you look in the vestibular epithelia the patch of cells in any one neighborhood generally have their kinocilia facing the same way. The situation is comparatively simple in the cristae: the kinocilia of hair cells in the horizontal canals face toward the utricle; in the vertical canals they face away. This morphological arrangement compared with the electrophysiological data suggests that when the stiff hairs bend toward the kinocilium and it in turn is pushed over, the cell is depolarized and triggers an increase in nerve activity. When movements are away from the kinocilium the cell is inhibited and there is a lessening of activity—in keeping with Ewald's Laws. Ades and Engström further suggest that the stiffer hairs may be auxiliaries; they might protect the cells, especially in the maculae, under conditions of strong shearing forces or increased pressures of otoliths, and their bending action may build up to the kinocilium's movement which would be the crucial event for generating the receptor potential.

The arrangement in the maculae is more complex. The surface of

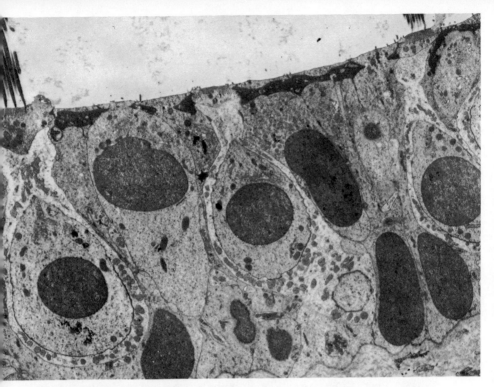

An electron micrograph of the sensory epithelium from the utricular macula of a guinea pig. Note the size gradations in the hairs of the sensory cell at the far left. × *4200.*

the utricular macula is creased along one side and there is a curving ridge down the middle in which the otoliths are heaped as in a snowdrift. Generally speaking cells in the same neighborhood have the same kinocilium orientation except for those facing each other across the ridge. Here the cells on one side are oppositely polarized from those on the other. These variations probably account for the fact that the utricle can respond sensitively to any deviation from the horizontal plane, with cells in different areas having peak reactions when the angle of tilt coincides with the orientation of their hairs.

The electrical changes that occur when the kinocilia are pushed over trigger impulses in nerve endings which reach up to form either flower cuplike holders around one type of hair cell (type I or flask shaped), or else attach at certain sites along the body of a second type, presumed to be an older form in nature, the cylindrically shaped type II hair cell. Again in any batch there are exceptions, cells which do not fall into either category, or ones whose kinocilia are out of place. It is tempting to think that such cells are the ones that show up as exceptions to the general rule in the electrode studies, becoming inhibited when

211

every other cell is excited, or producing other odd patterns of activity. These are not aberrant cells. On the contrary they may be very important in the peripheral coding of information, involved in signaling the onset, duration, or offset of the stimulus, for example, so that greater details or discriminations are possible in the long run.

This, in the case of the vestibular organs, is a very long run indeed. The reflex pathways that are set in motion by semicircular canal and otolith organ stimulation enter the brain and relay to four groups of cells, the vestibular nuclei. From here some paths lead to the eye muscle control centers, some to the cerebellum, some enter the broad stream of reticular formation fibers, and some continue to the cortical level. Others descend to the spinal cord to make final connections with the large motor nerve cells at the front of the cord, the last switchpoint before impulses leave the central nervous system to go to the body's muscles.

While canal and otolith organ fibers follow similar pathways it appears that the impulses preserve their origins and identity en route. Thus the nervous system distinguishes between stimulation due to gravity and stimulation due to angular acceleration. This distinction exists at the outset, of course, because even though the hair cells and the type of nerve innervations are similar in both organs, the cupola and the otolith membrane are very different in operation.

Magnetic Shrimp

One difference is immediately clear. You don't need to move your head to know where it is. Unlike the canals, the gravity receptors work all the time, adapting very slowly to a constant position of the head. From a theoretical point of view this seems reasonable considering that we are normally subject to the force of gravity all the time. The proof that the otoliths really were reacting to G-forces, however, awaited the outcome of an ingenious experiment with shrimp devised by an Austrian scientist named Kreidl.

The shrimp has a much simpler gravity organ than vertebrates, the statocyst, a spherical bag of tissue lying at the base of its first pair of feelers. The shrimp fills the bag with sand particles to serve the same function as otoliths, slipping them in through a tiny slit. It must do this every time it grows and sheds its shell. What Kreidl did was to remove the sand from the laboratory tank and replace it with iron filings just before moulting time. The shrimp had no choice but to fill its bag with these highly magnetized particles. When Kreidl placed a magnet over the tank the filings were immediately drawn to the upper wall of the statocyst, exactly the position they would have been in if the shrimp had turned over on its back and the sand particles were responding to gravity. Kreidl's shrimp obviously felt that this is what had happened and reacted by promptly flopping over.

For most animals it is the otoliths in the utricle that play the dominant role in maintaining posture in response to gravity. The role of the saccule itself, while analogous in structure, remains something of a mystery. Complete removal of the saccules on both sides seems to have little or no effect on animals. This leads some scientists to believe that its function may be more closely related to hearing. It may be a primitive low frequency vibration receptor arranged so that the pebbles might bounce up and down and cause the hair cells underneath to turn on and off in rhythm. But as mammals developed the more exquisitely functioning cochlea the saccule may have lost its purpose, perhaps only contributing to activity in response to very loud sounds or explosions, which can make you dizzy and start your head turning.

Tonic Action

On the other hand removal of the utricles does severely change an animal's behavior. A dog so deprived loses muscle tone and looks slumped over. This is further evidence that the utricle normally works at all times, in concert with the proprioceptors and the muscle and tendon spindles, to maintain the proper muscle tone in legs to support the body against gravity. The semicircular canals then can exert their influence in refining control, modifying activity to accommodate the body when the head is turned or twisted. If the semicircular canals on only one side are removed, animals generally develop a rolling or flexing posture turning toward that damaged side. If both canals are lost the situation in a way is better for there is no involuntary twisting or turning and, with the eyes open, equilibrium can be maintained. Without visual aid, however, it is very difficult to maintain a steady posture. If both the canals and otolith organs are gone, the symptoms are very much like a general cerebellar disturbance, with unsteady gait, poor judgment of the position of objects, and difficulty in coordination. There is the added danger of loss of sensory cues when swimming: a blind labyrinthine-defective person swimming underwater may not be able to tell which direction is toward the surface.

Automation

One indication of the importance of the vestibular senses is seen in the degree to which the nervous system has assumed subcortical control

213

over them. The orientation of the body in space in response to constant or changing forces is so vital that nature has automated control.

There are some signals that do reach the cortex, either via a direct route from the labyrinthine organs themselves, or else through the multiple inputs from the body's muscles, eyes, or viscera in response to movement. There is also evidence that the cortex quietly is at work inhibiting labyrinthine responses to prevent over-reactions. When such inhibiting influences are lost, for instance when the cortex is removed experimentally, dogs or cats exhibit a hyperextension of the limbs, as though bracing themselves mightily against the floor in a posture known as "decerebrate rigidity."

The cortex can also affect the course of labyrinth reactions through voluntary controls. You can stop postrotational nystagmus by fixing your eyes on an object. You can block some of the dizziness, or vertigo, of rotational stimulation by consciously bracing yourself against a wall or holding on to a railing. (In brief tests of weightlessness in airplanes monkeys also seem to bring some voluntary control to their behavior. Some back up against the sides of their cage. Others may float, but with an attitude that suggests they are ready to make a four-point landing.)

Finally when volition or inhibition fails there are drugs that can ward off the effects of too sensitive a labyrinth system. Space scientists laughingly refer to a "gravity" pill, which would be the magic answer to the weightless state. Though this has yet to be pulled out of the hat, there are an increasing number of drugs of various kinds and combinations which are effective in raising the nausea threshold. For purposes of comparison a standardized test is needed. One such is provided by the Slow Rotation Room at Pensacola's Aerospace Medical Institute. While the room is rotated at certain speeds volunteers are given a prescribed set of duties, knobs to turn and levers to pull, which involve standard head and body movements. The investigators can then study the drugged and undrugged performance, both in a single individual with himself as his own control, or in comparison with the group as a whole.

In one series of tests Dr. Charles Wood of the University of Arkansas Medical School reported that some of the better-known anti-motion sickness drugs like hyoscine (Scopolamine) and meclizine (Bonamine) did what they were supposed to do, but that the stimulant drug d-amphetamine (Dexadrine) was surprisingly effective as well. In combination with hyoscine the results were better than with either drug alone.

Dosage level and side effects are particularly important factors to take into account in recommending the use of such drugs, since in their service of preventing nausea and vomiting, they sometimes induce drowsiness, blurred vision, vertigo, or other symptoms hardly desirable in ship's officers or aircraft personnel. The answer may be in combinations of drugs where the sum of the various modes of actions enhances the desired effect and cancels out the undesirable.

Certainly there is no lack of zeal on the part of the investigators to try combinations of drugs and use themselves as guinea pigs. Here is how G. Richard Wendt describes his procedure to prevent motion sickness prior to flying weightless patterns at the Wright-Patterson base:

I took hyoscine to depress my vestibular nuclei and Marezine to depress my reticular activating system. I mistakenly took tigan hydrochloride to depress my vomiting center, and I took paregoric to keep stomach sensations from bothering me. I took amphetamine to make me cheerful and a very small amount of Seconal to make me self-confident. In the aggregate, there were no significant side effects of any kind, but as a motion sickness preventative, this mess of stuff actually turned out to be rather effective.

X

Believing Is Seeing

In some ways the most paradoxical, certainly the most studied of man's senses, is vision. The statistics alone are awe-inspiring. Seventy percent of all the body's sense receptors are in the eyes. Their sensitivity to light is of the order of 1 quantum—the smallest packet of energy physicists deal with. The ratio of nerve to muscle, about 1 to 200 in other parts of the body, is close to 1 to 2 in the eye, allowing superb control of eye movements. The size of the optic tracts, over a million fibers, is only equaled by one other pathway in the brain—the fibers that go out to control all voluntary muscles.

Yet the human eye is not perfect. Eyeballs may be too long or too short for proper focusing. Lenses distort colors and blur the images of rays coming in at the rim, elementary faults that would make an optician ashamed, as Hermann von Helmholtz noted a century ago. Lenses also dull and harden with age. People who have never worn glasses often need them in their forties.

The eye is easy to fool, so easy in fact that it seems to delight in delusions. Nor is its vulnerability purely psychological. If one eye suffers disease or injury, the other occasionally suffers, too. On the other hand if one eye is weak from birth, the brain may turn off signals from it altogether. A child may grow up for all intents and purposes one-eyed, no one noticing the defect until it's too late.

Usually both eyes work together with one eye dominating. You may be right-eyed just as you are right-handed ° (the two need not correspond). This physiological linkage may explain why one eye may be vulnerable when the other is injured. But the eyes also possess a kind of eerie independence. Normally if you project a beam of pure red light to one eye and pure green to the other you perceive the color yellow, exactly as if you had shown yellow light or a previously blended mixture of red and green light to either or both eyes. But the blending fails if you sever the parts of the optic nerves which cross in the brain along with the major connections between the cerebral hemispheres. Then each eye acts alone and appears capable of independent observations and judgments. It's as if you had become a two-headed cyclops, with the single eye in each head hooked to a separate brain.

Sometimes the eyes seem miraculously able to compensate for injury. A lesion in one eye—a piece of scar tissue where the eye's screen, the retina, has been damaged—may make no difference in a person's vision. The picture he sees has no hole in it. Yet some mentally ill persons with no overt eye damage see a figure-eight world as though they were looking through twin gun barrels.

Physiologically some of these oddnesses can be explained, and some are correctable. Others raise more fundamental questions about the nature of perception. The eye's imperfections perhaps may never be solved by some future, more evolved species if that species persists in using eyes for the many purposes man does. We use our eyes to see color and to see black and white. We see in broad daylight and on moonless nights. We see borders and surfaces and volumes and depths. We see objects that stay put and objects that move, while we stand or move ourselves. If we agreed to give up some of these talents we might gain more perfect but more limited eyes. So it is with night-prowlers: cats, opossums, and cockroaches may see better than we do at night. Rattlesnakes, vultures, and pigeons may do better by day. Our eyes might become extremely motion-conscious like the frog, or extend the range of radiation sensitivity to the infrared range like the rattlesnake, or into the ultraviolet as some insects do (not forming images on screens, but

---

° You can test this by focusing on a distant object with both eyes open. Now close each eye in turn. You are right-eyed if the object jumps to the right when you close the right eye, but is stationary when you close the left. This means that the object is lined up with reference to your right eye which dominates your gaze.

concentrating the light in each of their myriad-lensed eyes so that a mosaic of light and dark spots is formed).

Man does many things with his eyes, however, and does them very well, chiefly because they are linked to a better brain. If at times the eye's form seems a little wanting, at least it is wed to a content-bearing structure, so that the sum—vision—attains excellence in man. Descending from that height are all the other eyes found in nature: eyes with lenses and screens, as in the vertebrates; eyes with a screen but no lens, as in the charmingly named sea creature, the chambered nautilus; eyes with many-splendored double-screens, as in the blue-eyed scallop; or eyes that are only photosensory spots, like a worm's. These are all examples of specialized cells or organs that enable creatures, plants as well as animals, to respond to light, to use its energy for seeing or to convert chemicals into food, acting either automatically by instinct or reflex, or with a degree of self-consciousness dependent on the sophistication of the link to the central nervous system.

In man that link is of the highest order. The eye is an outpocketing of the brain. Like the brain, it starts developing early, within the first few weeks of life. At birth the visual system will have reached a stage of enormous neurological complexity, but it will still need years to mature. Some superficial parts of the eye will also continue to grow. The eyeball itself enlarges until about the age of eight; the lens will add new layers of cells, albeit very slowly, up to the point of death.

Like the gray matter of the cortex the cells that make up the retina are in layers. The stalks that originally carry the eyes forward in the head later become the cables that return to the brain what is really a part of it—the tails of certain retinal cells, or the optic nerves.

As the stalks push forward in the embryo the lumps of tissue at their tips go through a series of infoldings to form what are known as the optic cups. In so doing a single layer of tissue doubles back on itself. This second layer will become the sensory part of the retina. When the optic cup and stalk reach the surface they call the lens into development by chemical means not yet understood. The surface skin turns in, starts to proliferate, and takes the shape of an ingrowing mushroom. Investigators experimenting with chick embryos have found the change will occur even if the optic cup is transplanted to other parts under the body surface, to the back or stomach. The reverse is not true: a budding lens elsewhere brings forth no optic cup.

Two things form the fundamental camera parts of the eye: the lens and a screen on which to focus an image. Eventually the screen will be composed of several layers of tissue interwoven in a complex of nerves and photoreceptors. The last of the nerve cells to form, always farthest from the light, are the very ones which will respond to that light. These rods and cones are the final flowering of the rudimentary fast-proliferating tissue at the back of the optic cup.

At birth the eyes appear to be finished products. They come equipped with lashes, lids, lacrimal glands, a rich blood supply. But neurologically they are tender; psychologically they are innocent. More than any other sense organs the eyes must learn, must take on associative, maturing, memory-forming tasks which will both shape and be shaped by the personality of the individual and his culture. Insofar as man's future arises out of a past richly documented in the written word, his perceptions, his metaphysics, his imagination, are visual. Human dreams and nightmares, inspirations and hallucinations, are tinged with every sense, but vision above all dominates.

At birth a baby's eyeballs are actually foreshortened so he is farsighted. He uses only one eye at a time, practicing, guided by curiosity and reflex. Gradually he may come to favor, perhaps smile, at the round, moving thing that looms close when he cries. Tests noting an infant's attention span when presented with a variety of patterns and shapes almost always report that attention is greatest when the shape resembles a human face.

In time the baby keeps both eyes open and moves them together, but it is long before he has any real understanding of the world and its objects. Concepts of color and shadow, perspective and distance only slowly mature. Ask a child to look at a picture with white space in it, and he is likely to say that the space is snow; ask a child what is the sky, and he may say that it is made of blue; yet ask a child to pick the bigger of two circles when each is drawn against deceptive background patterns, an illusion which deceives adults, and he may have no difficulty.

There is both a literal and practical quality to a child's vision which only slowly evolves into adult perception. Interruptions or blocks at the earliest stages of this progression can have dire consequences for visual perception. The most dramatic examples of such abnormal vision occur among congenitally blind persons who have had operations for removal of cataracts (a clouding of the lens) and all at once can "see." Show such a person a figure, a circle say, and then show him a larger circle and a square and ask him to choose the similar figure. He will not be able to pick the circle. The change in area has been enough to make the second circle seem a completely different form. A change of color of two circles of the same size will also confuse him. It is as though in this vision perception were arrested, and the process of abstraction halted, as in languages where there may be words for many kinds of tree, but no word for tree.

Very little is known about the processes of synthesis, abstraction, deduction, and induction that develop as the eye matures. To ask how seeing passes into observing, how flashes of light become patterns of movement, of shape, depth, hue, and position, involves unraveling the lines of association that tie psychology to physiology. It is a tricky business to define what an image is—even trickier to trace its source.

What is possible is to follow the route, to dissect and analyze and show something of the mechanics of visual perception, starting first of all with the eye itself, distinguishing its crucial camera parts from the many accessory aids to the business of light catching.

The foremost aid, of course, is the location of the eyes up front and toward the top of the body. This placement may seem obvious until you realize that it is not always necessary. In addition to the rods and cones of their superficially placed eyes, birds have photoreceptor organs that are buried inside their heads. In spite of this position the organs can respond to seasonal light changes; in the spring birds lay eggs.

Certain crayfish have a pair of photoreceptor nerve cells within the central nerve cord which respond to light shining through their translucent exoskeleton. Investigators have also found light-sensitive cells within the heart muscle of certain snails, the brains of some insects, and in some of the smooth muscle cells in the walls of tiny branches of arteries in mammalian skin.

To compensate for their exposure our eyes lie buried in bony sockets under overhanging brows that can take the brunt of punishment from blows and falls. The eyebrows fringing the surface prevent sweat from running down into the eyes. Contrary to popular opinion the movable skin flaps that encase the eye, the lids, do not protect the eye so much as they bathe and lubricate it. Fish don't need and don't have lids, as their watery habitat accomplishes this purpose nicely.

The eyeball itself lies in a bed of fat in the socket, supported by muscles and ligaments which enable it to swivel around. The tension the muscles exert, combined with the pressure of fluids inside the eyeball, are responsible for its taut globular shape. These pressures are immensely important. If the external ties were cut the eye would cave in. If internal pressures build up, usually by a block in the fluid drainage system, glaucoma results. This disease, if uncorrected, can lead to blindness.

A healthy eyeball in the living state looks like a glossy white globe, enclosed in several layers of "skin," three to be exact. It gives somewhat to the touch for its interior is mostly fluid. Many of the complex parts of the eye are derived from the three skins according to the way they differentiated during development.

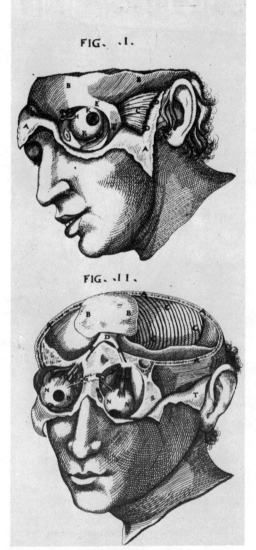

TAB. II. ORGANI VISVS.

FIG. .I.

FIG. .II.

An illustration of the eye muscles from Giulio Casserio's Pentaestheseion *("The Five Senses"), published in 1610.*

The white of the eye, the outermost layer, is the sclera, a tough, fibrous jacket which, according to Gordon Walls in his excellent treatise, *The Vertebrate Eye and Its Adaptive Radiation,* at one time in the course of evolution was transparent throughout. Now it retains its transparency only at a small bulged-out and thickened area in front, the cornea.

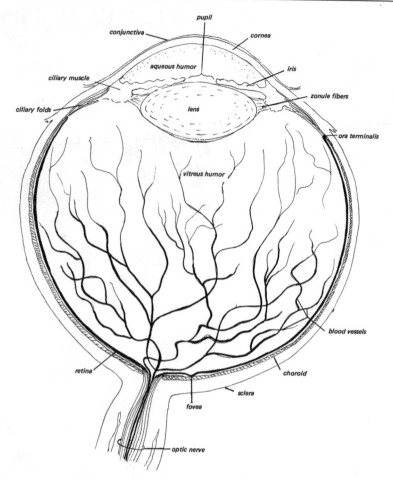

A cross section of the eye, showing the principal parts.

The True Lens

If we distinguish between accessory and essential camera parts, the cornea at once stands out as essential. It is the cornea plus the crystalline lens which constitute the true lens of the eye. The cornea is the first solid matter that airborne light rays hit. Here the major refraction of light, its change in speed and direction as it passes from one substance to another, takes place. In this the cornea behaves like any convex lens. It can be thought of as being built up of infinitely many wedges or rectangular glass prisms.

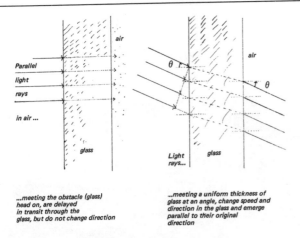

...meeting the obstacle (glass)
head on, are delayed
in transit through the
glass, but do not change direction

...meeting a uniform thickness of
glass at an angle, change speed and
direction in the glass and emerge
parallel to their original
direction

Diagram illustrating the refraction of light.

It is easier to understand this if we first consider the simpler case of light passing through a block of glass, a rectangular instead of a wedge-shaped solid. To borrow an analogy from Walls, the block represents an obstacle to light rays in the same way as a wheat field does to a regiment of soldiers crossing open country. If the soldiers meet the field head on, they may be delayed getting through, but they will press on in the same direction. If they meet it at an angle, there will be one column that gets delayed first, and this reduction in speed brings about a change in the direction of the column. By the time all columns have entered the field the whole group will have swung around as though pivoted to the first column. When the ranks emerge again the process reverses, and the group continues moving in a direction parallel to their original line of march.

If you substitute a wedge shape for the rectangular plane of the field you are in effect altering the contours so that some columns of soldiers may meet the field head on, while others will enter at angles; some columns will come out sooner, some later than others; some will be bent more, some less. Now if you think about a whole stack of such "fields" or prisms arranged symmetrically around a central plane, and you increase their numbers so that the edges smooth into a continuous curve—an arc of a circle—you arrive at the form of a convex lens. The lens will focus parallel rays entering it at some point beyond the lens whose distance depends on the degree of curvature.

The region behind the cornea of the eye is filled with a fluid, the aqueous humor. Behind it in turn stands the lens and then a slightly stickier fluid, the vitreous humor. The fluid substances have nearly the

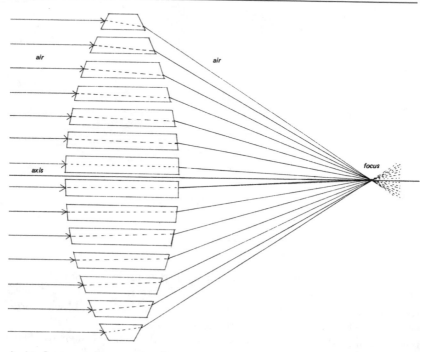

A simple convex lens can be thought of as being made up of many rectangular glass prisms symmetrically arranged about a central axis. The nonparallel sides of the prisms approximate arcs of circles. Parallel rays of light are refracted upon entering the glass and again upon exiting, with the result that they converge at a point—the focus of the lens.

same optical density as the cornea; they refract light by about the same amount. So whatever happens to light after it has passed through the cornea depends on the refinements in focus produced by the lens.

Because of the cornea's function as the major light receiver it has several unique features. There are no blood vessels coursing through it (they would mar its transparency); its nutritional needs are supplied differently. The aqueous humor provides these at the rear of the cornea while on the surface, the fuel is the tear fluid which is constantly pumped out in minute amounts by the lacrimal glands. Usually the excess evaporates. (Visible tears only occur when irritation or emotion swells production to the point where they can break through a thin film over the eyes.)

The cornea's surface layers are rich in nerve endings which are extremely sensitive to pain and probably to other sensations as well. Its ability to repair itself is extraordinary, and it is one of the few body tissues which can be transplanted from person to person with less chance of rejection. Presumably the lack of a blood supply means a lack of a channel for arousing antigen-antibody reactions.

The next two layers of eyeball serve so many purposes and cooperate at so many points that it is best to describe them together. The one farther out, lining the sclera, is the uvea. Lining it, in turn, is the retina. Both layers wrap almost completely around the eyeball. The reason the retina is usually thought of as the screen "in back" is that its most forward parts are not light-sensitive.

The rear of the uvea complements the retina's sensitivity by being dark-pigmented. This is the choroid coat, the black box of the camera, which absorbs light and so helps prevent rays from reflecting back and forth once inside the eye, and in this way confusing the image forming on the retina. The choroid is also rich in blood vessels to serve the intensely active retinal cells. Of course if in the course of evolution man came to live in the dark and needed the ultimate in light sensitivity a different kind of layer might have developed, one that would deliberately act like a mirror throwing any unabsorbed light back into the eye to give it another chance to stimulate the receptors. This is exactly the function of the tapetum, a luminous screen that makes cats' and other nocturnal creatures' eyes gleam in the dark.

At a rim five-sixths the way from the rear of the eyeball, the *ora terminalis*, the sensitive portion of the retina stops. The choroid, too, also ceases to be as deeply pigmented and blood-rich, changes shape, and proceeds forward as a bundle of thickened muscle tissue called the ciliary body, which, further along, fans out into a series of folds called the ciliary processes. The processes actually are derived from the non-sensitive part of the retina. The aicordion-pleated folds presumably provide a greater surface area for the secretion of the aqueous humor. This is produced nearby in a section of the retinal tissue covering the ciliary body.

Both uvea and retina continue forward on both sides now, turning inward slightly to form a cone of tissue with a hole in it. This is the iris and the pupil. The iris is the camera's diaphragm, closing down or opening wide the lens opening. It is the iris that determines the color of the eyes. Strangely enough, eyes appear blue through a trick of light. The tissue layers forming the iris contain only brown pigments. If there is much pigment in both layers you see brown or black eyes. If there is just a scant amount from only the retinal layer, you see blue because the shorter (blue) waves of light have been scattered, deflected from minuscule non-pigmented particles in the iris, just as dust, moisture, and air molecules act as reflectors in sunlight to make the sky blue.

The iris both contracts and dilates the pupil. Contraction occurs when rings of concentric muscle fibers tighten up, pulling the circular opening close together like a drawstring purse. Crossing these fibers at right angles, however, are radial fibers. When they contract they ruffle up the rings of tissue like a circular venetian blind, opening wide the pupil.

The two sets of muscles have opposing innervations: the dilatators are controlled by sympathetic nerves and the contractors by parasympathetics, so it is not surprising that each reacts differently, and often very sensitively, to drugs. Indeed this is one of the telltale signs of drug effects. The powerful hallucinogenic drug LSD, often thought to exert its maximum power on subjects within five or six hours after taking it, still causes dilatation of the pupils after 12 hours—a time when subjects say they are well over the drug experience and physiologically long after the drug has been excreted from the body.

The movements of the iris are involuntary and are involved in a number of reflexes, some of which are "consensual," for instance, if you cover one eye and look at a bright light *both* pupils contract. The iris' chief reflex function is to protect the retina by contracting in bright light. It will also contract when the eyes focus on nearby objects. Dilatation occurs in dim light, in states of emotion or excitement, and as a reflex response to pinching or other painful stimuli applied to the skin of the neck.

Dilatation or contraction may also occur involuntarily according to the interests or associations of the viewer. Professor Ekhard Hess of the University of Chicago owes his discovery of this phenomenon to an observation by his wife, a painter. She remarked one night that the light he was reading by must be weak because his pupils were dilated. He was sure the lighting was adequate and speculated that the reason might be because he was very interested in what he was looking at, some photographs of wild animals. The following day he decided to test his colleagues informally. He showed them a series of landscape photos in which he had slyly slipped a pin-up picture from a magazine. Sure enough when the pin-up was found the pupils enlarged. Hess went on to show that dilatation generally occurs when the subject matter is interesting or when a person is engaged in problem-solving. Computing your income tax may make your eyes get bigger and bigger.

Conversely, there is a degree of diminution in eye size if a person is bored or repelled by something he is shown. Even a "neutral" portrait photograph may trigger such a contraction if the person is told, for example, that the photo is of an ex-commandant of a concentration camp.

Behind the iris, pushing on it and making it bulge into a tiny

226

volcano shape, is the lens, a glassy substance that grows increasingly yellow with age and feels a bit like hardened jelly. It is fitted into a lining, the lens capsule. Helping to buoy it from behind is the vitreous humor. Its main support, however, comes from a rigging system of "zonule" fibers, which extend from the ciliary body surface and grasp the lens at front and back near the rim like many-fingered hands.

The chief purpose of the lens is to make subtle adjustments in the eye's optical system so that light rays come to focus on the sensitive parts of the rods and cones. These brush against the back of the retina over a length of a hundredth of an inch or so. Since the image from a distant object is exceedingly small anyway, the lens usually does not have to make any adjustment for distance viewing. Objects as far away as the horizon and up to about 20 feet away will normally form images on the sensitive part of the retina. The lens makes no adjustment when you watch a plane land or a train arrive in a station.

When objects are closer than 20 feet, however, the lens has to sharpen its focus. This might be done if we could vary the lens—slip in slimmer or fatter versions depending on the need—or if you could move the lens or screen forward or back. Human and vertebrate eyes use a method all their own, however. They alter the shape of the lens as it sits in place. The adjustment comes about through the contraction of the ciliary muscles. This contraction has the effect of moving the zonule fibers forward and relaxing the tension that flattens the lens. Since the lens is elastic, the release of pressure makes it bulge into a more balloon-like shape, thus providing a stronger curvature and a shorter focal length.

As you read the ciliary muscles are in constant tension. This is why it helps to stop what you're doing occasionally and stare off into the "middle distance"—the muscles can then relax. Perhaps the brown study of the scholar is just a subconscious way of giving the eyes a chance to rest up before the next round of close work.

The change of curvature of the lens is called accommodation. For the normal adult eye the bulge at its maximum brings into focus an object some 8 or 10 inches away—the normal reading distance. If the eyeball is abnormally long or short to begin with, however, no amount of accommodation will keep light in touch with the rods and cones. The familiar solution is to add lenses or a pair of spectacles in front. The power of the lens is usually measured in diopters, a unit inversely proportional to focal length. A 1-diopter lens brings parallel rays into focus a bit over a yard away; a 2-diopter lens focuses at approximately half a yard, and so on.

If you place a 1-diopter lens in front of a normal non-accommodating eye, the image of an object a yard away will fall on the retina. Since the lens when it is accommodating maximally manages this feat for objects between 5 and 10 or more inches away (depending on age), accommodating powers range up to 10 or more diopters.

Accommodation depends on the condition of the muscles and the elasticity of the lens. Unfortunately as the lens ages, its center cells die out and harden. A point may even be reached when the lens loses all its springiness and no amount of ciliary action will alter its shape.

This hardening begins to be felt in the forties, when husbands begin holding the newspaper at arm's length, and wives ask their children to read the measurements in a recipe. The condition is called presbyopia, literally, old sight. Of course in a previously shortsighted person, the gradual failure to accommodate, which is involuntary, may be of some help. Occasionally nearsighted people can throw away their glasses in middle age. In some cases of severe myopia, the person may even do better with no lens at all—the focal length of the cornea itself will permit images to form on the abnormally distant retina.

The journey of light from cornea to retina described so far has been a manipulative one. Light has been welcomed with open arms or more discreetly treated by the iris. It has suffered its major bending by the cornea and been further coaxed into line by the aqueous, by the bulged or unbulged front of the lens and by the unchanging but slightly more curved rear of the lens, on through the vitreous and to the retina. If you draw a line between the centers of curvature of cornea and

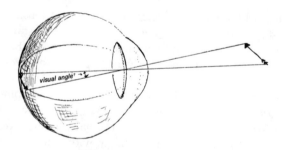

This simplified drawing of the eyeball shows how images are projected onto the retina. Because the screen is bowl shaped, the image of the straight arrow is curved. Positions on the retina are measured in degrees from the fovea, and the size of an object is expressed in terms of the visual angle it subtends. The full moon, for example, subtends an angle of approximately 0.5 degree on the retina. In linear measure, a millimeter of retina (approximately 1/25 inch) represents approximately 3 degrees of visual angle.

lens to define the optical axis, and let the rim of the lens be the equator, rays coming into the upper left-hand corner of the eye will cross from the upper to the lower half of the equator and go from left to right across the axis by the time they reach the retina. The result is the typical inverted image of a camera.

It is even possible to see this inverted image in the case of fair-skinned people (who have less pigment in the choroid). If they are taken into a darkened room and asked to look at a lighted candle placed to the far side of the eye, the flame will appear upside down shining through the inner wall of the eyeball.

But you don't see things upside down and backward, for at this point, light's optical journey comes to an end. Its energy will now trigger chemical changes in the visual cells which will eventually be spelled out as electrical impulses in the optic nerves. Not until these fibers relay their signals along the optic pathways in the brain will you see anything. What you see then—the wealth of image or its chiaroscuro vagueness—will be as much a function of the nervous system's skill at decoding the electrical impulses as it is the rods' and cones' in setting them down in the first place.

At this point analogies between eye and camera cease. The retina is no passive film emulsion, subject to the whims and caprices of light. No sooner do rays strike it than it starts behaving in the manner its origins suggest—like an inch of brain. It will weigh, balance, measure, and judge the flashes of light, decide what is interesting and worth emphasizing, and what is dull and to be rejected. In the process the retina sometimes behaves like a physicist paying attention to certain qualities of light, such as intensity or wavelength, but the measurements it makes are not identical with those made in a laboratory. Sometimes it will see things as brighter or dimmer, larger or smaller, nearer or farther than they are in reality. Sometimes it will pass on signals that will indicate color when there is no color, or movement when there is rest. Indeed such paradoxes and illusions are very much the stuff of art and visual research. To find out how the eye sees we must study how it distorts reality.

But in any case the retina must first be excited. Without that initial event there is no change of light to electricity, no message or code, no sight.

Visual Pigments

The locus for that essential change is in the next-to-last layer of retina. This is where the skinny rods or slightly fatter cone-shaped outer segments, the parts that give the cells their names, stand to catch light that has come into the eyeball and passed through the transparent neural layers of retina in front. Here in these outer extremities whose tips point away from the light and into the rear layer of pigment epithelium are the critical substances, the visual pigments. The behavior of the visual pigments is dramatic. When light strikes them they are bleached, only to

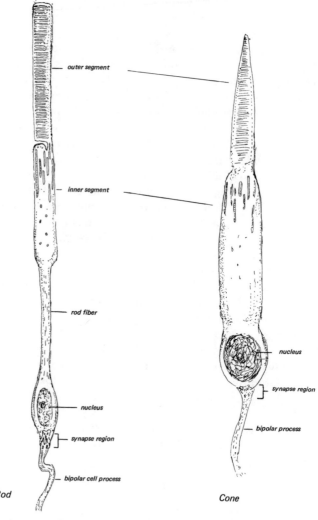

Diagrams of a typical rod and cone. The cones in the foveal region are much like rods in structure.

be regenerated again. Bleaching the pigment irritates the cell, changing its electrical state to provide the kickoff for the nervous activity to follow. Regeneration insures that after a time the cell can be light-struck again; that you will not be blinded after a few moments in bright daylight.

Much is known about the details of this process in the case of rhodopsin, a reddish-purple pigment (called visual purple), that is found in rods but not in cones. It was discovered in the frog's retina by Franz Boll in 1876 and soon after was seized upon as the only begetter of the eye's myriad activities. Doubts and reactions set in, however, so that its role was disputed. Gradually a balance was restored and in recent years rhodopsin's structure and function have been beautifully analyzed and described by many researchers, but in particular by George Wald and his colleagues at Harvard.

Rhodopsin is a large molecule composed of two parts. One is opsin, a type of protein peculiar to retinas; the other is retinene, a yellowish-colored substance that is related to carotene, the same color substance found in carrots and most green leaves.

Retinene comes in a variety of shapes, but the shape that combines with opsin to form rhodopsin has a special kink in it. When light strikes rhodopsin it dekinks the retinene, severing the union. Left alone, the straightened out retinene undergoes a further change—to vitamin A. The reaction is exciting to watch, either in the test tube, or in an animal like

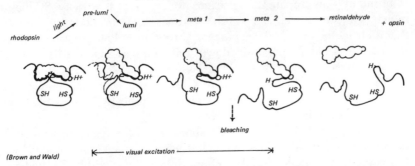

Stages in the bleaching of rhodopsin. Retinene fits closely a section of opsin. When light strikes the molecule it changes the shape of the retinene, ultimately severing the connection between the two parts of the molecule and exposing two sulphhydryl (SH) groups and a hydrogen ion binding group (H.+). The molecule undergoes a series of transformations, from pre-lumi-rhodopsin to lumirhodopsin to meta-1-rhodopsin to meta-2-rhodopsin, until the final separation into retinene and opsin. Bleaching occurs in the passage from meta-1- to meta-2-rhodopsin; visual excitation is presumed to have occurred by this stage.

the alligator whose white choroid provides an ideal backdrop. For the red pigment visibly fades to intermediate oranges, then to the yellow of retinene, finally losing color altogether in the change to vitamin A, for this, like opsin, is colorless. How the breakdown of the molecule alters the electrical state of the visual cell is still a matter of conjecture. One theory holds that the now naked opsin molecule exposes new reactive sites (including two sulphydryl groups and one hydrogen ion-binding group). Another theory is based on the intriguing structure of the outer segments. They are built up from identical thin wafers, each bounded by a double membrane rich in pigment, the whole suggesting the geometric regularity of a crystal. If light hits a single molecule of rhodopsin in the membrane of only one layer, it may kick an electron out of place, which, given the quasi-crystalline structure, may then be free to move down and kick an electron in the next layer, and so generate a current through a chain reaction comparable to the process operating in the semiconducting material of a transistor.

Regeneration of rhodopsin occurs by a reverse process: vitamin A (which may be brought in fresh from the bloodstream to the pigment epithelium) is converted to the rekinked form of retinene and this combines with free opsin to form rhodopsin.

The initial bleaching of a few molecules of rhodopsin has marked effects on vision; it greatly decreases sensitivity. Similarly the final restorations of rhodopsin—the last few molecules to be made to fill the reservoir to brimming—are apparently necessary for maximal sensitivity. Studies of human subjects as well as test-tube analyses of cattle rhodopsin indicate that a bleaching of only 0.006 percent of rhodopsin lowers visual sensitivity 8.5 times, while breaking down 100 times as much, still only 0.6 percent, makes the eye 3,300 times less sensitive. Conversely when rhodopsin is fully restored the gain in sensitivity is such that under ideal atmospheric conditions at night it would theoretically be possible to see the light of a candle almost a mile away.

Rhodopsin is by far the most abundant of the four pigments so far discovered in animal retinas. As such it has been the easiest to study and has served as a model for the others. Indeed the world of visual pigments seems a small one. Wherever it has been possible to extract pigments from eyes, be they the newt's or the pigeon's, the trout's or the rat's, they turn out to be simple variations on the rhodopsin theme—large carotenoid-protein molecules that undergo bleaching and recombination cycles. From an analytical point of view the only differences are in the kinds of opsin or forms of retinene and vitamin A. It would seem that all seeing creatures handle light, in particular that prime source of light, the sun, in much the same way.

An Octave of Light

Moreover all are stimulated by much the same band of rays out of the vast bundle of electromagnetic radiation the sun emits. When analyzed in terms of frequency or wavelength, this is a very thin sliver, a single octave in the middle of a grand 70-octave "piano" of radiant energy that extends from the miles long, low frequency radio waves to the infinitesimal (10 trillionths of an inch), high frequency cosmic rays. The visible spectrum, the familiar rainbow you see in sunlight, ranges from the longer red waves—1/40,000 inch (about 700 millimicrons in the usual units used, abbreviated mμ†)—up to the violet at a little over half that length, about 400 mμ. These dimensions, incidentally, set the limits on the power of a light microscope. You can't magnify an object smaller than the wavelength of violet light because the rays illuminating it are too big. It would be like trying to thread a needle with a length of rope, or measuring a hair's breadth with a 12-inch ruler.

Handling light photochemically is not the same as seeing. A single beam of light, a single set of molecular changes does not necessarily mean you see a flash, much less an image. It is possible to ask questions of human subjects, of course, but ultimately the meaning of the answer must be sought not only in terms of the reactions of pigments, but in the labyrinth of connections within the retina and brain, and this has to be looked at microscopically.

Blind Men and Elephants

The search is a complicated business, for one of the most distinguishing characteristics of the human retina is that it is different everywhere you look at it. Were you to deduce its behavior from any one microscopic section you might get as fallacious a picture as the blind men who described only that part of the elephant they touched. Toward the center of the retina, for example, a section might reveal only cones, very thin almost rodlike cones, squeezed into a tiny pit, less than 0.02 inch in diameter. Slice around this area and you might continue to intersect cones, with rods appearing now and then. Go out toward the rim of the retinal bowl and just the opposite will happen—there will be an abundance of rods and few cones.

Now if you trace the connections of each rod or each cone as it trails off to carry nerve impulses to the next layer of the retina you would continue to find differences. There will be exceptions, of course,

† One micron is 0.00004 inch approximately. A millimicron is 1/1000th of a micron, approximately 0.00000004 inch.

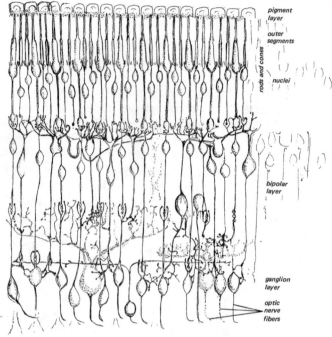

A semischematic drawing of a portion of retina containing both rods and cones; the bottom of the drawing represents the layers near the front of the eye. Note that the rods and cones are at the rear of the retina, with their outer segments penetrating the pigment epithelium. Light must pass through the preceding transparent neural layers before it can stimulate the photoreceptors. A variety of cell types are shown at the bipolar and ganglion levels. Some cells branch widely, some are more discrete. The cells differ in size, shape, and position, as well as in their input-output connections. In addition to the rods, cones, and bipolar and ganglion cells, the retina also contains a number of other nerve cells which interact with these, and fibers presumed to come from cells in the brain.

but the chances are that the rods will be promiscuous. Hundreds will tie into one or more second-order nerve cells, the double-ended bipolars that constitute layer three of the retina (counting as layer one, the pigment-epithelial layer that swings around to contribute color to the iris and layer two, the rods and cones themselves).

The rods' promiscuity continues, with several bipolars tied into one or more cells of layer four, the ganglion cell layer. The innermost fibers of these cells in turn form the optic nerves. The cones on the other hand seem more like prima donnas, especially in the central pit. Here a single cone may excite a single bipolar, for example.

It is interesting to speculate whether a cell "archaeologist" at some future date would be able to piece together these anatomical facts with a knowledge of photochemistry and optics to deduce what this meant. It could be that the two types of visual cells with two kinds of distribution and two sets of connections add up to a sort of double vision in man. This double vision would be nothing else than the ability to see in color and by day, "photopic" vision, and in black and white in very dim light or at night, "scotopic" vision. The early theoreticians of visual physiology came to this conclusion; and they were right.

The rods with their greater number—100 million at a rough count compared with 6 or 7 million cones—their multiple connections, and their rich stores of rhodopsin have evolved to squeeze the last drop of energy from the feeblest glimmers of light. These are your night eyes. Selig Hecht of Columbia University put this to a test some thirty years ago, asking subjects to tell when they could just detect light in a darkened room. When the intensity of the just noticeable flash was translated into photons or quanta, irreducible particles of light like the protons or electrons of atoms, and suitable corrections were made, it turned out that the energy of only 1 quantum was needed to bleach 1 molecule of rhodopsin in a rod. Only 5 to 10 rods are needed to experience such a change (within a tenth of a second) for normal eyes to perceive the flash. Even with the best present-day equipment it is not easy to detect such small amounts of light. If our threshold for perception were any lower than this it would lead to distraction or confusion: we'd see the occasional random event, such as the spontaneous unzipping of molecules of pigment. Spots would appear before the eyes whether they were open or not.

Primarily because of the rods' great convergence, but also because of their dominance at the optically poorer periphery of the retina (the rays here are bent more and are likely to come to a focus ahead of the true focus), the rods' sensitivity is at a sacrifice to sharpness. In dim light they may produce a fuzzy image. Yet that image is better than nothing at all, and indeed, if you are a stargazer given to looking at the heavens with your naked eyes, you will not be able to see a feeble star if you look at it straight on. Its light will only intercept the high-threshold cones. Light may have to be as much as 100,000 times brighter for even the most sensitive cones to react! Better to follow the French physicist Arago's advice—to see a dimly lit object, you must not look at it directly.

The cones with their best optical location near the center of focus, and their more discrete connections into the brain, can pin down with greater precision the place where light strikes the retina. These are your discriminating cells. The ones at the central pit, the fovea, or close by in

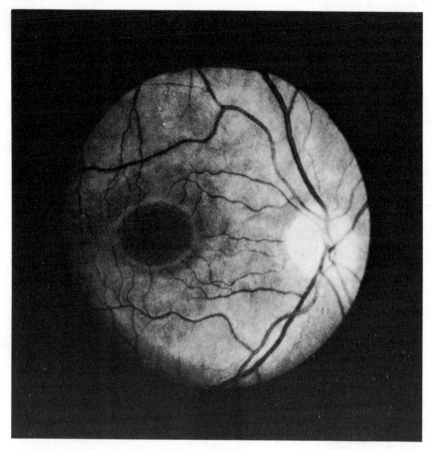

A photograph of the central portion of the retina of the left eye. The dark spot on the left is the macula, at the center of which is a lighter spot, the fovea. A number of blood vessels are shown; these, along with the optic nerve, exit at the optic disk at right.

the surrounding *macula lutea* (literally, the yellow spot, because of the presence of yellow pigment in the area), yield the sharpest images. Here acuity, usually measured in terms of resolving power—your ability to discriminate the fine details in a picture—is best. Your fovea is to vision what your fingertips are to touch, the optimal area for two-point discrimination. The foveal cones can detect the dots that make up a newspaper photo just as Meissner corpuscles in your fingertips can sense the grade of fine sandpaper. In both cases the peripheral "fine grain" of the receptors is complemented by central connections of great subtlety.

The letter chart in the doctor's office is one of the more familiar ways of testing acuity. Other methods make use of checkerboards or line gratings in which the widths of the black and white spaces are equal. In good lighting conditions the normal eye can detect adjacent line gratings as separate when the space between them forms a visual angle of only 30 seconds.

A less exacting test of acuity measures how fine a line can be, and still be detectable against a background. This is your minimum *visible* as opposed to *separable* acuity. Here the width of line need only subtend a visual angle of 1 second for a normal eye to distinguish it. This is equivalent to seeing a wire 0.01 inch in diameter at a distance of 100 yards. For such maximal acuity, however, the wire must be fairly long and the background illumination good.

Adaptation

Which kind of sensitivity and what degree of acuity your eyes have will depend on whether rods or cones are in the ascendancy and on the rates of bleaching and regeneration of pigments going on in each at any time, internal chemistry that in turn depends on the supply of materials [†] and the demand of light. Like most dynamic living systems the retina is ever seeking equilibrium, a balance of pigment bleaching and regeneration that will be achieved at lower or higher levels according to the available light. The passage from bright light to darkness, or the gain in sensitivity with rod vision, is known as dark adaptation. Conversely the loss of sensitivity (but gain in acuity) with more light is called light adaptation.

With a change in illumination come dramatic alterations of perception, the most dramatic change of all being the appearance or disappearance of color. Here the individual idiosyncrasies of the rod and cone pigments are most responsible. These show up in the different ways they respond to light of different wavelengths. Rhodopsin looks red because it doesn't absorb the long red wavelengths but instead reflects them. It can absorb all the other wavelengths, but in varying amounts. To study this selective action you need a source of spectral colors. Special filters, which absorb certain wavelengths and transmit others, can be used as well as fine line gratings, or most familiar of all, glass prisms. When ordinary "white" sunlight which is composed of all the visible wavelengths is passed through a narrow slit in front of a prism, the shorter wavelengths are refracted more than the longer ones. The result is that the colors of the spectrum line up behind the prism in order, from violet

---

[†] A lack of vitamin A, vital as a precursor of pigment, shows up as "night blindness." The antipellagra vitamin, nicotinamide, is also important.

nearest the glass, through blue, indigo, green, yellow, orange, and finally red, farthest away.

Next the strength of the spectral beam has to be measured. If this is very feeble you literally see "as through a glass darkly." The whole spectrum under such rod conditions appears in shades of gray. If the radiant energy is strong enough, however, you may remark on how bright all the "colors" now are. But just as the ear's perception of loudness is only roughly proportional to the decibel scale of sound intensity, so the eye's reading of brightness is not reliable and is at variance with the light meters or photometers that photographers use.

The basic unit for measuring intensity is the lumen. This is a unit of flux, or flow of radiant energy, 1 lumen being the amount of light falling on 1 square foot 1 foot away from an arbitrary light source, usually a standard candle. All other measures of intensity can be derived from this, and their usefulness depends on the point of view of the experimenter. If he is interested in the intensity of light measured at the source, the unit used is candlepower—one candlepower being the intensity at the point of the flame of a standard candle. If he is interested in the density of the flux—the intensity of light incident on a unit surface some distance from the source—he is concerned with illuminance. This is usually measured in foot- or meter-candles. One foot-candle represents the intensity of light at the surface of an imaginary sphere centered at the candle source and 1 foot in radius. A point to remember is that intensity falls off as the square of the distance. Thus 2 feet from an electric bulb the intensity is only one-fourth what it was at 1 foot; at 3 feet the intensity is one-ninth, and so on. At a rough estimate the illuminance supplied by the noonday sun on a bright day is about 9,600 foot-candles. On a dull afternoon it would be about 100 foot-candles.

In vision experiments it is usually more important to know the amount of light reflected from a surface, its "luminance," rather than the intensity of light incident upon it. The unit frequently used in this case is the lambert or millilambert. One lambert is the intensity of light reflected uniformly from a surface whose illuminance is 10,000 meter-candles.

Spectral Sensitivity, Visibility Curves, Action and Absorption Spectra

Once the wavelength and intensity of a beam of spectral light are known, the effects of the beam on extracts of rod or cone pigments, or on the eye itself, can be studied. A pigment exposed to various spectral beams is bleached by some wavelengths more than others. The measure

238

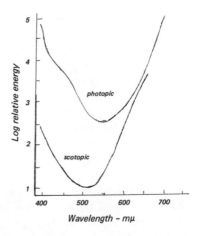

The absolute visual thresholds, in relative-energy units, as a function of wavelength. Note that the photopic curve is higher— the cones are not as sensitive as the rods— and its minimal point is shifted toward the red end of the spectrum, as Purkinje first noted.

of differences in absorbing power can then be used to determine the action spectrum of the pigment, typically a bell-shaped curve whose peak represents the wavelengths the pigment absorbs best, i.e., light of very low intensity in this region will still excite the molecules. For rhodopsin the peak is around 505 mμ, in the green portion of the spectrum (even though the rods don't see the color green). For iodopsin, a violet-colored pigment found in the cones of the chicken, the peak is at 562 mμ in the yellow-green region of the spectrum.

When the eye itself is tested more complex measurements have to be made in keeping with such variables as how large is the area, what part of the retina is being stimulated, and what are the effects of absorption and reflection by non-retinal parts of the eye. If a human subject is asked to state when light at various wavelengths is just visible as the intensity of the test beam is increased in steps, the results are used to draw threshold visibility curves.

There are two such curves for human eyes, corresponding to rod and cone vision. Both are U shapes, a fact of some interest for it shows that the eye in either dim or bright light is about 1,000 times more sensitive to rays at the middle wavelengths than at either end of the spectrum. Loosely speaking, middle wavelengths are to the eyes what human speech frequencies are to the ears.

The Purkinje Shift

If the rod (scotopic) and cone (photopic) visibility curves are drawn against the same scale, the photopic curve is both higher up, reflecting the over-all higher threshold of the cones, and also shifted toward the red end of the spectrum. Its lowest point is in the yellow-green, at about 550 mμ. This is known as the Purkinje shift, since it was first noted by Johannes Purkinje, a versatile Bohemian scientist who in 1842 established one of the first physiology laboratories in Europe.

If visibility curves are turned upside down, so that the points which represent the lowest thresholds are at the crest, the curve represents spectral sensitivity. This is a simple way of visualizing that sensitivity measurements are the inverses or reciprocals of threshold (minimal energy) measurements. If, in relative terms, you need ten times the intensity to see light at wavelength X than you need at wavelength Y, you are obviously only 1/10th as sensitive to X as you are to Y.

Sometimes the criterion in eye tests is not the report of the human subject or the brightness matches he may make to some standard, but the amount of electrical activity in the retina or in the optic nerve fibers that results from light stimulation. Usually the intensity of the test beam is altered until electrical responses at each wavelength are equal. Such tests conducted in animals suggest that there is wide similarity in the way vertebrate eyes see; visibility peaks may be displaced to the right or left, thresholds may be higher or lower (some animals have pure rod or pure cone eyes), but the limits are similar and the distributions usually U shaped.

One further comparison between rods and cones relates to the ability to detect just noticeable differences in brightness. On a moonless night, for example, where the total illumination is on the order of 0.01 millilambert, the intensity of the light of a firefly may have to be doubled (it would have to fly that much closer to you) before you could detect a just noticeable difference in brightness. In broad daylight, however, when the background illumination is several million times brighter, the cones apparently can perceive an increase in brightness by the fantastically small fraction of 1/167th.

These extraordinary differences in rod and cone behavior go far to explain the ever-changing qualities of vision that occur in the course of the day. At dawn your eyes may be fully dark-adapted and your vision will be restricted to black and white in the style of the rods. Red flowers will look dark (remember, rhodopsin absorbs very little in the red portion of the spectrum), while wavelengths close to rhodopsin's absorption peak, the blues and greens, will appear the brightest and lightest shades of gray. The other wavelengths will be graded down accordingly. "When a white thread can be distinguished from a black thread," according to Moslem tradition, "so must the day's fast of Ramadan begin. . . ." As the sun rises higher more rhodopsin is bleached than is made, so sensitivity goes down. At the same time light will begin to excite the cones and color will begin to be perceived. First the most sensitive cones are stimulated. Then as intensity is increased, cones of successively higher thresholds will be excited. For each wavelength of light there is an interval of grayness, a range of intensity called the photochromatic interval which must be passed before color is seen. For red the interval is almost nonexistent since you either see red as nearly black with the rods, or else you see it as red with red-sensitive cones. (Note that the scotopic and photopic visibility curves approach each other toward the red end of the spectrum.) The interval widens over the spectrum so that the gap between rod and cone vision is greatest at the violet end.

As the day wanes the visual processes reverse. "When white and black threads are no longer distinguishable one from the other, so the day's fast may end and night begin." But it takes the rods a long time to be roused from their lethargy. Even though the manufacturing process has been going on slowly in daylight, rhodopsin only approaches a peak level about a half- to three-quarters of an hour after the onset of darkness.§ That's why it takes so long before you can see your neighbors in a

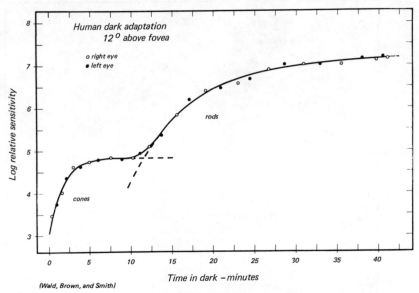

The dark-adaptation process in the human eye, measured in a peripheral area that contains both rods and cones. Cones complete adaptation within about 5 minutes; rods need about 45 minutes to reach maximum sensitivity.

§ The cones also regenerate in darkness and at a much faster rate. However they play no part in dark vision since their thresholds are so much higher.

movie theater, or the details of a room in a dimly lit restaurant. So crucial was this period in wartime that soldiers and pilots often wore glasses with red-filtered lenses while it was still daylight. The rods, less sensitive to the red light, were fooled into believing it was dark out and started to manufacture rhodopsin so that when night came they were already dark-adapted.

Fingerprinting the Eyes

If the rods or cones made use of only one kind of visual pigment it would be reasonable to expect that the eye's behavior in dark or bright light would correlate nicely with the activity of the appropriate pigment, which in turn would be a function of its absorption spectrum. Since absorption spectra are unique (this is true not just for the visual pig-

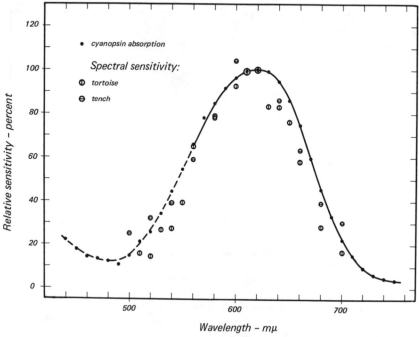

The absorption spectrum of cyanopsin compared with Granit's electrophysiological measurements of the spectral sensitivity of cone vision in the tench, a freshwater fish, and in the European tortoise (Testudo graeca).

242

ments, but for any substance that absorbs and reflects light selectively), the spectral record itself would indicate the presence of the substance. If you found an animal with a visibility curve that exactly matched the absorption spectrum of a known pigment, for example, you'd make the obvious deduction that the pigment was there; you wouldn't have to remove the retina and try to isolate the pigment.

Something very like this kind of pigment fingerprinting was used in reverse fashion in George Wald's laboratory at Harvard. He and his associates had investigated the various forms of retinene and the rod and cone opsins that constituted the then three known visual pigments and concluded that there should be a fourth possibility. They combined the suspected ingredients—a cone opsin with one form of retinene—to produce what seemed like a perfectly good blue pigment they called cyanopsin (cyan- means blue). If it existed in nature, they naturally decided the pigment should be found in the cones of some animals. Its peak absorption lay in the orange-red region of the spectrum around 620 mμ. But were there any animals around who might see according to this absorption mode? Indeed there were. The eminent Finnish neurophysiologist Ragnar Granit had made very careful spectral sensitivity analyses of the European tortoise, *Testuda graeca*, and the tench, a freshwater fish. When the data were compared the points marking the spectral sensitivities fell close to or on the curve of the absorption spectrum of cyanopsin. This experiment showed clearly that in animals that cannot perform psychophysical tests one can still obtain much information about the visual system.

Color Vision

The nuances of daytime vision in the tortoise and the tench can be understood completely in terms of a single photopigment. This is also the case whenever rod eyes or night vision is studied. Not all animal rods contain rhodopsin; some freshwater fish and amphibians have rods that contain porphyropsin (a pigment whose absorption peak occurs about 522 mμ). But generally speaking, the absorption spectra of one or the other match the animal's sensitivity curve so closely that no one disputes that a single pigment alone is responsible for black and white vision.

This has never been true for human color vision, or indeed, for any animal presumed to be able to recognize colors. This is an oddly assorted group that includes many birds, some snakes and fishes, but very few mammals. Only the higher primates and man are presumed to have true color vision. Not only at night are all cats gray, but the world is ever gray to cats. Remember, too, that the bull responds to the movement of the matador's cape, not to its red color.

To explain how a woman chooses between a dozen different lipsticks, or a man selects which tweed jacket suits his fancy, color theorists have generally assumed that there were either several types of cone, each with a different pigment, or that each cone contained more than one kind of pigment. Their differential absorbing powers would then lead to different mixtures or blends, which would make it possible to see all the colors of the rainbow—as well as the 160 different hues trained observers are able to discriminate, according to wavelength within those limits.

This presumption underscores a metaphysical truth about color: it is a function of the eye of the beholder. It has been convenient to relate the sensation to wavelength, just as pitch is subjectively associated with the frequency of sounds, but we neither see wavelengths nor hear frequencies. At best both the eyes' and ears' abilities to act as frequency or wavelength analyzers are conditioned by a number of factors.

For the eyes these include obvious spatial considerations: you see little or no color if only the rod-rich periphery of the retina is exposed. Nor do you see color purely and simply whenever cones are stimulated. Recent experiments by investigators Robert Boynton, William Schafer, and Mary Ellen Neun of the University of Rochester bear out studies dating as far back as Helmholtz's time that indicate that as you move farther away from the fovea your ability to judge color deteriorates considerably. You seem to lose reds and especially greens first, so that somewhere between 20 and 40 degrees from the fovea, all colors are seen as blues or yellows.

To some extent your analysis of color is always an abstraction from an event which has to be put into historical, physical, and psychological perspective. What has happened just before or just after you see a flash of light affects your analysis of it. Similarly the source of light, the duration of the stimulus, the background illumination, the state of adaptation of your eyes, the presence of drugs, and even your emotional state "color" your experience of color.

Some of these influences can be studied in terms of space or time variables. Adaptation or the effects of prior stimulation obviously involve the visual system's response as a function of time. The multicolored afterimages you see after staring at the setting sun are one of the more spectacular color effects that fit into this category as an example of "successive contrast."

Simultaneous contrast, on the other hand, is a quality of perception that depends on the juxtaposition in space of different colors, or shapes,

An example of simultaneous brightness contrast. Against the black
squares the white lines appear
very bright. At the intersections of
white with white, however, gray
spots are seen. When white is
bordered with white, there is no
contrast and hence no brightness
enhancement.

Rotating Benham's top produces
color sensations which vary with
the speed of rotation.

or brightnesses. If you stare at a gray circle against a red background, for example, the gray takes on a greenish hue. Put it against green and it will look red. Yellow looks brighter against a dark background and darker against white.

A mixture of spatial and temporal effects is involved in some of the most unexpected color phenomena, like that of Benham's top. The "top" is actually a disk variously striped or shaded in black and white. When rotated the observer sees a variety of colors that depend on the speed of rotation.

Underlying these spatial and temporal characteristics of color perception are the basic physical properties of the stimulating light. In addition to wavelength and intensity there is also saturation, the degree of pure color or "chroma" present as compared to tints, shades, or other adulterations that give hues a washed-out appearance. Here the differences between the eye and laboratory measuring instruments show up in the eye's inability to separate these qualities. Each is a complex function of the other two.

Most of the colors of the spectrum shift in hue with a shift in intensity, for example. The longer wavelengths approach yellow as intensity increases; the shorter ones, blue. This phenomenon, known as the Bezold-Brücke effect, means that if you were asked to match reds you would find that a very intense red at 650 mμ would look the same as a less intense red at 625 mμ and these would both match a very faint red at about 610 mμ. Only three points of the spectrum are invariant with respect to intensity: a yellow at 572 mμ, a green at 503 mμ, and a blue at 78 mμ.

The Bezold-Brücke effect has a counterpart in hearing for your perception of pitch is similarly a function of intensity. The louder you hear a pure tone of low frequency the lower it sounds, while for high frequencies just the opposite happens: the louder the squeak, the higher it sounds.

Brightness and saturation values are also bound up with wavelength and energy levels. The Purkinje shift is precisely an illustration of how your estimate of brightness varies with the wavelength and energy of the beam presented. Saturation judgments are such that yellow and violet appear the least colored of all the spectral hues, over a wide range of intensities. Reds and greens, on the other hand, the most saturated colors, appear at their deepest at middling intensities.

Contrast and Constancy

These examples suggest that the visual system is extremely capricious in its color judgments. In fact the capriciousness is of great advantage. A closer analysis of the interplay between light and man's visual system indicates that there are two forces at work. One sharpens contrast, making any changes in the visual world stand out. The other allows for some flexibility within the perceptual scheme. Whatever it is that stands out and is recognized should not change dramatically with changes in the seeing conditions. This "constancy" force, which affects size, brightness, and shape, as well as color, explains why the roses you cut in the noonday sun don't suddenly look orange in your house where they are illuminated by incandescent bulbs at night, or why the white shirt a man puts on in the morning doesn't look "tattle-tale gray" as he leaves for work on a cloudy day.

Unfortunately constancy creates a stumbling block for reality. It tends to take color from the eye of the beholder and put it back into things as an external quality. In due course we realize that the sky isn't blue and that water taken from the ocean is not green, but somehow the idea of the "coloredness" of solid objects is hard to give up. Cheese is yellow; meat is red; grass is green.

Even when we wear sunglasses we have a tendency to regard a change of hue as a distortion of the object's "real" color. It is only when we conclude that this real color more often than not is due to the selective reflection and transmission of sunlight, itself a most variable commodity, or when careful experiments are done, that the notion of color as a sometime thing strikes home.

Thus it's hard to believe that red and green light filtered from sunlight through prisms will combine to produce yellow; that blue can be made of violet and green; or that if you take the colors of the spectrum and arrange them in a circle, the pairs of opposites (complements) across the center will produce white. Yet all these experiments have been made since Newton's time and in due course have led to the concept of primary colors—primary in the sense that they did not look as though they could be made from any other colors (as orange looks like red and yellow), while in combination they could produce the whole spectrum.

Trichromatic Vision

A seventeenth-century printer named LeBlond was one of the first to exploit these possibilities. Before his time printers had to resort to hundreds of colored inks to achieve their effects. LeBlond first showed that he could produce all colors from just seven inks and black. Later he did it with three. By and large, every color theorist has started out with at least three to build a theory.||

But which three (or four or five) colors to choose from; what arbitrary wavelength to select within each color band; these were the problems. The English chemist Thomas Young who is credited with one of the earliest hypotheses first chose red, yellow, and blue as spectral primaries. Later he changed these to red, green, and violet, conveniently

|| It must be pointed out that color mixing with inks, paints, or pigments, while analogous to spectral mixing in that there are primaries, secondaries, and complementary pairs, is based on a very different principle. In any pigment the color you see depends on the wavelengths that have been reflected, all others being absorbed. Thus the yellow of yellow paint derives from the fact that the pigment absorbs blue light and reflects red, green, and yellow. (The red and green mix and are also perceived as yellow.) Blue pigment, on the other hand, reflects blue and some green and absorbs all other colors. Mix blue and yellow paint and the only light left over, subtracted after all the absorptions, is the green which both the yellow and blue pigments reflect. Spectral mixing is always additive. What you see is the transmitted combinations or sums of frequencies.

247

located at the extremes and middle of the spectrum. This is the formulation that Helmholtz also agreed upon in the theory which now bears both their names. On a purely physical basis there is no reason why red, green, and violet are any better since combinations of other wavelengths will also yield all the recognizable hues. Yellow bears no trace of its red and green progenitors and hence was frequently a candidate for a primary receptor. Blue and violet were also traded back and forth, and for the purposes of the Young-Helmholtz theory are treated synonymously.

The controversies that stirred rancor in the hearts of the theoreticians were physiological rather than physical. Did the eyes actually contain photosensitive substances corresponding to Young's choice or not? Were they to be found in the nerve fibers or in the outer segments of cones? Was each pigment isolated in a separate cone or did the cones contain pigment mixtures? What about some of the later theories that came along? Ewald Hering postulated that the receptor mechanisms involved antagonistic or opponent pairs of colors: red-green, blue-yellow, black-white. One or the other of each pair emerged as victor under a given light stimulus. Constantine Ladd-Franklin proposed an evolutionary theory about pigments, proposing that they evolved by a sort of fission process. First black and white developed, then white split into blue and yellow, and finally yellow split into red and green, a theory which might account for the varied color sensitivities as light plays upon areas more removed from the fovea.

Color Blindness

Any theory proposed not only had to explain normal color vision, but sooner or later had to come to grips with the disturbances known collectively as "color blindness." Half the time this seemed a stimulus to ingenuity; half the time a *bête noire*. For no sooner had a theory coped with one sort of color blindness when two others would be discovered.

Apparently the aberration was not noted before the eighteenth century, or else earlier records have been lost. One of the first accounts appeared in 1777 when it was reported that a certain Mr. Harris of Cumberland, England, had, at four years of age, picked up a stocking on the street and brought it to a nearby house. It puzzled him that the article was referred to as a "red" stocking, since from his point of view, the word "stocking" was a sufficient description. Later records make it clear that he was color blind. About twenty years later, John Dalton, the English chemist and contributor to atomic theory, discovered he too suffered from defective color vision, writing:

I find that persons in general distinguish six kinds of color in the solar image . . . to me it is quite otherwise. I see only two or at most, three distinctions. These I should call yellow and blue, or yellow, blue and purple. My yellow comprehends the red, orange, yellow and green of others; and my blue and purple coincides with theirs.

Dalton's perceptions were so novel that the French even coined the word *daltonisme* to describe the condition.

In retrospect it may not be a coincidence that such texts and testimonies appeared at a time when philosophy itself, stimulated by the works of Descartes and Newton, and exemplified in the essays of philosophers like Berkeley, Locke, and Hume, was concerned with questions of subjective appearance vs. objective reality. Phenomenology, the belief that what is is only what appears to be, rivaled the idea that there were absolutes, that beyond what could be sensed was the ultimate, the "really real." Sensory defects were fascinating because one could speculate what knowledge of the world would still be possible and what would happen if the defect were corrected.

The visual disorder Dalton suffered from was a form of the now familiar red-green color blindness, a hereditary sex-linked trait that affects about 2 percent of men and 0.03 percent of women.

The other forms of color defective vision, as well as *daltonisme*, have been codified in a system that pays homage to the Young-Helmholtz theory: the affected colors are referred to by the prefixes prota- , deutera- , and trita- to correspond to the first (red), second (green), and third (blue) color-sensing mechanisms. A reasonably complete listing of the types would include:

(1) Anomalous trichromacy. In this condition all colors are distinguished and presumably all pigments are present, but in abnormal amounts. Thus more intense red light may be needed to mix with green to match a standard yellow, or vice versa.

(2) Dichromacy. Dichromats see only two colors in the spectrum, usually separated by neutral gray or white areas. The most common forms are protanopia (red-blindness) and deuteranopia (green-blindness). In either case the only colors seen are blues and yellows. However the sensitivities differ. Vision for the red-blind person is greatly foreshortened in the red end of the spectrum. It's as though this part of the spectrum didn't exist. On the other hand the deuteranope can see out to the normal limits of the spectrum but he reports that it looks yellow. A third form of dichromacy, tritanopia, or blue-blindness, is much more rare. Such a person confuses blue with yellow and sees the spectrum in shades of red and green, with a neutral gray area around 570 mμ.

(3) Monochromacy. This very rare condition is the only one for which the term color blind is technically correct. No colors are seen at all, the whole spectrum appearing in shades of brighter or dimmer grays. Usually there is a major defect in the cones themselves, so that acuity is very bad and the eyes may even make wandering (nystagmic) movements as though avoiding focusing on the foveal area.

Acuity is seldom affected in protanopia or deuteranopia, however, so that the color defect is not one which means that the cones are deficient in number or have lost any power to respond. It may be that one pigment is reacting indiscriminately to two separate wavelengths. There might also be a coupling of transmission lines further on in the system.

Glimmers of support for some theories of color vision arise from certain classifications of color blindness. The rarity of tritanopia might be some evidence for the Ladd-Franklin theory, for example. However more recent evidence suggests that yellow need never be invoked as a primary receptor. The reasons for this involve several methods of testing which have been eminently successful in verifying the essential truth of the Young-Helmholtz theory. But before describing them, it is pertinent to mention why, in a century which has wrested so many secrets from irascible atoms, elusive cells, or intransigent forces of nature, the cones of the human retina should prove so intractable. Certainly there have been many direct analytic attacks on them, and some partial successes, but as yet the extremely small size of the cells in man, especially those at the fovea, has been a stumbling block. Attempts to isolate the minute traces of pigment present (much less than the rhodopsin found in the rods) are likely to yield incomplete or questionable results. Nor is it yet possible to apply the highly developed techniques of electrophysiology. The cone size eludes even the most delicately fashioned mircroelectrodes that might hope to tap the cone's discrete response to a light stimulus.¶

A number of investigators in England and America have circumvented these problems by devising ingenious techniques for studying the visual pigments. W. S. Stiles, an English investigator formerly on the staff of the National Physical Laboratory at Teddington, has studied the changes in spectral sensitivity at the fovea when a test beam at a given wavelength is seen against background illumination at various wavelengths and intensities.

¶ Though perhaps not for long. A Japanese scientist, T. Tomita, has recently reported some success with microelectrode implantations in cones. The technique involves using a loudspeaker to amplify vibrations set up in the individual cones of a fish. ˙

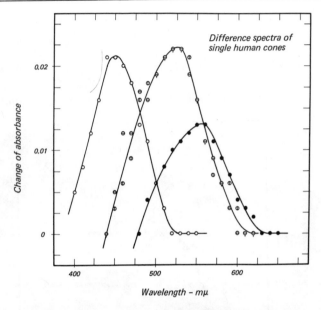

Difference spectra of visual pigments in single cones of the parafoveal region of the human retina. One of the cones, apparently a blue receptor, has a wavelength maximum at about 450 mμ; two cones, apparently green receptors, have wavelength maxima at about 525 mμ; and one, apparently a red receptor, has a wavelength maximum at about 555 mμ.

William A. Rushton of Trinity College, Cambridge, has developed a technique of reflectance densitometry. He has measured the changes in intensity of light reflected from the back of the eye (having passed through the retina twice), from test beams aimed at the fovea. The measurements are made before and after the fovea is partially bleached by light at certain wavelengths. If red light is used, for example, any red-sensitive pigment present will be preferentially bleached. When test beams at selected wavelengths are then aimed at the fovea those in the red portion of the spectrum should find less pigment available to absorb them, and hence be reflected more. Rushton's data revealed exactly this sort of phenomenon and he was able to draw "difference" spectra for foveal photopigments. (The points on the curve represent the postbleaching absorption data subtracted from the prebleaching data.)

In the late fifties and early sixties George Wald and Paul K. Brown at Harvard began to study the fovea in human and monkey retinas using microspectrophotometric (MSP) techniques. Essentially they aim a beam of light at a tiny patch of fovea taken postoperatively in a fresh, dark-adapted state, and then use a microscope to measure the

251

amount of light that gets through. They do this at selected wavelengths before and after bleaching with white or colored light and again obtain difference spectra.°°

Later this technique was refined so that the beam of light could be aimed at a single rod or cone. W. B. Marks, W. H. Dobelle, and E. F. MacNichol, Jr., at Johns Hopkins University perfected a similar tech-

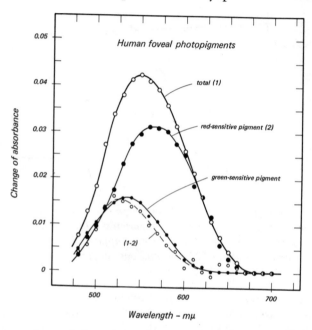

Difference spectrum of photopigments of the human central fovea, where there are few, if any, blue cones. The difference spectrum of a red-sensitive pigment (curve 2), wavelength maximum at 565 mμ, obtained by differential bleaching in deep red light, accounts for virtually all the absorption at wavelengths longer than about 625 mμ. This curve is adjusted in height, therefore, so as to coincide with the total difference spectrum (curve 1) above this wavelength. Subtracting curve 2 from curve 1 should then yield the difference spectrum of the green-sensitive pigment; this is shown as a broken line (1–2) with the wavelength maximum at about 530 mμ. It is to be compared with the directly measured difference spectrum of the green-sensitive pigment, shown as a solid line (wavelength maximum at about 535 mμ), obtained at the end of a successive series of bleaches with red light.

°° These difference spectra can be considered true absorption spectra for wavelengths above 510 mμ. Below that the difference spectrum falls below the absorption spectrum owing to the production of certain colored products of bleaching (which are themselves photosensitive).

nique at the same time. Because the cone pigment will undergo some bleaching during the course of the experiment certain corrections must be made. Brown and Wald first record the absorption data of the receptor from the red to the blue end of the spectrum, then they reverse the process. The two sets of results are averaged to compensate for the progressive bleaching.

Finally Wald, using a variation on Stiles's technique on human subjects, was able to isolate the behavior of single photopigments (as opposed to single receptors) in the fovea through a process of elimination of the others presumed to be present. After first measuring the overall spectral sensitivity of the fovea (the photopic luminosity curve), he would shine an adapting light stimulus on the area, say a bright yellow light containing all wavelengths longer than 550 mμ. After a time the pigments whose primary absorptions are in these limits will be exhausted. Keeping this light on as a background field, Wald then repeats the spectral sensitivity test moving down the spectrum from blue to red in graduated steps. The observer would then report at what point light at certain wavelengths was just visible. The resulting curve, with certain corrections, would represent the absorption characteristics of the blue-receptor mechanism. Using red and violet light (i.e., purple) as the adapting stimulus, Wald mapped the eye's green receptor sensitivity, while a blue background yielded data on red sensitivity.

Each of these techniques represents an impressive achievement in the face of formidable odds. The MSP work involves delicate surgery in which the retina must be carefully removed from the eye and the fovea extracted, mounted, and focused in the microscope. All these operations must be performed quickly and in deep red light in order to preserve the integrity and state of dark-adaptation of the tissue. The reflectance technique involves measuring quantities of light emerging from the eye at intensities that are only 1/20,000 that of the incoming beam. That beam itself must be sufficiently weak so that it does not appreciably bleach the pigments in the course of the experiment. Work with human subjects involves making corrections for the absorption of light by non-retinal parts of the eye like the yellow lens and macular regions, as well as for the bleaching that goes on during measurements.

It is all the more heartening to find that the results from these varied and independent techniques, while not in complete agreement, essentially confirm the brilliant intuitions of Young and Helmholtz. There are three, and only three, pigments which are responsible for normal color vision in man.

Stiles's sensitivity curves showed maxima at 440 mμ, 540 mμ, and 575 mμ, in the blue, green, and red portions of the spectrum. Rushton, working in the central fovea region which is poor in blue receptors, was able to demonstrate the existence of red and green photosubstances which he called erythrolabe (red-catching) and chlorolabe (green-catching). The first peak absorptions he reported were about 590 mμ and 540 mμ respectively. (He has since lowered the red and raised the green peaks somewhat.) Rushton also showed that the common forms of red-green color blindness occur because of a lack of pigment. When he tested the spectral sensitivity of protanopes (red-blinds), he found that the typical curve he obtained essentially matched that of the absorption curve for chlorolabe. In other words, the protanope primarily depends on this pigment for photopic vision. The deuteranope on the other hand lacks green pigment, and relies on his store of red for daylight vision. (Rushton was not able to test for the presence of blue pigment, but it is generally known that its over-all contribution to color vision is small.)

While the work of Stiles and Rushton is strong evidence for the existence of the three kinds of foveal pigment the MSP work with single cones perhaps offers the most dramatic proof. The Johns Hopkins group found individual cones with absorption spectra that clustered around peaks at 445 mμ, 535 mμ, and 570 mμ. They had reason to believe that the lower peaks represented pure blue or green cones, while their "red" receptor may have represented cones that contained both red and green pigments. The comparable data of Brown and Wald showed cone peaks at 450 mμ, 525 mμ, and 555 mμ, and added a figure of 505 mμ for several rods tested. They also felt that the long wavelength peak may have represented cones containing mixtures of red and green pigment.

Having analyzed the roles of individual photopigments in color vision it was natural for these investigators to check to see if the sum of the separate spectral curves they found added up to the whole of color vision. Again the single cone data confirmed this, but there were even earlier indications that this was so in Brown and Wald's results with foveal patches. They found that the difference spectrum they obtained after total bleaching of the sample—a curve representing the composite working of all the photopigments present—was a close match for the photopic luminosity curve when that was suitably corrected for the absorbance of light by the yellow lens and macular regions.

If further corroboration is needed that three photopigments are not only necessary but sufficient to account for normal color vision it can be found in Wald's most recent work with spectral sensitivities obtained after using light-adapting stimuli. The sensitivity peaks he found, after correction for the lens and macular absorptions which particularly affect the blue receptor, came out to be 430 mμ for the blue, 540 mμ for the green, and 575 mμ for the red. The individual curves, weighted according to the amounts of pigment present (there is more red than green and very little blue pigment in the eye), again approximated the luminosity function.

One of the more interesting by-products of this method is that it can reveal individual differences in color sensitivity that may never have been noticed. One of Wald's subjects was especially sensitive to blue—and it could be demonstrated that this was primarily due to a more powerful blue receptor mechanism, and not to a more transparent lens or less pigmented macula. Another subject showed an increasing decline in sensitivity toward the violet end of the spectrum.

Wald went on to compare the sensitivity data he obtained for normal eyes with the curves for protanopes and deuteranopes. He confirmed Rushton's earlier experiments that individuals suffering from the

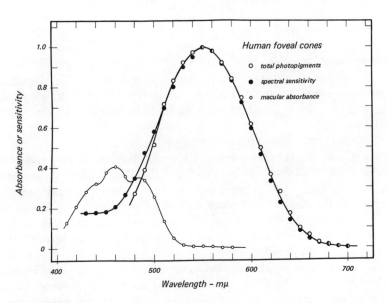

Brown and Wald compared the difference spectrum of the total number of photopigments of the human fovea (an average of five subjects) with the spectral sensitivity of foveal vision, measured as at the level of the cones. To obtain the latter function, the experimenters converted the average photopic luminosity curve data to a quantum basis and corrected for ocular and macular transmission. The spectrum of a human macula is shown at the left. The corrected luminosity curve agrees with the difference spectrum of the foveal photopigments down to about 510 mμ. Below this wavelength the difference spectrum falls off, owing to the formation of colored products of bleaching.

255

most common forms of color blindness lack either the green or red pigment. Their over-all sensitivities are close to the green or red curves of normal individuals. (The blue contribution to over-all sensitivity is very weak.) These people could be thought of as having a double dose of one pigment so that their cones respond indiscriminately to a broad band of wavelengths but with no loss of acuity.

Considering the degree of overlap that exists within the normal population of pigments—the wide range of middle wavelengths that will excite some activity in all receptors—it is remarkable that color sensations are as vivid as they are. After all, pure light is something of a laboratory artifact. The eyes are always exposed to broad, impure mixes. The retina's ability to measure the minute differences that do exist (in effect, the differences in the heights of the red, blue, and green curves when drawn on the same scales), and to enhance these differences through neural mechanisms, are very impressive.

The Long and Short of It

Such eye-brain subtlety has struck other investigators, notably Edwin Land, the ingenious inventor of Polaroid and of the Land camera. Several years ago Land startled the scientific world by producing color images from only a pair of what appeared to be black-and-white photos of a scene.

He accomplished this by shooting what he calls "long" and "short" photos of a scene. He may use a red filter for the long record and green for the short. The results in both cases are black-and-white photographs (the film is black and white); but in these prints the grays vary in brightness. He then makes black-and-white transparencies of the two records and projects them on a screen. This time he illuminates the long record with a band of long wavelength light and the short record with a short wavelength band, allowing the images from each projector to overlap on the screen. The surprising result is the original scene in color. If the illuminating lights are reversed, the short band shining through the long transparency and vice versa, the colors in the image reverse.

It makes no difference how wide at least one of the original bands may be; Land has used white light for his "short" record and red for the long. Nor is there much difference in the intensity of color in the image as the illuminating bands are varied in intensity. All that is necessary is that the long and short records offer some minimum separation (which may be surprisingly close in certain parts of the spectrum), and that the original scene presents a random collection of wavelengths to the camera, which a natural scene will always do.

Land concludes that the eye is capable of an amazing kind of adaptive behavior. Given a random mix of wavelengths in the landscape it sets up an arbitrary fulcrum point dividing light into longer or shorter wave groups. The division point itself depends on the aggregate of wavelengths displayed in the scene.

Land's experiments form an important bridge between the precise laboratory techniques necessary for delineating the apparatus of color vision and the psychological plane of everyday observation. Neither is complete in itself; neither can adequately explain the roster of phenomena recorded over the past few centuries of experiments in vision, or indeed explain the very interest in color itself, over and above all other aspects of vision.

From a philosophical point of view this interest is extraordinary, though not without a parallel in the emphasis on pitch in hearing. Western music since the Renaissance has stressed melody, while a concern for color can be traced much further back—from the anonymous craftsman Solomon sought "skilful to work in purple, crimson, and blue . . . for the veil of the temple at Jerusalem" down to the present-day extravagances of dealers in op art or Carnaby Street clothes. The prestige and expense of certain colors like the famous "imperial purple" of antiquity or the Turkey red of the Middle Ages, the elaborate etiquette that proscribed the use of green, for example, except for the lying-in chambers of medieval French queens, the long history of alchemical, emotional, and sexual connotations of color speak eloquently for its importance in man's social and cultural history. At the same time the value of the dyer's craft, the zeal with which his secrets were held, bespeak color's economic importance. As good a case can be made for the search for dyestuffs and fixatives as an incentive to the voyages of exploration and discovery as has been made in terms of the quest for salt and spices. "Brazil" even gets its name from the fact that forests of brazilwood were discovered in this New World territory, a tree whose bark was the source of a prized red rye.

Scientifically this concern for color led to early advances in chemical techniques, and, in the nineteenth century, to the discovery of the synthetic dyes which have vastly increased the number of distinguishable colors. Unfortunately these gains did not affect the physiology of color vision. The problem of color-in-the-eye remained. Some scientists were fascinated by the problems of photochemistry; others by the transducer problem or how light energy could trigger electrical events. Any time psychology raised questions about contrast, or afterimages, or constancy; any time someone asked how was it possible for the unique sensation of yellow to be produced by showing red to one eye and green to the other, science was embarrassed to answer, or at best, simply removed the question to the brain, where it remained, along with the other qualities of vision: the perception of shape, brightness, motion, depth, and distance.

More recently a number of scientists working with different species have made a fresh attack on the problem of color-coding in the nervous system with impressive results. These form part of a body of experiments aimed at tracking down still more fundamental qualities of vision like pattern or motion perception, however, and will be dealt with in that context. The elaboration of these qualities will disclose certain structural features of the visual system, not the least of which is that it is a paired system. Man has two eyes, and for good reasons.

XI

The Mind Is Blind

It seems intuitively clear that doubling the inputs of light by providing two sense organs does not result in a quantitative doubling of perceptual information. If you mix batches of red and green light ahead of time and show the results to each eye you don't see twice as much yellow. Similarly if you're driving on an overcast day the road is not very much brighter if you keep both eyes open, nor is the license plate three cars ahead any easier to read.

Why then do human beings and other animals have two eyes? One obvious reason is the insurance that a duplicate system provides. Should one eye fail, the organism is not completely at a loss. In certain fish and birds, whose eyes are widely separated, there is a considerable gain in the area the eyes can survey. Overlapping regions on the other hand might lessen any ambiguity in perception, in the same way that a letter may make things clearer than a brief note.

None of these reasons, however, comes close to the real reason why man has two eyes. The great virtue of the system is that it automatically endows human vision with something more than brightness, color, wider

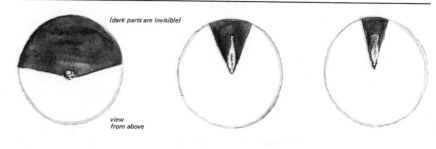

(dark parts are invisible)

view from above

If the world were a goldfish bowl,
man's view, a fish's view, and a bird's
view would be quite different.

view from inside

screens, or less ambiguous information. It adds depth and dimension, and it is the automatic and precise handling of these qualities that is the contribution of a pair of eyes.

There are many cues to distance or solidity which either eye alone can master, but only after learning and remembering. The size and details of familiar objects are familiar monocular cues. You judge how far away a friend stands by the relative size of his image on your retina. As he walks toward you the image grows, and gradually you see him in more detail; you note if he's gained weight, you observe the pattern of his tie or the name of the paper he is carrying. As he looms larger he in turn obscures objects behind him, completely hiding them or casting shadows over them so you know they are more distant.

Shadows in their own right provide useful information about shapes. We infer that objects are convex or concave, hollow or humped, according to the pattern of shadows they cast. Unconsciously we refer to the overhead position of the sun as the natural source of light and deduce the contours of a figure accordingly. If you turn a shadowed photograph or drawing upside down, you may still think of the light as coming from above, only now the contours of the figure may reverse: what was a crater or a lake may appear to be a mountain and vice versa.

Linear perspective is also important. The sides of an object appear to taper at a distance and in the extreme seem to meet at a point on the horizon, as in the familiar railroad track image. When you look out this far you also raise your head so that your line of sight is more nearly horizontal than when you examine things close by. Atmospheric conditions are also helpful. In addition to being blurred in detail, the hills beyond the railroad tracks may look bluish because of the light-scattering effects of dust and moisture particles in the air.

In recent years the psychologist James J. Gibson has suggested that some of these monocular cues may be special applications of a general principle he calls gradients of texture. Thus any time a two-dimensional drawing shows a row of similar objects, say circles, in a line at the bottom of the drawing, and these objects are then reduced in size in successive rows of decreasing length, the illusion of objects receding

The left-hand figure illustrates Gibson's gradients of texture. The density of the rows increases with each higher row; the over-all impression is of objects in depth, receding beyond the plane of the drawing. The right-hand figure shows how shadows provide a cue to contour: right side up it looks like trees by a lake; upside down the lake becomes a hill.

into space is immediately apparent. The density of each row increases as you move from the bottom to the top of the drawing. The converging lines of linear perspective would be an example of this. Pictures of wheat fields, soldiers on parade, or housing developments are other familiar examples of texture gradients. Gibson also emphasizes the importance of motion, either of the observer or of the object, as a guide to dimension. In this way the eye receives a succession of images in which the perspective is constantly changing. These spatial transformations of the object create a strong sense of solidity. An observer watching the shadow of a wire triangle slowly rotated behind a translucent screen is easily fooled into assuming that the figure is solid.

Most parents can testify that clues like these are learned and not innate. Typical is the story of the three-year-old girl who cried on being taken to the airport to see her father off. After much questioning (it was not the first time she had been to an airport), the answer came out: she hated to see daddy get small.

Stereoscopic Vision

What two eyes do to mold the world, however, and do unconsciously, is to scan that world together. When one moves to the right or up or down, so moves the other. These "conjugate" movements wouldn't make much sense except that in the course of evolution human eyes have rotated to the front of the head. Still their fields are not identical. The right eye sees more shadows around the right side of a sphere in the center field of vision; the left more on the left. In addition, objects farther to the left or right are seen at slightly different angles by each eye. These disparate views make for "roundness," or stereoscopic vision, when the signals are channeled to the brain.

Seeing in stereo usually involves another kind of eye cooperation as well. In zooming in on a target not only does one eye parallel the gross motion of the other, but each eye converges, turning toward the nose slightly, so that the target is lined up on the fovea. All points in the

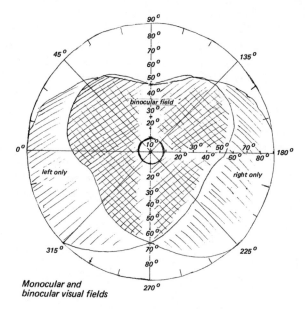

The extent of overlap in the fields of vision of the eyes is mapped in degrees of a circle. For each eye there is a temporal crescent, representing that portion of the field seen exclusively by that eye.

vicinity of the target then fall on corresponding points in the retina of each eye.

If for any reason one eye fails to converge properly, the two retinal images do not correspond and you may see double. This condition, called diploplia, is a typical symptom of "cross eyes." You can demonstrate double vision for yourself by focusing on a distant object and then putting your finger in front of your nose. Your eyes' accommodation, convergence, and corresponding points are one set of things for a distant object, something else again for an object near at hand. This kind of double vision is clinically called convergent or crossed squint, for rea-

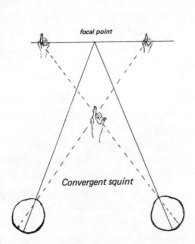

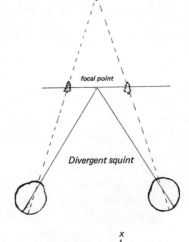

Demonstrating diplopia. If you fixate on a far object, a finger held close to the nose will appear doubled. The diagram shows that in this instance the images are crossed. You also can experience doubling of a far object if you fixate on something nearby. In that case the images are not crossed.

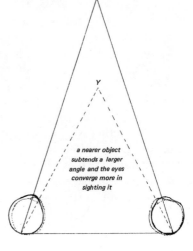

The eyes converge more in gazing at a nearby object than at a distant one. The extent of muscular movement provides a clue to distance.

sons the optical diagram makes clear. An object beyond the focal plane may also appear doubled, but here the images are not crossed and the condition is called divergent squint.

Accommodation and convergence are dynamic processes, occurring over a period of time. Several sets of muscles are at work, and there may be a certain amount of over- or under-shooting before a target is seen singly, "locked" in place. For the mechanically minded, and for the early investigators of visual physiology, it seemed clear that the eyes, in judging depth, behaved like range finders. The problem was to find out how far X, say a tree in a field, was from the eyes. The solution was to treat this as a problem in trigonometry. X was at the apex of a triangle whose base was the distance between the eyes. The eye muscles themselves were analogue computers. As the eyeballs moved, the muscle fibers registered amounts of tension which varied with the size of the angle and thus could be used to solve the triangle. The advantage of having two eyes lay in the simultaneous readings that could be made from two locations. This process, called binocular parallax, was obviously more efficient and faster than monocular parallax. One eye would have to take successive readings each time the position of the head changed. In this way you would observe that nearby objects seem to move in the direction opposite to head movement, a farther one moves in the same direction, and a very far object may not seem to move at all. This is a learned cue. You associate nearby objects with those that move opposite to your head movement, and so on. The direction of motion thus becomes correlated with distance.

There is no doubt that accommodation and convergence are important aids to depth perception over a short range (accommodation works up to 20 feet; convergence up to 100 feet), and they certainly figure in relative distance judgments, as the diagram shows.

But a number of experiments suggest that feedback from eye muscles plays far less a role in determining depth than the pattern-matching game that goes on as a result of binocular parallax. Left- and right-hand views contain sets of corresponding points, but because of parallax certain clusters of corresponding points will be displaced from one eye to the other. The displacements are along horizontal arcs (meridians, since the retina is bowl shaped), because the eyes are lined up along a horizontal base line. By comparing the amount of displacement and knowing in which eye the shift is taking place, the visual system in man apparently can make accurate depth judgments.

A simple experiment illustrates this. Hold a pencil in your left hand at arm's length, keeping it upright and directly in line with your left eye. Now if you take a second pencil in your right hand and move it

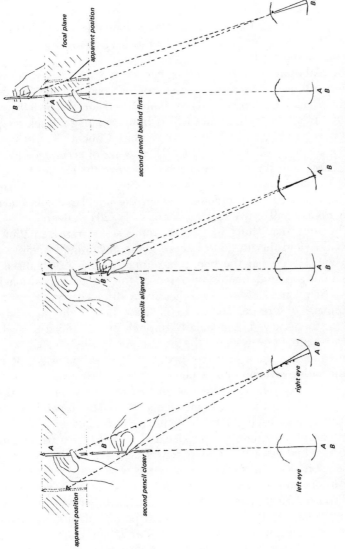

A simple experiment in stereoscopic acuity. Note how the image of the pencil on the right retina varies for each position of the second pencil.

forward or back under the first pencil and in the same line of regard, the left eye will see no parallactic shift (the direction of travel is along the line of regard), but the right eye will: As the pencil moves forward it will appear to the right eye to lie to the left of the stationary pencil. A move back will look like a shift to the right. The diagram shows what is happening on the right eye's retina. There is an angular displacement to right or left along a horizontal meridian as long as the second pencil is not aligned under the first.

An elaboration of this test is one of the methods used in the laboratory to measure stereoscopic acuity, or how well the eye detects these differences in depth. Rods are subsituted for the pencils; one is suspended from above, the other is free to move along a track regulated by the observer. The stationary rod is placed about 20 feet away to minimize proprioceptive clues (from the muscles of accommodation and convergence), and the observer is asked to move the second rod until it appears to him to be exactly under the first. The best observers can detect a departure from alignment when the angular displacement on the retina is as small as five seconds of arc, or 1/720 of a degree.

The idea that shifts in the two-dimensional representation of a scene could yield the illusion of depth is the governing principle of the stereoscope. Here what the two eyes normally do is externalized by a camera taking paired photos of a scene, the camera's position being changed from one view to the other by a distance equivalent to the interpupillary difference, about 2.5 inches. These right- and left-eyed scenes are then viewed monocularly through prisms which project each image to a common focus where the fused stereo image is seen.

Investigators soon realized that the stereoscope was not just a Victorian parlor diversion but a powerful research instrument for studying depth perception. If instead of photos of people or natural landscapes, abundant as they are in monocular clues, stereo pairs were made abstract, "rigged" to eliminate the familiar, you could test just how far the eyes can go in conjuring up space and what the relative importance of monocular and binocular guidelines were.

Geometrical figures and line drawings were used; sets of diagonals leaning in one direction in the left field, another in the right, or vertical lines, displaced so that in one field the distance between parallels was consistently greater than the other. Such pairs still produced convincing and instantaneous illusions of depth—"walls" going off at an angle, or "floors" or "ceilings"—suggesting that binocular parallax with its disparate views was the all-powerful depth determinant. Indeed the death knell to the importance of muscular sensations was dealt in an experiment of H. W. Dove in 1841 that employed a tachistoscope with a stereoscope. The tachistoscope is a device that can deliver a very brief flash of light or an image. Stereo pairs of line drawings flashed tachistoscopically still produced sensations of depth in which observers could say unerringly which pairs seemed in front, which behind, a given reference plane, in spite of the fact that the brief flash allowed no time for convergence or accommodation.

It might still be argued, however, that very simple line drawings or geometric figures offered monocular information of the gradient of texture variety, that the brain was in fact recognizing monocular patterns and then fusing them into a binocular image in depth. To answer this criticism a series of ingenious experiments has been performed by Bela

A schematic diagram of the stereo-scope. Light rays from the left- and right-hand slides are bent through the prisms so that a fused image is seen at F.

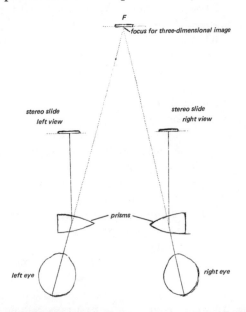

In the heyday of the stereoscope Victorian families could delight in such exotica as slides of Africa. The crocodile has just been landed beside the upper Nile in East Africa. Close observation will reveal subtle differences in the photos. The position of the gun is farther to the left in the right photo, for example.

Julesz of the Human Information Processing Department at Bell Telephone Laboratories in New Jersey.

Julesz uses a computer to generate stereo patterns which are random grids of light and dark spots, devoid of recognizable features. They are like completely asymmetrical crossword puzzles, with the black and white squares densely filling out the grid. He pairs these grids in such a way that all the black and white patches are matched except for a central cluster in the shape of a square, in which the right-hand view, for example, may be displaced four units to the left. (The "holes" this leaves in the right-hand view are then filled with more random black and white patches, which, since they are seen only by the right eye, will not figure in the fused field.) When viewed in a stereoscope this central square appears to float out in front of a background. The first time one views such pairs the effect is novel and rather exciting. It may take several minutes before the square is discovered, but once it is, the image is very stable.

Julesz, however, playing the role of his own devil's advocate, thought that even though the central square was clearly not discernible as a monocular pattern, perhaps small "micropatterns" were perceived unconsciously by each eye and used to create an image in depth. To eliminate this possibility he systematically altered the pairs, blurring one, changing its over-all dimensions slightly, making every other square of every other row black in one of the pairs, white in the other, and so on. None of these "confusion" factors disturbed the illusion of depth. As long as the displaced cluster was of a minimal size, and there was minimal linear connectivity—unbroken border lines, for example—the square stood out.

The only times depth was not perceived coincided with those times when there was no fusion: when the differences between right- and left-hand views were radical enough to produce "binocular rivalry." In such instances all or parts of one field were seen to alternate with all or parts of the other.

These and still more subtle experiments lead Julesz to believe that while monocular cues are enormous aids to depth perception in everyday life, they are only auxiliary channels in an information-processing system which essentially recognizes patterns in a binocular field. He theorizes mathematically that patterns-in-depth may be derived from a subtraction process: The nervous system may temporarily store information about left- and right-hand points in a combined field and, prior to subtracting the two fields, horizontally shift them with respect to each other by increasing amounts. For each such shift a difference field is obtained in which clusters of "zero-valued" points will give the cross sections of an object surrounded by random dots (without the nervous system's having to "recognize" these clusters).

While the gains binocular vision offer are usually expressed in terms of behavioral value—the ability of a monkey to judge how far away a lion lurks or how far he has to jump from tree to tree—there are many advantages to "civilized" man as well. Surgeons performing operations, or even truck drivers backing into a tight parking place, are typical examples of those whose performance is enormously enhanced by binocular vision. Less well known is the use of binocular perception in analytical work: comparing a real and a counterfeit bill in a stereoscope, for example, may make the differences stand out in relief. Similarly, aerial reconaissance photos taken from two different angles and viewed stereoscopically can reveal camouflaged areas almost impossible to detect monocularly.

Dr. Hans Lukas-Teuber of the Massachusetts Institute of Technology has also suggested that binocular vision plays a role in the size constancy of an image. Generally speaking, the size of a familiar object projected on the retina is not actually correlated in perception with real size, except over large distances. As you walk across a room to examine books in a bookcase they don't suddenly swell in size any more than a friend shrinks as he walks away from you, although optically the retinal images are changing continuously. Such constancy effects are seriously disturbed under certain conditions of monocular viewing. The famous "Ames Room" illusion provides one example. In this life-sized model of a room the rear wall goes off at a diagonal, while ceiling and floor diverge. When an observer using one eye views the room through a

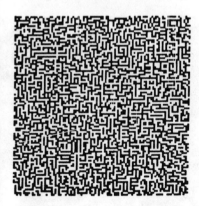 

Stereo pair. In the left field the diagonal connectivity is broken, and 75 percent of the picture elements in the pair are identical. Stereopsis is easy to obtain.

The Ames Room illusion. The camera as well as the human eye when placed at the peephole in the front wall of the model room captures the illusion of size distortion. In the absence of binocular and other cues to depth (such as objects in the room), the room is assumed to be a rectangular solid and the windows equal-sized rectangles. People in parts of the world who are used to living in conical or round houses may not experience this illusion.

Adelbert Ames also designed this ingenious illusion. Viewed from almost any angle with both eyes, the tubular and plane sections appear to be an abstract composition.

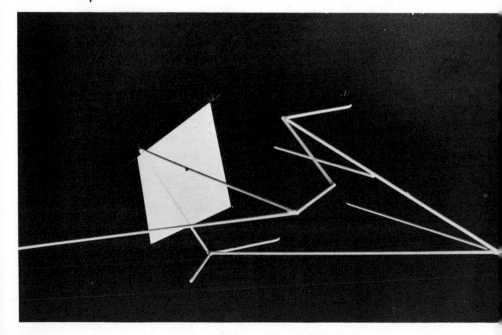

peephole in front, people standing against the back wall appear to be giants or dwarfs, depending at which end of the room they stand. Without binocular clues, or reference objects in the room itself, the brain assumes the room is of normal rectangular shape, and sees distortions in the people. Photographs of the room preserve the illusion since the camera, too, is one-eyed.

An interesting experiment by A. H. Holway and E. G. Boring furnishes additional evidence that binocular vision is important in size constancy. The psychologists first tested individuals' ability to judge the size of a small disk held at various distances along a long corridor. The observers were free to use both eyes. Though the position of the disk varied from 10 to 120 feet, size constancy was preserved. When the experiment was repeated under the restrictive conditions of monocular viewing, and with increased limitations on the size and details of the background, constancy suffered. Finally when the disk was viewed monocularly along a dark tunnel the judgment of its size increasingly reflected the actual size of the image on the retina.

Visual Coding

The work of Julesz along with the body of psychophysical experiments is of enormous value in documenting *what* the eye sees, but it essentially leaves unanswered, except in theoretical terms, the basic question of *how* the eye sees: how, when, and where, for example, information from each eye comes together in the brain. In many ways these are the knottiest questions of all. Our conceptions of the answers also require

Viewed through a single peephole placed at a critical position, however, the visual system interprets the various angles and intersections as a three-dimensional chair.

the most "unlearning." After all it took man many years to be convinced that optically the eye worked like a camera—that images were transmitted through a lens system that inverted and reversed them. Clearly you didn't see things upside down and backward. When the camera principle was finally accepted, people then assumed that it was the brain that turned the images right side up. Somehow it could look at the retinal "film" and make the appropriate corrections. The embarrassing dilemma of an eye within an eye, looking at a picture of a picture, with the infinite regressions that this invokes, was largely ignored. Only when

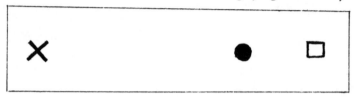

To find the blind spot, close your left eye and fixate on the cross. As you move the book toward you, the square and then the dot will disappear. If you continue the forward motion, each will reappear in turn.

this seductive analogy was given up, when it was realized that the mind is indeed "blind," having at its disposal only a pattern of electrical signals changing in time and space, could some progress be made. Even now it falls far short of the mark. Electrical signals simply don't add up to the "whole" of perception. They never will. But the partial analysis of one side of the equation has proven to be immensely exciting.

Anatomically the pathways visual signals take are relatively direct (compared, say, to the auditory pathways). Electrical activity originating at the level of the rods and cones is eventually relayed to the ganglion cells whose fibers gather at the back of the eye and pass out through a small exit called the optic disk. There are no receptors in this area, so that it represents a true blind spot in each eye.

The exiting bundles constitute the optic nerves which meet at the chiasm, a crossroad in the brain just in front of the pituitary gland. Here fibers from the nasal halves of both eyes cross to the opposite hemisphere, while those toward the sides, the temporal halves, remain uncrossed. The bowl shape of the retina suggests that all information about the left field of vision seen by each eye is transmitted to the right hemisphere; all right-field information to the left.

Past this switching point, the fiber bundles are termed the optic tracts. They continue toward the rear, the bulk of them terminating in a small knob of tissue that sticks out like a knee from the thalamus, hence

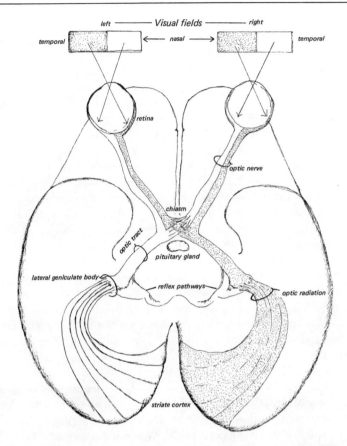

The visual pathways in man and in the higher primates are very similar. They are shown here against a background of the cerebral hemispheres. The stippled areas represent the left-hand portion of the visual field as seen by each eye. The diagram shows how the partial crossing of the optic nerves at the chiasma results in a mapping of the cortex on the right side with information about the left visual fields of both eyes; the left cortex is mapped with information about the right fields.

its name, "lateral geniculate body." The small group of fibers that bypass the geniculate relay to muscle control centers involved in eye reflexes.

New fibers arising from geniculate cells swoop down, around, and up again in a great fan called the optic radiation, which terminates in the occipital lobes at the extreme rear of the cortex. Here many fibers, especially ones associated with the fovea, branch out to supply more than one cortical cell. At the same time separate fibers may converge on

273

the same cell. There is a topographical orderliness about this, however. Fibers associated with the same place in the retina terminate near each other in the cortex. The effect of the various convergences and divergences is simply to distort the cortical map of the retina in the same way that the somesthetic cortex distorts the body surface. The visual "homunculus" consists of a giant fovea and a relatively dwarfed periphery.

The cortex represents at least the fifth stage in optic signal relays. Three occur in the retina, a fourth in the geniculate. Even if the cortex influences activity in the early stages via fibers traveling in the opposite direction in the optic nerves, as some physiologists think, a logical place to start cracking the visual code is within the retina itself. Unfortunately the small size of the cells at the first two stages, bipolars as well as rods and cones, has prohibited direct study of them with microelectrodes. Almost all the electrophysiology of vision currently begins at the ganglion cell level, admittedly a stage of considerable complexity in the pathway. Compounding this complexity is the double computer function of the retina: it is known that certain ganglion cells receive inputs from either rods or cones. That means that at different times of day the impulses moving down a particular fiber will have different meanings. This is a nice bit of economy. Nature has seen fit to connect the elements of its day and night computers to the same relays, with the understanding that the demand for the relay's service will be competitive—either rods or cones will win out, but not both.

In spite of this dual behavior, there are many subtleties in the organization of visual information which ganglion cell studies have revealed. This is particularly true with reference to the perception of form, the chief quality of visual perception. Without the organization of light into patterns or shapes, the visual world would be bizarre, almost unimaginable. For it is through the perception of form primarily that man experiences the visual environment. Color,° depth, and dimension are embellishments that enrich this basic quality of perception. They provide additional, but far less essential information.

On Seeing Form

Before we examine the microelectrode studies, however, it will be useful to mention the main theories of pattern perception and the ingenious experiments designed to test them before the days of single-cell recording.

The best known is the Gestalt theory associated with the names of Wertheimer, Koffka, and Köhler, in the thirties. This theory is based on the idea that man is inherently a pattern-forming animal; that given random assortments of points, lines, or more complex assemblages he will tend to group certain parts together, to separate a "figure" from its "ground," to organize the pieces into wholes, or "gestalts." For some people all-digit telephone numbers are excellent candidates for gestalt-making. They look for rhythms or relations between the digits to aid the brain in storing and remembering.

Gestalt theory asserts that there are certain inborn forms which are always perceived as wholes. In terms of vision such figures include circles, straight lines, and triangles. Even when these figures appear incomplete, the brain tends to "close" them. In addition to "figure and ground" and "closure" there are also certain other inherent principles of organization based on contiguity, segregation or differentiation of parts, and something called the "good gestalt"—by which one perception tends to dominate other, weak perceptions.

An alternative to this theory maintains that visual perception is based on learning and experience. Patterns are not innate, but built up from raw data elements, "percepts," which the brain cells assemble according to individual or cultural dictates.

In either case conflicts and even headaches can result when the eyes are presented with two different patterns simultaneously (as in binocular rivalry), or when a single pattern suggests more than one interpretation. The latter case gives rise to the familiar, ambiguous figures of optical illusions: the cube which looks hollow one moment and solid the next, or the step figure which looks like a staircase one way and a cornice another.

More interesting, perhaps, are some of the "impossible" figures or the psychological versions like the wife–mother-in-law figures or Rorschach inkblots. There are also artistic experiments in ambiguity, ranging from the symmetrical tile patterns that date back to antiquity, down to the Picasso profile-full face paintings typical of early Cubism. Other artists have produced works in which a human skull turns out to be a woman in front of a mirror or a group of chattering ladies becomes a horse's head.

Most of the time the duality of these figures is exclusively either-or. You don't see both versions simultaneously. Theorists generally cite this as evidence that the brain never adds up all the visual content available to it at any moment, but seizes bits and rejects others. It's as though the eye constantly samples the scene, compiling data that has been checked against some mentally stored image.

° Some scientists suggest that the only behavioral advantage color confers in higher species is the ability to tell ripe from rotten fruit at a distance.

Each of these figures can be interpreted in two ways. The figure may be a youthful lady with her head up and neck showing, or else an older woman with a big nose, small mouth, and chin wrapped in a furpiece; this is the wife–mother-in-law drawing (adapted from E. Boring, after Katz). The others are the staircase-cornice figure; the Necker cube (here doubled), named after the psychologist who studied the illusion; the pedestal-profile figure that the Gestalt psychologists made famous; and two examples of geometric tile patterns wherein figure and ground are ambiguous.

wife or mother-in-law ?

double Necker cube

cornice or steps ?

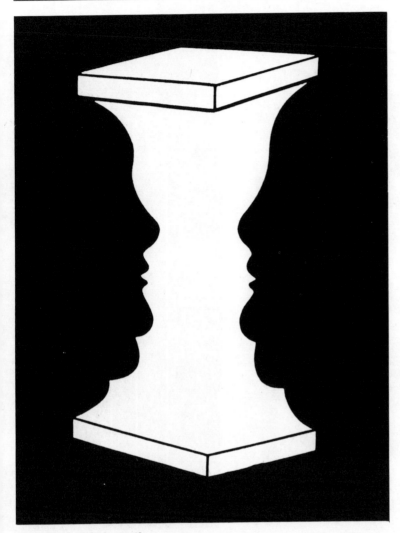

Which is figure? – Which is ground?

Geometric tile patterns

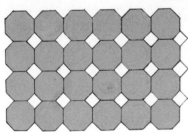
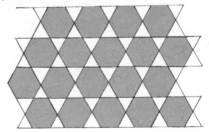

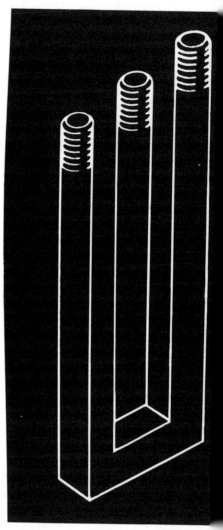

These impossible figures are examples of situations in which the brain is given insufficient information about depth in a two-dimensional representation. As a result it is impossible to construct a unique three-dimensional image of a "real" object.

Stabilized Images

One of the most ingenious experiments designed to test whether the laurels of perception theory should go to the Gestaltists or the cell

278

assemblers makes use of a contact lens and a projector tube. This device keeps an image fixed on a particular place in the retina, compensating for the rapid (50 to a 100 per minute) tiny shifts the eyeball makes, even when it is fixating on an image. Various forms of the apparatus have been used by R. W. Ditchburn and J. C. and T. N. Cornsweet in England and Floyd Ratliff and Lorrin Riggs in the United States. Essentially what happens is that every time the eyeball makes one of its "saccadic" jerks, as these involuntary movements are called, the contact lens also moves. Since this in turn is coupled with the image projector tube, the image follows the eye's motions exactly and the result is that the image stays fixed on the same spot of retina. Oddly, after a few moments, the image fades, only to return again after a time. What psychologists D. O. Hebb, Woodward Heron, and Roy M. Pritchard of McGill University in Montreal wanted to find out was how the image faded and reappeared: Did it disappear in wholes or parts, via inborn gestalts or learned perceptual elements?

At times the evidence strongly suggested that learning dominates.

Roy M. Pritchard was himself a subject for experiment with stabilized images on the retina. The right eye is covered with a contact lens upon which a tiny projector is mounted; the left eye is covered with a patch. Wires lead from the projector to a battery through a connecting jack taped to the forehead.

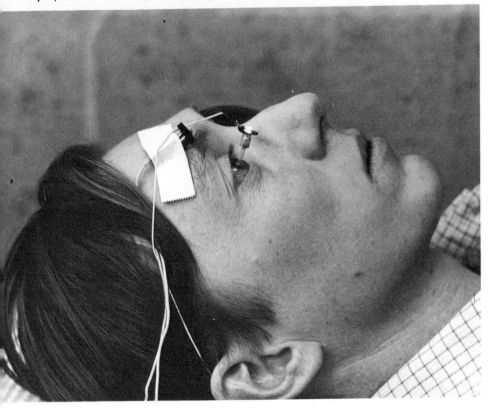

When whole words were projected for a short period of time, for example, the parts of the word or letters that were remembered were still meaningful words rather than nonsense syllables. So BEER became PEER, BEEP, PEEP, BEE, or BE, but never EER or EEP. Similarly a human profile was analyzed into constituent parts such as forehead, nose, mouth, chin and would fade and reappear in logical sections. An abstract curlicue pattern, on the other hand, evoked no associations or memories and at first parts would fade and return at random. After the fourth or fifth time, however, certain curlicues were grouped together into formal elements which persisted longer and would fade and reappear together, suggesting that some concentration and learning had taken place.

Gestalt theorists might argue that organizing principles like the contiguity of certain curlicues, or the desire to shape them into a harmonious whole, could explain the last result, the gestalt having been found after a few trials. They could also point out that patterns that depicted amorphous shapes like an amoeba crossed by lines sometimes fade as wholes, either the shape or the crosshatches disappearing, but sometimes would blend to form a semicurved semi-straight-edged shape, approaching a circle, for example. Here the result was an abstraction from both patterns, but one that tended, in Gestalt terms, toward a more pleasing simplicity—even including the hallucinating of parts to "close" the figure.

What was most striking, however, was not so much the evidence that both operations may go on, and indeed complement each other in the normal individual, but where observations supported both theories. They established the line as a basic unit. No line ever faded in part leaving broken segments or a gap at one end. Either the whole line disappeared or those segments cut off from it by intersections with other lines. This and one other characteristic—the fading of an over-all plane figure (say a colored square against a contrasting background) in a certain consistently reported pattern—were repeatedly observed. The middle portion of the figure was lost first, followed in turn by the corners.

These observations take on all the more significance as we return to the electrophysiological laboratory and follow the stunning microelectrode work that has been done to probe the nature of perception at the cellular level.

Such have been the contributions of Torsten Wiesel and David H. Hubel of Harvard Medical School. These investigators have recorded the activity of individual cells at the ganglion, geniculate, and cortical levels of monkeys and cats under normal and abnormal conditions. Their results suggest a beautiful structural and functional organization all along the visual pathways, culminating at the cortex in a system by which edges and contours of objects can not only be detected but also abstracted from the particular part of the retina originally stimulated. The nervous system connections are there to explain how you can recognize that a square is a square is a square whether it's big or little, seen at the right or left, or above or low down in the visual field.

The process of abstraction begins in, the retina where Hubel and Wiesel were able to confirm earlier studies of Stephen Kuffler, also of Harvard, and others, concerning the most effective light stimulus for a given ganglion cell.

Kuffler had backtracked to find the cell's receptive field—the region of retina where changes in light change the cell's electrical activity. He found that there were two kinds of ganglion cell in the cat, both with "bull's-eye" receptive fields. One kind responded by an increase in its firing if light was shone precisely on a small circle in the center of its field. Surrounding this, however, was a larger ring where light would have just the opposite effect—decreasing or eliminating the cell's discharge. The other type of ganglion cell had just the reverse arrangement of its bull's-eye. Light hitting its center inhibited it; light touching its ring elicited a brief burst of impulses. Accordingly the two cells were christened "on-centers" and "off-centers." The size of the fields varied through the retina, as large as a few tenths of an inch in some parts, as small as a few hundred-thousandths of an inch for the center fields of certain foveal cones.

Light shining on both parts of a cell's receptive field at the same time had less of an effect, suggesting cancellation due to summing of positive and negative influences. Adjacent ganglion cells have overlapping fields so that for any given pattern of light some cells may be maximally excited, others strongly inhbited, and still others may exhibit all shades of activity in between.

The next step was to observe what changes took place at the lateral geniculate body. Incoming fibers both converge and diverge here, but Hubel and Wiesel found that there was usually one "major" fiber for each geniculate cell which completely governed the location and behavior of the receptive field for that cell. The effect of the convergences, or the greater number of inputs per cell, makes the geniculate an area of sharper focus: cells here are less excitable than ganglion cells when diffuse light shines throughout their fields.

Visual Area I

The fibers from the geniculate which form the optic radiation project to the "striate" cortex of the occipital lobes. Like most parts of the cortex the striate is a layered structure, though the name striate here refers not to the layers but to a darkish stripe visible upon inspection of this part of the brain. Incoming fibers relay with cells in the fourth layer from the top, whereupon new fibers send impulses up or down several layers. This arrangement, combined with the observations that fiber connections are much denser going up and down than from side to side, provides anatomical evidence for what the experiments functionally suggested, namely that the cortex is arranged in columnar units, cells in any vertical (perpendicular to the surface) section cooperating as a unit.

The cortex is so rich in cells, however, there being about 50,000 cells in each square millimeter of cortex (about 0.0016 of a square inch) that it seemed unlikely that the same on-off bull's-eye behavior would be observed here.

Instead a great jump in abstraction and sophistication in image-forming seems to take place through the interaction of two types of cortical cell which Hubel and Wiesel have called "simple" and "complex." The simple cell no longer has a circular receptive field, but now responds to line stimuli, its excitable region may be a narrow strip between inhibitory areas (or vice versa), or it may respond to edges, becoming excited on one side of a border, inhibited on the other.

Naturally every line has a particular orientation; it is like an arrow whose angle can be measured with reference to a pair of axes. There are simple cells that respond to horizontal lines at precise places in the retina, others to verticals, and many others corresponding to all directions in between. The same observation applies to the edge detectors. The particular direction is known as the field orientation of the cell.

How are bull's-eyes one stage before translated into lines? How is it possible to pass from spots to edges? The answer is very simple when you consider that a line is nothing but a set of points. If you took a whole bunch of bull's-eyes and stacked them like coins, either neatly in vertical columns or turned sideways in horizontal rolls, or if you carefully staggered them in a diagonal, the line could be defined as the set of points corresponding to the coin centers from one end of the stack to the other. In the cortex the arrangement would be that dozens of geniculate cells with closely overlapping centers synapse with the same simple cortical cell. That cell would then be excited only if most of the feeding cells were individually excited, i.e., if a narrow slot of light originally crossed their receptive fields in the retina.

The situation is not quite this simple because a line of light in the retina that cuts across a bull's-eye will obviously intrude on the negative as well as positive parts of the field. However all that is necessary is that the excitation override the inhibitory effects. This in fact happens, since

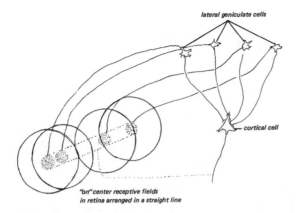

lateral geniculate cells

cortical cell

"on" center receptive fields
in retina arranged in a straight line

To explain how the receptive field of a simple cortical cell can be a straight line or edge, Hubel and Wiesel suggest that a large number of lateral geniculate cells all project onto a single cortical cell. If the geniculate cells all have "on-center" receptive fields aligned in a straight line, and if their inputs to the cortical cell are all excitatory, the receptive field of the cortical cell should correspond to the line or bar figure enclosed by the dashes in the diagram.

a narrow bar of light crossing a bull's-eye may cover all of the center but only a small part of the total surround, and so naturally the center effect prevails.

Now is it possible to conjecture under what circumstances a number of simple cells in the same region of cortex may be excited? The clue here is "same region," for the hookups are such that simple cells in the same column of cortex receive inputs from neighboring geniculate cells, which in turn reflect neighboring regions of retina. Furthermore simple cells in the same column have the same field orientation. If a horizontal line crosses the retina at some part and moves up or down a few degrees, hundreds or thousands of simple cortical cells in the same column will be excited. Now tie all these in turn to a single "complex" cell again in the same column. The result is the anatomical and functional basis for the kind of "aha" experience which allows you to recognize a line as horizontal, whether it's shorter or longer, higher or lower in the field of vision. This is an enormous leap forward in sophistication. Hubel and Wiesel have been able to estimate the leeway complex cells have in various parts of the striate cortex and found it could be measured in degrees or tens of degrees. Note, however, that at this stage the complex cell is still carefully attuned to orientation. It has made allowances for parallel displacements but not angular transformations.

By the time electrical signals reach the cortex it is evident that visual perception is very little concerned with neutrality. If the cortex is exposed to a mass of same-color or same-intensity light spread over a large region (remember the square that faded in the middle in the stabilized image experiments), it pays little attention to it, less than the geniculate and much less than the ganglion cells. The chief concern of the cortex is to sharpen the differences that exist at the edge or border of the mass, to pick out the outlines that break up neutral space blobs, noting the changes in intensity or color in passing from one part to another, or noting when a particular shape changes position. Light alone is a very poor stimulus. As Hubel himself wrote some years ago:

. . . *after five years we are still amazed each time we record from striate cortex to find that a cell which reacts so vigorously to a very special stimulus does little or nothing when a bright flashlight is shone right into the eyes. Perhaps this is because it is so natural to assume that the best stimulus for a cell in the visual system should be the one that affects every receptor in the retina. It is hard to swallow the notion that it is exactly the worst!*

The last few years of cortical recording have revealed the same kind of behavior in the auditory cortex. Again the role of the higher centers is not so much to heed steady sounds, whether they be musical tones or noise, but to pay attention to changes in intensity or frequency, relative differences that occur over a period of time rather than absolute qualities. For "time" substitute "space" and the statement will be true of visual cortex.

Visual Areas II and III

Hubel and Wiesel have extended their exploration of visual areas to two adjacent regions in each hemisphere called Visual Areas II and III. Cells here seem to be receiving depots for fibers from the striate cortex (though they may also have other inputs) and in general behave like complex cells, oriented to edges or narrow slits of light or dark lines. But in addition Hubel and Wiesel have found what they call low- and high-order hypercomplex cells.

These cells also respond to lines or edges, stationary or moving, but in the case of the low-order hypercomplex cell the stimulus must be limited at one or both ends. One way this could happen would be if a pair of complex cells representing adjacent edge regions of the same orientation both fed into a single low-order hypercomplex cell, but in such a way that cell A excited the cell and cell B inhibited it. The most

A lower-order hypercomplex cell behaved as though it had received both excitatory and inhibitory inputs from complex cells. The cell responded to a light edge stopped at one end (with dark below), which was moved upward in the receptive field (A through C). The receptive field apparently is divided into activating and antagonistic portions. When the "corner" moved up, filling the activating part of the field exactly, the electrical record was maximal (C). If the corner intruded on the antagonistic half, responses dropped (D and E). This cell did not respond to downward movements at all (second part of electrical record, A through E).

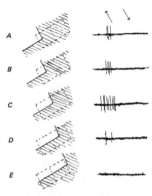

exciting stimulus for such a cell would then be a corner—a right angle of brightness next to darkness, or vice versa.

The high-order hypercomplex cells in turn behave as though they were stimulated by several low-order hypercomplex cells. They too respond to stimuli limited at one or both ends, but in addition they can respond to a line in two different orientations 90 degrees out of phase, and the point where the line or edge ends need not be as precisely fixed in the visual field. In other words slight displacements in space are allowed which could be thought of as linear transformations in *two* dimensions—a cross or a corner can move up or down or to the right or left.

Optical Dominance

Each time Hubel and Wiesel tapped a cortical cell they had to find out which eye, what part of the retina, and what kind of stimulus triggered the maximum response. In doing this they were able to accomplish three things:

(1) Confirm previous maps that showed that each hemisphere receives signals from both eyes: the left hemisphere gets information about the right field of vision from both eyes, and vice versa.

(2) Establish that cells in the same column have the same field orientation, while adjacent columns, though with different orientations, nevertheless correspond to neighboring fields in the retina.

(3) Discover that the majority of cells can be driven by signals originating in either eye, as though the cell were tied to left or right switches. Either one or both can "turn on" the cortical cell.

This last finding is of great interest in the light of Julesz' conjecture about binocular depth perception. At just one stage before, incoming signals are carefully segregated, with crossed optic tract fibers relaying with layers 1, 4, and 6 of the geniculate, uncrossed with layers 2, 3, 5. Suddenly at the cortex there is enormous interaction: About 85 percent of the cells respond to either eye, with the majority showing no marked bias toward one or the other. The remaining 15 percent were exclusive in their tastes.

This amount of binocular cooperation impressed Hubel and Wiesel very much and immediately started them thinking about what happens in abnormal situations. Suppose the eyes are not aligned at birth and cortical cells receive non-corresponding messages from each eye. Suppose there is congenital blindness due, say, to a cataract, in one or both eyes. Does the cortex fail to develop? If so, what happens when surgery later corrects defects?

To explore these possibilities the two performed a number of experiments with kittens. They sewed one or both lids shut at about the time the eyes normally open—eight days. They designed translucent eye patches that would not eliminate light altogether, but would prevent form perception, and then covered one eye, or in some experiments alternated, covering the right eye one day, the left the next. They tried severing a muscle of one eye and leaving both eyes open, but no longer aligned. After varying lengths of time they removed the patches or reoperated and observed the degree of recovery and the brain changes that occurred. They then compared their findings with similar experiments in adult cats.

Almost every experiment was a revelation. Kittens with one lid shut acted as though they were blind in that eye when it was re-opened a few months later. There was very little recovery in time, although the retina itself appeared normal and pupillary reflexes were present. Surprisingly, too, cells at the geniculate level that were tied to the closed eye, though smaller than normal, behaved typically, with clear-cut bull's-eye receptive fields.

Changes in behavior did show up at the cortex and these were striking. Here the pattern of optical dominance was radically altered. In cases where one lid was shut some cells were completely silent, while the rest responded only to stimulation from the good eye. Where the eyes were used alternately, or were crossed, the pattern of dominance was completely inverted from normal. The majority of cells now attended only to signals from one or the other eye, rarely to both.

In cases where the geniculate showed more or less evidence of thinning or shrinking of cells, the cortex remained active. A kitten that had had both lids closed possessed cortical cells that actively responded to light once the lids were opened. The responses admittedly were bizarre sometimes—there being no field orientations—but as often as not the cells responded quite normally.

Hubel and Wiesel wondered whether this meant that there was much more visual potential laid down at birth than had previously been thought. Then when vision is eliminated it is not that the visual pathways fail to be laid down, but that existing ones change. To test this hypothesis they recorded the cortical responses of "naïve" eight-day-old kittens. Indeed field orientation patterns were already firmly established.

The two conclude that sensory deprivation, as far as vision is concerned, involves a loss or change of inherent connections, not a failure in development. All the more reason, in humans, to detect and correct eye defects early—perhaps within the first few months of life. The chances for recovery are greater the sooner repair measures are taken, and indeed, once experience enforces the normal pattern, the eyes are less vulnerable. Tampering with the vision of adult cats produced none of the permanent behavioral changes or cortical dominance inversions observed in the immature animals.

Goldfish, Crabs, Monkeys, and Frogs

What Hubel and Wiesel have done for the cat's visual system has been paralleled for other species by a number of investigators. At the invertebrate level there is the classic work with the horsehoe crab, limulus, of H. K. Hartline of Rockefeller University. Hartline recorded the electrical activity of single nerve fibers leading off from the individual facets, or ommatidia, which make up the crab's compound eye. He noted how activity in any one fiber varied with the intensity or duration of light, and how the discharge pattern was affected according to whether light was shone on its associated facet alone or also played upon neighboring facets. He examined the more complex retina of the frog, describing "on" cells, whose associated fibers fired a burst of electrical impulses when light was shone on the cell's receptive field; "off" cells that were inhibited by light but fired when the stimulus was turned off; and "on-off" cells which did both, firing briefly at the onset and again at the cessation of light.

At the vertebrate level, of course, one expects higher orders of complexity. The similarities in structure across species lines, however, make the study of vertebrates advantageous when one wants to make the jump to man. It is as though all vertebrate eyes used the same grammar and basic rules of operation, but each species elaborated a language peculiar to its evolutionary adaptations and behavior. For example, because the cat's retina possesses cones it may be assumed to have some rudimentary color sense; but its nocturnal mode of life has not led to development of this part of the language. The goldfish, the pigeon, monkeys, and man all have excellent color vision, however, so that for those interested in color physiology these are "species of choice."

Some of the most interesting color studies to date are associated with the work on goldfish carried out by H. G. Wagner and M. L. Wolbarsht of the Naval Medical Research Institute in Bethesda, Maryland, E. F. MacNichol, Jr., of Johns Hopkins, and Gunnar Svaetichin of the Karolinska Institutet in Stockholm. In 1958 Svaetichin and Mac-Nichol reported that they were able to pick up electrical activity from the goldfish retina in a region between the receptor and ganglion levels. They labeled this activity the graded photopic response, or GPR. What was fascinating was that this gradedness, a rise or drop in the level of electrical activity present, was dependent on wavelength. Some colors were exciting; some inhibiting.

Later MacNichol, Wolbarsht, and Wagner showed that similar responses could be picked up from cells at the ganglion level. A cell they had thought of as a typical "on-off" cell, firing vigorously at the onset or offset of white light, changed its behavior dramatically when the wavelength of light was specified. The same cell became a pure "on" cell in response to certain wavelengths (say short ones) then changed to a pure "off" cell in response to others (long wavelengths) with a sharp transition point between, as small as 10 m_μ in some cases. Further alterations of the stimulus revealed other subtleties: if intensity was raised at certain wavelengths the cell's response might change from "on" to "on-off," and at still higher intensities to "off."

All this began to sound very reminiscent of the color theory proposed by Hering in 1875, which stipulated that there were opponent color mechanisms at work in the retina. When Wolbarsht and his colleagues traced the receptive fields of the color-sensitive ganglion cells they found certain spatial characteristics that lent greater weight to the idea. If they shone a small spot of long wavelength light at various positions in a particular cell's receptive field (previously mapped under general illumination), they discovered that the strongest "off" response was elicited when the spot struck positions in the center of the field. Moving out toward the periphery it was still possible to elicit a response though it was much weaker. This was interesting because one might suppose that the fields of excitation or inhibition would be strongly delimited in bull's-eye fashion. That this was not the case was confirmed when Wolbarsht repeated the experiment, this time using small spots of short wavelength light. Again excitation was strongest when the light hit the field center, diminishing toward the boundary, but it did not drop

A close-up of the goldfish eye and the experimental setup used by Wolbarsht, Wagner, and MacNichol in their investigations of color vision. The probing electrode is mounted in a hypodermic needle; a wire stretched across the experimental chamber completes the circuit. The glass plate that the eye rests on is a hollow one containing circulating cold water. The light comes up from underneath the retina. The white material around the edge is a moistened wick to keep a high relative humidity inside the chamber, which is covered.

off as significantly as in the long wavelength case. In other words the cones that relayed to these ganglion cells reflected the same retinal fields, even though their color sensitivities were at opposite ends of the spectrum. How the ganglion cell reacts is determined by the relative strength of one or the other influence. On the whole long wavelengths are relatively more sensitive in the center, short wavelengths in the periphery, but the cell is capable of subtle integrations over the whole field, and hence sometimes exhibits pure "on" responses, sometimes pure "off," and in between, a variety of transitional "on-off" responses.

Simultaneous Contrast

This model of a color-sensitive "on-off" ganglion cell has temporal characteristics as well. It is important to know not only the wavelength and energy of the stimulating light and the portion of receptive field it strikes, but also how long it lasts. A red light continuously shining at the center of the field of the above cell, for example, would sooner or later fatigue the receptors connected to it. Adaptation to the light takes place, with a resultant decline in activity. In this way the ganglion cell may be released from inhibitory inputs and whatever excitatory inputs exist; either the resting level of activity or that which is stimulated by light shining in the peripheral region of the receptive field would have a free hand to excite the cell. Thus even though red may have been the original strong inhibitory stimulus, the net effect would be to stimulate the sensation of green nearby. By such quirks of physiology the phenomenon of simultaneous contrast—seeing a gray disk as greenish when it borders something red—begins to make sense.

Independent evidence that the kind of color coding that exists at the goldfish level may extend to man comes from the work of Russell De Valois of the University of Indiana, who has worked with a much more highly developed species, the macaque monkey. De Valois has found several kinds of color-sensitive cells segregated in various layers of the monkey's lateral geniculate. Some are "on" cells that respond to sufficiently narrow bands of wavelengths to be called "red" cells or "yellow" cells; some are "off" cells that are highly sensitive and inhibited by somewhat broader bands of wavelengths; but the majority he found were of the "on-off" variety. These he classified as "red-on, green-off" (or vice versa) and "blue-on, yellow-off" (or vice versa), depending on whether the switching point from excitation to inhibition occurred at wavelengths greater than 560 mμ (the red-green cells) or less than 560 mμ (the blue-yellows). These cells also exhibited a kind of rebound effect. For example, shining a red light on an R + G − cell would increase

290

its rate of firing, but as soon as the light was turned off it would be inhibited. Similarly if green was the stimulus, the cell would decrease its rate of firing, and when the light was turned off, become excited again. These cells were indifferent to light at intermediate wavelengths and did not respond to white light either, presumably because excitatory and inhibitory inputs canceled each other.

Successive Contrast

The behavior of the "on-off" geniculate cells suggests the physiological mechanism underlying the phenomenon of negative afterimages, or successive contrast. If, for example, you stare at the bright red setting sun, numbers of R+G− cells increase their firing rates, thereby signaling red. When you look away, however, these same cells are inhibited, thereby signaling green. If in addition you turn to look at something green it will seem even greener, because there is now the positive inhibition green exerts added to the post-red-seeing inhibition. You've supplied the cell with just what it will reject the most vehemently at a time when it already is being inhibited.

The Physiology of Motion

If the cat is a model for form perception, the goldfish or monkey for color, it is the frog that has revealed much about motion perception. Frogs use their eyes in hunting for food and in avoiding predators. But they notice only moving objects. They will catch a bug on the wing or a crawling worm, but ignore a resting fly or a dead caterpillar. Larger and presumably more sinister objects must also be moving to be seen, before the frog will try to protect itself by jumping to a darker place, under a bush or into the water. What is interesting about this behavior anatomically is that the eyes that do this detecting are essentially stable. They move to compensate for the excesses of gravity, if the frog's whole body bobs up and down on a lily pad, for example; otherwise they stay put, incapable of purposefully gazing at or following an object, incapable even of making saccadic motions. This makes the frog a fine test animal: investigators do not have to anesthetize or paralyze eye muscles. Moreover the frog's visual system is relatively simple. There is no fovea in the retina, and the optic fibers relay to only one brain station after leaving the eyes, a layered structure called the colliculus, or tectum. (This is comparable to the relay station for those optic tract fibers in man which bypass the geniculate.) Given such an amiable animal with interesting behavior to boot, investigators J. Y. Lettvin, H. R. Maturana, W. S. McCulloch, and

W. H. Pitts of the Massachusetts Institute of Technology set out to analyze the frog's visual system. They wanted to find out how it was equipped to abstract just the pattern-and-motion details it needed from the outside world.

They constructed an ingenious test apparatus, a bowl-shaped world for the frog to look at, placing the animal so that its eyes were approximately positioned at the center of an aluminum hemisphere about 14 inches in diameter. The inner surface of the bowl was silvered to a matte gray finish. A variety of test objects attached to small magnets—geometrical figures, arrays of dots, or shapes that might mimic natural objects—could be introduced along the inner surface of the sphere, manipulated by a larger magnet held against the outer surface. An opening in the frog's head allowed the experimenters to isolate single fibers in the optic nerves, and note changes in electrical activity in response to the varied positions, motions, shapes, and illuminations of the test objects. In other studies the fibers were traced to their terminations in the tectum, or to connections back in the retina itself.

The M.I.T. group discovered five varieties of fiber whose discharge patterns suggested functional definitions. Class I fibers, for example, were "sustained contrast detectors." They fired long bursts of impulses whenever a light or dark boundary moved into their fields. They continued to fire if the contrast-making object stopped. If the lights were turned out for a moment, the fibers would be quiet, but when the lights were switched on and the object was revealed, still in the field, the fibers would again fire, as though they had "remembered" it. Other fibers were more selective. Class II fibers only noticed small, dark, convex objects that moved or came to rest in their fields. Turning out the light momentarily erased these fibers' memories. So special were they that the M.I.T. workers couldn't help but think of the II's as "bug perceivers." They even tried an amusing variant on their test procedure introducing a facsimile frog's world to their aluminum bowl, a close-up of grasses and flowers that would be a natural terrain from the frog's-eye view. Into this they introduced facsimile bugs. The II fibers fired every time the bug moved into their receptive fields; never when the background alone or bug-plus-background was moved.

Class III fibers were sensitive to moving edges crossing their somewhat larger fields, and within limits, the faster the motion, the more excited they became. Class IV reacted to a sudden darkening of their fields, as might be caused, for example, by the shadow of a moving object. The response was prolonged if a large dark object stopped in the field. The remaining class of fibers differed from the rest in paying attention not so much to subtleties in contour or contrast, but relayed information about the general level of light in fairly large patches of retina. They were termed "darkness detectors" because their discharges were inversely proportional to the total level of illumination. In contrast to the Class V fibers the others' behavior was almost independent of the total amount of light. As long as there was sufficient contrast they reacted. Presumably the frog eats as well on overcast days as on sunny ones.

While these functional descriptions were fascinating in their own right, what was most satisfying was that generally speaking, each of the separate classes of fibers fitted neatly into an anatomical and morphological scheme. Class I fibers were the smallest, slowest-conducting fibers. They had the smallest receptive fields and terminated in the uppermost layer of the tectum. The remaining fiber classes lined up in order behind Class I, successively bigger, with larger receptive fields, terminating in layers lower down in the tectum. Follow-up studies of the morphology of retinal cells suggested that the fiber connections inside the retina were also distinct, each class associated with a specific type of ganglion cell and in turn with particular bipolar cells.

The distribution of the various ganglion cell types is uniform throughout the retina. Given the multiplicity of branchings at each level, plus the extensive overlapping of receptive fields, this means that any one fiber will ultimately be in contact with hundreds or thousands of rods or cones, while each receptor will be in touch with many fibers of all classes.

If you think about this in terms of a particular spot "X" on the retina you can visualize what happens: four (or five if you count the darkness detectors) "TV" channels are beamed to pick up what's happening in successively larger neighborhoods of X. Each is biased toward reporting its own brand of news which it transmits to a particular terminal down the line. These terminals in the tectum are also arranged in order: the layers are congruent to each other and in register. Moving from the top down, the different sets of information about X can be read out against larger and larger contexts. Thus the ultimate "meaning" of the news depends on integrating, or pooling, the separate reports. This the M.I.T. workers believe to be the function of the tectal cells. These, for the most part, lie toward the base of the tectum and reach up branches to contact the terminals in order. It is this integrated news-handling which is the key to understanding what the frog's brain learns from the frog's eye.

Perhaps the most striking feature of this elegant arrangement is that the frog's eye has so much to tell—much data-processing goes on within the retina itself. There is no need to postpone the reckoning to the "black box" above. Of course the frog may be special in this, having chosen a particular feature of the visual world to elaborate at the expense of many others. (A frog will stick its tongue out as readily after a moving shoelace as a worm.)

Man's motion perception may be more fallible in comparison, not only because many other qualities of the stimulus are being analyzed, but also because the analyzing equipment itself is subject to motion, both voluntary and involuntary. Whatever the reason, the fact remains that we cannot distinguish real from apparent motion. Like color, it belongs to the eye of the beholder, a sensation deduced from a sequence of electrical events. Just as we are prey to contrast, constancy, intensity, or afterimage effects of color, so are we vulnerable in judging motion. We see stationary objects whirl, and whirling things stand still. Perhaps because motion is so inherently compelling such illusions are the most beguiling of all.

The "Flicks"

The movies are a classic example of an illusion based on a time lag. We see always a fraction of a second after the fact, and what we see persists for another fraction as an afterimage. The movie projector "beats" this slice of time by feeding the still frames onto the screen at 24 frames per second—beyond the "critical frequency of fusion," or CFF. No longer can the single stills be distinguished, and because each is so like its predecessor, the images blend into an impression of continuous smooth movement. Short of the CFF, movies are literally "flicks."

The Phi Phenomenon

The illusion of movement also occurs when stationary objects close in shape and position are illuminated in sequence. The bulbs of movie marquees or advertising signs make use of this effect, called the "phi" phenomenon by Wertheimer (who chose Greek letters to describe a number of illusory effects of movement). Phi impressions can range from headlines moving around a building to liquid filling a glass, or figures jumping out from a billboard, flipping over in three dimensions.

Stroboscopic Effects

The speed of a camera can be used to make still things move, but it can also "stop" moving objects. This is the trick of the stroboscopic camera,

294

which, in principle, can be thought of as making use of a slotted disk placed in front of the lens. When the disk is rotated, light can enter the camera only during the brief instant the slot passes the lens. Suppose you want to photograph a fan in motion. If you set the disk rotating at the same rate as the fan, whenever the camera clicks it will catch the blades in precisely the same position of each rotation. When the film is projected it will appear as though the fan is standing still. Now suppose you set the strobe at a slightly slower rate. Then each successive image will catch the fan blade at a point further along in its cycle, and the fan will appear to rotate slowly in the true direction of its motion. Set the strobe faster and the fan will appear to rotate backward.

Your own fusion rate makes it possible for you to observe strobo-scopic effects without a camera. If you watch a fan or a plane's propellers warm up or slow down they too may pass through clockwise, counterclockwise, and stationary (or invisible) stages.

Afterimages of Motion

Observing motion when there is no motion is also possible if a spirally painted disk is rotated in one direction and then stopped. If the spiral seemed to coil inward during rotation it will expand when stopped. Counter-rotation produces opposite effects. Another afterimage of movement is the waterfall illusion. Moving a horizontally striped surface up or down in front of a person induces movement in the opposite direction of the surroundings. When the movement is stopped, there is a negative afterimage—a sensation of motion opposite to the original movement of the striped surface.

Some of the frenzy of optical art is also due to afterimages. The repetition of simple patterns such as straight lines radiating from a common center induces the sensation of shimmering circles, or arcs of circles, at right angles to the radii. These can be projected onto a neutral surface and appear to rotate.

Figure-Ground

The frame of reference is very important in judging movement. Gestalt theory points out that we tend to think of the background of a scene as the fixed backdrop against which action takes place. Thus on a cloudy night it appears that the moon, the central figure, bustles through the clouds rather than the opposite. Similarly it is the sun that "sinks slowly into the west," slipping behind a stand of trees or a hillside.

The surround is also important in judging the apparent speed of motion. A horseback rider passing from open field to woods may feel that he has doubled his speed when in fact the rate is the same. Similarly anyone driving along a flat monotonous turnpike knows that doing 70 doesn't "feel" very fast at all, but would notice that speed in town.

Learned monocular clues like changes in size, brightness, or clarity that aid in judging the shape and position of stationary objects also figure in motion. So does motion parallax, of course, the business of seeing the telegraph poles stream past you going in the opposite direction while far-lying hills travel with you when you're riding in a train.

Art and Reality

For every learned experience corresponding to a "real" change in the world there are visual effects mimicking it. When these are instituted in the laboratory we call them illusions; when they are created as expressions of imagination we call them art. An artist paints on a flat canvas. To the extent that the space enclosed by the frame mirrors a universe, conjures up a real world, he has successfully fooled our eyes.

We know that he may use color—thus a master landscape painter such as Turner or Constable may tinge the distant hills with mauve or blue to suggest the effects of aerial perspective. He may blur outlines and use shadows and perspective to give depth and suggest the time of day. The horizontal lines of the painting may lead the eye beyond and behind the frame to some common meeting point "at infinity."

But it would be wrong to assume that because the artist has skillfully mimed nature he has mastered his art. His version of reality may have nothing to do with the everyday world. Indeed he may very well have had to unlearn some of the constancy effects we bring to perception. Not only do we hold to the color and size of the rose under varieties of lighting conditions and viewing distances, but we alter perspective and optics so that we see it as round. When we look at a plate on a table viewed from an angle, it is not the skinny ellipse the optical diagrams require, but some pleasing oval between thinness and roundness—shaped by our familiarity with the object.

Sometimes architects make use of these vagaries of human vision. So the Greeks, recognizing that human eyes saw temple columns seemingly taper towards the middle, added a bit of a bulge to make the sides appear straight and parallel. Similarly they bowed the temple steps, again to make them appear straight. And of course they were endlessly fascinated with the dimensions supposedly universally pleasing to the eye, those of the "golden section."

Eye-trickery continues today in some of the familiar parallel line or arrow illusions of psychology texts. Sign painters, too, know that they should make their A's a bit taller than other letters because something—perhaps perspective, perhaps a basic feeling of closing in that the acute angle gives—makes the A look shorter than a neighboring T or B. Anyone who has climbed a pyramid knows the effects of this illusion in three dimensions. The height of the pyramid viewed from the base seems considerably shorter than the frightened and weary climber finds it when he reaches the top.

For these reasons it is dangerous to assume when you see a painting or examine the art of some past culture that this corresponds to the way people actually saw the world. Nor should the frontality of archaic art, the flatness of Egyptian painting, the varied-sized persons of medieval art, the strange inversions of perspective in Chinese art, suggest that they are in any way lesser works of genius. The artist picks and chooses and his work is a manifestation of metaphysics rather than physics. So the medieval painter may seem to be preoccupied with verticals, with Gothic heights and proportions, but this may be his way of mirroring the hierarchical structure of life, the order imposed by church and feudalism.

The Renaissance with its turning toward man, its re-appreciation of the world and the individual brought a new impression of the universe to the world of art. All at once there seems a fascination with the toy of perspective and the viewer is treated to endless variations on themes like the "Annunciation to Mary," set in pillared hallways with tiled floors which carry the eye dutifully back and out into the hills of Tuscany.

Yet even within that framework there was no rigid adherence. No sooner had he demonstrated his skill at the new art of perspective than Mantegna produced "Christ Dead"—an almost grotesquely foreshortened figure of Christ, supine, with no common meeting point for the horizontal lines in the painting. Instead there is a dual perspective so arranged that the eye traversing the figure experiences a weird sense of motion—wherever the observer stands or moves to look at the picture, the feet of Christ appear to follow, always confronting him.

This very sensation of motion is one of the greatest illusions of painting. As Georg von Békésy remarked in his Nobel Laureate speech, he found in Leonardo perfect examples of the two extremes—absolute rest and captured motion—the first in a drawing of flowers and the second in that of a storm. One could point to sculpture too, and observe that in this most "heavy" of media, someone like Degas could eminently succeed in making bronze move.

It is in the eye's readiness to look and be seduced by looking that vision maintains its endless fascination and power. So quickly do the eyes accustom themselves to a new view that the old becomes dated. Yesterday's Impressionism, Cubism, Futurism, are distinctly old hat. While reverting to the laboratory again, there is ample proof that the most bizarre alterations of perception are often completely absorbed.

Perhaps the weirdest demonstrations of this eerie adaptability comes from experiments with goggles. Some of these use prism lenses that create color fringe effects according to the way the prism differentially refracts the various wavelengths. The edges of an object may be red or orange on one side, blue or violet on the other. Prisms can also alter the shapes of things, making straight lines curve or bow. Some switch right and left and up and down, creating the dizzying phenomenon of seeing the world upside-down and backward. In almost all cases however, given time and practice while wearing the goggles, persons again saw the world right-side up; curves were straightened, color haloes vanished.

The explanation offered by Ivo Kohler of the University of Innsbruck, Austria, and his colleagues, who were guinea pigs in these experiments, is that the distortions are consistent. If, whenever you look to the right you see a blue world, and whenever you turn left you see yellow (this happens when ordinary lenses are made up of blue and yellow filters and are split down the middle), you have a basis for adjustment and adaptation. In all such cases taking off the glasses creates an equally bizarre complementary situation, until, after a few days, the eyes again react normally.

One occasion when this did not happen was when Kohler's subjects wore prismatic lenses which were oppositely aligned. The thick part was on the right for the right eye, say, and on the left for the left eye. Wearing such glasses had the effect of making them squint—they learned to turn the eyes inward or outward depending on the orientation of the prisms. This created certain stereoscopic effects—a vertical line appeared to bend away or a flat wall bulged in the middle.

The color-stereo effects were particularly unsettling. As one of the experimenters reported:

A woman carrying a red bag slung over her back seemed to be transparent, and the bag to be inside her, somewhere near her stomach. . . . Most peculiar was a woman wearing a red blouse. She had no upper body, and the red blouse seemed to be following her about a pace behind, moving its empty sleeves in rhythm with the movement of her arms.

298

What was happening was based on the greater refraction of short waves over long. With the prism bases outward, blues were deflected outward more than reds, so in order to focus on blue objects the eyes had to converge. But this has the effect of making blue objects appear nearer than red ones. The colors line up with blue closest and the remaining spectral hues receding with red the most distant.

Nobody who wore prisms arranged this way ever got used to the effect, even though they may have worn the glasses for weeks. Probably this is so, Kohler conjectures, because there is no color consistency in the world. As the eyes roam about they will light upon a woman in a red print dress, a child carrying a blue balloon, or a bookstore window with all colors of the rainbow displayed.

Kohler suggests that it should be possible to make use of these effects to aid color-blind persons. Provided with prism glasses and the instruction that green looks nearer than red, and yellow appears to be between them, they would have no trouble at traffic lights.

Several American psychologists have also experimented with goggles, with particular emphasis on the conditions of adaptation. Austin Riesen of the University of California at Riverside and Alan Hein and Richard Held at M.I.T., along with Kohler, stress the importance of body movements if adaptation to a drastically altered visual environment is to take place. Held tested adults before and after wearing goggles in such situations as marking the corners of a square that is seen reflected in a mirror, or aligning the body to face in the direction of a dimly lit slit, after swinging around on a rotating chair in a small test room.

The persons were divided into three groups: the first was allowed to move freely after putting on the glasses, the second was not allowed to move at all, and the third was moved passively, either by being wheeled around in a kind of stroller, or else, in the drawing test, having the arms lifted by the experimenter. The only persons who showed any adaptation to the prisms were those allowed to move freely. Held's interpretation of this is that normally there are feedback signals from hand or body muscles which are coordinated with sensory information from the eyes. In the ordinary environment such feedback establishes eye-hand coordination, and continually works to orient the body in space in relation to surrounding objects. Wearing goggles creates a situation in which information from the retina conflicts with motor feedback. With repeated practice, however, the central nervous system in man can apparently establish new sensory-motor coordinations. Some individuals may even show 100 percent adaptation in the goggle experiments after some weeks of practice. When they take off the glasses they suffer a reverse impairment. The adapted set of coordinations is now in conflict with the old "reality." Thus the problem of re-adaptation.

Whenever the conditions of adaptation are inconsistent, if, for example, the prisms can be rotated continually so that the location of objects in space is always fortuitous, the feedback from hands or body can establish no new rules. A movement of the hand 2 inches to the right may appear to be now a smaller, now a larger displacement in some other direction, depending on the position of the prisms at the time. Such circumstances (comparable to Kohler's randomly colored world) lead only to confusion.

The goggle experiments are among a variety of investigations that are of considerable importance because they accent the fact that perception is a two-way street. We are not passive receivers of sensation, but are actively engaged in a continual sensory-motor interplay which can have serious consequences any time there is tampering with traffic one way or the other. The goggle experiments are one means of tampering in which there is a rearrangement of the sensory input. Other kinds of experiments involve sensory deprivation. Adult volunteers may be kept in soundproof, lightproof rooms, their bodies contained in such a way as to prevent tactile stimulation, or animals may be reared in darkness. Surgical intervention in animals or procedures to prevent movement may also be used to examine the dynamics of sensory-motor interaction with particular reference to vision.

As these examples suggest, visual experiments have grown considerably complex over the years. Even the classic optical illusions, the "short" and "long" arrows, or the circles that seem to bend, are not so much thought of as amusements or tricks as considered genuine indicators of how "real" perception works. One theory has it that many of the line and angle illusions result from misplaced constancy judgments, combined with a reduced or simple field background. The eye adds width or changes angles in its customary compromise between geometrical optics and the true size and shape of an object.

Twentieth-century contributions to psychology à la Freud and Jung also enter into current analyses. Some experimenters have observed that the distortions people experience in the Ames Room illusion may be related to their emotional state or attitude toward the people in the room. "Neutral" persons were distorted more than those that aroused fear or anxiety. Boot camp recruits saw their buddies distorted more than officers; normal individuals saw other normals more distorted than persons who looked maimed or had limbs amputated (whether real or sham).

In time, perhaps comparably sophisticated behavioral experiments

Familiar illusions, classified according to whether the illusion is of angle, extent, or shape. In each case the name of the investigator associated with the discovery or discussion of the illusion is given. A number of psychologists today believe that most or all of these classic optical illusions result from misapplied constancy. Our eyes tend to enlarge the more distant portions of a figure—say, a table top seen in perspective—and similarly to alter angles to "rectify" them, making those nearby seem less acute, those more distant less obtuse. Frequently the illusion presents the viewer with minimal information that suggests a drawing in two dimensions of what could be a three-dimensional object or scene. The brain builds on this minimal information, applying constancy principles or else adapting to the scene (as in the "rigged" Ames Room environment).

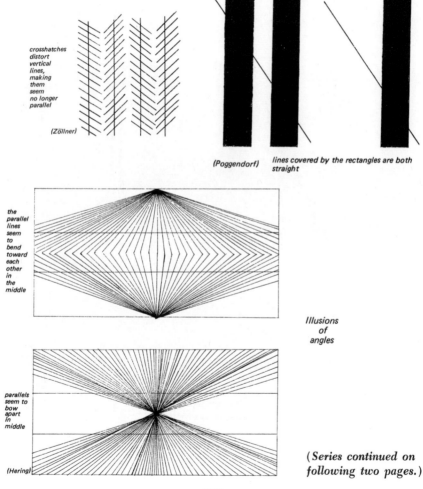

crosshatches distort vertical lines, making them seem no longer parallel

(Zöllner)

(Poggendorf) lines covered by the rectangles are both straight

the parallel lines seem to bend toward each other in the middle

Illusions of angles

parallels seem to bow apart in middle

(Hering)

(Series continued on following two pages.)

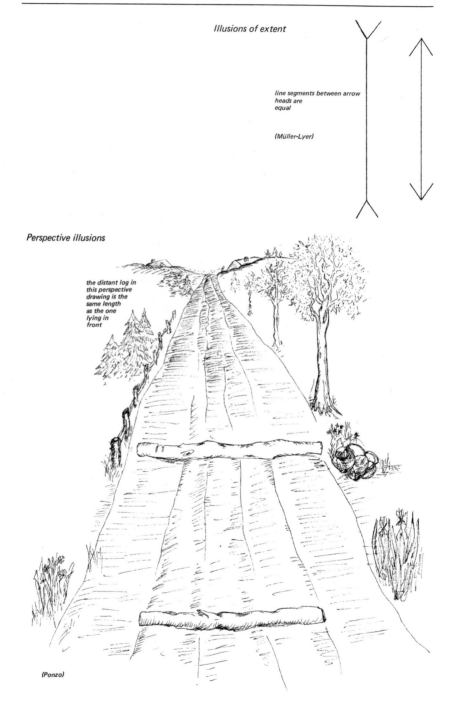

Illusions of extent

line segments between arrow
heads are
equal

(Müller-Lyer)

Perspective illusions

the distant log in
this perspective
drawing is the
same length
as the one
lying in
front

(Ponzo)

Pattern illusions

the square is perfect; patterned
background distorts sides, making
them appear concave

regular-patterned background
distorts perfect circle

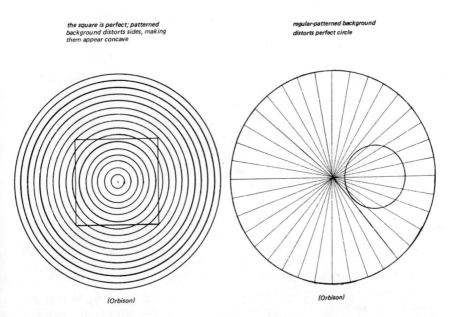

(Orbison)   (Orbison)

will be performed with animals, when it will be possible to record electrical activity at the various brain centers simultaneously. Some progress has already been made, with quite interesting results. R. W. Sperry of the California Institute of Technology has shown that if the great circle of nerve fibers that connects the left and right hemispheres of the brain, the corpus callosum, is severed, along with the crossed optic fibers of the chiasm, chimpanzees can be trained to make independent responses to visual stimuli. The right eye might be conditioned to recognize a circle, push a button, and get a reward, while a square might elicit a shock. The left eye, amazingly, could be trained to do just the opposite, a pattern of contradictory behavior that did not lead to the chimpanzee equivalent of a nervous breakdown.

Sometimes surgical cutting of the corpus callosum is tried on humans, as a means of preventing the spread of epileptic brain wave patterns to both sides of the brain. Such individuals appear to be little handicapped by the operation, a fact not too surprising since most of the time the right and left sides of the body actively cooperate. But these people have shown fascinating split-brain phenomena when the effects were specifically looked for.

Generally speaking the clues to brain activity in vision rely pri-

303

marily on the surgical intervention or implanted electrode techniques that have been so effective in the hands of investigators like Hubel and Wiesel, Wolbarsht, MacNichol, Lettvin, and others. Some progress has been made with external electrical recording from human subjects. It has been known for some time that the intrinsic wave patterns of the brain fall into a few stable forms, corresponding to waking or sleeping, resting or being highly attentive. One of these forms is the "alpha" pattern, a regular 8 to 10 times a second high-amplitude wave form displayed in particular in the posterior of the cortex. It is this pattern which is disrupted when you open your eyes to look at things. The conjecture is that attention and the great number of incoming visual signals disrupt the synchronized activity of brain cells, breaking in on it and taking over. Now, through the development of a computer analyzer by Manfred Clynes at Rockland State Hospital in New York, it has been possible to record surface brain wave activity over the visual cortex, and by means of repeated recordings using fixed stimuli, to pick out the changed signals against the background. A particular signal shows up, for example, when the subject is shown a blue object. Perhaps this procedure combined with the single cell work on goldfish or monkeys will completely unravel the color code some day.

These are among the most promising tracings on a map that is still largely unexplored. The number of surveyors will grow and gradually bridge the gaps between observation and anatomy, psychology and electrical signals. The exploration is surely one of the most fascinating of all fields of human knowledge.

XII

Non-Sense

Non-sense does not mean nonsense. It is a logical term used to describe matters that are neither sense nor not-sense, by the same principle that a non-friend is neither a friend nor an enemy. The label conveniently fits the host of weird and wonderful happenings continually being reported in mass media. Russian ladies who see colors with their fingertips; university students who call the throws of dice; hypnotized subjects who reveal lurid lives lived centuries ago; mediums who levitate; ghosts and poltergeists who play havoc with houses or their inhabitants.

Non-sense also applies to those strange crossings of the senses, synesthesias, in which persons may report they see green whenever they hear certain chords of music, for example, or to "superman" talents like X-ray vision or ultrasonic hearing. The category also includes the trances or pain-free ecstasies of fire-walking fakirs or human pincushions; the visions, hallucinations, or simply heightened sensibilities to color or sound that mark the effects of drugs like mescaline and lysergic acid diethylamide, LSD.

By extension of sensory inputs to brain and memory, non-sense also includes one of the most mysterious phenomena of all, the prodigious feats of idiot savants, exemplified today by a pair of mentally retarded twins who can give the day of the week corresponding to a given date for centuries past or future and who can instantly recall details of their own lifetime dating years back.

To be sure some of these happenings are out and out frauds, truly nonsense. The Bridey Murphy case, for example, in which a woman under hypnosis supposedly reported her previous life in Ireland, turned out to be nothing but memories of stories she had heard as a child growing up in Chicago. Other "remarkable happenings" may involve honest self-deceptions, unconscious biases, or faulty statistics. Still others are fascinating puzzles which at present stump the experts but may serve as new and interesting springboards to the study of the brain.

Extrasensory Perception

Unfortunately reports of such events seldom give rise to the logical neutrality of the "non" attitude. Friend and enemy camps tend to spring up. Nowhere is this more evident than in the sphere of extrasensory perception (ESP), the term that came into vogue through the work of one of its most distinguished and respected researchers, Dr. Joseph Banks Rhine, Director of the Institute of Parapsychology, formerly Director of the Department of Parapsychology at Duke University in Durham, North Carolina. ESP strictly defined includes telepathy (mind reading), clairvoyance (fact or event reading as opposed to mind reading), and precognition (knowledge of the future). In recent years Dr. Rhine and his colleagues have become interested in mind-over-matter control, for which they have adopted the word psychokinesis (PK). They have also extended the definition of ESP to handle cases where it may be difficult to decide which ESP talent is involved, labeling a general psychic intuition GESP, and associating it with the possession of "psi," the psychic force or power governing ESP.

Rhine's association with ESP reflects a lifelong interest in matters of science and spirit. As a young man he thought of becoming a Protestant minister. Later he obtained a doctorate in botany at the University of Chicago and taught for two years at West Virginia University. During this period in the twenties he and his wife Luisa attended a lecture on spiritualism given by Sir Arthur Conan Doyle. The lecture profoundly impressed them, and not long after Rhine wrote to Professor William McDougall, a British psychologist who had come to Harvard in 1920 as chairman of the department of psychology. At that time McDougall was president of the British Society of Psychical Research, an organization which had been formed at the end of the nineteenth century for the express purpose of conducting scholarly investigations of telepathy and related phenomena. Psychical research flourished at Harvard under Mc-Dougall, and when he moved on to Duke, he invited Rhine to join him.

Initially Rhine set out to discover who might have ESP abilities. He employed simple guessing games, asking children to guess a number between zero and nine. Later, with the collaboration of K. E. Zener, a colleague in the department, he worked with cards, now known as ESP cards, which Zener had designed. A deck typically consisted of twenty-five cards, five of which were marked with one of the following symbols: a star, a cross, a circle, a square, or a set of wavy lines. If in repeated tests a subject did better than chance (five out of twenty-five) in guessing the symbols when the deck was shuffled and the cards dealt one at a time, he was presumed to show ESP ability.

In the course of these investigations Rhine discovered a number of persons amazingly adept at card reading—even, in a few cases, when guesser and experimenter were hundreds of miles apart. With each success, confidence in the reality of ESP increased, books and journals were published, and persons reputed to have the talent were invited to be tested or perform experiments themselves. The odds against chance alone explaining the results were phenomenal. In the case of Hubert E. Pearce, who later became a Methodist minister, they were awe inspiring: Pearce once guessed 25 cards in a row, an event with the odds of 298,023,223,876,953,125 to 1 of happening by chance.

Astronomical odds against a chance event are one thing. The deduction that this proves the case for ESP is another. Whenever Rhine or other scholarly spokesmen for ESP such as the English mathematician S. G. Soal have elaborated experiments and published results to show statistically that ESP has been demonstrated, their claims have been found wanting, challenged on one or more of the following grounds:

(1) The special quality of the experimenter. If the outcome of A's experiments reveals ESP in some people most of the time, then experimenter B working with a comparable sample (university students), and duplicating A's methods should yield similar results—or if not B, then C, or D, and so on. This has not happened and is a major disappointment with Rhine's work. Rhine himself suggests that skepticism on the part of the experimenter mitigates against psi's showing up. The psi force apparently is elusive, shy, hidden, affected by attitude. But the scientific attitude calls for skepticism. If one accepts the notion that evidence is a function of the personality of the experimenter one closes the door forever to the very foundation of scientific proof.

(2) The error factor. Martin Gardner in his book *Fads and Falla-*

cies in the Name of Science * points to several occasions when hidden cameras or tape recorders were used during ESP experiments. One at Stanford University involved card reading, and one at Yale involved a PK test of students' abilities to control the throws of dice. In each case bias on the part of the person recording results showed up. Misses were recorded as hits if the person were pro-ESP, the reverse if he were strongly opposed. This is not to impute deliberate dishonesty to the workers at Stanford or Yale so much as a subconscious predilection. Looked at in this light, the mass of pro-ESP data, especially that derived from early experiments in the thirties, is open to question. Neither experimental design nor control was particularly sophisticated at that time, while those involved were almost exclusively sympathetic to the cause. The doubts seem all the more justified since ESP findings have gone down in recent years as experimental procedures improved. It also has been found that subconscious recording errors are most likely to occur at the beginning or end of an experiment, times when interest and emotional expectation run high. But these are just the times ESP enthusiasts regard as the most propitious to psi's appearance. In mid-course a monotony sets in that is antithetical to psi and this accounts for the low scores of this period. It also is the time when random recording errors are most likely to occur.

(3) Selection. Gardner reasons that another kind of unconscious bias may be in operation, one that favors the reporting of successful experiments to the exclusion of others. One could imagine, he says, a teacher successively testing a class of 100 students, each time choosing the half that scored better than chance on an ESP deck of cards, and ignoring the low scorers. At the end of six or seven runs there might be one person left who had scored consistently better than chance every time—clearly a psychic fellow! This argument is the same as the "Heroic Dolphin" folklore. As one delphinologist put it, a lot of people believe dolphins are lifesavers, helping the stranded swimmer by pushing him to shore. But suppose it was completely a matter of chance whether the dolphin directed the swimmer to shore or further out to sea. Half the swimmers would be lost—the very ones you never hear about. So it may be, in less obvious ways, with negative tests of ESP.

W. S. Taylor also raised the issue of negative evidence in a letter to *Science,* the weekly publication of the American Association for the Advancement of Science. He described an event that happened in his instructor days. He had had a dream that something dreadful had happened at home. When he woke up he promised himself to remember

* New York: Dover Publications, Inc., 1957.

the day and hour and check up. A week later a student in class asked "What about those feelings you get that something bad has happened at home, and then you get a message that it has happened?" It was only then that Taylor remembered that (a) he had forgotten to remember; (b) things at home were as usual.

Taylor was remarking on the innumerable instances of non-coincidence in our lives, when thought is neither father, brother, nor son to the event. In another letter to *Science* Luis W. Alvarez of the Physics Department of the University of California at Berkeley addresses himself to another problem. He had thought of a person and then within five minutes read of that person's death. Dr. Alvarez was reading a newspaper whose front page contained a reference to Dr. Carleton S. Coon, the University of Pennsylvania anthropologist. This triggered a youthful memory of another Carleton Coon who with a partner, Joe Sanders, had led a popular dance band in Chicago. Turning the pages of the newspaper Alvarez was startled to read of Sanders' death. The question interested him enough to begin to calculate the chances of such an event happening every day somewhere in the United States. His reasoning, summarized, went along these lines: †

Assume that an average person may know the names of about 3,000 persons each of whose death he will hear about at some time in the course of 30 years. Now if you restrict your attention to the five-minute interval before such knowledge, the probability of some random event triggering the thought of the person in question is, within a factor of 2, the ratio of a five-minute interval to 30 years, or 3/10,000,000. (If you think of the person more often than once in 30 years the probability rises—one thought a year, say, multiplies the probability by 30 to 90/10,-000,000 or roughly 1/100,000.) The probability that one will have such an experience when learning of the death of any one of 3,000 is 3,000×3/10,-000,000 or approximately 1/1,000 in 30 years or 1/30 of that, or approximately 3/100,000 a year. If we assume there are 100,000,000 adults in the U.S. then 3×1,000 experiences should occur per year or about 10 a day.

Alvarez concludes that it is not surprising, given the large U.S. population to draw upon, that such astonishing coincidences are reported in the literature as evidence of ESP.

Not so, says Dr. Rhine in answer, asserting that such instances of "spontaneous" ESP do not belong in the scholarly assemblage of ESP experiments. Unfortunately this is easier said than done. While scholarly

† Letter in *Science*, Vol. 148, No. 3677 (June 18, 1965), 1541.

ESP researchers may abjure spontaneous accounts they are almost always seized upon by the true believers as signs of the omnipresence if not the omnipotence of psi. Moreover in the publicity given such stories there is little concern for the kind of mathematical probabilities Alvarez proposes. There may even be a clear sin of omission of follow-up studies.

(4) Physical, logical, and psychological cues. Better-than-chance results in card guessing can derive from a variety of human idiosyncrasies that a good student of psychology or a trained observer may pick up. Hesitations in speech, pauses, changes in inflection, minor muscular movements, alterations of limb positions and gestures can all give clues to the guesser facing the experimenter. The good poker player knows how valuable such hints are in playing the game; the percipient, the person who is being tested, may likewise make use of them either consciously or unconsciously, unaware of his "subliminal" perceptions—his ability to absorb and make use of sensory data he has not consciously attended to.

In addition there may be flaws in the design of the experiment. These may range from such gross faults as being able to see the symbols through the backs of the cards or detecting edgewise differences, to less obvious but equally serious statistical flaws.

For example in some tests the percipient sees the results at the end of each run of five cards. If the cards are not replaced in the deck he can keep track of cards still out and score higher toward the end of the run.

A seasoned observer may also make use of psychological inferences in certain telepathy experiments. Here the agent, the person whose mind is being perceived, was sometimes asked to think of a group of five Zener symbols which the percipient would try to name in order. The trouble with this, as psychologist C. E. M. Hansel of the University College of Swansea, University of Wales, explains in his book, *ESP: A Scientific Inquiry*,‡ is that people seldom produce random series. Randomness would permit occasional repetitions or runs of three or more of the same symbol, but rarely does a person think this way. He is more likely to permute the five symbols, using each only once in a given quintet. The same disinclination to repeat a symbol occurs in longer series, where the agent may be asked to generate a list of thirty-five or fifty symbols. Knowing this habit, the guesser can formulate a rule to guess a particular symbol until he is told he is correct and then abruptly change his guess.

(5) Fraud. It was partly through statistical analyses like these that Hansel and others have discovered patterns of correct guesses in some

‡ New York: Charles Scribner's Sons, 1966.

well-known ESP experiments, a tendency for the percipient to be right, say, on the third or fourth symbol in a group of five. There is no ESP explanation for this; such a non-rational power would hardly be expected to appear in mathematical cycles. Hansel concludes that fraud may very well be the explanation. In this case he postulates collusion in marking the answer sheets ahead of time, with no one taking the trouble to randomize the positions of the phonied answers.

Accusations of fraud have traditionally been the least popular route in explaining away ESP data. As George Price, formerly of the University of Michigan Faculty of Medicine, stated in an article in *Science* some years ago, "Surprisingly it is not only the believers who are reluctant to imagine fraud, but virtually all skeptics as well prefer almost any other type of explanation."

Yet Price, Hansel, and a host of other investigators over the years have shown that fraud was not only possible but the most likely explanation in many instances. Further, it is well documented in the history of psychical research. The learned scientists who witnessed mind reading between G. A. Smith and Douglas Blackburn in the 1880's went away convinced of the performers' honesty. After all, Smith was wrapped in blankets, his ears were plugged, and his eyes swathed in bandages, yet he was able to produce an accurate copy of a complex design which had been shown to Blackburn by the observers and on which he had concentrated very hard. Some thirty years later Blackburn explained how it was done. He drew the design secretly on cigarette paper, transferred it to the tube of a brass projector on the pencil he was using, and, following a prearranged symbol, stumbled against the rug near Smith's chair. Smith at once exclaimed, "I have it.. . . Where's my pencil?" Blackburn obligingly placed his on the table, Smith seized it and buried his hands under the blanket again. Now the luminous plate he had concealed in his vest was put to use. He managed to push the bandage up from one eye just enough to see and copy the drawing as it lay on the plate and after five minutes of seemingly intense mental labors, threw back the blanket and produced the copy.

Modern readers may scoff at the naiveté of the Victorian gentlemen, but the record strongly suggests that people today are just as easily deceived. For the more sophisticated, there are more sophisticated techniques, in keeping with advances in technology. Just as cops and robbers, counterfeiters and treasury agents and spies engage in endless rounds of technological warfare, so mentalists too can benefit from the fruits of twentieth-century invention.

It is not necessary to invoke high-powered methods in discussing some of the classic experiments cited as foolproof demonstrations of ESP.

One of the most famous was a series of tests in which Pearce was the subject and Rhine's colleague Joseph G. Pratt was the card handler. Pearce was ostensibly seated in a room in the library on the Duke campus, while Pratt was in an office in the psychology department in a building 150 yards away. Watches were synchronized, and at certain time intervals Pratt was to place a card face down in front of him. Pearce was to write his guess and then Pratt was to remove the card to the left of the desk, still keeping it face down. At the end of the run Pratt turned the cards over and made two copies of their order, one of which was to be put into an envelope to be sealed and handed over to Rhine. The room Pratt sat in was visible through a window and door. There was nothing to prevent anyone from going across the hall to an empty room, standing on a stool and peering over the door's transom to read the cards when they were being recorded. In a recent visit to Duke, Hansel himself demonstrated this method of cheating to a member of the psychology department.

A classic experiment in which cheating was detected on at least one occasion involved the English investigator Soal and a pair of supposedly telepathic Welsh schoolboys. Observers noted that the boys were augmenting their ESP talents with coughs, creaks, and stamping of the feet. When placed in separate hotel rooms with the doors closed, or when test conditions were otherwise carefully controlled and observed, they scored at chance levels. Whenever there was opportunity for visual or auditory contact however their scores showed marked improvement. Hansel further points out that in tests with children there is the possibility of using auditory codes based on high-pitched dog whistles concealed under clothing and operated by a rubber bulb: the high sounds are within the range of youthful ears but elderly professors in attendance would fail to detect them.

The value of Hansel's analyses of these and other famous experiments lies in his meticulous delineation of loopholes: the variations that exist in the reports of the experiment, the alterations in test conditions during the experiment, the chances for recording errors, the failure to use random series, and the various ways fraud could be perpetrated. Even in experiments in which elaborate screens were used to prevent any communication between an agent and an experimenter (so that the agent would have no idea which cards were being dealt, he would only touch them) it was possible to detect the key position of a test symbol by observing the shadows of the experimenter's arm or noting the order in which certain cards were picked up and replaced.

He points out too that there are a number of incentives for cheating, not the least of which is money: Pearce, the Welsh schoolboys, and others were offered financial rewards for good guesses. Prestige, publicity, and something akin to the subject's desire to please the experimenter—to guess the cards and prove ESP—by one means or another, may account for the situations in which several persons including or excluding the percipient are involved in cheating.

Sadly there are many cases of known deception which swell the canon of ESP literature. The records may admit that some of the time a famous medium cheated, but there is invariably the statement that at least X percent of the time he or she was on the up and up. Apparently the ESP personality is not subject to a Caesar's wife code of conduct.

It is for these reasons that the popular press accounts of parapsychology must be examined with great care. A recent illustration of this was the color-seeing-with-fingertips reported about a Flint, Michigan, housewife, Mrs. Patricia Stanley. When questioned, Rhine and others were hopeful that such talents would add new luster to the power of psi, though naturally only after a thorough investigation. One such interested investigator was a Barnard College psychology professor Richard Youtz. He experimented both with Mrs. Stanley and a class of Barnard girls to see whether such abilities existed more generally. Earlier accounts of Russian women possessed of the talent had stirred the curiosity of more than one academician who was willing to conjecture that color discrimination might be possible if nerve receptors could be found which were sensitive to infrared rays that would be differentially given off by the various colors. The first tests gave positive results. While many newspapers and magazines reported the initial sensational accounts, only *The New York Times* later pointed out that in the presence of one of its reporters the housewife working with Dr. Youtz was no longer possessed of the power.

In a recent article in *Science* Martin Gardner firms up the case against skin-vision by revealing some of the tricks of mentalists, magicians, and other seers. He also declares that the Russian journals have taken a second look at the evidence, finding that celebrated dermovisionaries lack their powers when tighter controls are used. It appears that the cotton wads, masks, blindfolds, or turbans used to seal the eyes invariably leave tiny areas between the bottom of the eye and the bridge of the nose where light can enter. Typical gestures like probing the brow, lifting the head in profound concentration, or stroking the chin are just added gimmicks to make cheating that much easier. To Gardner's eternal exasperation it would seem that no one thinks of conducting and reporting the results of tests of blind-vision by making the seer wear a lightweight aluminum hood that would completely cover the head.

Similarly it would appear that no one has taken up Clayton Rawson's suggestion for foolproof PK tests, either. Rawson, an expert on the tricks of magicians and mentalists, as well as gamblers and card sharks, suggests that instead of trying to prove PK by mental maneuvering of cubes of dice, as cumbersome and open to the same statistical suspicions as the cards, PK tests be conducted using a delicate arrow pointer set in a vacuum jar. The subject's power to cause the arrow to deflect would then be the criterion of PK.

Until such antifraud tests are made, until the cards are properly shuffled or procedures automated to prevent human error or bias, the case for ESP remains unproven. This does not mean that research should not go on. The U.S. Air Force Research Laboratories have set aside funds for a year's investigation of ESP using a computer called VERITAC. If, under such conditions, persons are found with ESP prowess there may indeed be genuine cause for excitement and further study.

In the absence of such studies the world of ESP is left to the enthusiasts, those who ride the coattails of the college professors, insisting that there is a real "sense" here to be investigated, while at the same time devoutly pleased that they have found something which lies beyond the scientific pale. Their essentially antiscientific posture has been aptly described by the noted psychologist Edwin G. Boring of Harvard: "The parascientist as does his complement pits his ingenuity against the inscrutability of nature, and when the parascientist has failed, he has succeeded, for he has discovered the inexplicable."

(6) If all this seems too harsh an attack on ESP there is yet a final argument which in a sense both praises the long and conscientious efforts of Rhine, Pratt, Soal, and the others, but points to the extreme difficulties of the research. It is a needle-in-a-haystack argument which says that if persons with psi do exist their number within any generation may be so small that one could spend a lifetime trying to find just one. Even if successful in this, the discoverer would be severely limited in finding anything about the individual's ability. A microbiologist investigating bacteriophage or other viruses, or a geneticist experimenting with molds or bacteria, has the advantage of simpler systems and vast numbers of lifetimes in which to isolate and propagate a mutant in the general population.

Some recent investigators of ESP have seized upon just such a genetic approach with man, deciding to examine the brain wave patterns of individuals who in some sense are mentally related. Drs. T. D. Duane and Thomas Behrendt of the Department of Ophthalmology of Jefferson Medical College in Philadelphia, Pennsylvania, have been working with identical twins. It is clear that two people who have known each other or have lived together for long periods of time, such as husband or wife or good friends, are more likely to perceive the shape of each other's mind, to know the mental habits, the dreams, images, and thought processes.

Duane and Behrendt attempted nothing as complex as this. They tried to determine whether or not an identical twin could evoke the alpha brain wave pattern in his partner seated in a room some 18 feet away. The 8–10 cycle-a-second alpha pattern is one of the brain's resting rhythms, a surge of synchronous nerve cell activity that goes on when the individual is relaxed. It normally can be induced when a subject closes his eyes in a lighted room.

The idea was to seat both twins in lighted rooms and instruct them to keep their eyes open and to be relaxed and calm. At some point the sender twin would be told to close his eyes. If the alpha rhythm was then picked up not only from the eye-closer, but from his twin in the other room whose eyes were still open, ESP induction was presumed to be the reason. This supposedly happened in two cases out of fifteen. When the successful senders were paired with unrelated subjects, no alpha pattern was induced.

Unfortunately the experiment as reported in *Science* admits of too many uncertainties to warrant drawing ESP conclusions. To begin with no blood or other tests were performed to determine if the twin pairs were identical. Also the two successful pairs "possessed a prior knowledge of biological sciences and were relatively unconcerned about the tests." (The others were anxious.) The reader by this time may be able to think of a number of questions he might like to ask: Did the successful pair know the investigators? Were all proper measures taken to prevent any cooperation, conscious or unconscious? Were attempts made to "fool" the participants, i.e., running tests in which no eye closure was asked for, or to "fool" the interpreters, or at least to avoid letting them know when the records being compared were of twins or not. In addition there are some doubts about how reliable the alpha criterion is. The pattern can be induced by sheer boredom; it can happen spontaneously, or be triggered by the sound of recording equipment being turned on or off, or similar disruptions in keeping the eyes open.

In short, while the experiment may have some merit, the conclusions are doubtful. Even the investigators admitted qualms, for while they were fully capable of saying, "Thus extrasensory induction of brain waves exists between individuals when they are completely separated," they concluded with the cautionary words, "Because of the paucity of controlled data, contrasted with the voluminous controversial information available on the subject of extrasensory perception, it appears unwise to draw any conclusions or to make any statements regarding these aspects of our investigations."

Synesthesia

Cases of crossed reactions to sensory stimuli, seeing colors that correspond to particular sounds for example, are reported from time to time, and some authorities think the experience is not uncommon. Dr. Peter F. Ostwald of the University of California Department of Psychiatry in San Francisco estimates that as many as 14 percent of men and 31 percent of women experience some kind of double sensation, usually color hearing, and he notes that medical papers describing the phenomenon date back at least 200 years.

Usually there is a pitch relationship: low sounds are associated with dark colors and higher ones with brighter and lighter colors. Vowels and pure tones come through as more defined in hue than consonants or noise. Ostwald cites several reactions of a woman patient: the numbers 1, 2, 3, 4, 5 recited aloud evoked silver gray, dark green, cherry red, yellow, and lavender, while the short sentence "You get the cat" was dark green, beige, putty, and cream colored, in that order.

Whether such associations represent true crossties that are present in the brain at birth, or occur as a result of accident or mental illness is hard to say. They may simply represent early conditioning experiences. Today's children may very well have permanent color associations with numbers if they work with blocks and hear the teacher say "Take the green bar from the red slab . . ." when subtracting three from five.

To some extent all language and art are elaborate constructs of symbols which can act as secondary evokers of sense organs—a Tamayo painting of a watermelon may make your mouth water. Respighi's *Pines* and *Fountains of Rome* may evoke pastoral imagery, though even in such well-known "program" music there is cause for doubt. Insofar as the music is not pure sound effect, i.e., when there are no birds twittering or fountains overflowing, the mental associations individuals make are often completely different from what the composer had in mind. They are also subject to suggestion. A music teacher who implies that a certain theme (say Wagner's *Liebestod*) is the strongest embodiment in music of the physical act of love may have a readily assenting audience, as assenting as those who have seen Walt Disney's *Fantasia* and other films in that tradition who forever will associate a cartoon-devil world with *Night on Bald Mountain* or see dinosaurs cavorting in the swamps whenever they hear Stravinsky's *The Rite of Spring*.

Some composers, notably the Russian Scriabin, were supposed to have been possessed with true auditory-visual synesthesia and to have written music according to color associations. Certain contemporary composers, too, express a deep debt to visual art. The American composer Morton Feldman comments that the abstract expressionist painter Philip Guston strongly influenced his approach to music, making him think of using sound like paint. Feldman's scores are abstract designs, squared-off spaces in which instrumentalists are free to improvise over an indicated time interval. He has commented that if "it doesn't look right visually . . . then there's something wrong with the whole sound conception. It's as if the rightness of the sound is right visually." §

Gestalt psychologists have also studied synesthesia, suggesting that there may be some associations of sound and sight which are universal. When Köhler made up lists of nonsense syllables and asked groups of people to pair the words with abstract drawings there was remarkable consistency: smooth-sounding words like "maluma" were matched with undulating curves, while a word like "takete" was associated with jagged angles. Results were the same whether the children tested were from the Mahali peninsula, Lake Tanganyika, or from America or England.

Hyperesthesia

The question of supersensibility on the whole is easier to investigate than synesthesia. We know in the course of a lifetime that our threshold sensitivities dull, just as our muscles lose tone, our skin sags, our healing ability isn't all it once was. Like cars we simply run down. We are not surprised that children's hearing often extends into higher or lower ranges than an adult's; that they have more taste buds or keener senses of smell. We may regret, with Shaw, that youth is wasted on the young, or be a little envious when the abilities persist in friends our own age who don't need glasses or hearing aids.

But all this is not too surprising. Especially when we consider that the threshold levels themselves are arbitrary. For every sense there is a "loudness" or intensity factor, which if increased makes it possible for us to stretch that threshold. So it is with hearing low or high notes, and so it is with seeing into the ultraviolet || or infrared ranges. That there are "hyperesthetes," people who can do this without the extra amplification the "normal" person needs, is simply a statistical reality. Most of us

§ Article in *The New York Times*, February 2, 1964.
|| Often, persons who have had the lens removed in cataract operations can see in the ultraviolet range easily. The yellow lens is one of the major obstacles, strongly absorbing ultraviolet rays.

cluster around an average, swelling up the hump of a typical bell-shaped distribution curve. The rare ones tug at the tail. Sometimes the hyperesthetes are aware they have the ability, sometimes not.

Members of a family in a suburb of Schenectady, New York, did not realize how sensitive their hearing was until a group of Air Force technicians from a nearby base conducted tests. The six-year-old boy could hear frequencies of 21,000 cycles, and the rest of the family was presumed to do nearly as well. This, the Air Force conjectured, was undoubtedly the reason they complained of the whirring sounds in the air around their home. They were within sight of the transmission towers of three radio stations.

Scientists are often the ones who discover normal or abnormal abilities in the course of their self-testing. Several researchers in vision have reported that when spectral intensity is very much increased their range of vision extends into the infrared—until some point when they begin to feel the radiant energy as heat.

Normal vision is usually described as 20–20, the ability to resolve letters or symbols of a certain size at a distance of 20 feet. But some people may have 20-12 vision, seeing at 20 feet what a normal person would have to be at 12 feet to make out. Such a person is astronaut Gordon Cooper, a fact seldom mentioned in the news accounts of his supposed sightings of railroad tracks in northern India or houses with smoking chimneys in the Himalayas, while in orbit some 100 miles above the earth.

Most psychologists have said that this might be explained as a typical case of "visionary" vision as opposed to real vision—that is, the use of intelligence and experience to deduce an accurate perception from sketchy clues—something we do everyday when we judge a friend at a distance by his size or gait. But Cooper's far-better-than-average acuity, combined with training; the very clear atmospheric conditions; and the time of day (it was 7 A.M. by local time so that there would be good shadows) make his space feat more credible. That and one other fact seldom mentioned in the papers: in his space capsule he was breathing pure oxygen.

This last point introduces the fascinating realm of the effects of drugs on the senses. There is reason to believe that pure oxygen may exhance vision, for a while at least, perhaps by aiding the synthesis of visual pigments in the active rod and cone cells, perhaps by exerting a central pep effect.

Even more spectacular are the effects of the hallucinogenic drugs such as LSD, mescaline, or psilocybin which dramatically enhance color perception, distort shapes of everyday objects, making them curve, move,

318

loom larger or smaller, or amplify sounds so that, in the words of one self-testing psychologist, the sound of a typewriter in the next room makes it seem an infernal machine.

There seems no doubt that these effects are real. There is a body of literature and a history to testify to the drugs' importance in many religious rites of tribes in Central and South America, or as close to home as in the Christianized Native American Church, most of whose members are Indians in the southwest.

How and where in the body these drugs work are questions that have stimulated much research in the past few years. But like the heart of the atom to the physicist the more research that is done the more complex the picture seems to be. There are almost as many theories on facilitation or inhibition of nerve cell action, on repressing or stimulating of inhibitors, on differential stimulation on brain centers, of effects on the distribution, release, or storage of brain chemicals or secretions in the nervous system, as there are researchers reporting results.

There are those who use LSD to simulate mental illness, relating the sensory distortions to the altered perceptions characteristic of schizophrenic patients. There are those who are using sensory images to evoke an LSD effect: physicist-cum-painter Gerald Oster of the Brooklyn Polytechnic Institute believes that staring at moiré patterns which confront the eye with an ever-changing kaleidoscope of moving lines or circles may produce as many mental disturbances as doses of LSD.

One of the most interesting applications of LSD was its use in the design of a mental hospital. A Japanese-Canadian architect Kyo Izumi took the drug to see what effects it would have on his perceptions of space and time in the setting of a typical mental institution with wards, long corridors, and barred windows. One of the first things he noticed was that he could read without his glasses even though he is normally astigmatic and requires strong lenses. But his enhanced vision in the hospital setting was marked by more emotional reactions. Time seemed to stand still; normal activities like eating were seen in extreme slow motion. Familiar patterns of linoleum tiles took on a third dimensional aspect so that walking meant lifting or putting down each foot as though climbing or going downhill. Reflections from the smooth walls of the corridors added to their already depressing length, while an ordinary crack in the wall became a menacing crevice. Izumi incorporated what he learned from these experiences into the design of the Yorkton Psychiatric Centre in Saskatchewan, breaking up spaces, giving patients more privacy and quiet, using the colors, textures, and lighting arrangements he had found most pleasing under the drug, and supplying the rooms with calendars and clocks to keep patients time-oriented.

The potency of LSD in helping scientists understand something of mental illness extends as well to the study of normal behavior. Drugs as stimulating as this present a challenge, something to be tamed for man's benefit. If a drug can be found which increases our sensibilities and is safe, then it stands a chance of increasing intelligence, simply by enlarging the capacity for data that the system can handle. If the same or other drugs could enhance storage, manipulation, or retrieval of these sense perceptions mankind would actually better its perception by deepening it.

And with it perhaps would come a glimmer of understanding of how the brain functions. For in the long run the drug studies, the measures of sensibility, the recording of the odd fact, the unrelated phenomenon, are all routes to knowledge not even partially now in man's grasp, i.e., of how the brain works.

When two obviously disturbed young men, identical twins aged twenty-six, stunted in growth, one rocking back and forth in a way commonly seen in the retarded, can stand before an audience of neurologists, neuroanatomists, and psychiatrists and proceed to answer such questions as what day of the week will February 15, 2000, fall on, or what date was the first Wednesday in July, 1911; when one can say infallibly what the weather was like five years ago last Thursday, one dismisses any idea of fraud and turns at once to ponder the extraordinary workings of the brain.

The twins in question, Charles and George, are the idiot savants mentioned in the beginning of the chapter. They have an I.Q. of 70 and had been institutionalized at Letchworth Village in Thielle, New York, for fifteen years before Dr. William A. Horwitz of the New York Psychiatric Hospital first encountered them and brought them to New York in 1963. They apparently are the only known cases of twin idiot savants. There might even have been three—since a sister had been born with them, but died shortly after. Interestingly the more the pair has been studied the more have unusual talents shown up. First their memory of days and dates was discovered. Then the less disturbed of the two, George, displayed knowledge of the weather for dates extending five years back, adding sufficient personal details to make his account seem based on sensory impressions rather than on newspaper accounts of the day. More recently it appears that both twins have exceptionally keen senses of smell, being able to distinguish each other's clothing by smell alone.

Idiot savants of the past have generally shown some wizardry at calculation or music. While retarded in most ways they are fast at arithmetical computations, or they know the notes for any instrument in any measure of a given symphony. But little else has been recorded. At least with the present pair more questions are being asked. What is interesting is the degree to which the twins know they are objects of scientific curiosity. As long as they are a challenge to science they need never be sent back to their former hospital. This obviously makes them happy—and less likely to reveal any secrets—if they could. As it is now they simply say they do not know when asked how they know.

This makes the pursuit of such knowledge all the more tantalizing. Perhaps someone will link their keen sense of smell with a well-developed "old brain" as opposed to the layers of cortex which are the key to man's intelligence as we generally recognize and test it today.

Perhaps the elusive field of subliminal perception will get more attention. Researchers find it increasingly plausible that the brain is stirred by vast amounts of sensory stimuli that never rise to consciousness except perhaps in the rare cases of the savants. Psychologists and advertising researchers have examined such phenomena, usually testing the effects of very brief flashes of words or pictures on a screen alone, or along with images of longer duration. More recently several investigators compared the associations people made with two figures—one of a tree and one of a tree with a "hidden figure" of a duck—and found that the hidden figure evoked more "ducklike" images even when viewers were unaware of what they had seen.

All such amusing, seemingly peripheral adventures of the mind seeking explanation of the mind may be just the clues to solve the puzzle some day, and the goal of the parascientist's complement, to quote Boring, will be accomplished—the inexplicable will be explained.

SOURCES OF ILLUSTRATIONS

Page 2:   H. F. Harlow and R. R. Zimmerman, in *Science*, 130:421–432, Aug. 21, 1959, fig. 9.

Page 3:   *Ibid.*, fig. 23.

Page 13:   *A Preliminary Atlas of Early Fetal Activity.* Copyright 1939 by Dr. Davenport Hooker. Courtesy of Dr. Tryphena Humphrey, University of Alabama Medical Center, Birmingham.

Page 14:   *Ibid.*

Page 15:   *Ibid.*

Page 16:   T. Humphrey, "Some Correlations Between the Appearance of Human Fetal Reflexes and the Development of the Nervous System" (edited by D. P. Purpura and J. P. Schadé), *Progress in Brain Research*, 4:93–135, 1964.

Page 25:   Albert Einstein College of Medicine, New York.

Page 41: TL   G. C. Huber and L. M. A. DeWitt, in *Journal of Comparative Neurology*, 7:169–230, 1897, fig. 39.

Page 41: TR   *Ibid.*, 10:159–208, 1900, fig. 22.

Page 54: T   N. Cauna, University of Pittsburgh School of Medicine.

Page 54: B   N. Cauna and G. Mannan, in *Journal of Anatomy*, 92:1–20, fig. 1.

Page 55:   *Ibid.*, 93:271–286, fig. 28.

Page 56:   N. Cauna, in *Journal of Comparative Neurology*, 113:169–210, fig. 27.

Page 57: TR   *Idem*, in *Bibliotheca Anatomica*, 2:128–138, 1961, fig. 1.

Page 57: BR   *Idem*, in *American Journal of Anatomy*, 99:315–350, fig. 14.

Page 58:   *Idem*, in Proceedings of Ciba Foundation symposium "Touch, Heat, Pain" (edited by A. V. S. de Reuck and J. Knight), Little, Brown and Company, Boston, 1966, fig. 8.

Page 59: BL   *Idem*, in *The Anatomical Record*, 124:77–94, fig. 28.

Page 59: BR   *Ibid.*, fig. 23.

Page 60:   N. Cauna, in *Journal of Comparative Neurology*, 113:169–210, fig. 51.

Page 61:   *Idem*, University of Pittsburgh School of Medicine.

Page 62:   *Idem*, in *Journal of Comparative Neurology*, 113:169–210, fig. 31.

Page 65:   After a drawing supplied by A. Iggo, University of Edinburgh, Scotland.

Page 68:   After O. Foerster from W. Haymaker and B. Woodhall, *Peripheral Nerve Injuries*, W. B. Saunders, Philadelphia, 1945.

Page 70:   After H. B. Cantlie, in W. G. Penfield and T. Rasmussen, *The Cerebral Cortex of Man*, The Macmillan Company, New York, 1950, fig. 17.

Page 71:   *Ibid.*, fig. 22.

Page 77:   After A. S. Dogiel, in *Archiv für Mikroskopische Anatomie*, Vol. XXXVII.

Page 85:   Naval Medical Research Institute.

Page 86:   *Ibid.*

Page 87: T   *Ibid.*

Page 87: B   *Ibid.*

Page 90:   After a drawing in R. Descartes, *Tractatus de Homine*, Amsterdam, 1677. Courtesy of the National Library of Medicine.

Page 97:   Germanisches Museum, Nuremberg. Courtesy of the Picture Collection, New York Public Library.

Page 100:   N. Cauna, *Verhandlung der Anatomischen Gesellschaft, Ergänzungsheft zum 111 Band (1962) des Anatomischen Anzeigers*, Gustav Fischer Verlag, Jena, fig. 7.

Page 101:   Camera lucida drawing after G. C. Huber, in *Journal of Comparative Neurology*, 10:135–151, 1900, fig. 1.

Page 103:   After a diagram supplied by R. Melzack.

Page 113:   G. Casserio, *Pentaestheseion*, Frankfort, 1610. Courtesy of the National Library of Medicine.

Page 135: T   P. Mascogni, *Anatomia Universale*, V. Batelli, Florence, 1833, tav. ix, fig. 1. Courtesy of the National Library of Medicine.

Page 137:   N. Cauna, in *Journal of Comparative Neurology*, 113:169–210, fig. 5.

Page 160:   After G. von Békésy, in *Akustische Zeitschrift*, 6:1, 1941.

Page 162:   After B. J. Melloni, in *An Atlas of Some Pathological Conditions of the Eye, Ear & Throat, Together with Drawings Showing Structures of the Internal Ear*, published by Abbott Laboratories, North Chicago.

Page 164:   After S. S. Stevens and H. Davis, in *Hearing: Its Psychology and Physiology*, John Wiley & Sons, New York, 1938.

Page 165:   After Melloni, *op. cit.*

Page 167:   *Ibid.*

Page 168: T   *Ibid.*

Page 168: B   *Ibid.*

Page 170:   Detail of organ of Corti after H. Davis and others, in *Journal of the Acoustical Society of America*, 25:1180, 1953.

Page 173:   G. von Békésy, *Experiments in Hearing* (translated and edited by E. G. Wever), fig. 13-8. Copyright © 1960 by McGraw-Hill Book Company. By permission.

Page 174:   After S. S. Stevens and H. Davis, in *Journal of the Acoustical Society of America*, 8:1–13, July 1936, fig. 8.

Page 176:   After von Békésy, *op. cit.*, fig. 11-21. Copyright © 1960 by McGraw-Hill Book Company. By permission.

Page 177: T   *Ibid.*, fig. 13–17. Copyright © 1960 by McGraw-Hill Book Company. By permission.

Page 180:   After H. Ades, H. Engström, and J. Hawkins, research report "Structure of Inner Ear Sensory Epithelial Cells in Relation to Their Functions," U.S. Naval Aerospace Institute, Pensacola, figs. 16 and 17.

Page 187:   E. F. Evans, Laboratory of Neurophysiology, National Institute of Neurological Diseases and Blindness.

Page 197:   After Melloni, *op. cit.*

Page 198:   H. Ades and H. Engström, in Proceedings of symposium "The Role of the Vestibular Organs in the Exploration of Space," U.S. Naval Aerospace Institute, Pensacola, published by Scientific and Technical Information Division of National Aeronautics and Space Administration, Washington, 1965, fig. 21.

Page 206: T   *Ibid.*, fig. 18.

Page 206: BL   *Ibid.*, fig. 20.

Page 206: BR   *Ibid.*, fig. 19.

Page 210:   *Ibid.*, after fig. 1.

Page 211:   *Ibid.*, fig. 22.

Page 221:   Casserio, *op. cit.* Courtesy of the National Library of Medicine.

Page 231:   P. K. Brown and G. Wald, "Human Color Vision and Color Blindness," Proceedings of Cold Spring Harbor symposium, Vol. XXX, 1965, fig. 2.

Page 234: After S. L. Polyak, *The Retina*, University of Chicago Press, Chicago, 1941, fig. 95.

Page 236: National Institute of Neurological Diseases and Blindness.

Page 239: After A. Chapanis, "How We See," Chap. I in *Human Factors in Undersea Warfare*, published by National Research Council, Washington, 1949.

Page 241: G. Wald, P. K. Brown, and P. H. Smith, in *Journal of General Physiology*, 38:623–681, May 20, 1955, fig. 20. By permission of the Rockefeller University Press.

Page 242: *Idem*, in *Science*, 118:505–508, Oct. 30, 1953, fig. 3.

Page 251: P. K. Brown and G. Wald, in *Science*, 144:45–51, Apr. 3, 1964, fig. 3. Copyright © 1964 by American Association for the Advancement of Science.

Page 252: *Idem*, in *Nature*, 200:37–43, Oct. 5, 1963, fig. 6.

Page 255: *Ibid.*, fig. 8.

Page 260: After I. Mann and A. Pirie, *The Science of Seeing*, Pelican Books, Penguin Books, Ltd., Harmondsmith, England, 1946.

Page 269: B. Julesz, in *Science*, 145:356–362, July 24, 1964, fig. 5. Copyright © 1964 by American Association for the Advancement of Science.

Page 270: T Courtesy of the Pepsi-Cola Company.

Page 270: B *Ibid.*

Page 271: *Ibid.*

Page 273: After Polyak, *op. cit.*, fig. 1.

Page 276: T After E. Boring and D. Katz, based on a similar figure in D. Krech and R. S. Crutchfield, *Elements of Psychology*, Alfred A. Knopf, New York, 1958.

Page 277: T Courtesy of the Pepsi-Cola Company.

Page 278: TL *Ibid.*

Page 278: TR *Ibid.*

Page 279: John Langley Howard, in *Scientific American*, June 1961.

Page 283: After D. Hubel, "Information Processing in the Nervous System," Proceedings of International Union of Physiological Sciences, 22nd International Congress, Vol. III, 1962 (from Excerpta Medica International Series No. 49), fig. 2.

Page 285: After D. Hubel and T. N. Wiesel, in *Journal of Neurophysiology*, 28:229–289, 1965, fig. 8.

Page 289: T M. L. Wolbarsht, Naval Medical Research Institute.

Page 289: B *Ibid.*

BIBLIOGRAPHY

The following is a partial list of books which were found useful in preparing this volume. The first references are the most comprehensive and detailed sources. Following these are other general references and then books appropriate to particular senses. Where more than one book is listed in these latter categories the attempt has been made to order them from the most popular to the most advanced. Not included in this bibliography are many articles in professional journals and in popular general science periodicals like *Scientific American*.

Comprehensive

Handbook of Physiology. Section 1, *Neurophysiology*. Vol. I. Washington, D.C.: American Physiological Society, 1959; also Volume III, 1960.

Truex, Raymond C., *Strong and Elwyn's Human Neuroanatomy*. 4th ed. Baltimore, Md.: The Williams & Wilkins Company, 1959.

Crosby, Elizabeth C., Humphrey, Tryphena, and Lauer, Edward W.,

Correlative Anatomy of the Nervous System. New York: The Macmillan Company, 1962.

Wyburn, G. M., Pickford, R. W., and Hirst, R. J., *Human Senses and Perception.* Toronto: University of Toronto Press, 1964.

Rosenblith, Walter, ed., *Sensory Communication.* (Contributions to the Symposium on Principles of Sensory Communication, July 19–August 1, 1959.) Cambridge, Mass.: The M.I.T. Press, 1961.

Walsh, E. Geoffrey, *Physiology of the Nervous System.* New York: Longmans, Green and Company, 1957.

Granit, Ragnar, *Receptors and Sensory Perception.* New Haven, Conn.: Yale University Press, 1955.

Geldard, Frank A., *The Human Senses.* New York: John Wiley & Sons, 1953.

Manter, John T., and Gatz, Arthur J., *Essentials of Clinical Neuroanatomy and Neurophysiology.* 2d ed. Philadelphia: F. A. Davis Company, 1961.

Netter, Frank H., *Nervous System.* Vol. I. The CIBA Collection of Medical Illustrations, CIBA Pharmaceutical Company, Summit, N.J., 1962.

Adrian, E. D., *The Basis of Sensation.* New York: Hafner Publishing Company, 1964.

Rawdon-Smith, A. F., *Theories of Sensation.* (Cambridge Biological Studies.) New York: Cambridge University Press, 1938.

General

Von Buddenbrock, Wolfgang, *The Senses.* Trans. by Frank Gaynor. Ann Arbor, Mich.: University of Michigan Press, 1958.

Milne, Lorus J. and Margery, *The Senses of Animals and Men.* New York: Atheneum, 1948.

Dröscher, Vitus B., *The Mysterious Senses of Animals.* Trans. by Eveleen Huggard. New York: E. P. Dutton & Co., Inc., 1965.

Sherrington, Sir Charles, *Man on His Nature.* 2d ed. Garden City, N.Y.: Doubleday & Company, 1953.

Mueller, Conrad G., *Sensory Psychology.* Englewood Cliffs, N.J.: Prentice-Hall, 1965.

Development

Flanagan, Geraldine Lux, *The First Nine Months of Life.* New York Simon and Schuster, 1962.

Watson, Ernest H., and Lowrey, George H., *Growth and Development of Children.* Chicago: The Year Book Publishers, 1951.

Piaget, Jean, *The Origins of Intelligence in Children.* Trans. by Margaret Cook. New York: W. W. Norton & Company, 1963.

Langman, Jan, *Medical Embryology.* Baltimore, Md.: The Williams & Wilkins Company, 1963.

Proprioception

Galambos, Robert, *Nerves and Muscles.* (Science Study Series.) Garden City, N.Y.: Doubleday & Company, 1962.

Smell

Bedichek, Roy, *The Sense of Smell.* Garden City, N.Y.: Doubleday & Company, 1960.

Taste

Dethier, Vincent G., *To Know a Fly.* San Francisco: Holden-Day, 1962.

Brillat-Savarin, Jean Anthelme, *The Physiology of Taste.* New York: Dover Publications, 1960.

Hearing

Griffin, Donald R., *Echoes of Bats and Men.* (Science Study Series.) Garden City, N.Y.: Doubleday & Company, 1959.

——, *Listening in the Dark.* New Haven, Conn.: Yale University Press, 1958.

Von Helmholtz, Hermann, *Popular Scientific Lectures.* New York: Dover Publications, 1962.

Kock, Winston E., *Sound Waves and Light Waves.* Garden City, N.Y.: Doubleday & Company, 1965.

Littler, T. S., *The Physics of the Ear.* Vol. III in International Series of Monographs on Physics, G. H. A. Cole, gen. ed. New York: The Macmillan Company, 1965.

Vinnikov, Ya. A., and Titova, L. K., *The Organ of Corti.* Authorized translation from the Russian; updated by the authors for the English edition. New York: Consultants Bureau, 1964.

Vestibular Senses

The Role of the Vestibular Organs in the Exploration of Space. (Symposium at the U.S. Naval School of Aviation Medicine, Pensacola,

Fla., January 20–22, 1965.) Washington, D.C.: National Aeronautics and Space Administration, 1965.

Vision

Walls, Gordon L., *The Vertebrate Eye and Its Adaptive Radiation*. New York: Hafner Publishing Company, 1963.
Gregory, R. L., *Eye and Brain*. New York: McGraw-Hill Book Company, 1966.

Non-Sense

Smith, Susy, *ESP for the Millions*. (Psychic Self Improvement Series.) Los Angeles: Sherbourne Press, 1965.
Gardner, Martin, *Fads and Fallacies in the Name of Science*. New York: Dover Publications, 1957.
Hansel, C. E. M., *ESP: A Scientific Inquiry*. New York: Charles Scribner's Sons, 1966.
Rhine, J. B., *Extra-Sensory Perception*. Boston: Bruce Humphries, 1964.

INDEX